Kant and Phenomenology

Kant and Phenomenology

TOM ROCKMORE

The University of Chicago Press
Chicago and London

The University of Chicago Press, Chicago 60637
The University of Chicago Press, Ltd., London
© 2011 by The University of Chicago
All rights reserved. No part of this book may be used or reproduced in any manner whatsoever without written permission, except in the case of brief quotations in critical articles and reviews. For more information, contact the University of Chicago Press, 1427 E. 60th St., Chicago, IL 60637.
Published 2011
Paperback edition 2021
Printed in the United States of America

30 29 28 27 26 25 24 23 22 21   1 2 3 4 5

ISBN-13: 978-0-226-72340-2 (cloth)
ISBN-13: 978-0-226-81785-9 (paper)
ISBN-13: 978-0-226-72341-9 (e-book)
DOI: https://doi.org/10.7208/chicago/9780226723419.001.0001

Library of Congress Cataloging-in-Publication Data

Rockmore, Tom, 1942–
Kant and phenomenology / Tom Rockmore. p. cm.
Includes bibliographical references and index.
ISBN-13: 978-0-226-72340-2 (cloth : alk. paper)
ISBN-10: 0-226-72340-2 (cloth : alk. paper) 1. Knowledge, Theory of.
2. Phenomenology. 3. Kant, Immanuel, 1724–1804. I. Title.
BD161.R594 2011
121—dc22
                              2010019949

CONTENTS

Introduction / 1

ONE / From Platonism to Phenomenology / 17

TWO / Kant's Epistemological Shift to Phenomenology / 41

THREE / Hegel's Phenomenology as Epistemology / 71

FOUR / Husserl's Phenomenological Epistemology / 101

FIVE / Heidegger's Phenomenological Ontology / 139

SIX / Kant, Merleau-Ponty's Descriptive Phenomenology, and the Primacy of Perception / 187

CONCLUSION / On Overcoming the Epistemological Problem through Phenomenology / 209

Notes / 217
Index / 249

INTRODUCTION

This book studies phenomenological approaches to epistemology, using a very broad interpretation of the term *phenomenology*. A number of the most important modern thinkers are concerned with a phenomenological approach to epistemology. Phenomenologists who contribute to a phenomenological approach to knowledge include Kant, Fichte, Hegel, Husserl, Heidegger, and Merleau-Ponty; perhaps we could also include Cassirer as well as Gadamer.

The term *phenomenology* is used in many ways; for instance, we use it to refer to first-person moral experience.[1] In restricting phenomenology to the epistemological domain, my concern here is to examine a promising approach to knowledge already suggested by Kant that is carried forward by Hegel, Husserl, and others; since Heidegger, however, it has, with the exception of Merleau-Ponty, been largely abandoned. Kant is crucial in this narrative. He is, depending on the understanding of the term *phenomenology*, arguably the initial figure of the first rank to turn to a phenomenological approach to epistemology. Through his so-called Copernican turn, he works out a claim for knowledge based on the "construction" of phenomena as distinguished from appearances. This basic claim is later reformulated or rejected in interesting ways by Fichte, Hegel, Husserl, Heidegger, and Merleau-Ponty. Hence one reason to study this progression is to call attention to the considerable epistemological resources of a phenomenological approach to knowledge that, after Husserl, and certainly after Merleau-Ponty, was, at least "officially," quickly but perhaps unwisely abandoned.

In focusing on the relation of phenomenology to epistemology, I intentionally limit the scope of the investigation. Phenomenology is both wider and narrower than epistemology, understood as theory of knowledge of all kinds. It is wider in that phenomenologists who make explicit or implicit epistemological claims often understand theory of knowledge as a subset of a broader phenomenological domain. Hegel examines phenomenological themes without ever raising epistemological claims for his position. Husserl frequently seems to equate phenomenology with epistemology. Heidegger, who turns from epistemology to fundamental ontology, "officially" regards theory of knowledge as lying outside his phenomenological concerns. Yet phenomenology is also narrower than epistemology, many of whose questions cannot be resolved or even addressed merely through analysis of the appearance of the real on the phenomenal plane.

Phenomenology in all its forms differs from phenomenalism.[2] The latter derives from a specific way of reading the critical philosophy as an approach to knowledge of a mind-independent external world. Phenomenalism is routinely understood as the general view that talk about the mind-independent real world is just talk about sensory experience, since what we call *external objects* are merely logical constructions out of sense data.[3] *Phenomenology*, on the contrary, as I will use the term here, does not distinguish between external objects and the sense data on which phenomenalism depends.

The present discussion is primarily interested in the phenomenological contribution to epistemological concerns in the widest possible sense and only secondarily interested in the history of phenomenology. Thus I do not attempt to provide a history of phenomenology, even in outline. Yet, since I am studying a phenomenological approach to knowledge in general and not merely versions of it formulated by Husserl and his successors, I contest the widespread conviction that he and he alone invented phenomenology, or at least phenomenology worthy of the name. This story, which has been repeated and embellished by successive historians of phenomenology, is simply false for a number of reasons.

Husserl seems to have believed, and on occasion even explicitly claimed, that he discovered phenomenology.[4] Yet if "phenomenology" is understood in a widened sense, since there are significant pre-Husserlian phenomenologists, such as Lambert, Kant, Fichte, and Hegel, he can at most have invented a form or forms of phenomenology. Further, it is widely known that Husserl himself never settled on a view of the phenomenological discipline he found acceptable. Hence, in attributing to him the invention of phenomenology, it remains unclear in what the invention can be said to consist.

Epistemological questions are often raised about Husserl,[5] but less often about Heidegger, in virtue of his explicit turn away from epistemology,[6] or about those who succeed him. Others who are not often associated with phenomenology, such as Cassirer, turn to phenomenology for epistemological purposes.[7] There is at present little explicit interest in the link between phenomenology and knowledge; hence there is little explicit interest in a phenomenological approach to epistemology.

Yet there are indications that the situation is now changing. After a period of around a hundred years in which twentieth-century phenomenology and Anglo-American analytic philosophy followed separate, independent paths, there are now incipient signs of at least limited convergence around selected themes. Husserl's early breakthrough to phenomenology is closer to naturalism than his later position. The rapprochement based on reinterpreting selected aspects of twentieth-century phenomenology along naturalist lines[8] that are currently dominant in analytic circles[9] narrows the gap between so-called analytic and continental approaches. Others utilize specific phenomenological insights for current scientific concerns. Michael Wheeler, for instance, develops a phenomenological approach to philosophy of mind based on Heidegger.[10] And Thompson relies on phenomenology, especially the views of Husserl and Merleau-Ponty, in his effort to reconstruct biology.[11] The many writings of Oliver Sacks, the widely known neurologist, read as if he were a practicing phenomenologist.[12] Yet others, such as Carl Craver, eschew any recourse to phenomenology in neurological science.[13]

Henry Pietersma, who is an exception to the general disinterest in phenomenological epistemology, has studied this theme in Husserl, Heidegger, and Merleau-Ponty.[14] Pietersma opposes classical realism to the entire transcendental tradition; hence he opposes phenomenology, which he interprets as internalist, to externalism. Yet he fails to realize that Kant is already concerned not with "externalism," but with "internalism" of a particular kind. In the critical philosophy, the distinction of subject and object is only internal to the mind.[15]

All approaches to knowledge share an interest in grasping, knowing, or cognizing the cognitive object or objects, sometimes also called nature, or the world, or the real. What I call the general problem of knowledge can be initially understood through such terms as *reality*, *phenomena*, and *appearance*, which have become familiar since Kant but go all the way back to ancient philosophy.[16]

Since these terms are often taken as synonymous, differences between them are often overlooked, especially in ordinary language, in which phenomena are routinely taken as appearances and conversely. Phenomena in general are often distinguished from appearances understood as a special kind of phenomena. Appearances further refer beyond themselves to mind-independent cognitive objects. Understood in this way, all appearances are phenomena, but only some phenomena are appearances.

Since the early Greeks, phenomena and appearances are often either taken to differ in kind or to be identical. The epistemological consequences of these and other ways of comprehending the relation between phenomena and appearances have continually been drawn in different ways throughout the Western philosophical tradition. As concerns knowledge, phenomenology turns on the analysis of the relation of phenomena to cognitive objects, which are variously said to appear or not to appear in the form of phenomena for a large series of reasons by an even longer series of thinkers from Plato up to contemporary phenomenology.

This distinction, though not in these terms, emerges very early in the tradition, perhaps as early as Heraclitus and certainly as early as Parmenides. The Parmenidean distinction between the way of appearance (opinions) and the way of truth (or reality) presupposes a related distinction between what appears to be but is not, or false appearance, and what is and cannot be otherwise, or what, since it is, cannot not be. What, on the contrary, appears to be but is not cannot be and hence cannot be known. And what is, since it is, can be known. For this reason, some observers think that, at least informally, Parmenides introduces the basic distinction between truth and appearance. Or if truth, or reality, is phenomenal, then Parmenides already points toward the later distinction between phenomena and appearances.

Plato, who lacks the requisite vocabulary to refer to the difference between phenomena and appearances, is already concerned with this relation, which much later becomes central to Kant. Kant's critical philosophy literally turns on different ways of drawing the distinction between phenomena and appearances, which he studies in detail. This Kantian concern remains central to later phenomenological investigations of knowledge. It is not often noted that Kant features two different, incompatible approaches to knowledge. In adopting and then later turning away from representationalism in favor of constructivism, he turns toward an influential view we can state informally as the claim that we know only the phenomena we construct. All the main post-Kantian German idealists, including Marx, who is typically misrepresented as abandoning philosophy, follow Kant down the phenomenological path. All are in that sense also phenomenologists, committed to a phenomenological approach to knowledge.

Plato, Kant, and later phenomenologists differ radically in their understanding of the relation of phenomena and appearances to reality. Platonism is the body of theories routinely taken as describing Plato's position. We do not know and cannot now determine what (if any) theory Plato himself accepts. Yet if his writings are a reliable indication, then Plato, who denies that reality appears in a way that can be known, implicitly draws a sharp distinction between what, in Kantian language, are called *phenomena* and *noumena* and hence between phenomena and appearances as well. For Plato, phenomena are not appearances, or not cognizable appearances of reality. Kant, who clearly distinguishes phenomena and noumena (also called *things in themselves*),[17] both distinguishes as well as conflates phenomena and appearances, which later phenomenologists often identify. Though the views of "reality" differ, it seems that all later phenomenologists are apparently committed to some version of the anti-Platonic claim that reality is phenomenal and hence can be known.

In distinguishing between phenomena and noumena, Kant follows Platonism, and perhaps even Plato. Yet it is not clear how to understand this relation. Commentators, including Aristotle,[18] sometimes identify Plato's position with his writings. Yet the difficulty of identifying Plato's position, if he has any, if in fact he ever makes up his mind, has never been overcome.

It is useful, for present purposes, to distinguish between Plato and Platonism, which is a construction based on a reading and interpretation of Plato's writings, and whose relation to Plato's view remains uncertain. Platonism concerns a complex, influential position combining interlocking epistemological and ontological claims, a position that, depending on the favored interpretation, develops chronologically in Plato's writings or is virtually complete, in a single complex vision as it were, from the beginning. Ontologically Platonism is committed to a basic distinction between objects of thought, which are intelligible and invisible, and objects of sensory experience, especially sight, which are visible. This leads to the familiar dualism between appearance or phenomena and reality, between physical things and ideas. This dualistic ontology is linked to the notorious theory of ideas that emerges in the *Phaedo* and is developed further, criticized, but never accepted or rejected in such dialogues as the *Republic*, the *Theaetetus*, the *Sophist* and the *Parmenides*. For instance, it is thought that in the *Sophist*, though he still holds that ideas are changeless, Plato softens his earlier view that they comprise the whole of reality. If we recall that in the *Phaedrus* and again in the *Laws* he suggests that the soul is self-moving, and that in the *Timaeus* he suggests that reality includes divine intelligence that functions as a cause, then we can understand that Plato later seems to come to believe that what, in more modern language, we can call an idealist view of the real must include what is sometimes called spiritual motion as well as the unchanging ideas.

A peak of sorts is reached in the *Republic*. In the famous passage on the divided line, Plato distinguishes between the visible objects of opinion and the invisible objects of knowledge. Here he describes the familiar triple distinction between representations of physical objects, then the physical objects themselves, and finally the immaterial objects of mind—what Kant later calls *things in themselves* as well as *noumena*—which in the Platonic position are cognizable through mathematics, natural science, and above all through philosophy, but which in the Kantian position are simply beyond cognition.

In Plato's day, the claim that reality in fact appears was maintained in Protagorean relativism. According to Theaetetus, who follows Protagoras, knowledge is nothing but (infallible) perception (aesthesis).[19] Plato rebuts this view, through Socrates, on two grounds: difficulties in the identification of reality and appearance as described in his reconstruction of the Protagorean position, and prior acceptance of his own rival view that reality does not appear. Socrates replies that knowledge is not perception that does not have the real for its object. This amounts to claiming that phenomena are not appearances (phantasia), or, more precisely, not appearances of the real. To put the point otherwise, although phenomena are caused by the real, and through recollection the real enables us to identify things in the world of appearance in reference to their form or idea, one cannot follow the inverse path in order to arrive at knowledge of the real on the basis of phenomena. There is an asymmetry between the ontological claim that the real causes or otherwise brings about appearances and the epistemological claim that phenomena are not appearances, or not appearances of the real. For the ontological claim is not convertible into an epistemological claim.

This approach to theory of knowledge depends on a complex view of causality embedded in the theory of forms, which is the centerpiece of Platonism. It has been well said that this theory, which is never explicitly expounded, and which hence never attains a definitive formulation, is a rational reconstruction by Plato's readers. Everything about the theory of forms is uncertain, including whether there is such a theory, whether Plato subscribes to it, and, if so, which version he accepts. Yet since early Greek philosophy, most prominently Aristotle, and over the intervening centuries, many of Plato's readers have routinely claimed to find what is widely known as the theory of forms in his texts and even to identify it with Plato's own position.

The theory of forms attributed to Plato is regarded as a reliable way to know the mind-independent real that lies beyond appearance as it is. If Plato subscribes to Platonism, then it commits him to what is sometimes called Platonic realism, also widely called metaphysical realism, according to which to know is to uncover, to discover, or to reveal the mind-independent external world, or what is as it is in independence from us or, as is often said, in independence from mind.

The Greek word *idea*, which is usually translated as "form" or "idea" and is derived from *idein*, "to see," means the "look of a thing" as opposed to its reality, or to its kind, sort, or nature. Through different versions of this theory, Plato appears to identify cognitive objects of mind, which are beyond the changing world of appearances and hence really are, and which, as eternal, or unchanging, neither come into being nor pass away. A minimal, "average" statement of this view includes two related claims: the epistemological conviction that we know and only can know a particular because of a universal, or what is now also called *universal predication*; and the ontological belief that there are particulars only because of the causal relation to a universal, as in the well-known example of a craftsman with an idea of a bed in book 10 of the *Republic*.[20]

Causality figures in Platonism on different levels: first, as concerns the explanation of ordinary, everyday events; then as concerns the origin of physical objects; and finally with respect to knowledge of the mind-independent external world, or reality. The theory of ideas can be regarded as a nonstandard theory of causality. In the *Phaedo*, in answer to Cebes, as part of the argument in favor of the immortality of the soul, Socrates indicates his interest in the explanation of nature. After giving a list of possible explanations, as he also does in the *Sophist* and elsewhere,[21] he rejects causality as it arises in natural science or in earlier philosophers, such as Anaxagoras, in favor of the theory of ideas.[22] According to this view, ideas function as causes—more specifically, as the causes of sensible things in the surrounding external world.[23]

The rejection is based on a specific, controversial view of causal explanation. In rejecting such alternatives as the pre-Socratic theory of opposites, Anaxagoras's conception of mind, and natural scientific views of causality, Socrates seems to accept as his norm the specific explanation of each single thing allegedly furnished by the theory of ideas. In other words, it is not sufficient to explain a given thing or situation through a general scientific law. A view that each thing or occurrence must be explained individually would rule out an appeal, say, to the law of falling bodies to explain why a given physical thing falls or to the law of gravitation to account for planetary motion.[24]

The theory of forms, which is not, say, like contemporary string theory, intended as a theory of everything,[25] is presented as having distinct explanatory limits. According to the theory Socrates quickly sketches, physical things are said to be "caused by," hence "explained by," "participation" (*methexis*) in ideas or forms, as beautiful things are "caused" by the Beautiful. The central insight seems to be that the intelligible world is related to the sensible world as cause to effect.

Plato can be read as making a complex ontological and epistemological claim. He asserts that it is plausible to believe that reality causes appearance in general, more plausible than to adopt any of the alternatives. Hence, ontologically, each thing presupposes as its cause an idea. Yet ideas that function ontologically as the causes of things cannot be known through a backward inference from effect to cause through sensory experience of appearances, or physical objects. In other words, since the causal relation is not "reversible," one cannot infer, other than in a general way, from the effect to the cause.

The result is a paradox. Well before Kant disqualifies a representational approach to cognition, Plato paradoxically holds that the world, which, according to the likely explanation formulated in the theory of ideas, "causes" the objects of experience that are its effects, cannot be known. This paradox, which has never been resolved, runs throughout the entire later discussion up to the present, in which we continue to wrestle with this problem on theological, philosophical, scientific, and perhaps other levels in formulating different ways to justify the backward inference from effects to causes.

Plato denies a representational approach to knowledge in different ways throughout his writings. In the *Theaetetus*, he confronts a contemporary version of this approach in Protagoras's view that perception is knowledge.[26] This claim can be interpreted as asserting direct, or naïve realism, or even representational realism. *To represent* is often understood as to correctly depict or to make a true statement about some thing.[27] The "real" can be understood as a physical thing or as the mind-independent external world—in short, as the way things are in independence of the observer.

Plato can be read as developing this (Platonic) argument in different ways throughout his writings. The argument as it unfolds in the *Theaetetus* has two parts. In virtue of the relativity of perception, anticipating the argument that Berkeley will develop two thousand years later, Plato draws a distinction between the appearance and what appears, between the physical object and its representations. Socrates, who interprets this argument in connection with the Heraclitean doctrine that all things are in motion and the Protagorean doctrine that man is the measure, draws conclusions applying to any formulation of this argument. And, anticipating Kant, a further distinction is drawn between the object of sensory perception and the object of intellection, or reason, which is not given in experience but can be thought.

The denial that perception is knowledge is linked to Plato's famous account of art and art objects in the *Republic*. Plato, who interprets art along mimetic lines, creates aesthetics and art criticism at the same time as he denies art an epistemological function in suggesting, on the basis of the theory of forms, that it is at most an imitation of an imitation, hence thrice removed from reality. It follows that art is not a reliable indication of reality.

Plato, who parts company with Socrates on the issue of skepticism, seems, at least in the *Republic*, to offer two positive approaches to knowledge of mind-independent reality. In the famous passage on the allegory of the cave at the beginning of book 7, he imagines the process of knowledge as an ascent from darkness to light (514A–521B). Later, in the description of dialectic near the end of the book (536D–540C), he suggests the possibility of going beyond hypotheses, on which mathematics and science rely in directly grasping their truth. Taken together, the allegory of the cave and the account of dialectic suggest ways to reach knowledge if knowledge is to be possible.

We do not know, since we do not know Plato's position, if he accepted these or indeed any approach to knowledge of reality. If he did, then he was committed to the view that reality, which does not appear and which hence is not given in experience, can nonetheless be known. This is a view he seems to affirm strongly in the *Seventh Letter*, if that text is genuine (see, e.g., 342A–343D). If he thinks there is nonsensory knowledge of the real, then Plato is an anti-phenomenologist. In other words, in denying that reality appears in phenomenal form, he rejects any phenomenological approach in favor of a direct grasp of mind-independent reality. In that sense, Plato's suggestion that under appropriate conditions mind-independent reality can be directly grasped is analogous to the more familiar direct, or naïve realism. Beginning with Kant, later phenomenological approaches suppose that under appropriate circumstances phenomena grasp the real.

Plato is an anti-phenomenologist, and Kant is in some ways a phenomenologist who restricts knowledge to knowledge of phenomena but is also committed to the idea that under appropriate circumstances reality can indeed appear and hence be known. More precisely, in different places Kant defends both anti-phenomenological and phenomenological approaches to knowledge, whose difference correlates to his relation to Platonism.

Kant is sometimes viewed, as he himself suggests,[28] as a sophisticated Platonist.[29] His relation to Plato is extremely complex and hence difficult to depict simply. Kant follows the Platonic distinction between noumena and phenomena while holding that (1) knowledge requires the analysis of the relation of representations to mind-independent cognitive objects, and that (2) a minimal condition of knowledge is to construct mind-dependent cognitive objects. The former, anti-Platonic view fails because it commits Kant to knowledge of noumena, which, by definition, cannot be experienced and hence cannot be known. The latter view is potentially successful if Kant could explain how a finite human subject "constructs" cognitive objects, or phenomena. An important theme in post-Kantian idealism consists in explaining the relation of cognitive claims to the finite human subject, which Kant's theory of the subject as a transcendental unity of apperception excludes.

The insight that cognitive claims depend on the subject is specifically modern. The modern idea of the epistemological subject is largely influenced by the Augustinian view of the human subject as ethically responsible.[30] The transition from the specifically religious question of individual human responsibility, which presupposes a conception of the subject, to the modern epistemological subject only occurs much later in Montaigne and Descartes. The change in the conception of the subject is a central difference between ancient and modern philosophy. A key Platonic theme in Kant concerns the relation between objects of experience and knowledge. Plato's theory of ideas provides an explanation of the relation between ideas and physical things through the notorious, never sufficiently clarified term *participation*. Kant's Platonism consists in working out a conception of participation that links mind-independent reality, which cannot be known, to objects of experience that can be and in fact are known.

With respect to knowledge, Kant is both an anti-phenomenologist, though in an anti-Platonic sense, as well as a phenomenologist in a Platonic sense. In his earlier representational phase, Kant is committed to representing mind-independent reality on the anti-Platonic assumption that reality appears. In this sense he follows the widespread modern anti-Platonic effort, including both continental realists and empiricists, to account for knowledge through the relation of ideas to the mind-independent external world. In his later constructivist phase, Kant is rather committed to the view that reality for us is identified with phenomena.

Kant's representationalist, anti-phenomenological, anti-Platonic approach to knowledge fails for a Platonic reason. As for Platonism, so for Kant the distinction between noumena and phenomena, or reality and appearance, is close to the center of the position. Kant, who accepts the Platonic distinction between noumena and phenomena and denies that noumena can appear and hence be known, cannot, for this reason, successfully claim to represent them. Since representation is a form of appearance, it would be inconsistent to represent what cannot be known. In depicting the problem of knowledge along the lines of the analysis of the relation of representations to objects, an insuperable difficulty arises. Kant cannot distinguish between phenomena and noumena and also maintain that through phenomena one can know noumena. In that sense, he follows Plato, who also refuses a cognitive inference from appearance to reality. At a minimum, Kant would need, to make this argument, to claim that phenomena lead to noumena. Though versions of this view are routinely asserted, it seems difficult to make out. Thus Thomas Nagel suggests we can get down to ontological bedrock by subtracting the subjective dimension to reveal the objective dimension.[31] Similarly, Paul Boghossian thinks we can agree about the way things are in independence of our opinions, and that constructivist arguments are incoherent.[32] Yet if objects can only be known by representing them, then it can never be shown that the representation adequately represents. This line of argument supports Kant's later turn away from representationalism as well as his turn toward constructivism.

Kant begins the *Critique of Pure Reason* by famously affirming that knowledge begins in, but is not necessarily limited to, experience.[33] Kantian constructivism is intended as a second-best, substitute theory that abandons the anti-Platonic claim to know reality through experience, for which no convincing argument has ever been devised, in favor of a weaker but arguably sustainable claim to know the contents of experience. Unlike Kantian representationalism, which presupposes the existence of a mind-independent reality that appears, Kantian constructivism gives up any reference to reality in itself. Constructivism turns away from metaphysical realism as the standard for knowledge and toward empirical realism; that is, it turns away from a claim to know the way the world is in itself for a claim to know whatever is given in experience.

Representationalism and constructivism are basically different approaches to knowledge, which cohabit uneasily in Kant's critical philosophy. At its limit, representationalism presupposes an "identity" between a representation and what is represented, for instance, an idea in the mind and a cognitive object interpreted as a mind-independent physical thing. Constructivism, which accepts the same standard, claims that a minimal condition of knowledge is that the subject must in some sense, which varies according to the thinker concerned, "construct" what it knows.[34]

Representationalism and constructivism propose different conceptions of the cognitive object. Representationalism claims to uncover, discover, or reveal what is as it is. Constructivism makes the very different, incompatible claim to construct, produce, or make what it knows.[35] The constructivist claim to know is based on the presupposed identity between subject and object, which is brought about directly or indirectly through the subject's activity.

The theory of activity as the mediating factor between subject and object, knower and known, goes all the way back to Aristotle. In response to Plato's inability to do more than name the relation between ideas and things, Aristotle formulated a conception of activity (*energeia*) as distinguished from movement (*kinesis*). The central theme of Aristotle's conception of activity is an underlying unity, such as the unity of ideas and appearances in Plato's position, or the unity of a life in Aristotelian ethics. An example might be the idea of realizing oneself in what one does, in one's actions. This idea is well known in the aesthetic realm, where we recognize a painting as the work of a particular painter, or a literary work through its style of composition; in all cases the work, of whatever kind, and its creator are two versions of a nonstandard "metaphysical" identity.

This Aristotelian insight has an extremely wide application to many situations. It is, for instance, the basis of the well-known idea of self-development in and through objectification of oneself in what one does. It is also the underlying view in the theory of alienation, which presupposes that in appropriating the object one also appropriates the person in the form of the object. This insight is further applied to epistemology in the view of knowledge as requiring an identity in difference between knower and known, between the subject that knows and what it knows, between the epistemological subject and the epistemological object, or between epistemology and ontology. In constructivism, the correspondence between the representation and the represented epistemological object, on which representationalism insists, is restated as an identity brought about through the subject's activity.

Platonism asserts the direct, intuitive grasp of reality that does not appear in ordinary experience, and which appears only through recollection in making it possible to recognize particular objects as instances of general forms or ideas. Kantian constructivism is based on the anti-Platonic claim that reality in fact appears and is known in ordinary experience. Epistemological constructivism, which entails a shift from metaphysical to empirical realism, refers not to the mind-independent real but to what is given in empirical experience.

Kantian constructivism brings together constructivism and phenomenology in a single epistemological argument. Constructivism goes back to ancient Greek mathematics. Euclidean geometry relies on the construction of plane figures with a straightedge and a compass as a form of proof. In the *Critique of Pure Reason*, Kant explains more than once that mathematics, which constructs concepts, differs from philosophy, which analyzes them. Epistemological constructivism applies this mathematical principle to the general problems of knowledge. The result is a theory of how the subject knows phenomena that, as a necessary presupposition, it is said to construct.

Kant's epistemological constructivism, and hence his incipient phenomenology, is clearly promising but fraught with difficulties. In his Copernican turn Kant stresses that the subject knows only what it constructs while famously failing to explain what that entails. Kant never provides an account of the activity through which the subject constructs its cognitive objects, an activity which, he claims, cannot be brought into consciousness.

Kant's critical philosophy is crucial to understanding the epistemological thrust of phenomenology. From the phenomenological angle of vision, Kant is an epistemological pioneer. Kant, who was preceded by Lambert as well as many ancient writers who speak about phenomena, did not invent phenomenology. But he advanced it in ways that are still not well understood. All later phenomenologists stand in Kant's debt. As concerns epistemology, later phenomenology consists in a series of efforts to improve on the Kantian version.

Phenomenology after Kant deepens and broadens his effort to exploit the ancient distinction between phenomena, appearances, and reality for epistemological purposes. Kant continues the modern, anti-Platonic revival of representationalism, which runs together phenomena and appearances. Later phenomenology takes phenomena as appearances in identifying phenomena with things themselves, or, in Kantian language, "things in themselves."

The most important post-Kantian phenomenologists are Hegel, Husserl, Heidegger, and Merleau-Ponty. Each of them reacts to Kant in developing a distinctive phenomenological theory centered on, or at least strongly concerned with, the problem of knowledge. And, with the possible exception of Merleau-Ponty, who sharply rejects the critical philosophy he seems not to know well, phenomenological theories can be read as carrying central facets of the critical philosophy beyond Kant.

This book develops in six chapters. Chapter 1, "From Platonism to Phenomenology," discusses the Platonic background to an approach to knowledge through ideas, culminating, as Kant implies in a famous remark about understanding Plato better than he understood himself, in Kant's critical philosophy. This chapter takes up the notorious Platonic theory of ideas, in which forms or ideas cause appearances, through which they cannot be known; and then considers the modern, anti-Platonic relation of ideas as appearances to the mind-independent world in causal theories of explanation. Anti-phenomenology is analyzed in the Platonic attack on aesthetics. The final section takes up the shift from the old way of ideas to the new way of ideas leading up to the representationalist dimension of Kant's crypto-Platonic position.

Chapter 2, "Kant's Epistemological Shift to Phenomenology," discusses Kant's representationalism in the context of modern causal theories of perception, beginning with his Platonism. It analyzes the new way of ideas and its later avatar in Kant's representationalism. It identifies difficulties in Kantian representationalism that lead him to turn toward constructivism, above all the inability to show that ideas in the mind can reliably be said to correctly represent the mind-independent world. The chapter further analyzes post-Kantian efforts to "save" representationalism and hence to defend Kant against himself in arguing for an epistemological approach that he formulated and then abandoned. Kant's constructivist turn in the B preface to the *Critique of Pure Reason* is described, with special attention to his reading of the history of science, including Copernican astronomy, for its possible contribution to what he calls the future science of metaphysics. The chapter concludes with separate accounts of the relation between Kantian constructivism and modern phenomenology, as well as the relation of modern phenomenology to Platonism, the *terminus ad quem* and the *terminus a quo* of the ancient and later forms of the notorious theory of forms.

Chapter 3, "Hegel's Phenomenology as Epistemology," provides a detailed argument that his phenomenology is not simply opposed to Kantian epistemology. I argue that his phenomenological epistemology is opposed to the letter of Kant's phenomenological epistemology but is arguably compatible with its spirit. The chapter addresses the wider theme of Hegel, post-Kantian German idealism, and the philosophic tradition by examining the specific roles played by such intermediaries between Kant and Hegel as Reinhold and Fichte. The chapter ends by considering Hegel's phenomenological turn before examining the following question: Is Hegel's *Phenomenology* phenomenological?

Chapter 4, "Husserl's Phenomenological Epistemology," turns from German idealism to twentieth-century phenomenology. In the *Critique of Pure Reason*, Kant criticizes Locke's "physiological" theory, in fact an incipient philosophical anthropology emerging under Locke's influence, in working out an anti-psychologistic approach to knowledge. Husserl's anti-psychologism is key to his protean position. This chapter depicts his effort to overcome psychologism as an ongoing concern from his early breakthrough to phenomenology to his final unfinished texts. It considers Husserl's early descriptive approach to what he calls *things themselves*, and then an intermediate step in the evolution of his position between *Logical Investigations* and *Ideas* in *The Idea of Phenomenology*, and finally his mature theory of phenomenology as transcendental idealism in *Ideas* and selected later writings.[36]

In differentiating his position from others since early Greek philosophy, Heidegger claims that phenomenological ontology is not epistemology. In chapter 5, "Heidegger's Phenomenological Ontology," I argue that in Aristotle, Heidegger's favored ancient philosopher, and in his own position, the analysis of being is in fact a restricted form of epistemology. The chapter studies the complex relation to Husserlian phenomenology, especially psychologism and categorial intuition, and then offers accounts of Heidegger's critical readings of Descartes and Kant in *Being and Time* and of Kant in *Kant and the Problem of Metaphysics*. Other sections address specific Heideggerian concerns with the history of ontology, the relation of phenomenology to things themselves, interpretation and the hermeneutical circle, and the ontological theory of truth as *aletheia*.

The sixth and final chapter is entitled "Merleau-Ponty, Descriptive Phenomenology, and the Primacy of Perception." It begins with remarks about Merleau-Ponty's descriptive conception of phenomenology, which depends on his reading and rejection of the critical philosophy. The chapter addresses his views of idealism, Kantian idealism, and perception as well as such specific themes as subjectivity, psychology and perception, and phenomenology and psychology. Examination of his thesis about the primacy of perception is followed by further remarks on his views of phenomenology, idealism, and epistemology.

It is widely believed that phenomenology worthy of the name arises with Husserl, who forges a link to epistemology that Heidegger dissolves in turning to ontology. This book argues that, on the contrary, Kant is already concerned to work out a phenomenological approach to epistemology, which is rethought by his main phenomenological successors. The conclusion, which is entitled, following Gadamer, "On Overcoming the Epistemological Problem Through Phenomenology," contains some final remarks about a phenomenological approach to epistemology. These remarks should not be taken as an argument but as an indication of what an argument might look like concerning the epistemological interest of phenomenology. If we take Kant's critical philosophy as the criterion, and if we further assume that all appearances are phenomena, but only some phenomena are appearances, we can reconstruct constructivist phenomenology as the familiar Kantian claim that the subject must construct its cognitive object. The crucial problem in a constructivist form of epistemology is this: What does it mean to construct what one knows? Kant never answers this question, and twentieth-century approaches to phenomenology abandon constructivism. The general interest of Hegel's approach lies in an account of how human beings construct the cognitive object, an account that I suggest requires reformulation.

ONE

From Platonism to Phenomenology

Phenomenology is an epistemological strategy that arises in dialogue with earlier modern and ancient Greek thinkers. This chapter further examines the origins of modern phenomenological epistemology in relation to Platonism. Studies of phenomenology, especially in English, routinely begin with Husserl, who is usually discussed in detail prior to more or less detailed accounts of Heidegger, Sartre, Merleau-Ponty, and others. There is rarely more than cursory mention of pre-Husserlian phenomenologists, such as Hegel, whose relation to Husserl (or even Heidegger) is not often analyzed and remains unclear.[1] In dealing with prior debate, students of phenomenology routinely make do with a rapid glance at such predecessors of Husserl as Brentano with perhaps scant mention of Lambert or Kant in referring to several appearances of the term *phenomenology* in his writings.

The typical approach to phenomenology centers on Husserl, and the phenomenological aftermath conceals as much as it reveals. In propagating the Husserlian myth that Husserl and he alone invented phenomenology worthy of the name, a myth for which Husserl and his interpreters bear responsibility, his theory, however understood, becomes the phenomenological norm. As a result, it becomes difficult, perhaps impossible, to assess Husserl's specific contribution to an ongoing approach whose origin lies in the pre-Husserlian history of the phenomenological debate at a time when, on the Husserlian perspective, phenomenology had not yet even begun. And it is not possible to evaluate the epistemological contribution of pre-Husserlian forms of phenomenology beginning with Kant's critical philosophy.

Though Husserl clearly defends a phenomenological approach to epistemology, a study of this theme does well to start with Kant and Plato. Even more than Plato, the author of the critical philosophy is key to an understanding of the relation of phenomenology to epistemology for two reasons. He is, as noted, arguably the initial figure of the first rank to turn to phenomenology as an approach to knowledge, and his approach to knowledge is enormously influential in the later debate.

Kant was aware of his link to Plato, though perhaps not to Platonism. Kant's complex link to Platonism is an important key to understanding his later turn toward phenomenology. His phenomenological approach to knowledge, which arises out of his Copernican revolution, is a replacement strategy that reverses (or inverts) Platonism.

Platonism, the Theory of Forms, and Phenomenology

We can distinguish between Plato, whose position remains unknown and cannot now be recovered, and Platonism. Platonism is the series of theories often ascribed to Plato. Platonism, without mentioning the term *phenomenology*, which only arises much later, presupposes the failure of a phenomenological approach to knowledge understood as the phenomenal appearance of the real. In other words, Platonism presupposes that the real does not and in fact cannot appear in cognizable form.

I will be calling Platonism the approach to knowledge based on the notorious theory of forms or ideas routinely but perhaps incorrectly attributed to Plato. Platonism is distinguished by doctrinal commitments to metaphysical realism, sometimes eponymously called Platonic realism, and the theory of forms.

There are obviously different kinds of realism, including aesthetic, scientific, empirical, and so on. Aesthetic realism, which is associated with claims about art and art works, is favored in Marxist aesthetics. Scientific realism is associated with scientism, or the view, espoused without reflection by the ordinary individual and, since the emergence of Vienna Circle positivism, increasingly by certain analytic philosophers, that science is the sole measure of the real.[2] Empirical realism is the doctrine, clearly related to the positivist reliance on the so-called empirical criterion of meaning, that what we mean by *real* is solely empirical. By *metaphysical realism* I have in mind what Peirce usefully called *ontological metaphysics*.[3] This includes many versions of the familiar idea, which goes back in the tradition to early Greek philosophy, according to which, under proper conditions, there is reliable knowledge about mind-independent objects as they in fact are, that is, about the mind-independent world, not only as it appears, but as it is.

Metaphysical realism in all its many varieties presupposes three related claims. First, there is a way the mind-independent world, what Kant later influentially called the thing in itself, or noumenon, in fact is. One might paraphrase this informally as the claim that facts are facts, or that there are at least some facts which hold in all possible worlds. Second, "knowledge" by definition concerns the way the world "really" is in independence of an observer. If there is a difference between reality and appearance, however defined, then to know requires that one surpass mere appearance in grasping reality. Third, at least some of the time and in specifiable circumstances, one can reliably claim to know the mind-independent external world as it is and hence to escape epistemological skepticism through reaching knowledge.

Metaphysical realism spans the entire Western philosophical tradition from its pre-Socratic beginnings to the present day. Parmenides believes that what is, is and, for that reason, cannot change. To know is to know what is, and there is no knowledge of what is not. Fragment 2 commits him to the view that what he calls the "path of conviction" concerns knowledge of "true reality," namely, of what is and cannot not be.[4] In fragment 8, he goes on to deny that what is can change.[5]

There is scholarly controversy about how to interpret the Parmenidean view of the real, about whether he understands it monistically, dialectically, in relation to the so-called meta-principal interpretation, or in some other way. But there is no doubt that he believes that to know something is to know it as it is. This view has remained influential through the later tradition. It is repeated in two of the best-known and most influential passages in Plato's *Republic*, which describes reality as what one knows when one knows in different places, including the famous passage on the divided line and the perhaps even more famous allegory of the cave.

The familiar Platonic two-worlds ontology includes the visible world of appearance and invisible world of reality. Following this distinction, the passage on the divided line in book 6 draws attention to four stages of cognition, which are correlated to four levels of cognitive objects. The latter are divided into invisible and visible objects of knowledge and opinions situated respectively in the worlds of reality and appearance. The two worlds of reality and appearance are further subdivided into objects of reason and understanding situated in the former, and objects of belief and imagination located in the latter.

The Platonic problem of knowledge, which respects the ontological distinction between two irreducibly different kinds of cognitive objects, concerns knowledge of the mind-independent invisible real—in short, the forms or ideas. The series of views widely known as the theory of forms (or ideas) remains controversial. The theory of forms apparently centers on an effort to take a median position between materialism (identified with the

Sophists, for whom the real is limited to body, or the visible) and the very radical Eleatic view, according to which the true reality of the Sophists is no more than "a moving process of becoming" in the eyes of those who are referred to as the "friends of the forms."[6] If, in mentioning the friends of the forms, Plato is not referring to his own circle but, as seems likely, to the Eleatics, then he does not invent but only adapts an earlier version of the theory of forms, which is perhaps invented (and defended) before him, as Aristotle thinks, by Socrates, as a median position between the extremes in the battles of gods and giants that began between the defenders of materialism and the defenders of ideas. Some observers detect traces of the theory of forms throughout the Platonic corpus. Current Platonic scholarship accepts that this theory is first referred to in the *Symposium*; then stated, argued, and defended in the *Phaedo*; expounded and applied in the *Republic*; mentioned in the *Timaeus* and in the *Philebus*; and famously subjected to very thorough but puzzling criticism and, depending on the interpretation, perhaps also strenuously defended, in the *Parmenides*. In the *Phaedo*, where Plato examines the question of the immortality of the soul, a concept (or idea) is said to be immutable, timeless, unitary (or one over many), and knowable in virtue of its status as a mind-independent thing. Many passages in Plato's writings appear to refer to different versions of a doctrine that is often abbreviated as one over many. They include passages in the *Republic* (596A), where it is said that there is one idea for each type of object; in the *Hippias Major* (287CD), where it is suggested that good things are good because of the Good; in the *Phaedo*, where it is said that beautiful things are beautiful because they participate in the Beautiful (100C); and in the *Parmenides* (132DE), where it is suggested that things that participate in the same idea resemble each other in this respect.

The theory of forms (or ideas) is described, formulated in different ways, and criticized in a series of dialogues in the course of the discussion, as a nonstandard causal approach to knowledge. This theory is based on the familiar ontological dualism between sensible things, or appearances, and ideas, also called forms. This theory has two main functions: to explain the origin of appearances through a theory abbreviated as one over many; that is, one form or idea is invoked to account for the origin of many appearances and to deny knowledge of reality on the basis of appearance.

The theory of forms, which is earlier alluded to in the *Symposium*, seems to have been introduced for the first time in the *Phaedo*. From the *Phaedo*, for example, we learn that the young Socrates was interested in "the investigation of nature," which consists in a search for "the causes of everything," understood as "why each thing comes into being and why it perishes and why it exists."⁷ This calls for a general theory of causality, which Socrates presents in two main steps concerning the existence of ideas and their explanatory function. The existence of forms is proven by the argument from relativity at 65d4–66a3. At 100, Socrates proposes a theory of causation through the theory of forms in analyzing extant scientific and philosophical approaches to knowledge. Socrates mentions Anaxagoras, who claims mind is the cause of everything, as well as a "scientific" theory of causation, which makes no use of mind. He objects that the "scientific" theory does not explain individual situations before turning to the theory of forms as a better type of causal explanation. According to the hypothesis of the theory of forms, the essential properties of a thing are related to forms. Thus, a thing is beautiful because of the form of beauty. The form of beauty functions as a cause to explain the existence of the beautiful thing. In other words, reality is the cause of appearance that is said to partake of, or participate in, what it illustrates.⁸ This claim is generalized as the familiar view that appearances are caused by "participation" in the forms or ideas.⁹

Modern theory of perception, the main modern epistemological model, is based on a causal relation. The theory of forms, which joins together a nonstandard theory of causality as well as an exceedingly modern denial of a cognitive inference from effect to cause, is basically unclear and problematic on many levels. The inability to formulate an adequate causal explanation through the theory of forms is arguably one of the reasons, which leads Aristotle to focus on this problem. In the theory of forms, Plato appeals to a causal mechanism that he is unable to describe other than to attach a name to it. Aristotle, who seems to have no doubt about the relation of Plato to Platonism, seems to characterize Plato as the chief Platonist in clearly placing him among the friends of the forms. Aristotle sees the theory of forms in the context of a long series of efforts at causal explanation leading up to his own theory of four causes. We have Aristotle's testimony that Plato throughout follows Heraclitus's view that sensible things, which are in flux, cannot be known. He sees Plato as applying the Socratic concern with universals to the forms while neglecting nature.

Criticism of this theory has continued over the centuries, beginning with Plato himself. In dialogues after the *Phaedo*, Plato both reformulates and criticizes versions of this theory, most enigmatically in the *Parmenides*. Aristotle, who is one of the early observers to react to the Platonic theory of ideas, sees Plato's contribution as lying in the invention of the term *participation*, which is not yet an explanation of a causal relation. Aristotle lists a series of difficulties with the theory, such as the unnecessary multiplication of entities (*Meta.* 1.9), failure to prove that forms exist (*Meta.* 1.9), infinite regress

(*Meta.* 1.9), the claim that forms do not contribute to knowledge of sensible things (*Meta.* 1.9), and failure to arrive at a first principle (*Meta.* 2.1).

The Theory of Forms and Causal Explanation

The theory of forms is an early entrant in an ongoing struggle that runs throughout the entire later Western philosophical tradition between partisans of causal and noncausal explanation or, in an alternative formulation, between those committed to explanation through material causality or to causality based on forms or ideas. The latter view is later faintly echoed in the Kantian view, central to his theory of morality, of noumenal causality. There is a close relation between the theory of forms and scientific causal explanation. The theory of forms, which Socrates adopts in the *Phaedo* as an alternative to the early Greek form of causal scientific explanation, is later countered by the emergence of what became modern causal theory of scientific explanation.

The theory of forms explains the origin of sensible things through the causal influence of forms or ideas in which they are said to participate. "Participation" is the Platonic way of designating a causal interaction that the theory does not otherwise explain. The theory of forms is a very early form of the well-known general view, later restated by Kant and others in many different ways, according to which the problem of knowledge rests on a distinction between, in Platonic terminology, appearances, or what are given in experience as effects, and their causes, or supposed necessary conditions.

The Platonic theory of causality is difficult to defend, but the depiction of the problem is right up to date. In the *Phaedo*, Socrates' concern to explain the contents of experience through a premodern type of causal analysis based on forms as opposed to a scientific type of causality anticipates a widely accepted approach to the relation between the contents of experience and the mind-independent world. Even Berkeley, who is often wrongly criticized as denying the existence of the external world and hence as denying the commonsense view accepted by everyone, rather claims to be defending common sense. The theory of forms is invoked to explain sensible things as effects caused by a mind-independent world. Knowledge requires a grasp of causes; hence it requires following the causal network in reverse from sensible things given in experience to their causes, which, since they are only indirectly experienced, are not, therefore, known through their effects.

The Platonic reliance on causal explanation is modern, but the conception of causality is not. *Cause* is obviously a historical variable. The span of views about causality from the pre-Socratics to the contemporary period is simply breathtaking. In Homer, causality is understood as including fate (*moira*) as well as the intervention of gods and goddesses, as when Thetis intervenes to save her son Achilles during the Trojan War. Until the invention of quantum theory, the main modern view of causality depicted it as a mechanical relation among sensible objects in space and time. This view is attacked by Hume, defended by Kant, and described as a relic of a bygone age by Russell.[10] Quantum mechanics, which departs from the mechanical relation among sensible objects, understands causality in stochastic or statistical terms. As part of his rejection of the modern world, Heidegger returns to a premodern view of causality in appealing to destiny, fate (*Geschick*), and the destiny of being (*Seingeschick*) as explanatory concepts.[11]

Aristotle usefully contextualizes Plato's conception of causal explanation as one of many approaches, including all his main predecessors concerned with study of nature, leading up to his own position. The Platonic view of causality, hence of causal explanation, depicts a relation between visible and invisible sensory objects and ideas, or between objects in space and time (or things, what Platonism calls phenomena), and ideas outside of space and time. The former are given in sensory experience and hence are cognizable through it. But the latter are not given in sensory experience and are not cognizable through it. Platonic causality is teleological. The cause is the essence or *telos*, which the latter "imitates" through "participation," as when, in a famous example mentioned above, a craftsman constructs a bed according to an idea.[12]

Platonic causality is not general, but specific—focused, for instance, on explaining how beautiful things can be or become beautiful—as distinguished from general laws. Modern theories of causality are routinely understood as general, applying without exception to all spatiotemporal objects. An example is Newton's famous inverse square law, which quantifies the gravitational attraction between bodies having mass in terms of the inverse square of the distance between them. This law, which, according to Kant, holds throughout the material natural world, or nature,[13] holds in the critical philosophy between appearances, but not between appearances and things in themselves, since the latter are in neither space nor time, nor for that reason between things in themselves. The Platonic insistence on the causal link between essential qualities and forms points to a normative conception of explanation based on a one-to-one relation between a particular idea, such as beauty, and one or more phenomena exhibiting this quality, or between *explanans* and *explanandum*. Hegel, who was knowledgeable about modern science as well as ancient philosophy, may have a version of this Platonic view of causal explanation in mind in his otherwise surprising objection, which arguably suggests a blanket rejection of modern causal explanation in all its forms, that since modern natural scientific laws are general (hence nonspecific), they fail to explain individual things.[14]

Platonic causality, which is asymmetrical, justifies an inference from cause to effect, but not from effect to cause. On the Platonic model, one can infer that beautiful things are beautiful because they participate in and hence are caused to be beautiful by, the form of beauty. In denying the reverse causal inference from phenomena to forms, the Platonic theory denies the cognitive grasp of ideas on the basis of a reverse inference running from phenomena to forms. At stake is not the general inference that phenomena depend on ideas, which the theory endorses, nor the general relation, say, between the idea of beauty and beautiful things. Rather the Platonic analysis in the *Phaedo*, in rejecting such things as bones and sinews (98C) in favor of so-called real causes (98E), turns away from the explanatory use of general principles or rules to a more specific approach focusing on the causal link between ideas and phenomena.

The Platonic denial of a reverse causal inference, more precisely, the inference from effects to causes, is widely followed by later theories. If there is a collision signified by an impact in a Wilson cloud chamber, one can infer that subatomic particles, such as cosmic rays, were present, but one cannot identify the individual particle in reasoning backward from its effect. Similarly, modern genetics bases the genetic explanation of inherited traits of the most different kinds on the causal relation of parents to children. Blue eyes require the presence of a recessive trait. From a child with blue eyes, one can reasonably infer that the recessive trait is present in the lineage of that individual. But one cannot infer which parent possesses that trait unless, of course, both are blue-eyed. Marx's comment that human beings are a key to studying apes is counterintuitive but correct if and only if we concede that there is no way to trace the specific causal chain leading backward from human beings to primates.[15]

Anti-Phenomenology and the Platonic Critique of Aesthetics

The Platonic position is an anti-phenomenology, which rejects the view that reality appears. The Platonic theory of forms rejects any cognitive inference from phenomena, or sensible things, understood as effects, to forms understood as causes. The rejection of any cognitive inference from effects to causes justifies Plato's famous polemic against poetry and other forms of artistic representation.

Representation is a particularly widespread approach to knowledge. The appeal to representation in theory of knowledge is a constant in the tradition. As a translation of the Greek *phantasia*, the Latin term *repraesentare* was already employed in the sense of "vivid illustration" by Quintilian in the first century in ancient Rome. Brentano, who forged the modern conception of intentionality, relied on the medieval tradition, in which many thinkers understand mental concepts or signs in the mind as referring to external things. According to Foucault, from Descartes to Kant ideas stand in for the cognitive object, and theory of knowledge is based on mental representation.[16]

It is at least interesting that the tendency to refer to the Platonic two-worlds view in terms of such words as *phenomenon* and *appearance* is not authorized by Plato's texts. Plato, who may not have any position of his own, also has no specific technical vocabulary to describe it. The term *phenomenon* is only rarely employed by Plato and then apparently not in a technical sense. His well-known attack on artistic representation can be taken as pointing to a distinction, which is only later drawn, between *appearance* and *phenomenon*. The latter is derived from the late Latin *phaenomenon* and the Greek *phainomenon*, from the neuter of *phainomenos*. This comes from the present participle of *phainesthai* meaning "to appear" and the middle voice of *phainein* meaning "to show." The meaning of the ancient Greek *phainomenon* is roughly a "thing appearing to view," in other words, the appearance of something. Plato seems to be claiming that if what we understand as knowledge refers to what later came to be understood as mind-independent reality, then reality does not and cannot appear through things in a cognizable way in the misnamed world of appearance. This can be interpreted as a claim that reality does not appear and hence as an indication that the distinction is not drawn in the single Greek term *phenomenon* between phenomena and appearances. It follows that ancient Greek vocabulary does not by itself help us concerning a distinction in which appearances are not a reliable source of knowledge about reality. Plato's critique of aesthetics on cognitive grounds is only an illustration of a wider thesis. In criticizing art and art objects of all kinds as falling short of verisimilitude, or faithful representation, he rejects any form of representationalism in favor of his well-known suggestion, which can be paraphrased as the claim that on grounds of nature and nurture, some selected individuals can literally "see" the invisible real.

The Platonic critique of the mimetic form of representationalism is either alluded to or sketched slightly more fully in a number of dialogues, including the *Ion*, the *Cratylus*, the *Republic*, the *Sophist*, and the *Laws*. In the *Republic*,

Plato assumes a mimetic conception of aesthetics in attacking the view that representational forms of art, such as painting, can yield knowledge. According to the mimetic view, art is simply a copy of appearance.[17] In the second and third books of the dialogue, Socrates criticizes the supposedly pernicious views of the poets, particularly Homer and the tragedians. In the tenth book, he extends the criticism to other forms of representational art, especially painting. At 596 C6, Socrates refers to a craftsman who can make all things, which, he suggests, anyone can do by carrying about a mirror.[18] He goes on to describe the painter as someone who makes a picture, which is a mirror image of what it represents, and painting as a process of mimesis, or imitation. Plato's criticism, which is general, counts not only against art and art objects of the most varied kinds, such as painting, sculpture, literature, poetry, music, and so on, but also against any theory of knowledge based on representation. The critique is directed not against the successful imitation of a visible thing but rather against the successful imitation of invisible reality through imitation of phenomena.

This two-pronged critique concerns the likely success as well as social function of representational art. A painting, by inference, would successfully represent if and only if it correctly depicted shared features of an invisible reality, a possibility Plato denies on cognitive grounds. The criticism, which derives from the theory of forms, is that representational art of all forms imitates "sensible things" that are themselves mere imitations. An artist is merely "an imitator of things that others create" (597E) and hence not a party to truth. A painter does not imitate truth but merely imitates illusion. Such a person merely deceives others into thinking their paintings successfully imitate the real. Even Homer does not make us better, since, like other poets, he is a purveyor of mere imitations of virtue and other things they write about (600E). Literature and the arts in general are harmful because, as Iris Murdoch points out, like sophists, who blur the distinction between the true and the false, writers and artists lack knowledge and, for that reason, tend to lead us astray.[19]

The influential Platonic critique of art as neither true nor a source of virtue creates the aesthetic discipline while providing an important analysis of the social function of art and art objects, which remains of continuing interest. The Platonic critique depends on adopting the Platonic theory of ideas as well as a mimetic conception of art, which has been a continuing source of controversy from the time of Plato until today. The mimetic approach to art is immediately challenged by Aristotle, who contributes to broadening the view of art as an imitation of nature. In comparison to Plato, whose view he contests, Aristotle takes a wider view of artistic mimesis as including a series of arts.[20] Gerard Else helpfully points out that Aristotle gives the key term *mimesis* a different meaning than does Plato.[21] One way to put the point is that Aristotle reinterprets *mimesis*, which for Plato means "imitation," as "construction or production." According to Aristotle, both mimetic and nonmimetic types of art imitate nature. He has in mind the purposeful character of productive processes based on rational principles,[22] which is different from mimesis itself. Though all the arts imitate nature, only the specifically mimetic arts aim to represent the world as such. In the *Poetics*, Aristotle suggests that the mimetic arts represent actual reality, or popular views or beliefs about the world, or normative ideas of what ought to be the case.[23] Other views of mimesis are strewn throughout the later tradition.[24] Kant, who is an epistemological anti-Platonist, is an artistic Platonist in an Aristotelian sense. A version of the mimetic view of art survives in Kant's conception of aesthetics as the imitation of visible nature as distinguished from invisible reality.

Mimesis continues to be discussed. Sophisticated criticisms have been raised in recent literature about the very possibility of an uninterpreted imitation of objects of any kind. Ernst Gombrich, who denies that art consists in merely copying what one sees, considers pictorial representation as the source of illusion.[25] Nelson Goodman directly attacks the very idea of representation in the course of replacing the realist theory of representation, in which imitation is its most developed form, with conventionalism.[26]

Artistic mimesis is a form of artistic representation. The anti-Platonic, representational approach to art is central to the Christian religious tradition. Christian art contradicts the Platonic claim that we cannot reliably claim to depict or otherwise represent the mind-independent world as it in fact is. Over a period of centuries, illiterate Christians believed they could literally "read" the stained glass windows of the great Western cathedrals that, from their perspective, successfully depicted transcendent reality. The Christian claim for artistic truth is further maintained in the secular aesthetic tradition, which for a long time remained concerned with the relation of art to knowledge. The French impressionists, who followed Courbet and Manet, were aesthetic realists, concerned, as the phrase goes, to be true to nature. It is often said that in impressionism realism is transformed into subjective realism. Yet the focus on epistemological truth remains a constant, even for the post-impressionist, Paul Cezanne, who says, "I owe you truth in painting and I will tell it to you."[27]

Others turn away from a representational approach to art on religious or more closely aesthetic grounds. On doctrinal grounds, Jewish and Muslim religious art eschews graven images. It is accordingly non-representational, intended as referring to, or as symbolizing, but not intended literally or even figuratively as a depiction of, transcendent reality. The non-representational approach of certain forms of religious art later spread into modern art, which, in turning away from any representational function, became increasingly abstract. Cubism is a form of abstract art, which was begun in 1907–8 by Pablo Picasso and Georges Braque, and later joined by Juan Gris, that is also nonmimetic and non-representational. The early cubists brought together views of the same object from different angles of vision in which the parts were distributed in nonstandard ways, resulting in increasing fragmentation and abstraction. Cubism later led to such forms of abstract art as constructivism and neoplasticism.

The Old Way of Ideas and the New Way of Ideas

Plato's attack on mimesis belongs to the effort many observers attribute to him to solve the problem of knowledge through the theory of forms. The theory of forms analyzes the problem of knowledge through the relation of ideas or forms to things. Modern epistemology, which also approaches knowledge through the relation of ideas to things, features a very different version of this same approach.

Platonism, or the old way of ideas, and modern causal theory of perception, or the new way of ideas, feature basically different interpretations of the relation of things and ideas. The "new way of ideas" is a phrase apparently coined by Bishop Stillingfleet in reference to John Toland's non-Cartesian way of using ideas, based on his reaction to Locke's *Essay*, in *Christianity Not Mysterious* (1696).[28] In referring to modern philosophy, we will be using "new way of ideas" in a widened sense to refer not only to Locke, but also to English empiricism in general, as well as to continental rationalism—in short, to the main modern views of knowledge up to and at least partly including the critical philosophy.

The new way of ideas is the movement arising in the seventeenth century, which includes the continental rationalists (Descartes, Spinoza, Leibniz, and others) and the British empiricists (Bacon, Locke, Berkeley, Hume, Reid, and others) but excludes others, such as the Cambridge Platonists.[29] The new way of ideas—new by comparison to Platonism, or the old way of ideas—reverses the Platonic rejection of representationalism while maintaining without change a similar commitment to metaphysical realism. The Platonic approach to knowledge in the full sense of the term as intuitive, hence immediate, is rejected in the new way of ideas in favor of an anti-Platonic model of knowledge mediated by ideas, thoughts, or representations in the mind. In general, for the new way of ideas, *to know* is to know the way the world is, not directly but indirectly through ideas, which are said to represent, or depict, what is as it is. Understood in this way, the new way of ideas includes not only Descartes and perhaps the other continental rationalists, as well as the English empiricists, but also Kant, who, since he already has a role for the term *idea*, which designates a concept of reason going beyond experience,[30] substitutes the word *representation* (*Vorstellung*). These and many other thinkers who discuss epistemology in this period do so in terms of the same canonical, Platonic conceptual matrix comprising ideas and things.

Modern epistemology, which relies on the Platonic framework of things and ideas, is not Platonic but anti-Platonic, based on reversing a fundamental epistemological tenet of Platonism. According to Platonism, the relation of forms to things is ontological but not epistemological. The relation can be summarized as the claim that forms cause things but cannot be known through them. Platonism, which denies epistemological skepticism, holds that under appropriate conditions, and on the basis of nature and nurture, in leaving the world of appearance behind some selected individuals can reliably claim to grasp mind-independent reality directly. In other words, if there is knowledge, which remains unclear in Plato's dialogues, then it is reserved for some exceptional individuals known as philosophers, who, unlike sophists, are concerned with and sometimes actually reach truth. Modern epistemology, which reverses the relation between ideas and things as well as the cognitive relation between ideas, things, and knowledge, features variations on the anti-Platonic claim that things cause ideas, which are known through them. Since things cause ideas, this epistemological approach amounts to claiming that reality manifests itself in and through our ideas. In extending the cognitive domain to all observers, modern students of knowledge, who differ widely about the proper approach, nonetheless agree that there is knowledge of the way the world is.

Like Platonism, modern epistemological analysis relies on the term *idea*, which is understood differently by various observers. In interpreting the ancient and modern views of *idea*, we must avoid reading modern distinctions back into the early history of Western philosophy. Three main aspects concern their ontological status, causal role, and relation to reality.

Platonism contrasts forms or ideas, which are permanent and unchanging, or said to be real, or reality, and the cause of impermanent things, or particulars, which are their effects. Platonic ideas are invisible, immaterial universals not material particulars; they are objects of mind or reason but not of vision or the other senses. There is scholarly agreement that ideas are one, or unitary, hence simple, and that their sole property is the quality each exemplifies. Thus the idea of beauty is itself beautiful since its quality is predicated of itself. The interpretation of this claim, which is delicate, concerns the problem of self-predication leading to an infinite regress, an objection initially raised by Plato[31] and then by Aristotle in the so-called third-man argument.[32] According to Gregory Vlastos, the relation between the idea and itself is the same as that between a particular and the Form.[33] This interpretation, which suggests that beauty, like beautiful things, has a mind-independent status and hence is epistemologically significant. It is at least clear in Platonism that to know is to know ideas, so that to know beauty means to know the idea or form of beauty. Knowledge is the result of grasping the essence or true quality that cannot be known through the body, that is, through sight, but is knowable only through reason.[34] Unlike the world of appearance, which is constantly changing in a Heraclitean flux, ideas are stable. This agrees with the view going back at least to Parmenides, and exemplified by Socrates' search for universal definitions, that we can define and know what is as it is, what does not change, but we cannot know what does change.[35] Finally, ideas, which are permanent, hence unchanging, are unaffected by the passage of time and neither come into being nor pass away. Yet particulars, which, unlike ideas, are situated in space and time, change their qualities in the course of coming into being and passing away.

In later philosophy, the term *idea* is used in the most varied ways including the "idea" of God, Bolzano's "idea in itself" independent of thought and language, and so on. In modern philosophy, *idea* is used to designate an idea in the mind, which is neither universal, nor permanent, nor even stable. In modern times in epistemological contexts ideas are not said to cause but are said to be caused by and hence to be effects of the mind-independent external world. Modern ideas, which are not independent of but dependent on the outside world, change as the world, which causes them, changes. Unlike Platonic ideas, which are stable, permanent, and immutable, ideas in the mind are not stable or permanent but mutable and impermanent, subject to change, not as the causes of but as the effects of the surrounding flux; hence they are not independent of but depend on the surrounding world. In Platonism, sensible things, which are the effects of ideas, are not themselves on the road to knowledge. In modern times, the inversion of the relation of ideas and things leads to the view that through ideas we grasp the way things, which are reality, in fact are. In this period, the problem of knowledge is not addressed by circumventing things, or the world of appearance, in order to grasp ideas. Rather, it is addressed by formulating an account of the relation between ideas and things on the basis of which, under appropriate conditions, an epistemological inference is possible and plausible from ideas to things. The underlying analysis for the relation between ideas and things, which justifies the claim to know on the basis of ideas, derives from the familiar causal theory of perception. In one formulation, this consists in the claim that mind-independent things, otherwise referred to as nature or as the world, cause ideas in the mind, which are effects allowing a reliable inverse inference that yields knowledge of their causes.

Platonism rejects claims for direct knowledge on the grounds of perceptual relativity. Long before Berkeley, Plato points out that the same thing, in different conditions, appears differently. Platonism further rejects representationalism, or the view that ideas in the mind can stand in for or otherwise correctly represent the mind-independent external world as it is. Modern theory of knowledge, which centers on the relation of ideas to objects, and which features an interpretation of ideas as representations of things, is often representationalist. The anti-Platonic return to representationalism resulted from a revised conception of the term *idea*. In Platonism, an idea, or form, is an unchanging cognitive object. The concept of the Reichstag remains the same even when flames are lapping around the building. The view in the *Timaeus* of the forms as eternal and independent objects functioning as patterns for the demiurge was influential in later antiquity and throughout the Middle Ages. Through such thinkers as Plotinus, Augustine, Aquinas, and Montaigne, *idea* later came to mean "image" or "representation," often situated in the mind. By the time of Montaigne, *idea* apparently already meant "mental representation."

Descartes' position turns on the simple word *idea*, which, it is widely agreed, he uses in many different senses in what is sometimes called his theory of ideas.[36] Like a number of modern figures, he clearly has a view that depends on a variable conception of *idea*, yet is not anything like what is understood as the theory of forms in Platonism. The term *idea* suggests a strong continuity between Descartes and the philosophical tradition, especially with respect to Platonism, a link that is perhaps stronger than is warranted by an analysis of the texts. In Descartes, there simply is no theory of forms in the Platonic sense in which forms or ideas that do not appear in experience are said to cause things. Yet there is clearly a strong relation between Descartes and the prior tradition in various ways, including the relation to scholasticism,[37] to specific scholastic authors,[38] to specific themes such as skepticism,[39] and so on. We know at least since Gilson that the supposed break between Descartes and scholasticism is more gradual and less radical than is often supposed. It is at least clear that in appealing to the term *idea*, he is following a long tradition stretching over the centuries from ancient philosophy to the very beginning of the modern tradition. It is often observed that Descartes is heavily dependent on medieval sources in his theological, his scientific and other views.[40]

In appealing to ideas, Descartes seems less to break with than to be following scholasticism. There are various avenues for the transmission of the Platonic concern with the theory of ideas to modern philosophy that is concerned with ideas. One is the interest in the so-called problem of universals, which is a form of the Platonic concern with ideas.[41] This runs from the creation of this problem by Porphyry, through Boethius, Abelard, William of Ockham, Jean Buridan, and others. Another is the later Christian reliance on a quasi-Platonic, specifically Christian approach to knowledge, in which Platonic ideas become divine ideas. It is a commonplace that, beginning with Augustine, Christian philosophers insert Platonic ideas into the mind of God, where they function as models for the creation of the world. This view is held by Augustine and, following him, Aquinas.[42] The latter notes that whenever possible Augustine adopted Platonic doctrines.[43] Aquinas, who subscribes to a version of the Platonic doctrine as revised by Augustine, again restates it.[44] This view is once again restated by Descartes, without more than indirect reliance on the divine, who justifies his recourse to the term because it was already the standard approach. "I used the word 'idea' because it was the standard philosophical term used to refer to the forms of perception belonging to the divine mind."[45]

In part because of Descartes' enormous and continuing influence, the term *idea* is widely used in modern epistemological contexts. We can distinguish broadly between rationalist, empiricist, and Kantian critical perspectives, all of which rely on some form of causal relation between ideas and things but differ widely among themselves and, as concerns rationalism and empiricism, within each tendency. These distinctions, which are initially useful to separate broad theoretical options, later break down on examination or even tend to become obstacles since there is so much variety within the different tendencies, whose supposed members were sometimes in contact with and influenced by representatives of other tendencies.

The new way of ideas counters the old way of ideas, which rejects an approach to knowledge based on representation understood as resulting from a causal theory of perception. In different ways, all those associated with the new way of ideas, including rationalists, empiricists, and critical philosophers alike, approach knowledge through an analysis of the causal relation of ideas to cognitive objects variously understood as nature, the world, or even the thing in itself, or noumenon. This large and diverse group includes the main rationalists, such as Descartes, Spinoza, and Leibniz, as well as the Cartesian occasionalists, including Malebranche, whom Kant appreciates, Geulincx, de La Forge, de Cordemoy, and others who think that the relation of mind and body requires divine intervention. The empiricists include such important figures as Locke, Berkeley, Hume, and Reid, who was an opponent of all three, as well as such figures of the Scottish Enlightenment as Francis Hutcheson, Adam Smith, and others.

Plato famously mentions cutting up things according to their type along their natural joints.[46] But the world never divides neatly at a small number of conceptual joints uniquely identified by philosophical observers. The main philosophical terms usually (perhaps always) reflect different normative concerns. The web of distinctions surrounding such terms as *rationalism* and *empiricism*, and the relation of both to Kant's critical philosophy are highly complex. There is probably no way acceptable to all observers to characterize rationalist, empiricist, and other approaches to knowledge. Any description one proposes can always be criticized in terms of another normative view. Broadly speaking, in following Descartes many rationalists lay claim to innate ideas. In speaking of innate ideas, the quarrel between rationalists and empiricists is sometimes stated in terms of the idea of God. But this is not true for Kant, who is in many ways close to rationalism, for instance, in denying that claims for knowledge, which must begin in experience, can be limited to experience. Kant does not feature an innate conception of the deity and is not a rationalist in that sense, unless categories are taken to be innate ideas.

I stress broad differences between rationalism, empiricism, and critical philosophy as concerns the epistemological analysis of the common commitment to a causal analysis of the relation of ideas to things. Following Descartes, the rationalists tend to analyze this relation from the perspective of the subject who makes a justified cognitive inference from an idea in the mind to the mind-independent external world. Under the influence of Locke, empiricists reverse the direction of the analysis in arguing from the mind-independent world to ideas in the mind.

This minimal extent of agreement plays out differently in different positions. For present purposes, we can distinguish broadly between rationalist, empiricist, and critical approaches to knowledge in terms of three different approaches to the relation of ideas to things as illustrated in the first place by Descartes, Locke, and Kant.

The influential Cartesian view of ideas spans mathematical claims as well as adventitious thoughts neither innate nor formed by the subject, which are defined as "images of the [external] things."[47] This view is frequently criticized. It is often said that Descartes uses the term *idea* inconsistently to refer to an operation or act and to its content.[48] He introduces *idea* (*idée*) to mean "images of things."[49] In answering Hobbes, he maintains this definition in denying that he has an idea of God.[50] In the preface to the *Meditations*, he responds to the objection that an idea I have might be more perfect than me. He answers that the term *idea*, which is "equivocal," can be taken either "materially, as an act of my understanding" or "taken objectively, as the thing which is represented by this act."[51] R. A. Watson, who considers Descartes to be the father of representationalism,[52] argues that he consistently conflates image and concept, as in the discussion of the two ideas of the sun in the third *Meditation*, of which one is acquired from the senses and the other through astronomical reasoning.[53] This type of objection was already raised before the book was in print. Hobbes, for instance, complains that we could not have more than one idea of the sun at a time, and that Descartes conflates "idea" and "rational inference."[54]

Descartes is often taken as the canonical modern illustration of foundationalist epistemology. His foundationalist epistemology is intended to justify a representationalist approach to knowledge, which can be informally described as justifying a cognitive inference from an idea in the mind to the mind-independent external world. This approach can be further described as an effort to weave a seamless web in the form of a single deductive argument. The Cartesian theory begins in a first principle in theory known to be true beyond doubt of all kinds; hence, since any presupposition can always evoke doubt, it begins in an argument that supposedly has no presuppositions, leading from the cogito to knowledge of the mind-independent world. His familiar argument runs through a series of stages, including proof of his own existence, through proof of God's existence, then through the inference that, since God is no deceiver, clear and distinct ideas are true, and finally to the proof of material things. Descartes freely concedes his inability to prove the existence of external objects with absolute certainty ("I cannot derive some certain proof of the existence of corporeal objects").[55] But in relying on God, he arrives at the desired certain result ("Hence we must allow that corporeal things exist.").[56] Note that this is precisely the result that Kant later derives in his famous "refutation of idealism." Descartes, who tries but fails to prove the existence of the external world without invoking God, never doubts it exists. He rather entertains doubt as a step within his epistemological project. Hence Kant's claim that Descartes doubts the existence of the external world is mistaken.[57] And if he thinks, on the basis of his own position, that Descartes is not entitled to doubt, then his criticism is external, not internal to the Cartesian position.

For our purposes, it is not necessary to sort out the proper interpretation of the Cartesian position. Suffice it to say that his important distinction between the reliance on *idea* to refer to concepts and to images of things identifies a basic difference between Platonism, or the old way of ideas, and modern representationalism, or the new way of ideas. The antirepresentationalist Platonic theory of ideas takes them to be concepts, or exemplars of sensible things, whereas the representational approach to perception that flourishes in modern times regards them as images of mind-independent external things. In running together the ancient use of *idea* to refer to concepts and the modern usage to refer to things, Descartes conflates Platonism, which in this way enters into modernity and survives in his position, and the anti-Platonic, modern form of representationalism, of which he is an early, distinguished, and highly influential representative.

Descartes' residual Platonism was mainly discounted, but his influential appeal to *idea* as "an image of a thing" and hence the representationalism following from it was widely accepted. Those influenced by this Cartesian view include Pierre Gassendi and Thomas Hobbes, who were early readers and critics of his *Meditations*; such other rationalists as Spinoza and Leibniz; and, through Locke, the entire British empiricist tradition. Spinoza distinguishes between conception, or an idea in the mind, and perception, which is acted upon, in stressing that in conception the mind acts. He defines an idea as a concept in the mind when one thinks.[58] And he famously claims, in anticipating Kant's Copernican turn, that the order and connection of ideas and things is the same.[59] In the *Monadology*, on the basis of his conception of a preestablished harmony, Leibniz maintains that each monad represents, or mirrors, the whole universe.[60] In the "Discourse on Metaphysics," he further distinguishes between an idea understood as different thoughts about the same thing, and also as the object of thought—that is, as something permanent that remains unaltered whether or not one is thinking of it.[61]

The rationalist approach to knowledge through ideas in the mind exemplified by Descartes "officially" runs from ideas to things. We are meant to infer that ideas are effects caused by things, by the impact of the world on the mind, the world to which we return through an inference in part justified by the conviction that God would not deceive us. Reliance on God is intended to justify the anti-Platonic inference from effect to cause, or from ideas to the world. The difficulty lies in showing without invoking a deus ex machina that ideas in the mind match up with or otherwise correspond to the way the world is. Empiricists, who hold that a rationalist approach to knowledge cannot justify this type of claim, invert the rationalist strategy in an argument that in effect turns it upside down.[62] Though preceded by Hobbes and Bacon, Locke has the reputation of being the first great standard-bearer of British empiricism.

The term *idea* in the *Essay on Human Understanding* "stands for whatsoever is the Object of the Understanding, when a man thinks."[63] Locke believes that we think, and that when we think, we have ideas. According to Locke, "the mind perceives nothing but its own ideas," and "it is necessary that something else," or an idea "as a sign or representation of the thing it considers, should be present to it."[64] This view makes him out to be a representational realist about perception. But he has also been read as a skeptic, and as a direct realist.[65] Locke differentiates between simple ideas, which the mind cannot create, and complex ideas, or ideas composed out of simple ideas by the mind.[66] He claims that the latter are never wrong, and directly grasp the mind-independent, empirical world.[67] According to this and related forms of English empiricism, complex ideas represent the world, which is indirectly but unerringly known through simple ideas claimed in various ways to match up one-to-one, so to speak, with the world. Versions of this theory run throughout British empiricism and allied doctrines at least through the early Wittgenstein and even later in the early Carnap. Thus Wittgenstein typically asserts, but never shows, that so-called atomic ideas bear a one-to-one relation to atomic facts. And Carnap, supposedly following Wittgenstein, introduces the concept of protocol sentences (*Protokollsätze*), famously refuted by Neurath,[68] intended to weave a seamless web between experience and science.

Locke, who is sometimes said to adopt and make his own Descartes' way of ideas, in fact opposes the view of innate ideas favored by rationalism. In book 1 of the *Essay* he argues, following others as early as Aristotle,[69] that we do not have innate knowledge since the mind at birth is a blank slate. According to this view, there is nothing in the mind that does not come to it through the senses, where the latter term includes both sensation as well as reflection. The mind, which is passive with respect to the reception of simple ideas, is also active in combining them through reflection into complex ideas. But simple ideas, which match up one to one with the world, are necessarily true about the mind-independent external world.

Locke's view of knowledge of the world through ideas that are necessarily true about it was attacked directly and indirectly within the empiricist tradition by Berkeley, Hume, Reid, and many others, including in the twentieth century the later Wittgenstein, Neurath, W. Sellars, Quine, and

Davidson. It is an irony of the contemporary debate that analytic philosophy, which arose in the empiricism invoked by Russell and Moore at the time of its founding at the beginning of the twentieth century, had by the middle of that century widely rejected its empiricist roots.

In response to Locke, Berkeley denies we can ever know that our ideas resemble the objects independent of them.[70] He further maintains, as Reid also argues, that as soon as we distinguish between things and ideas of them we land in skepticism.[71] And Hume divides the contents of mind into impressions—or, as he says, sensations, passions, and emotions—and ideas. He claims that the latter are merely fainter, less vivid copies of the former, while denying that we can ever rationally infer to causal relations in the world. Through the influence of the *Port Royal Logic* and Locke's *Essay*, the term *idea* was gradually extended to mean literally "any object of thought." Further complications were introduced by distinctions between innate, abstract, and concrete ideas. One difficulty is the confused discussion about innate ideas between Descartes, Leibniz, Locke, and others. A second difficulty lies in the distinction between abstract ideas, arrived at through abstraction, and concrete ideas. Locke took over the conception of abstract ideas in the *Port Royal Logic*[72] as the basis of his own distinction between simple and complex ideas.

Berkeley's idealism arises out of his critique of Lockean empiricism through an original interpretation of the theory of ideas. Berkeley, who attributes many philosophical problems to the misuse of language, does not deny general ideas. But he rejects abstract general ideas in holding, as already noted, that an idea becomes general in being made to stand for similar particular ideas.[73] Berkeley employs a strongly a posteriori, empiricist approach. He holds that what exists is always particular, never general, and that whatever exists can be sensed or imagined. He applies this approach to natural science and to mathematics. For instance, he rejects as unintelligible Locke's conception of a general triangle[74] as well as, and well before Kant, Newton's conceptions of absolute space, time, and motion. Like Kant, Berkeley denies that an analysis of motion requires a conception of absolute space, understood as "distinct from that which is perceived by sense, and related to bodies."[75] Yet since he thinks it is not even possible to imagine space without body, Kant's objections that for Berkeley "space is impossible in itself" and that "things in space [are] merely imaginary" are simply mistaken.[76]

Locke's view of knowledge depends on the familiar distinction between primary and secondary ideas formulated by Descartes, Galileo, and other students of nature. This distinction is intended to isolate ideas that reliably inform us about the way the world is from those that do not. Locke distinguishes simple ideas, which are necessarily true about the independent external world, by separating them from merely secondary ideas. For Berkeley, there are only secondary ideas. His position turns on his rejection of any version of the distinction between primary and secondary ideas. In response to Locke, he denies we can ever know that our ideas resemble independent objects. Since for Berkeley there are, in effect, only secondary ideas, no ideas, none at all, can count as trustworthy representations of a mind-independent external world. Like Reid, he claims against Locke that as soon as we distinguish between things and ideas we land in skepticism.[77]

Berkeley regards the view that perceived qualities really are in the object (e.g., the apple is really red) as at once absurd, dangerous, and repulsive: it is absurd because it leads to skepticism; it is dangerous because this view inclines toward universal causal determinism, hence toward atheism, and for this reason apparently undermines all morality; and it is repulsive because it points toward a conception of the world as a vast machine, actually formulated in the mid-nineteenth century by the French anti-Cartesian materialist La Mettrie,[78] whereas on the contrary God's creation could not really be like that, despite the peculiar arguments of the philosophers, since apples really are red. The solution, Berkeley thought, must consist in immaterialism, which is best conceived not as a denial of but as an argument in favor of common sense, for instance, the commonsense view about the color of apples. His strategy, which is to deny that there is any quality that extra-mental objects can possess, consists in applying arguments about the relativity of perception already known to the ancient Greeks against the kind of general worldview then emerging out of modern science, as well as to the form of empiricism based on the emerging modern science.

Berkeley's main insight can be summarized as the view that we do not perceive tables and chairs; rather, we perceive ideas, so that objects merely are ideas.[79] He applies this insight in attacking contemporary representational claims to knowledge of things. Representational approaches to knowledge presuppose that ideas are like the things they represent. Berkeley denies this in criticizing the distinction between primary and secondary ideas. According to Berkeley, for whom this distinction is invalid, all ideas are secondary ideas, dependent on the perceiver. His view comes down to the commonsense claim taken up again in our day by Davidson that ideas cannot be like things since they can only be like other ideas.[80]

Berkeley is often described but rarely read, and when he is read, he is often understood in controversial ways.[81] Hume is more often read and clearly celebrated. His position depends on his view of ideas. Both the

Treatise and the *Enquiry* open with discussion of impressions and ideas, which, he thinks, are the only way to treat meaningful philosophical topics. In this respect, Hume anticipates Kant's later view that we cannot hope for knowledge beyond the limits of experience. As an empiricist, Hume limits the contents of thought to perceptions whose source lies either in sensation, or "outward sentiment," or in reflection, known as "inward sentiment."[82] Perceptions further divide into two types as concerns their force or vivacity. According to Hume, the weaker perceptions or ideas are traceable to the livelier impressions.[83] Like Locke, Hume further discusses the relation of simple and complex ideas. The former are constructed out of simple ideas. Simple ideas, which are fainter impressions of simple impressions, directly and exactly resemble, or correspond to, simple impressions. Hume, who is sometimes believed to take Newton as a model, takes this general proposition, which is also known as the copy principle, as his first principle of the science of human nature.[84]

Humean skepticism is moderate, less extreme than ancient skepticism, directed not to the possibility of knowledge as such but to particular types of cognitive claims. He accepts, for instance, that we have knowledge of human nature. He thinks we can understand human freedom, what he famously describes as a "reconciling project with regard to the question of liberty and necessity; the most contentious question of metaphysics, the most contentious science,"[85] through a compatibilist model,[86] which Kant restates in his moral theory. He also accepts the theories of natural science that in his view, which Kant later shares, peak in Newton.

Hume's view of knowledge through ideas is famously supplemented by a destructive attack on causality. His skeptical attack on the concept of cause is based on his view of ideas. In effect, he claims that what we initially take to be a causal relation between two sensible things in the mind-independent world is seen on inspection to be due to a misperception founded on reading a psychological cause, namely, the tendency of human observers to understand experience on a causal basis, into experience. According to Hume, causal relations, which cannot be justified by reason or understanding, are justified only by custom or habit that leads us to believe that the future will conform to the past.

Reid, who was a contemporary of Hume, is now best known for his critique of Locke. Like Berkeley, and later like Moore and Austin, Reid defends common sense. Reid's critique centers on his objections to the way of ideas. Like Berkeley, Reid argues that as soon as we distinguish between things and ideas of them we land in skepticism.[87] In arguing against dualism from Plato to the present, Reid claims that we have direct, immediate knowledge of the existence of things.[88] Like Moore, who also sometimes favors direct, or immediate, realism, Reid believes that most of the time we are directly aware of real objects. Reid's accusation that Berkeley and Hume, who, from this perspective, is reclassified as an idealist, deny the existence of the external world later recurs in Kant's famous "refutation of idealism."[89] In his own notorious "refutation of idealism" (1903), Moore reformulates Reid's complaint, as restated by Kant, in generalizing it to idealism as such.

In Reid's interpretation, in Locke's theory any thing present to mind is what Reid calls "perception," as distinguished from sensory perception. This view can be abbreviated as the claim that mental phenomena are perceptions of mental objects. Reid attacks Locke's view of the relation between simple ideas and things. According to Locke, simple ideas are caused by the mind-independent external world. Reid believes that what we call thinking implies the mind doing the thinking, then the thinking, and finally what we think about, or the object. Philosophers differ from ordinary individuals in substituting an idea in the mind as the immediate object for the mind-independent external thing. This leads to skepticism since we can draw no conclusions about the relation of ideas in the mind to their causes in the world.[90] Hence philosophy leads to skepticism that is avoided by common sense. We find a later echo of this view in Hilary Putnam's recent shift to a direct form of realism without a representational interface, a view that is in many ways close to Reid's.[91]

Modern causal theory of perception plays a central role in the transition between ancient Greek philosophy and modern phenomenology. Kant is in some respects a Platonist as well as a phenomenologist. The long road from Platonism to phenomenology becomes shorter and more interesting if we perceive the complex links between what we can call the old theory of ideas illustrated in Plato and Platonism, and what we can call the new theory of ideas, understood in a widened sense as including Descartes and perhaps other rationalists as well as Locke and other empiricists, especially Berkeley. Phenomenology arises in modern times out of the difficult distinction, which is still in the process of being drawn, between phenomena, appearances, and reality as it is or what is often referred to as the mind-independent real. An important step toward clarifying this distinction occurs in Kant's critical philosophy in the evolution of his epistemological approach.

TWO

Kant's Epistemological Shift to Phenomenology

Kant's relation to Plato is complex. Though in some senses a deep Platonist, Kant is also arguably the most important modern anti-Platonist. His position contains a shift from a causally explanatory approach to a phenomenologically descriptive approach to knowledge, which becomes the basis of later post-Kantian phenomenology. This shift occurs through the reinterpretation of a single epistemological model from competing perspectives. The first model continues and develops the canonical, anti-Platonic, modern causal theory of perception, according to which mind-independent things cause ideas in the mind—in Kant's theory, representations or appearances. The second model refutes this initial model in all of its many variations while suggesting another anti-Platonic alternative. The first very familiar model presupposes metaphysical realism in adopting a representational approach to knowledge understood as requiring the correct representation of the world as it is, beyond appearance. The criterion of truth in this model is the correspondence of the representation to its cognitive object. The second model is not representational but constructivist. It presupposes the failure of the initial strategy, which is replaced by the view that a necessary condition of knowledge is that the cognitive subject in some sense "construct" the cognitive object or objects. The criterion of knowledge in this model is the identity of the subject and object, knower and known.

The familiar representationalist model is a restatement of the causal theory of perception running throughout modern philosophy. The unfamiliar constructivist model goes back to ancient mathematics and comes into modern philosophy through Hobbes and, under his influence, Vico. Kant formulates both models of knowledge in the critical philosophy. I have described these models in detail elsewhere and do not wish to repeat that description here.[1] I concentrate instead on the Platonic and anti-Platonic aspects of the Kantian effort to analyze the cognitive relation between ideas and things understood as the mind-independent external world or, in his terminology, as noumena, or things in themselves.

The difference between these two models, which can be understood with respect to Platonism, can be briefly described with respect to a causal approach to knowledge. The initial, representational approach to knowledge is based on causality, or the causal influence of the mind-independent external world. On the contrary, the later anti-Platonic alternative effort abandons causality as usually understood in formulating a constructivist approach to phenomenology. In other words, in moving beyond the causal anti-Platonism typical of modern epistemology, Kant invents another, more powerful, but still anti-Platonic epistemological strategy—in short, phenomenology. Accordingly, this chapter also focuses on the further development and final breakdown of the old causal model of knowledge and the discovery of a new, postcausal model as well as the relation of both to Platonism.

Kant's "Platonism"

Kant's Platonism is often mentioned but not often studied in detail.[2] His precise relation to Plato and Platonism remains unclarified. According to Mihaela Fistioc, we do not know if Kant ever read any of Plato's texts,[3] or if his knowledge of Plato and Platonism is indirect, say, through Johann Jakob Brucker's *Historia Critica*.[4] Yet observers have never hesitated to discuss the relation of Kant and Plato. Hamann, for example, was bothered by Kant's Platonism in the first *Critique*.[5] Manfred Kuehn, who says Kant seems to have read Plato, thinks Kant's idealism derives from his reaction to Plato's ideas.[6] Paul Guyer depicts Kant without hesitation as reacting to Plato.[7]

I have been stressing the importance of the anti-Platonic reaction in the modern formulation of the problem of knowledge not, as Platonism suggests, through a direct grasp of reality, but by appropriating the Platonic model of the relation of ideas to things in the causal theory of perception. This leads to the familiar claim that we grasp things in the world through ideas in the mind. This rethinking of the Platonic model of the relation of ideas to objects continues in Kant's critical philosophy.

In sorting out Kant's view of Plato, whom he does not distinguish from Platonism, it will be useful to distinguish between Kant's reading of Plato in terms of his own position, which remains on the superficial plane; his view of the interaction between philosophical positions, which is very suggestive;

and the more complex question, which Kant does not directly address, of the relation of his own position and modern epistemology to Platonism.

Kant mentions Plato early in the *Critique of Pure Reason*. In the A preface, he refers critically to Plato's propensity to venture beyond the world of experience into "the empty space of pure understanding."[8] In a passage on ideas in general at the beginning of the chapter entitled "Transcendental Dialectic," he notes, in recalling the view expressed in the famous Herz letter, that for Plato ideas are "archetypes of things themselves"; hence, unlike categories, they are "the key to possible experience" (B370, 395). In the famous letter to Herz, Kant rejects the view he attributes to Plato of "an archetypal intellect (*intellectus archetypi*), upon whose intuition the things themselves are grounded."[9] In the passage in the Transcendental Dialectic, he rejects direct intuition of the real, which is impossible in principle, since a relation to what is must be mediated through a categorial framework. Yet this objection is superficial, since there is no more than a distant analogy between ideas as cognitive objects in Platonism and sensible things of experience as cognitive objects in the critical philosophy. And he denies the tendency, supposedly illustrated by Brucker, to take the Platonic republic as a dream of perfection, which Hegel later restates as an *"empty ideal,"*[10] since "human reason shows true causality" and "ideas become efficient causes" (B372–75, 396–98), especially in morality. This would situate Kant's otherwise difficult comment that ideas are "the original causes of things" (B374, 398).

Though he declines to study the texts, which he disparagingly describes as mere "literary investigation," Kant further suggests a more general relation between the critical philosophy and Plato. He famously thinks that, since we are sometimes unable to express ourselves precisely or only do so carelessly, we often understand an author better than the author understands himself (B370, 396). In this observation, Kant is not advancing a version of Plato's claim that language falls short of grasping reality. Neither is he adumbrating the point that occurs later in the book that an original thinker often is able to use but not clearly state an original idea (B862, 692). Yet he is at least suggesting the possibility of a dialogue between an earlier and a later author, such as between himself and Plato, which the comments about the relation between Plato's *Republic* and Kant's view of morality seem to suggest. The remarks on Plato are helpful in situating Kant with respect to Platonism, which he evokes from epistemological, moral, and political perspectives. Yet Kant does not appear to detect a relation between his view of knowledge and the one he attributes to Plato, a relation that turns on the noncausal approach to knowledge through ideas for Platonism or categories for Kant.

The Way of Ideas and Kant's Representationalism

The passage on ideas in general discussed above is ostensibly intended to provide a plea for maintaining Plato's use of the term *idea* while preparing the way for an account of Kant's conception of transcendental ideas. Kant, who believes Plato's term should be maintained, employs *representation* in his position. The substitution of *representation* for *form* or *idea* should not be allowed to obscure differences between the critical philosophy and Platonism or similarities between the critical philosophy and the new way of ideas that arguably peaks in his position.

A basic statement of what later became the critical philosophy is contained in the Herz letter, which is probably the most useful indication of Kant's intentions early in the critical period. The problem of knowledge can be formulated in many different ways, none of which is more than normative. In the letter, where Kant considers various possibilities, he canonically depicts the epistemological problem as he then understands it, at a time when he is preparing the first edition of the *Critique of Pure Reason*, in terms of a single question: "I asked myself, namely: on what grounds rests the reference of what in us is called representation [*Vorstellung*] to the object [*Gegenstand*]?"[11] This way of stating the question mandates a representationalist response to the problem of knowledge, which continues to function as Kant's main understanding of this theme throughout the critical period. Though in the *Critique*, the term *appearance* often takes the place of the term *representation*, in which it functions as a synonym, the approach to knowledge does not change. This is also the approach to knowledge that is most often discussed by Kant's commentators.

Kant's answer, which he works out in the *Critique of Pure Reason*, consists in claiming that experience and knowledge of objects require sensation or a sensory input that is worked up by the mind in order to construct cognitive objects. In more technical language, the contents of the sensory manifold are brought under the categories, or rules of the understanding, in the process of producing objects of experience and knowledge. The latter function as representations of noumena, or things in themselves, in short, the mind-independent external world.

This Kantian model further develops the modern causal theory of perception in adding a crucial distinction between the mind-independent world, or the world as it supposedly is, which lies beyond appearance, and the world of human experience, which is mere appearance as distinguished from reality. Modern causal theory of perception, is, like Platonism, dualist, but it is also anti-Platonic in other ways, such as the reverse inference from effect to cause. The modern anti-Platonic dualism runs from things to ideas and back again. The new way of ideas formulates a theory of knowledge in which things in the world are understood to cause ideas in the mind that, through a backward inference from effect to cause, lead to knowledge of the mind-independent world as it is. This model is anti-Platonic because reality can be known through a reverse inference from ideas taken as effects to their causes. It is because Plato denies this reverse inference from effects to causes that he needs to invoke the privileged claim that philosophers are capable of being trained to "see" the invisible real. There is an ontological distinction but no epistemological difference in this modern epistemological model between the idea in the mind and the mind-independent object. At the point of knowledge, through the device of a background inference from effect to cause, the idea in the mind, which is caused by the mind-independent object or world, is said in various ways "to match up with" or "correspond to" the object in the world.

The Kantian representational epistemological model is a revised, improved, but not basically different form of the modern causal approach to perception running throughout the new way of ideas. In reinterpreting the cognitive object, Kant extends the modern causal loop between things and ideas at the cost of introducing a distinction between what appears and what is. In calling attention to the difference between objects of experience and knowledge on the one hand, and things in themselves on the other, Kant formulates a new and very powerful version of the ancient Platonic dualism between objects of experience and knowledge, between the world in which we live and the world we invoke to explain that world. This results in new conceptions of the subject, the object, and the relation between them that lead Kant away from the new way of ideas in the direction of Platonism.

The familiar Platonic model features a distinction between appearance and reality, between the visible world in which we live and the invisible world we invoke to grasp its origin as well as to justify any knowledge claim. In the modern causal model, since in appropriate circumstances we can reliably claim to know reality as it appears in and through ideas, there is no distinction between reality and appearance. In the Kantian model, this ancient Platonic distinction is reintroduced in distinguishing between the appearance and its cause. The real is now understood to be the mind-independent object in itself, what Kant calls the thing in itself, or noumenon, as distinguished from whatever it is that is given in experience and knowledge, whose relation to reality cannot be determined. Kant's straightforward assertion that the thing in itself can be thought without contradiction but not experienced, but whose effects are experienced (B566, 535), suggests what is called a "two aspects" theory. This theory depends on a distinction between cognizable and uncognizable aspects of the same object, which is understood from different perspectives (Bxxvii, 116). According to this view, a cognitive object, such as a table or a chair, is the result of some unknown and unknowable object affecting the subject in the form of sensations, which the cognitive subject works up into a cognizable object.[12]

The new Kantian model improves on the standard model in the new way of ideas, which in its various formulations has no way to allow for the limitations of human cognition. Though we can obviously claim to know, we can never convincingly claim to know any object as it is in total independence of the cognitive subject. Kant captures that crucial nuance in his seminal distinction between phenomena and noumena. He devotes an entire chapter in the first edition of the *Critique of Pure Reason* to this distinction, which he extensively revised in the second edition of the work.[13]

Kant's distinction between phenomena and noumena moves the discussion toward Platonism. The new way of ideas reverses the Platonic relation between ideas and things in making the former depend on the latter. If we grant that the noumenon is a mere idea introduced by reason to understand the possibility of human cognition, then, in again suggesting that ideas "cause" things, Kant decreases the "distance" between the new way of ideas and Platonism. Kant, who suggests that the noumenon causes sensations, attributes causality to it.

Kant's model transforms the conception of the subject. Early Greek philosophy often approaches the general problem of knowledge without taking the subject into account. Modern anthropological views insist on the central role of the human subject in analyzing knowledge. All the main British empiricists are concerned with human knowledge from the perspective of finite human beings. Kant, on the contrary, avoids any hint of philosophical anthropology because he is concerned to avoid the difficulty that, since Husserl, is known as psychologism, roughly the confusion between the analysis of epistemological conditions and their psychological description. I return to this point in the chapter on Husserl. From Kant's perspective, Locke's empiricism is a paradigmatic instance of the psychologistic approach to what Kant depicts as the transcendental logic of knowledge. In the course of working out his view of the subject, Kant refers several times, prior to the emergence of modern psychology, to Locke's "physiological" theory (Aix, 100; B119, 221). Kant's minimalist conception of the subject is not and should not be confused with a human being. It is rather a conception of the cognitive subject rethought from a resolutely epistemological perspective, which culminates in an abstract, purely epistemological conception with a series of specific functions, which allegedly identify the only conditions that make knowledge possible.

In its role as the recipient of ideas that are the effects of external objects, the modern epistemological subject is basically passive. On the contrary, the Kantian subject is both active and passive, passive as the recipient of sensation, which the subject in its active role works up into a cognitive object, which can be experienced and known. Kant breaks with earlier thinkers who believe that the world presents us with items of knowledge, so to speak, in arguing that what we experience and know is not produced solely by an object that exerts causal influence on the cognitive subject, who in turn can know the object as it is. Kant, who for the first time notes the consequence of the Cartesian view that the road to objectivity necessarily runs through subjectivity, argues that the subject in effect constitutes what it knows, although it cannot claim to know the world as it is.

A key epistemological difficulty lies in justifying the inverse inference from effect to cause, from the subject to the world that supposedly causes its ideas. Kant, like Plato, blocks any inference from the mind to the world on the grounds that the former causally influences the latter. Though in his representationalist phase Kant restates the familiar causal approach featured in the new way of ideas, his very way of formulating the problem of knowledge drives a conceptual wedge between his position and other modern epistemological approaches. Kant, who is aware of the difficulty of overstating the subjectivist side of the argument at the cost of any claim for objective cognition, explicitly claims that attention and practice will enable us to distinguish between what comes to us from outside and what the subject contributes to cognition (B2, 136). Yet this is a mere verbal flourish that cannot be justified. For, on strictly Kantian grounds, there is no way to go from a representation of the object to the world, or the object understood as a thing in itself, or noumenon, which, since it is not and cannot be given in experience, cannot be known.

Three Difficulties in Kant's Representational Model

Representationalism is a form of the canonical modern causal theory of perception. The difficulties in his representational model are so severe that Kant, who initially formulates a representational approach to knowledge, later moves away from the causal model of perception. In the *Critique of Pure Reason*, which features both a causal, representational model as well as a "noncausal," non-representational, constructivist epistemological model, he later turns from the former, which corresponds to the initial normative statement of the problem of knowledge in the Herz letter, to the latter.

Kant's theory of representation raises enormous interpretive difficulties that, despite extensive discussion during several hundred years, have still not been resolved. To begin with, it is not clear what he has in mind as the object of representation. He could be referring to nothing but objects of experience and knowledge, the stuff of ordinary experience, such as tables and chairs, but not cosmic rays or neutrinos. Or he could be referring to objects that lie outside experience but are invoked to explain it. If he were merely concerned with everyday objects, Kant's theory of representation would be limited to representation within the limits of experience. Since representation is a forerunner of modern semantic theory, which is often said to begin in Frege, the representational reading of the critical philosophy is the basis of the familiar view that Kant is, in effect, an early analytic thinker. According to this interpretation, which is widely shared, the critical philosophy is an earlier version of the standard analytic concern with the problem of reference.[14]

This approach is undermined if one thinks that objects are not in some sense already given as they are, full-formed, so to speak, but are "constructed" by the subject as a condition of knowledge. Kantian representationalism creates a complex, double causal relation. This includes the causal influence of the mind-independent real on the cognitive subject as well as the causal role of the subject in constituting the cognitive object. More precisely, Kant features a mind-independent source, which transmits sensation understood as an effect of the external world impinging on the subject, and which the cognitive subject works up by bringing it under a series of built-in mental categories, which are the same for all people in all times and places, in the process of constituting or constructing objects of experience and knowledge. As a result, the relation of the so-called representation to the mind-independent world is, as Plato would say, twice removed. The subject relates to the original cognitive object, which it seeks to represent, through the mediation of sensation, and then through the intervention of the cognitive subject in transforming sensation into a perceptual object.

In Kantian representationalism the difficulties that led Plato to deny a cognitive inference from appearances to forms or ideas return in ways specific to the critical philosophy. There are difficulties in Kant's representational approach to knowledge as concerns (1) the appearance or nonappearance of noumena, (2) the causal relation between noumena and phenomena, (3) and the link between constructivism of all kinds and representationalism. In each case, the difficulty is tied to the controversial concept of the thing in itself, or noumenon.

There is, to begin with, a contradiction between the view that noumena, or things in themselves, by definition do not appear and hence cannot be known, and the very different view that noumena can be (correctly) represented and hence known. These two views are clearly incompatible and cannot be reconciled. Representation is a form of cognition. What cannot be cognized cannot be represented, and what can be represented can obviously be known. Since a thing in itself cannot be cognized, either the cognitive object can be represented and hence be known since it is not a thing in itself; or, on the contrary, it is a thing in itself and hence cannot either be represented or known. It follows that the very idea of representation as Kant describes it is unintelligible.

A second difficulty in the critical philosophy, which also occurs in Platonism, concerns the causal relation between representations and things in themselves. In adopting a nonstandard form of causal relation between the subject as a noumenon and the object as a noumenon, Kant, like Plato, extends causality beyond the bounds of its legitimate application. Talk about causality as normally understood is intelligible as concerns the interaction of things situated in space and time only, things on the same causal level, as it were. The supposed causal interaction between Platonic ideas and appearances cannot be understood in that way; hence it cannot be understood on a standard causal model. An analogous difficulty arises in the critical philosophy, which relies on the causal influence of the world for arriving at our views about it. If the world did not have a cognitive effect on the cognitive subject, there would be no way to make cognitive claims about mind-independent reality. Yet the problem of relating our views of the world to the world is complicated in the critical philosophy by Kant's insistence that noumena are not in space and time. It is difficult to understand how there can be a causal relation to something outside the usual understanding of the limits of the causal framework. Kant compounds this difficulty in insisting that, as a category, causality is limited to objects of experience and knowledge and hence cannot apply beyond that sphere. It follows that Kant's view of representation depends on a causal link that he cannot explain and that is simply unintelligible on the basis of his theory.

The third difficulty concerns the inference from representations to what they represent, in Kant's position, from representations to noumena, or things in themselves. The difficulty is not related to misperception due to familiar problems of the relativity of perception. Berkeley, for instance, in following many predecessors, famously notes that on the basis of misperception we mistakenly believe the moon to be about a foot in diameter, the square tower to be round, and the oar seen in water to be crooked.[15] The difficulty is rather due to the fact that what we experience and know is the result of the subject working up sensory information in the form of a perceptual object. This view is now widely familiar. Modern physics and physiology tell us that, for instance, the wall is not off-white but we see it that way because light vibrating at a certain wavelength enters the eye and is processed in the optical nerve as that color. This is an instance of the way the cognitive subject constructs what it experiences and knows.

This point is crucial to the cognitive claim of a representative approach to knowledge. Consider the problem of the relation of scientific theories to the world. A basic assumption common among many working scientists and selected philosophers of science is that science enables us to know the world as it is. According to this assumption, science, in knowing the real, in fact realizes the ancient Parmenidean dream of knowledge as the unity of thought and being. The conviction that science reliably depicts the world as it is countered by the very different claim, apparently first formulated by Hertz, that science bears no more than a symbolic relation to mind-independent reality, with respect to which its relation cannot be measured, and whose existence can only be presupposed.[16]

Any claim to know the real as it is must show the mechanism through which this occurs. The difficulty lies in explaining how the cognitive subject can accurately represent a cognitive object. Both Descartes the rationalist and Locke the empiricist improbably suggest that certain ideas necessarily match up one to one with the real world, relying on divine intervention. Kant, who seeks a secular solution for this difficulty, suggests that the "fundamental material" can be isolated from whatever the subject adds to it in working up objects of perception and knowledge (B1, 136). If this could be done, then at least in principle the world as it is could be recovered. In that case, the subject could be understood as wholly passive and hence as a reliable source of information about the world, to which it adds nothing. In reference to the distinction between reality and appearance, if the subject were merely passive with respect to the world, which impinged upon it, then one could claim there was undistorted information about the world as it is.

This assumption is deeply problematic. In Kant's position, the subject is not passive but both passive as well as active in shaping what we experience and know. Hence, a representation can never be more than a mere appearance, which is transformed by the intervention of the cognitive subject. It is simply not possible to subtract what the subject adds to reveal the object prior to any action on it. As Hegel points out, acquaintance with either the instrument or the medium of knowledge will not permit us to eliminate, subtract, or otherwise remove whatever is due to the subject in order to reveal the object as it is.[17] Further, if the world as we experience and know it is merely an appearance, whose relation to the world as it is can neither be known nor analyzed, then we cannot claim to represent it. Hence a representational approach to knowledge fails.

Saving Representationalism: Fichte, Allison, and the Double Aspect Thesis

We still need, before we abandon the representational approach to knowledge, to consider the so-called double-aspect thesis. The double-aspect thesis, which is not a theory, is embedded within the critical philosophy, in which, depending on the interpretation, it is sometimes thought to play a central role. It is formulated by Kant in the B preface to the first *Critique* at a time when he has apparently already moved away from representationalism. It can be considered as a fallback effort, after Kant has acknowledged the failure of a representational approach to knowledge. It is intended to save his version of the modern causal theory of perception without demonstrating that representations in fact represent, hence without an analysis of the relation of representations to objects that is called for in the Herz letter.

In this respect, it is useful to distinguish between Kant and those influenced by him, who are sometimes more orthodox about the critical philosophy than he is. Kant, who hesitates to make up his mind, often defending incompatible alternatives, on occasion also changes his mind. His remarks in the B preface about Copernicus suggest that he later gives up representationalism, his initial epistemological strategy, for a replacement strategy for knowledge. But others, including some Kantians, continue to defend representationalism, in effect defending it against its author, by exploiting a remark in the text to maintain, against the author of the critical philosophy, that noumena in fact appear. Henry Allison, a leading contemporary Kant scholar, is an important defender of Kantian representationalism through a reading of the double-aspect thesis that goes back at least to Fichte.

In the familiar double-aspect thesis, to which Kant alludes in passing, he (1) draws attention to the distinction between objects of sensible intuition, or appearances, and things in themselves, and then (2) indicates that the human subject is both phenomenally determined and noumenally free. In this context, he then writes, "But if the critique has not erred in teaching that the object should be taken in a *twofold meaning*, namely as appearance or as thing in itself..." (Bxxvi, 116). In this complex passage, Kant is concerned, since he believes in strict phenomenal causality, to stake out room for morality, which he defends through a conception of noumenal freedom.[18]

This claim is important, beyond the defense of the possibility of morality, for three reasons. First, to show that an object is both an appearance and a thing in itself would go a long way toward making out Kant's representational form of the modern causal theory of perception. Kant innovates with respect to this epistemological approach. Second, it has already been noted more than once that the modern causal theory of perception fails to demonstrate the reverse inference from ideas to mind-independent objects. If Kant's improved version of the causal view of perception could be defended, it would vindicate an entire line of argument that, if Kant's representationalism fails, would no longer seem promising. It would further vindicate the entire anti-Platonic approach to knowledge that is widespread in the modern debate. The third reason concerns twentieth-century phenomenology, which can be read as routinely taking a phenomenon as both an appearance and as a thing in itself in the pervasive phenomenological effort to attend directly to things themselves (*zu den Sachen selbst*). This claim is epistemologically plausible if and only if, as the double-aspect thesis suggests, a phenomenological approach to grasping things is also a grasp of things in themselves. I return to this point below in discussing Husserl and Heidegger.

Allison defends Kant's idealism through a version of the double-aspect thesis, which has given rise to extensive discussion.[19] According to Allison, who has in mind the familiar contrast between ordinary and philosophical views of the same thing, the term *thing in itself* simply specifies the epistemic conditions of cognizing spatiotemporal objects.[20] This way of defending Kant is intended to make it plausible to analyze representations, as Kant seems to claim in the passage cited above, as both appearances and things in themselves. Hence, if the double-aspect approach could be defended, representationalism would be plausible because noumena would in fact appear.

This type of approach to the critical philosophy goes back at least to Fichte. The latter, who is one of the most influential of Kant's early interpreters as well as a major philosophical thinker, is also the most influential proponent of a double-aspect approach. After the publication of the *Critique of Pure Reason*, several of Kant's younger contemporaries each claimed to be the only one to understand him. Fichte's influential version of this claim was almost immediately accepted by the young Schelling and the young Hegel, who later continued to read Kant through Fichte's eyes.

Fichte's theory is in part an attack on a reading of the familiar, causal, representational approach to knowledge. He thinks, like Kant, that philosophy needs to explain experience, which he understands, unlike Kant, as representations accompanied by a feeling of necessity.[21] Yet in abandoning the thing in itself, he gives up the possibility of explaining representations as the result of the causal action of the mind-independent object on the subject, which he labels dogmatism.[22] He stresses instead the role of the subject as an explanatory factor, which he calls idealism. In rejecting the thing in itself as a dogmatic concept,[23] he restates Kantian representationalism in an updated version of the double-aspect thesis. The real causal order requires ideal explanation, that is, solely from the perspective of the subject.

According to Fichte, a causal theory of perception, which he calls materialism, leaves an unexplained gap between things and their representations. In rejecting materialism and hence a causal approach to perception, he sides with idealism against materialism, as well as against any version of the critical philosophy, which, according to Fichte, depends on the mere chimera of the thing in itself. In holding as Kant does that the a priori and the a posteriori coincide,[24] Fichte compares three forms of experience: (1) the experience of the ordinary person, who sees a specific metal a posteriori; (2) the experience of the chemist, who sees the same thing from the a priori point of view as a whole that can be analyzed into its constituents; and (3) the experience of the philosopher, who, on the assumption that the intellect is active and only active in a specific way, explains experience.[25]

Fichte's version of the double-aspect thesis reads Kant by dispensing with the thing in itself, which functions in the critical philosophy as an ontological cause of representations. Under Kant's influence, he turns to a conception of phenomena "constructed," so to speak, by the subject. According to Fichte, his contemporary J. S. Beck correctly shows that in Kant's transcendental idealism "the object is given neither entirely nor in part but is produced [*gemacht*]."[26] Fichte's form of the double-aspect thesis differs from Allison's mainly in that he presents this view independently of Kant, whereas Allison considers it more narrowly as the correct and defensible reading of the critical philosophy. We need, accordingly, to ask, Is this the correct reading of Kant? Can it be defended, even against Kant himself, as a viable approach to representationalism and hence as a vindication of at least one form of the anti-Platonic causal theory of perception?

It is difficult to present any version of the double-aspect thesis as the correct reading of Kant since, as is so often the case, he seems to hold two views about this theme simultaneously. Each is an aspect of the wider theory, within which they cannot be reconciled. One is the reading of the thing itself as an ontological cause of which the idea in the mind, or the representation, is the effect. The other advances the further claim that the representation represents, that is, stands in for and correctly identifies, an object that, in the double-aspect thesis, Kant presents through the view that appearance and reality are two sides of the same coin as it were.

The double-aspect thesis, as Allison's critics (e.g., Ameriks, Guyer, and Langston) point out, seems to deny or at least to threaten the familiar ontological reading of the Kantian object as an ordinary object of experience in pointing toward an unknown, transcendental object.[27] In the *Critique of Pure Reason*, many passages support an ontological reading of the thing in itself, which, if sustained, would run against a purely epistemic reading of this concept. Kant consistently maintains that the transcendental object, or thing in itself, functions as an entirely unknown and unknowable cause of representations.[28] It follows that it is not in space or time, cannot be an object of sensible intuition (B522, 513), and ought not to be accorded the status of a self-subsistent reality (B594, 550). On merely textual grounds, the double-aspect thesis simply fails. Kant, in responding to Hume, grasps causality along the lines of Leibniz's principle of sufficient reason. Since Kant requires a cause of which the appearance is the effect, he cannot dispense with some form of ontological input. Yet even if he could, the double-aspect thesis fails for other reasons. If we assume, as Kant claims, that, by definition, if there is an appearance, then something appears, it does not follow that a particular phenomenon is also an appearance. According to Kant, we can only decide on empirical grounds if we are dealing with an appearance or a thing in itself (B62, 186). This is possible if and only if there is a way to cognize a thing in itself other than through its appearance. Yet since there is no way at all to cognize things in themselves, this possibility is not open to us. And since there is also no way to show which phenomena are also appearances, in practice one cannot infer that if there is a phenomenon, something appears. It finally does not follow that a phenomenon is also a thing in itself. In fact, it could not be if a thing in itself does not appear. Hence the whole line of argument based on the double-aspect thesis appears flawed.

Kantian and Post-Kantian Representationalism

In substituting *representation* for *idea*, Kant improves on the causal theory of perception that runs throughout the new way of ideas. The anti-Platonic new way of ideas reaches a peak in the critical philosophy that is never later surpassed. Kant's innovation lies in understanding the subject as both passive as well as active, in broadening causality to include the impact of the world on the cognitive subject as well as the subject's role in "constructing" the cognitive object. Allison fails to save Kant's representational approach to knowledge, which Kant himself abandons and hence fails to save the critical philosophy understood as a representational approach to epistemology even against Kant. In Kant's wake, the representational approach to knowledge is immediately abandoned by the post-Kantian German idealists, who give up the causal theory of perception, and hence the causal relation of ideas in the mind to the surrounding world, in stressing not the passive but the active role of the subject. Thus for Fichte, the subject is solely active, never passive.

The representational approach to knowledge, which neither comes into existence nor disappears with the critical philosophy, arguably peaks in Kant. In different ways, a representational approach to knowledge goes back at least to early Greek philosophy, most often through some form of direct realism. Plato already rejects this approach in the passage on the divided line in his depiction of the lowest level of cognition of physical objects that takes the form of shadows or reflections.[29] He implicitly presupposes the view, later explicitly formulated by Aristotle, that the mental representation and the thing represented have the same form. Aquinas, who reformulates this view as the concept of intelligible species, believes that the idea representing the thing and the thing represented are two aspects of the same thing. This is roughly the claim behind Kant's double-aspect thesis. Duns Scotus later introduces a distinction between representing as a mental act or concept, or an ontological accident of the mind, and the object represented. According to Scotus, the cognizable, represented object exists *sub ratione cognoscibilis seu repraesentanti*, or "in keeping with the nature of something cognizable or represented."[30] It is sometimes said that in this way he anticipates Brentano's view of intentionality.[31]

After Kant, little if any progress has been made on the representational approach to knowledge running throughout the modern tradition. In Kant's wake, the original problem of the relation of ideas to things, which reaches its peak in Kant's theory of representation, fragments into a series of related but identifiably different domains. These include theories of artistic representation and their decline in modern art through the emergence of cubism early in the twentieth century, theories of reference in which representation may or may not play a role, causal theories of perception, and even causal theories of reference. As a result the conceptual unity illustrated by the anti-Platonic causal theory of perception gives way to a surprising welter of special theories on related but crucially different themes. But in the absence of a unified theory of reference with cognitive intent, they no longer serve to confirm any version of the Kantian claim to formulate an acceptable approach to knowledge.

One product of the post-Kantian fragmentation of the theory of representation is the modern theory of intentionality formulated by Brentano and others. The diverse views of mental representation and intentionality are further related in contemporary philosophy of mind on the grounds that the content of a mental state refers to something, or is representational; that is, it is about something other than itself. I return to this theme below.

Another result is what is known, following H. P. Grice, as the causal theory of perception. This approach is intended to exclude cases of hallucination from real perception in terms of causal theory.[32] Here there are obvious analogies with the Gettier problem and more distantly with Descartes' evil demon. Grice's original paper led to further contributions by Strawson, Goldman, and others.[33]

In the last century, attention was often devoted to artistic theories of representation but less often to epistemological representationalism. Over time, the very effort to base a theory of knowledge on perceptual representation that originates in the modern causal theory of perception and peaks in Kant's critical philosophy seems to have been forsaken in favor of discussion of conceptual puzzles that take on a life of their own.

An important instance is the problem of semantic reference. Reference is a later form of representation. The analytic treatment of reference is crucially influenced by Gottlob Frege's canonical distinction between sense and reference.[34] Frege was centrally concerned with linguistic reference. Reference, which has been close to the center of analytic philosophy since its inception, is related to but basically different from the form of the epistemological problem motivating Kant and his predecessors in the new ways of ideas. One way to put the difference concerns the question of how to relate words to things. Since ideas cannot be reduced to the words in which they are formulated, a satisfactory treatment of this difficulty would leave unresolved the further difficulty of how to relate ideas to things.

Nelson Goodman usefully links art, representation, and reference. Reference, which lies at the heart of representation, is more complex than simple linguistic denotation. He understands reference as the primitive relation of "standing for" that takes many different forms, more precisely as "the application of a word or picture or other label to one or many things."[35] The two most basic forms of reference are denotation and exemplification. Though works of art are invariably symbolic, Goodman, who gives up the cognitive dimension central to Kant, claims that a symbol represents or depicts in belonging to a conventional system of symbols similar to a language. Yet the resemblance of a symbol to an object does not determine the referential relationship that depends solely on the conventions adopted in the system of symbols.

Goodman maintains a tenuous link to representation that later disappears in Saul Kripke's and Hilary Putnam's causal theories of reference. The central question concerning reference, which takes precedence over questions about truth or the relation of meaning and reference, is to understand how words refer, or the mechanism of reference.[36] Ever since Frege, attention, from Russell through Strawson and more recently to Kripke, Putnam,[37] and others, has centered on devising a formal solution to the problem of reference. Putnam and Kripke focus on what the latter calls rigid designators. Yet after more than a century of concerted effort devoted to the problem, it remains unclear that an acceptable formal approach to reference, which W. V. Quine famously opposed,[38] can be successfully formulated. One of the reasons for the popularity of Robert Brandom's inferentialism is arguably that he appears to succeed in formulating an informal approach to reference.[39]

One can speculate that part of the interest of the problem of reference is that it appears, at least to some observers, as a slimmer, more acceptable version of the problem of representation. Thus Anandi Hattiangadi has recently tried to defend semantic realism against the skeptical consequences of Kripke's theory of reference.[40] Yet even if one knew how overcome the problem of reference, one would not have addressed the epistemological conundrum, which interests Kant, of correctly representing the mind-independent world. But this traditional theme, and hence the problem of knowledge as it comes into modern philosophy and as it is later formulated in the critical philosophy, seems to be increasingly uninteresting to those interested in the philosophical enigma of reference.

Kant's Constructivist Turn

Representationalism, Kant's answer to his initial formulation of the epistemological question in the Herz letter, simply fails. If this were his only approach to the problem of knowledge, then he would, as is sometimes claimed, and as was claimed in his own time by Maimon and then Hegel, be in fact an epistemological skeptic. Yet though he denies knowledge of things in themselves, he is not skeptical about the possibility of knowledge. It has been noted several times that, after formulating a representational approach, he apparently came to believe that representationalism fails. But

Kant has a second approach to the epistemological problem in reserve that he merely hints at but that was quickly grasped by his German idealist successors, Fichte, Schelling, Hegel, and Marx, who further develop it in various ways. Kant's second epistemological approach requires a turn to phenomenology. This turn follows from the canonical distinction between phenomena and noumena, to which Kant devotes a crucial chapter.[41]

The alternative epistemological approach, Kant's second best view, requires a critique of Kant's representational view (provided above), as well as a sketch of the constructivist alternative. By *constructivism* I have in mind the view that a minimal condition of knowledge is that the cognitive subject must "construct" the cognitive object. Constructivism, which precedes Kant, comes into modern philosophy through Hobbes and Vico. Kant knew Hobbes, whom he criticizes,[42] but not Vico, who was apparently not known in German philosophical circles prior to Marx.[43] Yet Kant seems to have arrived independently at epistemological constructivism, the basic insight of the so-called Copernican revolution in philosophy, not by reading his predecessors but by working through the problem of knowledge on his own.

Since Kant never uses the term *constructivism* and hence never uses it to designate his own position, a claim that it is centrally important for his view of knowledge is controversial. Discussion of Kant's Copernican revolution, especially in English, varies widely from efforts to interpret it to denials that Kant is even interested in Copernicus. Hans Blumenberg, the author of an extremely detailed study of this theme, concludes that Kant probably never read Copernicus.[44] Yet, even if this were true, it would not be decisive. It is known that Kant did not have a detailed knowledge of Hume, who was only partially translated in Kant's time, but he is obviously central to Kant's project.[45]

At least four reasons support a specifically Copernican reading of the critical philosophy. First, it is well known that Kant was a convinced, very knowledgeable Newtonian, committed to defending modern science against Hume's attack on causality. Second, and not surprisingly, since he came to philosophy from natural science, especially astrophysics and cosmology, which he helped to invent, Kant possessed a strong grasp of contemporary physics. He was, like Voltaire, committed to Newtonianism, but, unlike Voltaire, he was obviously familiar with Newton's *Principia*. In the preface added to the second edition of that work in 1713, Roger Cotes suggests, according to Blumenberg for the first time,[46] that Newton's epistemological contribution lies in proving from appearances that gravity belongs to all bodies.[47] Third, Kant's contemporaries, including Reinhold[48] and Schelling,[49] draw attention to the link between the critical philosophy and the Copernican astronomical revolution. Fourth, this relation can be verified from the second preface to the *Critique of Pure Reason*. In simplest terms, one can say that Kant generalizes Cotes's suggestion to relate Newton to Copernicus through a physical explanation of astronomical phenomena. According to Kant, Copernicus put forward as a hypothesis a theory, which was only finally proven through Newton's law of gravitation. Newtonian mechanics provided a physical explanation for the perceived phenomena. On this reading of the rise of the new science, through the successful application of mathematics to nature, Copernicus introduced a change in perspective that made possible the emergence of modern science in the seventeenth century, leading on to a peak finally attained in Newtonian mechanics.

Cartesian Method and the B Preface

Kant's appeal to Copernicus is linked to his Cartesianism. This is unexpected since Kant's references to his French predecessor are uniformly negative. The Cartesian undertone of the A preface becomes central in the B preface, which is organized along clearly Cartesian lines. In the A preface, Kant's emphases on certainty and clarity refer at least generally to Descartes' views of clarity and distinctness as the hallmarks of apodictic knowledge. Kant's implicit Cartesianism only becomes explicit in the B preface.

In the *Discourse on Method* and in other texts, Descartes famously insists that method is the key to theory of knowledge. According to Descartes, we disagree, and our disagreements can only be laid to rest through a method that guarantees apodictic claims to know. Here and in other places he works out the famous method that he calls for in the *Discourse* and that he later describes in the *Meditations*. But it no longer appears in such late works as the *Passions of the Soul*. According to Aristotle, there is more than one possible method, whose choice is dictated by the subject matter. Descartes, who disagrees, elaborates a single method that is allegedly valid for all cognitive domains.

In the B preface Kant partly follows but also departs from the Cartesian view of method in reformulating the criterion for the success of a method as reaching the secure path, or course, or the highway of a science. Though his position is a priori, Kant oddly invokes a pragmatic perspective. We can judge, he claims, that a domain has reached the "secure course of a science" through its "success" (Bvii, 106).

With this in mind, Kant quickly reviews four cognitive domains, each of which determines its cognitive object a priori. Logic, which describes the rules of thought, has always been on a secure path. Mathematics only reached that stage through a veritable "revolution in the way of thinking" (Bxi, 108). Empirical natural science, which progressed more slowly, finally arrived at the stage of science when, in the seventeenth century, Galileo and others comprehended in an "advantageous revolution" that, as Kant famously states, "reason has insight only into what it produces according to its own design" in reasoning on the basis of "principles" and according to so-called "constant laws" (Bxiii, 109). Kant is suggesting that the epistemological success of modern science depends on an epistemological reversal. Rather than attempting unsuccessfully to know the mind-independent world as it is, in reversing the relation modern science succeeded through making the cognitive object depend on the observer.

Like Descartes, Kant holds that the possibility of knowledge depends on a methodological revolution that guarantees claims for universal and necessary knowledge. The value of this approach has supposedly already been proven in the domains of logic, mathematics, and physics. Since logic, mathematics, and natural science have already reached the level of science, the only remaining problematic cognitive domain is metaphysics.

Metaphysics, since it leaves experience behind, is rife with disagreement. Hence, it has still not found a secure path nor become a science. It can only do this through a future methodological revolution. It is perhaps not surprising, since Kant began in natural science and only later turned to philosophy of science and philosophy, that, as concerns metaphysics, he is inspired by the example of natural science, whose methodological revolution is, he thinks, applicable to metaphysics. In referring to his methodological innovation, he specifically says that this revolution is based on the method of those who study nature (Bxviii, 111). Kant's standard of knowledge is a conception of natural science understood as the capacity to yield apodictic knowledge. To transform metaphysics into a science of this kind, he proposes to extend the same Cartesian procedure that guarantees the scientific status of the other cognitive domains to metaphysics, or theory of knowledge, by introducing a fourth methodological revolution based on the Copernican astronomical revolution. With this in mind, he famously suggests a reversal in metaphysics similar to that earlier undertaken successfully in natural science. Rather than understanding cognition on the traditional model in which it conforms to the object, Kant calls attention to the advantage of "assuming that," as he puts it, " the objects must conform to our cognition" (Bxvi, 110).

Copernicus and Kant's Methodological Revolution in Metaphysics

How does Kantian epistemology relate to Copernican astronomy? It is well known that Copernicus introduced a shift from a geocentric to a heliocentric view of the solar system in replying to Ptolemy. In the *Almagest,* the only comprehensive treatise of Greek astronomy we possess, Ptolemy sketches a theory without adducing theological considerations and relying on purely astronomical reasons. The heavens are spherical and move spherically, and the earth, which lies at the geometrical center of the heavens, is motionless. After giving reasons why the earth is spherical, he argues that it is in the middle of the heavens and motionless. He specifically claims that observed appearances can only be understood if the earth lies at the center of the heavens (1.5.9).[50] In the same way, he affirms that the earth can neither move nor fail to lie at the center of the heavens (1.7.10–12). According to Ptolemy, who insists that the appearances will be borne out by astronomical proofs (1.8.12), the heavens manifest two so-called prime movements: that from east to west and that through which the stars make local movements around other poles in the opposite direction, what we now call apparent retrograde motion (1.8.12–13).

Copernicus responds to Ptolemy and other astronomical geocentrists in the *Commentariolus* (1530) and in *De revolutionibus* (1543). Throughout he is concerned to save the uniformity of motion that he believes cannot be saved through a geocentric system, and can only be saved on the basis of a heliocentric hypothesis. In the *Commentariolus,* where he announces an early version of the theory, he outlines an astronomical view based on seven explicit assumptions.[51] The seventh assumption is that, as he says, "The apparent retrograde and direct motion of the planets arises not from their motion, but from the earth's."[52] He develops his position in *On the Revolutions of the Heavenly Spheres* (*De revolutionibus*).

In the preface, where he dedicates his book to Pope Paul III, Copernicus straightforwardly proclaims his intention to demonstrate the earth's movement.[53] He adduces as reasons the inability of mathematicians to agree with one another about the movements of the spheres of the world, an inability that results in his opinion from a general failure to follow "sure principles" (507). As he goes on to specify, what follows from true hypotheses can be verified, a claim Kant specifically makes about his own Copernican hypothesis. Copernicus further claims that his demonstrations are better than those of his predecessors on the assumption that the earth moves in a circular orbit

(508). He develops his claim in the first book of his great treatise in sketching a view of the earth as neither at the center of the heavens nor at rest but rather as a sphere moving in a circular orbit with three forms of motion.

Like Ptolemy, Copernicus acknowledges that, except for the earth, the whole world appears to revolve daily from east to west with antagonistic revolutions by the sun, the moon, and the so-called wandering stars (513). Copernicus, who holds that their regular, circular movements only appear to us as irregular, supposes the capacity to distinguish between appearance and reality (514). In a key move, he distinguishes apparent change with respect to "either . . . the thing seen or . . . the spectator" or, to vary the metaphor, with respect to the contained or the container (514, 515). With this in mind, he notes that although many think the earth is the immobile center of the world, a series of Greek predecessors (Herakleides, Ekphantus, Hicetas, Philolaus) believe that it moves at the center of the world. In announcing his hypothesis, he goes further in denying that if the earth were at the center of the world it would be possible to explain the apparent irregularity of perceived motion (515).

Copernicus next refutes those who believe the earth is the immobile center of the world, or that it is close to the center, because it is the heaviest element, and so on. He argues that movement belongs to the spherical shape of the earth, although so-called daily revolution appears to belong to the heavens (519). Turning now to the movements of the earth, Copernicus makes two points: more than one movement can belong to it, and the earth cannot lie at the center of the apparently irregular movements of the planets (520–21). In an account of the celestial orbital circles, he says that, on the basis of simplicity, the sun is immobile since its apparent motion can be attributed to the earth (525). He finally indicates that in specifying, or, as he says deducing, the terrestrial movements, he will explain why it appears that even the fixed stars move (526).

Copernicus's discussion reaches a crucial point in his demonstration of the threefold movement of the earth. He begins by saying that what we know about the planets is consonant with the movement of the earth. He then proposes to summarize its movement as a hypothesis to account for appearances. With this in mind, Copernicus discerns no less than three terrestrial movements: first, the so-called circuit of day and night, which traverses the earth's axis from west to east; second, the annual movement of the center around the sun, which is inferred from the movement of the ecliptic; and, third, the declination, which is inferred from the change in the length of day and night through the year (530). The remainder of the first book is taken up in a geometrical demonstration of this triple claim for the earth's motion, which is invoked, he clearly says, "to demonstrate all the planetary appearances" (557). Throughout, he has in mind the basic point that appearances need to be explained from the perspective of human beings situated on the earth, since "To us who are being carried by the Earth, the sun and the moon seem to pass over; and the stars return to their former positions and again move away" (557).

We can sum up the basic Copernican position, hence Copernicanism, as follows in five related points:

1. The motion of the planets must be explained.
2. It is not explained through a geocentric hypothesis.
3. It is explained through a heliocentric hypothesis.
4. This hypothesis entails a reversal in which the earth does not stand still but rather moves around the sun.
5. This hypothesis can be empirically confirmed.

Kant's complex relation to Copernicanism centers on his direct as well as indirect adherence to the basic Copernican position. In simplest terms, he transposes the basic Copernican scientific model, which he thinks lies at the basis of modern natural science, into epistemology. In other words, he relies on a Copernican reversal for a methodological revolution that has allegedly made possible the rise of modern science and that will supposedly make possible the future science of metaphysics. Kant's Copernicanism is evident on different levels, including specific references to Copernicus, his general understanding of the rise of modern science, and his specific analysis of the relation of Copernicus to Newton.

Kant's references to Copernicus are both explicit and implicit. He explicitly compares his crucial suggestion to reverse the priority between concepts and objects in metaphysics to Copernicus's suggestion that celestial motion is best explained by reversing the relation between the revolution of the celestial host and the observer. The celestial host is best seen as revolving, while the stars are, as Kant says, at rest. In reference to his own revolutionary methodological innovation in metaphysics, Kant writes, "This would be just like the first thoughts of Copernicus, who, when he did not make good progress in the explanation of the celestial motions if he assumed that the entire celestial host revolves around the observer, tried to see if he might not have greater success if he made the observer revolve and left the stars at rest" (Bxvi, 110).

Kant further follows Copernicus in holding that scientific theories rest on hypotheses that can be confirmed through their success in practice. Though he is "officially" a transcendental thinker, he seems "unofficially" to hold what today would be described as a pragmatic view, which applies equally to natural science and to philosophy. Kant makes this crucial claim in two ways: with respect to science and as concerns his own methodological revolution in metaphysics.

Kant's view of the confirmation of scientific theories appears odd. A theory that could be confirmed, or definitively confirmed, would no longer be a theory but something else, lying beyond theory. Today it is widely thought that scientific theories are fallible and hence can never be demonstrated with certainty, nor confirmed, but can only be disconfirmed. Peirce, the most important pragmatist, describes the process of knowledge as oscillating between doubt and belief, which cannot be surpassed.[54]

Kant, however, thinks that scientific theories can be confirmed empirically. He believes, for instance, that Newton proved Copernicus's conjecture. The Copernican theory is kinematic, since it is incapable of offering a causal analysis, which is the hallmark of genuine explanation. According to Kant, Copernican astronomy makes possible Newtonian mechanics, which proposes a causal analysis, and which cannot be formulated from a geocentric angle of vision. The Newtonian theory, which is dynamic, supposedly proves with certainty, through a causal explanation, based on "the invisible force," or gravitation, what Copernicus advanced only as a hypothesis (Bxxii, 113).

Kant makes a similar claim about his methodological revolution in metaphysics. In the same passage in which he discusses the relation of Newton to Copernicus, he insists that his proposed "transformation in our way of thinking," which he presents "merely as a hypothesis," is "proved not hypothetically but apodictically from the constitution of our representations of space and time and from the elementary concepts of the understanding" (Bxxii, 113). The justification for this suggestion perhaps lies in an earlier passage where he describes his methodological innovation as inspired by students of nature. He adds that his book concerns "the elements of pure reason in that *which admits of being confirmed or refuted through an experiment* (Bxviii, 111; Kant's emphasis). This can be read as suggesting, by analogy with natural science, that philosophy is also experimental. Philosophy proposes hypotheses, which are confirmed or disconfirmed on an experimental basis.

What this suggestion amounts to is unclear. There are at least two possibilities. One might be an empirical confirmation that the Copernican theory is correct, that is, that there is a proof on empirical grounds by analogy with the alleged Newtonian proof of the Copernican hypothesis. It is difficult to see what this might be. After Einsteinian relativity, it is widely believed that the Copernican and the Ptolemaic perspectives are exclusive alternatives, neither of which can be demonstrated. Another might be the ability to work out the theory, for instance, the analysis of space, time, and the categories. Yet here as well it is difficult to understand, without further argument, why merely formulating a theory counts as a proof of it. A possibility in this regard is Kant's belief, which he never tires of expressing, that from his transcendental standpoint he has identified the only possible set of arguments concerning the future science of metaphysics. If he could plausibly show that this was the case, then he could arguably claim with equal plausibility that the mere formulation of the theory counts as its demonstration, hence as its proof. Yet since he does not and arguably cannot do so, and since it is not possible to demonstrate closure,[55] this line of argument seems to fail.

Kantian Constructivism and Modern Phenomenology

The final step, to round out the argument, lies in showing that the shift from representationalism to constructivism, hence toward phenomenology, is also a qualified return to a form of Platonism. *Phenomenology* is difficult to define since, like all such general terms, it is routinely understood from widely different perspectives. Yet all observers agree that phenomenology concerns phenomena, a theme that was already under discussion in ancient Greece. It was later used in a scientific context, for instance, by Newton. In the scholium to the *Principia*, he famously claims to deduce his experimental philosophy from phenomena in eliciting the laws of nature directly from experience.[56] In a letter to Roger Cotes, the English mathematician who wrote the preface to the second edition, Newton similarly claims to deduce the first principles or axioms of physics from the phenomena and generalize them through induction.[57]

The term *phenomenology,*" which only emerged in the middle of the eighteenth century, was used slightly earlier than 1762 by both F. C. Oetinger[58] and J. H. Lambert.[59] The latter, with whom Kant corresponded, was apparently the first to use *phenomenology* in a specifically philosophical manner. Francis Bacon discusses four kinds of idols, or illusions, that impede us from correctly knowing the world.[60] Under Bacon's influence, Johann Lambert developed a theory of phenomenology as false appearance (*Schein*) in *Das neue Organon* (1764). The term does not occur in the *Critique of Pure Reason*, although Kant uses it in different ways in other writings.

Phenomenology has several distinguishable meanings in Kant's writings. In the precritical period, Kant intended phenomenology to precede science as a separate discipline, whose role consists in testing the validity and limits of sensory knowledge. In the immediate aftermath of his *Inaugural Dissertation* (1770), Kant defined the positive part of this work as a *phaenomenologia generalis*. In a letter to Lambert, he calls attention to the difference between general laws of sensation as opposed to concepts and basic principles of pure reason with respect to metaphysics. Perhaps under Lambert's influence, he describes *phaenomenologica generalis* as a special, but negative science that precedes metaphysics in order to avoid confusion over judgments about objects of pure reason. Understood in this way, phenomenology is a propaedeutic, which preserves true metaphysics from any sensory contamination.[61]

In the famous Herz letter, early in the critical period, *phenomenology* is synonymous with what will later become the critical philosophy that Kant formulates in the *Critique of Pure Reason*. What was earlier understood as a preliminary, negative discipline in the precritical period has meanwhile apparently become equivalent to the entire discipline in general. At this point critical philosophy is phenomenology and phenomenology is critical philosophy.

Phenomenology further plays a central role in Kant's view of philosophical physics. *The Metaphysical Foundations of Natural Science* studies the a priori conditions of physics. In its last chapter, which is entitled "Phenomenology," this term refers to a modal account (possibility, actuality, and necessity) of the experience of matter in motion. Kant here describes phenomenology as a theory of true appearances (*Erscheinungen*) or, more precisely, as a theory that explains how within the realm of material natural science empirical phenomena become experience.[62]

This passage is important. Kant indicates, as he also indicates in the B preface to the *Critique of Pure Reason*, the significance of the natural scientific approach to empirical knowledge. He refers in this passage, as he also does in the B preface, to a natural scientific approach, presumably the Copernican astronomical model, which he imports into the philosophical domain.

We can infer that about the time he composed the *Metaphysical Foundations of Natural Science* (1786) and the second edition of the *Critique of Pure Reason* (1787), Kant understood the critical philosophy as, in whole or in part, phenomenology. It is worth emphasizing this point, since there is little discussion of the relation between Kant and phenomenology. There is the so-called phenomenological interpretation of Kant by Heidegger and others.[63] But the specifically phenomenological dimension of the critical philosophy is not well understood and only occasionally even mentioned. When it is mentioned, the references are very general and often presuppose a Husserlian view of phenomenology, as in vague claims that in describing perception, thought, and imagination Descartes, Hume, and Kant are practicing phenomenology.

In now turning to the phenomenological theme, I follow Kant's own suggestions that the critical philosophy is itself phenomenology. For present purposes, I will understand *phenomenology* in the first instance in terms of Kant's canonical distinctions between phenomena, appearances, and noumena, or things in themselves. We have repeatedly noted that Kant's distinction between phenomena and noumena suggests two approaches to knowledge. One is based on cognition of noumena, which appear (or fail to appear) in the form of representations. The other is based on phenomena, in Kant's case on the construction of phenomena.

Kantian phenomenology is constructivist because the phenomena are constructed and hence can reliably be known by the cognitive subject. Kant, who denies a direct, intuitive grasp of cognitive objects, offers no less than three different versions of the constructivist side of his theory. All three versions rely on the way in which the subject is affected by something different from itself through sensory intuition, whose contents it works up into the object of experience and knowledge. First, there is the familiar causal view of perception in which the subject is causally affected by an external object. This presupposes a distinction between noumena, appearances, and phenomena as well as the causal influence of noumena to produce the contents of sensory intuition, which are worked up into the object of experience and knowledge that is also an appearance. Second, there is the noncausal view based on turning away from noumena. According to this view, the subject works up sensory intuition into objects of experience and knowledge, which are not appearances and hence are no more than mere phenomena. Third, there is the enigmatic, frequently cited passage in the schematism chapter where Kant asserts that we simply cannot elucidate the relation of schemata to appearances (B181, 273).

Kantian Phenomenology and Platonism

I conclude this chapter with a brief remark about the complex but crucial relation between Kant and Plato. In part, this relation turns on different appreciations of the role of causality in theory of knowledge. This theme, which is very old, is already, as noted above, a concern in pre-Socratic cosmology. The Platonic theory of ideas arises as an explanatory alternative to scientific causal explanation as it was emerging in Plato's time. Platonism is an early form of idealism. The theory of forms or ideas constitutes an important chapter in the struggle between idealism and materialism that, after Plato, echoes throughout the entire later Western tradition. Plato, who regards this struggle as the central problem of philosophy, describes it in the *Sophist* as the battle between the gods and giants.[64] A version of this same struggle between idealism and materialism takes place at the heart of the critical philosophy, which, in the form of representationalism and constructivism, opposes two very different materialist and idealist analyses.

Analytic philosophy emerged around the beginning of the last century through the revolt against British idealism and, by extension, against idealism in all its forms. In our time, with the exception of Nicholas Rescher, idealism has no important representative. Yet this battle is still being fought in different ways in analytic philosophy of mind, which in various ways seeks either to eliminate the mind in favor of the body, to eliminate idealism in favor of materialism, or at least to reduce the mind to the body. Yet if Fichte is right, these two epistemological approaches are locked in a battle that neither side can win. The solution, then, cannot be to adopt idealism to the exclusion of the material external world, nor to adopt materialism, which denies the role of the subject in knowledge; it requires a third approach that appeals to both.

It would be an error to describe this opposition merely in terms of an acceptance or denial of causality since Platonism is itself a causal theory. Platonism replaces the nascent scientific version of external causality with a theory of forms that, through the unexplained claim of participation, can be regarded as the causal source of the so-called, but misnamed, world of appearances. This world is misnamed since a reverse cognitive inference from appearances to reality, or from things to forms, is not possible.

The Greek term *phenomenon* means both "phenomenon" in the modern, restricted sense as well as "appearance." In Platonism, forms or ideas manifest themselves through phenomena. With respect to science, Platonism is backward-looking in rejecting scientific causality in favor of a nonscientific, wholly speculative form of causal theory in which things are supposedly better explained through the causal role of ideas leading to things as their effects. After Plato, science developed in reasserting different forms of scientific causality in place of the Platonic model.

Modern phenomenology, which is opposed to causal explanation, hence to materialism, in that limited sense brings Western philosophy back to its Platonic roots. In its constructivist moment, in which it stresses phenomena against noumena, Kant's critical philosophy is Platonic as well as phenomenological. Like Platonism, phenomenology turns away from noumena and hence from a type of explanation that depends on an inexplicable causal influence of the world on our perception of it, a causal influence fully as mysterious and inexplicable as Platonic participation.

The strictly Platonic dimension of Kant's critical philosophy is finally very limited. Kant rejects both the ancient, Platonic, idealist approach in limiting the causal function of ideas to morality as well as the modern, anti-Platonic, causal approach to knowledge. In its place, he insists on the role of the subject, influentially formulated in the critical philosophy, in constructing objects of experience and knowledge. Kantian epistemology is both constructivist and phenomenological: constructivist in that the subject constructs what it knows as a condition thereof, and phenomenological because what it constructs are not appearances, hence not representations, but mere phenomena. In sum, phenomenology as it arises in Kant is neither wholly Platonic nor anti-Platonic, but non-Platonic in its stress on the constructivism of phenomena that represents a third way, a new approach to knowledge.

THREE

Hegel's Phenomenology as Epistemology

Kant has been enormously influential, both in his own time and in later debate. Phenomenology after Kant is decisively influenced by and can be regarded as an effort to respond directly and indirectly to Kant. Since Kant turns to phenomenology to resolve the problem of knowledge, we can assess later phenomenology in terms of its capacity to progress with respect to Kantian epistemological themes.

It is a deep error to think epistemology ends in Kant or to overlook Hegel's persistent concern with this theme. Hegel, who reacts to Kant and intervening figures, as well as to the entire history of philosophy in formulating his own position, is strongly interested in developing if not the letter of Kant's position, at least the spirit of the Kantian approach to knowledge. Epistemological considerations, though not epistemology as Kant understands it, are central to Hegel's position. Hegel, like Kant and Fichte, also adopts a phenomenological approach to the overall problem of knowledge. Hegel's specific contribution to knowledge includes at least (1) analyzing the problem of knowledge from a historical perspective, (2) drawing attention to the epistemological resources of a phenomenological approach, and (3) establishing a firm link between a phenomenological approach to epistemology and history. Though Hegel identifies his position as phenomenology, this aspect of his thought is, ironically, only rarely discussed.

Phenomenology after Kant consists in a series of reactions to its pioneering form in the critical philosophy. This chapter examines Hegel's phenomenological epistemology. Hegel is a post-Kantian German idealist, but what that means requires detailed discussion. The phenomenological dimension of German idealism is rarely mentioned and little understood, but, beginning with Kant, it is significant for German idealist efforts to come to grips with the problem of knowledge.

Post-Kantian German Idealism

In the reaction of Kant's contemporaries to the critical philosophy, various themes emerge. They include most prominently further concern with (1) system and (2) knowledge; (3) a gradual turn away from the a priori and toward the a posteriori as transcendental philosophy as Kant earlier understands it is progressively abandoned; (4) a basic revision in the concept of the subject, which as early as Fichte, hence at the very beginning of post-Kantian German idealism, takes on anthropological characteristics strongly opposed to Kant's anti-anthropological "reduction" of the subject to a mere epistemological principle; and (5) the slow but decisive move toward history (and historicism), which is arguably the single most important innovation of the post-Kantian German idealist debate.

A systematic conception of philosophy is as important for post-Kantian German idealism as it is for Kant. Kant famously calls for the formulation of philosophy as system.[1] The shared concern to formulate an acceptable form of the system Kant insists on, but supposedly does not provide, and hence to take the critical philosophy beyond Kant, unites the main post-Kantian German idealists, beginning with Karl L. Reinhold, the first in a line of later thinkers who strive to take the critical philosophy beyond the point at which Kant left it.

Reinhold is a protean figure, someone who quickly ran through successive interest in his contemporaries Kant, Fichte, and C. G. Bardili. In the period in which he was interested in reformulating the critical philosophy, he was an epistemological foundationalist; hence, he was concerned to reformulate the critical philosophy in an epistemologically foundationalist form. Epistemological foundationalism of all kinds consists in a specific type of claim about the extent as well as the way or ways to which epistemological theory, hence claims to knowledge of any kind, can be justified. In modern times, epistemological foundationalism is often identified with Descartes, whose influential form of foundationalism relies on a mathematical model best illustrated in geometry. This is not surprising since Descartes was both a mathematician as well as a philosopher. His contribution to mathematics, especially to geometry, is fully as important as his contribution to philosophy.[2] Epistemological foundationalism in its strongest form can be described as a normative view of philosophical theory in which, as in the Cartesian position, there is finally no more than a single initial principle, which can be shown to be true and from which the entire theory can be rigorously deduced. In his pioneering effort to improve on Kant, Reinhold appeals to a quasi-Cartesian model in restating the critical philosophy in clearly foundationalist form.

It is unclear if Reinhold's concern to put the critical philosophy on an epistemological foundation is consistent with Kant's position. Kant, depending on the interpretation, may or may not be an epistemological foundationalist. Once one penetrates behind the rhetoric, Kant's epistemological claims appear surprisingly modest. If there were any place where the critical philosophy is epistemologically foundationalist, it would be in the transcendental deduction. The transcendental deduction eschews any form of empirical justification in claiming to provide an a priori justification of the general possibility of knowledge. An a priori justification must satisfy the twin criteria of universality and necessity. Yet Kant, who indicates that the deduction responds to the juridical question (*quid juris*)[3] and describes it as an "exhibition" (*Darstellung*) of the pure concepts of the understanding,[4] casts doubt on any claim to provide an absolute demonstration. A juridical justification, however understood, is less than an absolute proof, and an exhibition, no matter how rigorous, is less than a conclusive a priori demonstration of the uniqueness claim that is required to justify an assertion to provide the only possible set of categories.

Reinhold, who was not himself an important thinker, was, despite the modesty of his own theories, very influential. Reinhold, who is not an idealist thinker in any obvious sense, is also not a post-Kantian idealist. But his effort to recast the critical philosophy in systematic form in effect marked the beginning of post-Kantian German idealism. Like Kant, and like Reinhold, whose efforts led to post-Kantian German idealism, such post-Kantian idealist thinkers as Fichte, Schelling, and Hegel are all strongly systematic thinkers. Systematicity is often identified as the central component of German idealism.[5] Unlike the foundationalist Reinhold, who began a movement to which he did not belong, the main post-Kantian German idealists are all epistemological anti-foundationalists or at least postfoundationalists, unconcerned with the Cartesian problem, restated by Kant, of providing an absolute justification of claims to know. Close inspection of the post-Kantian German idealists shows that they are all concerned with the foundations of knowledge. Kant, though not his German idealist successors, follows Descartes' insistence on apodicticity as the criterion of knowledge. Unlike Descartes, and unlike Kant, the post-Kantian idealists reject the very idea of a single identifiable principle or set of principles that can be demonstrated to be true and from which the remainder of the theory can be rigorously deduced. For this reason, they reject indefeasible epistemological claims in proposing weaker, defeasible epistemological claims.

System for Kant and post-Kantian German idealists is not an end in itself but merely a means to an end that lies in working out an adequate epistemological approach. This commitment echoes through the views of Kant and his successors. In his account of architectonic as the art of systems, Kant insists on viewing a system as involving unity under a single principle.[6] A strong concern with system animates Kant's immediate idealist successors, though what that means varies widely. Fichte is concerned with the form of system.[7] Schelling deduces a system from the concept of the absolute.[8] Hegel is already focused on the problem of system as early as his initial philosophical publication, the *Differenzschrift*, where, like Fichte, he argues for a circular conception.[9]

This shared theme of the relation of system to knowledge is vitally important for an appreciation of German idealism. On this point, there is a wide range of views. A representative sample of the best recent contributions to the discussion might include the views of Terry Pinkard, Frederick Beiser, Paul Franks, Manfred Frank, and Nectarios Limnatis. Pinkard describes German idealism without ever discussing the problem of knowledge, which on his account, is not an important concern in the thought of this period.[10] Beiser is persuaded by Schelling's later critique of Hegel, and thinks, to paraphrase his view, that post-Kantian German idealism illustrates the decline and fall of objective cognition from the level already attained in Kant.[11] Frank reads Fichte as an epistemological foundationalist against which the early German romantics revolted.[12] Franks takes a quasi-Kantian line in holding that either there is total system or there is nothing.[13] Limnatis believes that the problem of knowledge is central to post-Kantian German idealism.[14]

These scholarly disputes are important but outside the scope of the present discussion. Suffice it to say here that the post-Kantian German idealists are united in their concern with the problem of knowledge as central to their positions. It is, then, a misconception to believe that epistemology, or even rigorous epistemology, theory of knowledge worthy of the name, comes to an end in the critical philosophy. At most a certain kind of epistemology exemplified by a priori epistemology, which Kant officially takes as his norm for philosophical theory, ends with Kant.

Unlike Kant, who was, at least "officially," an a priori thinker, the post-Kantian German idealists are all, to varying degrees, a posteriori thinkers and, in that sense, non-Kantian, even anti-Kantian. Kantian transcendentalism is regulative but perhaps not constitutive of the critical philosophy. It is not often noted that Kant's position is also not transcendental in his specific sense. He consistently conjoins a priori and a posteriori claims, for instance, in his view of the subject as both a transcendental unity of apperception as well as a human being, which immediately raises the twin specter of philosophical anthropology and psychologism. Though the post-Kantian German idealists are strongly indebted to Kant, and though they use Kant's transcendental terminology, they all move toward the a posteriori plane. This move is already underway in Reinhold's effort to rethink the critical philosophy on the empirical basis of the principle of representation (*Vorstellungsvermögen*). Reinhold's effort to defend Kant by reformulating the critical philosophy in foundationalist form runs counter to Kant's commitment to the a priori approach, which is one of his most deeply held insights.

Kant and the Idea of a Philosophical Tradition

German idealism includes Leibniz, if he is an idealist,[15] as well as Kant and the post-Kantian German idealists.[16] "Post-Kantian German idealism" refers more narrowly to thinkers who react to Kant in further developing the critical philosophy. In the *Differenzschrift*, Hegel invents the conception of German idealism in taking stock of the main contemporary figures at the very beginning of the nineteenth century. The Hegelian conception of post-Kantian German idealism implies German idealism, which in turn implies the philosophical tradition. Hegel extends this view in a philosophical conception of the philosophical tradition, which receives its most developed account in his *Lectures on the History of Philosophy*.[17]

Hegel's "invention" of the post-Kantian German idealist tradition follows from two basic Kantian insights: Kant's claim that there is at any given time only one true theory,[18] and the suggestion that all texts, including his own, should be understood in terms of a suitably updated version of the distinction between the spirit and the letter. Kant's related belief that the critical philosophy was the one true theory was intended to fortify his own position against possible competitors in suggesting that any other theory that could be described as "true" was only a variation on his original theme.

If Kant's position were true, then others, which were also true, could only be forms of the critical philosophy. This explains Hegel's claim in the *Differenzschrift* that Fichte's and Schelling's positions are merely two forms of a single system, which, insofar as it is true, is Kantian and hence correctly identifies the "spirit" of the critical philosophy. Hegel extends this basic insight in a conception of the history of philosophy in which a supposedly "true" view precedes the critical philosophy, in which it reaches its apogee and is then further worked out by post-Kantians. This Hegelian approach suggests that, despite the obvious differences among the views of the later German idealists— Fichte and Schelling, or even Kant —Fichte, and Schelling are committed to a single overall position. This approach is further supported by Fichte's many claims to be a "seamless Kantian," if possible even more Kantian than Kant, and the young Schelling's own assertions, before he broke with Fichte after publishing the *System of Transcendental Idealism*, to be a Fichtean.

The second Kantian insight consists in an adaptation to textual interpretation of the ancient Pauline distinction between the spirit and the letter. This is one of the many sources of Hegel's conception of spirit, which becomes central in the *Phenomenology of Spirit*.[19] According to Saint Paul, non-Christians, who can grasp only the letter but not the spirit of Christianity, cannot understand it.[20] Kant, who believed that he was misinterpreted by his initial readers, influentially introduces a version of this Pauline distinction as an aid in grasping his position.[21] In the context, Kant's effort to focus attention on the spirit of his own position was triply important: for hermeneutics, for the view that positions can be improved, and for the further view that this describes the process of the philosophical tradition.

Kant's distinction suggests interest in isolating the spirit of a theory such as the critical philosophy from its letter. It further indicates the need to interpret texts through different possible readings, which may or may not agree with the author's intentions. There is no difference in principle between the special problem of determining the spirit of Kant's position and the more general problem of how to interpret any philosophical position. In this sense, even though Kant never appears sensitive to the difficulties of textual interpretation, and though the very idea of interpretation is inconsistent with his consistent claim that his theory is apodictic and cannot be modified, he is himself an early hermeneutical thinker. Yet, perhaps because he is apparently not himself aware of the difficulty of ascertaining the supposedly correct, or best, reading of a text, or even the most plausible reading, he does not anticipate the difficulty of determining the spirit of a given position, including his own.[22]

The series of disagreements about the correct way to read the critical philosophy indicate that it is not simple and perhaps in practice not possible to come to agreement about even the main features of the critical philosophy. The ongoing discussion of Kant, which more than two centuries after his death shows no signs of abating, mainly concerns the proper interpretation of his theories. It can be described in Kantian language as an incessant effort to determine the spirit of the critical philosophy through its texts. This effort is problematic since, according to Kant, for the critical philosophy and in all other cases the spirit must be determined through the letter, or through the texts. A straight line leads from efforts to resolve the difficulty, which Kant does not foresee, of identifying the spirit of a given text with later theories of hermeneutics as intrinsically historical.[23]

A second theme suggested by Kant's distinction, assuming that the spirit of the critical philosophy can be reliably determined, is the possible improvement on the very theory that, he repeatedly claims, successfully reaches an end in his position. From his ahistorical perspective, Kant believes that philosophy has already been completed in the critical philosophy. Yet his distinction between its spirit and letter suggests the possibility of future improvement in the overall position. Kant in part concedes this point in a minimal sense in at least admitting the possibility of stylistic improvements.[24] But the difficulty is deeper than he admits. The theory, which Kant presents as destined to stand for all time, appears in a different light as soon as it becomes clear that not only its specific details but even its main contours cannot reliably be determined. Different readings of the theory suggest different ways of developing it and hence different ways of bringing it beyond the final point that it allegedly reaches in Kant's writings. In short, in the context of its immediate reception, Kant's very effort to assert the unrevisable, inalterable, absolutely final status of his position contributed to its anti-Kantian understanding as imperfectly defined and hence capable of further development.

A third theme is the idea of the German idealist tradition and hence, by inference, of the philosophical tradition. The idea of a philosophical tradition is inseparable from the further idea that philosophy is essentially historical. Kant is a resolutely ahistorical thinker, who acknowledges prior philosophical thinkers, but who, from his ahistorical perspective, does not acknowledge the historicity of either claims to know or of the philosophical discipline. To put the point sharply but not unfairly, if, as Kant believes, critique is the criterion of philosophy worthy of the name, then prior to Kant there were no philosophers in his sense of the term. Kant, who is a dualist on many levels, thinks of philosophy in terms of exclusive alternatives, in short, either as philosophy in his own specific sense or, on the contrary, as nothing at all. From this perspective, though there are earlier thinkers who claim the title of philosopher or to whom it is routinely accorded, there is not and cannot be a philosophical tradition, or a tradition through which philosophy develops. Kant believes that philosophy, which in his particular sense can only be critical, finally, after more than two thousand years of debate, only comes into existence in his own critical period. Descartes believes his predecessors lack a method adequate to guarantee truth. Kant considers earlier thinkers, including Descartes, as dogmatic, hence as pre-philosophical— as thinkers who are not philosophers at all. Kant, who implicitly denies that he has philosophical predecessors, further implicitly denies that he will have philosophical successors in asserting that nothing can be altered in his position, which has supposedly already brought philosophy, which both begins and reaches its high point in the critical philosophy, to an end.

Kant's anti-traditional, normative view of philosophy amounts to the idea that the critical philosophy is the only philosophy there ever has been or will be. Though he is clearly reacting to a long line of preceding thinkers, for Kant, from his transcendental point of view, as for Descartes, there is, at least "officially," nothing, nothing at all, that he needs to take into consideration, no prior philosophical theories he can reliably build upon in formulating his own perspective. Hegel, on the contrary, who routinely gives credit to earlier positions, takes an entirely different view of his predecessors, on whose theories he claims to build in formulating his own.

Kant's complex claim to invent, to formulate for the very first and also for the last time, and to complete philosophy in a single position, namely, his own, runs against the idea of a philosophical tradition. His claim is sharply contradicted by his canonical distinction between the spirit and the letter of a theory, which paradoxically opens the way to a view of philosophy as a traditional discipline to which the critical philosophy belongs. From this perspective, the critical philosophy would not be the only philosophy, the only important philosophical position, or even the philosophical *terminus ad quem*. Despite its important contribution and its undoubted influence, Kant's position is finally merely another in a series of positions that together constitute the ongoing philosophical tradition, to which it belongs and within which its theories are meaningful in respect to other positions. In other words, and despite his intentions, in particular despite his wish to interdict any later modification of his own position, which is allegedly already complete in itself, Kant unwittingly helped to bring about a post-Kantian reaction that, at least on the part of Kantians who did not reject but struggled to perfect Kantian doctrines and themes, consists in a series of variations on Kantian theories, which in effect build on and hence modify the very position its author explicitly claims could not be altered.

The modern idea of the philosophical tradition, which is due to Hegel and is modeled on the Platonic depiction of the confrontation of competing positions in ongoing dialogue, has never been popular. Kant's conviction that nothing or nearly nothing can be rescued from the prior debate is widely shared. A straight line runs from Descartes' concern to distinguish between prior theories that are possibly in error and hence to turn away from the history of philosophy to Quine's reported distinction between the history of philosophy and philosophy.[25] Plato, who presents the Socratic model of dialogue between different positions that need to prove themselves in the give and take of debate, contradicts it in the view of the philosopher as someone who can grasp invisible reality through intellectual intuition. Aristotle is routinely attentive to prior theories, which he lists but also refutes before working out his own position.[26] His approach is both Kantian and anti-Kantian. It is Kantian in the sense that the spirit of a position can be developed in succeeding positions. But it is non-Kantian or anti-Kantian in suggesting that there is, for this reason, a historical dimension to philosophy, which, despite Kant's claims about the critical philosophy, has not been and arguably cannot be brought to an end in any single final theory.

Hegel's *Differenzschrift* and the Idea of German Idealism

In the *Differenzschrift* Hegel works out the main lines of the view he later extends and deepens but never basically changes. This early text is unfortunately still relatively neglected in the immense and growing Hegel discussion. When he composed his article, Hegel was still unknown—known mainly as Schelling's older but "slower" colleague. The "excuse" for the text consists in responding to Reinhold's recent discussion of philosophy at the turn of the nineteenth century. Hegel takes the occasion to formulate his own position in reaction to the views of Kant, Fichte, and Schelling—the only contemporary philosophers he thinks are worthy of the name—and to criticize Reinhold, whom regards as a leading nonphilosopher.

In the *Differenzschrift* Hegel is both influenced by and critical of Kant. He is influenced by Kant's claims that there can never be more than a single true theory and that his theory is true. In distinguishing between the intention and the accomplishment of Kant's position, Hegel points to an unresolved problem, which is later addressed by Fichte and Schelling, and misunderstood by Reinhold. In this way, and at a single stroke, he creates German idealism and post-Kantian German idealism. In applying Kant's revised form of the ancient Pauline distinction to the critical philosophy, Hegel suggests that Kant's critical philosophy is idealism in spirit but not according to its letter, which falls below its intention and is further developed, in effect through carrying the critical philosophy beyond Kant, by Fichte.

Under Kant's influence, Hegel calls attention to the distinction between the views of Fichte and Schelling within a single overall philosophical system. He begins from Kant in considering Fichte, a professed Kantian, and Schelling, at the time a professed Fichtean, as presenting variations on a single, common idealist position. The main difference lies in Schelling's interest in the philosophy of nature (*Naturphilosophie*), which, after the publication of the *System of Transcendental Idealism* but before the appearance of the *Differenzschrift*, quickly led to the break between Fichte and Schelling. The point of contention between Fichte and Schelling was the latter's insistence on a philosophy of nature. Hegel later follows Schelling on this point in developing his own philosophy of nature.[27] In the *Differenzschrift*, he considers the differences in the views of his contemporaries with respect to the critical philosophy. He interprets the critical philosophy immanently according to the distinction between the spirit and the letter. He reads Fichte and Schelling as denying its letter while carrying further its spirit, and Reinhold as comprehending neither its spirit nor its letter. Hegel is concerned to distinguish Fichte's and Schelling's variations on the overall (Kantian) system of philosophy that Reinhold, at the time under the influence of Bardili's supposed reduction of philosophy to logic, simply conflates.[28]

In the preface, Hegel begins by pointing to the need to distinguish between the spirit and the letter of Kantian philosophy in identifying its speculative principle. For Hegel, who follows Fichte's identification of the identity of subject and object as the spirit of the Kantian philosophy,[29] the deduction of the categories is authentic idealism. He criticizes Kant's attachment to things in themselves as "empty forms of opposition . . . posited as absolute objectivity," which is simply dogmatic. He further objects to the conception of categories, which are simply static and conflict with our capacity to grasp the absolute, understood as Spinoza's "substance."[30]

Though he credits Kant with genuine idealism, he refuses Kant's assessment of his own accomplishment. Hegel detects a significant difference between Kant's intention and his result. In Hegel's opinion, the critical philosophy is, at least in intention, a true idealism since it offers a deduction of the categories. The *Critique of Pure Reason* reaches a high point, early in the book, in the transcendental deduction of the categories, whose role is to account for the unity that is the condition of the cognition of objects of experience and knowledge. If the deduction, which is central to the Kantian project, fails, then there is a clear difference between Kant's intention and his accomplishment. The principle of speculation lies in the identity of subject and object, which should be situated in reason, but which Kant mistakenly locates in the understanding. In this way, he creates an absolute opposition between the a priori identity featured in the categories and what Hegel calls the a posteriori realm.

Since the criterion of "true" idealism is a system of speculative thought leading to an identity, which Kant does not deduce, the letter of Kant's idealism falls below its spirit. Fichte further develops the spirit of Kant's idealism, but also fails to realize it. According to Hegel, the principle of Fichte's system is the identity of ego = ego.[31] Yet this turns out to be a merely subjective identity of subject and object. The result is an unresolved dualism between what is and what ought to be, between reason as infinite and reason as finite. This basic distinction and hence the character of Fichte's position is simply "overlooked" by Reinhold. The latter also misunderstands Schelling's effort to depict an objective subject-object in the philosophy of nature and to unite both in his conception of the absolute.[32]

Kant's normative model of the philosophical discipline is apparently based on the Cartesian idea that through a decisive methodological innovation, the problems can be finally solved through working out an ahistorical conception of the discipline. Hegel's normative model resembles a Socratic dialogue, in which theories are advanced as proposed solutions with respect to ongoing concerns. All theories enter into debate, in which their respective merits are assessed, and in which further theories are formulated to improve on their predecessors. Emphasis in this model does not lie on finality but on progress with respect to earlier contributions to the discussion. And all contributions are assessed in relation to the ongoing debate.

If philosophy consists, not in a single, decisive methodological transformation but in the progressive unfolding of ideas through dialectical debate in historical space, then there is no reason to accept Kant's claim to complete philosophy. Hegel's view of the difference between the spirit and the letter of the critical philosophy implies five related insights, which, taken together, point to a conception of German idealism in relation to the ongoing philosophical tradition: first, philosophy is an intrinsically historical discipline that, hence, cannot escape from history. Since no position is beyond time and place, all positions, including Hegel's, can, as he explicitly notes, be treated historically.[33] It follows that there is no philosophical way to end philosophy,[34] and that claims to bring philosophy to an end—for instance, the well-known claim of the young Hegelians that philosophy reaches a high point and an end in Hegel, a claim Hegel never makes but which is, for instance, integrally related to Engels' "invention" of Marxism,"[35]—are not only incompatible with Hegel's own view but also false.

Second, the critical philosophy fails to reach its goal and hence is incomplete because it only points to but does not in fact deduce the categories. Hence, it fails to realize the principle of speculation that lies in demonstrating the deeper unity underlying diversity. For Hegel, what he calls "the need of philosophy" only arises through difference.[36] Since Kant does not overcome difference, he does not respond to this existential difficulty. In that sense, the critical philosophy fails the test.

Third, the critical philosophy, which does not reach its high point and end in Kant, can be further developed with respect to its intrinsic goal and even in principle completed by carrying its spirit, which can be separated from its letter, beyond Kant. In fact, the history of philosophy consists in a series of conscious and often largely unconscious reactions among different thinkers with respect to a small set of basic philosophical concerns. The critical philosophy belongs to these concerns, which Hegel later traces back to early Greek philosophy, at least as early as Parmenides, to demonstrate the unity of thought and being.

Fourth, Fichte takes the critical philosophy beyond the point at which Kant left it. Kant, who thought Fichte misunderstood the critical philosophy, sharply rejects his disciple's position.[37] In this dispute, Hegel supports the disciple, who implicitly suggests that the critical philosophy is unfinished and needs to be carried beyond the place where Kant left it, against the master, who claims it has been completed; hence, he supports Fichte against Kant. The critical philosophy remains incomplete since, as noted, it fails to deduce the categories, which Fichte, in building upon Kant, in fact accomplishes for the first time. It follows that the critical philosophy fails to make good on the principle of speculation that lies in demonstrating the unity underlying diversity. In Hegelian language, Kant fails to respond to the need of philosophy.

A fifth insight concerns the relation of Hegel to Kant. If philosophy is historical, if the critical philosophy falls short of its goal but can be further developed, if Fichte takes it beyond the point at which Kant left it, and if Hegel identifies with Fichte (and Schelling), then it follows that Hegel is a Kantian. To put the same point differently: Hegel sharply rejects the letter of the Kantian position, but he does not reject—in fact he explicitly accepts—its spirit, namely, the speculative principle that Fichte identifies as the spirit of the critical philosophy. It is then incorrect to regard Hegel and Kant as basically opposed, for instance, in the opposition between Kant's epistemology and Hegel's phenomenology. It is crucial to understanding Hegel, who so strongly relies on the history of philosophy, to see that he regards the main figures in post-Kantian German idealism as rejecting the letter but as further developing the spirit of the critical philosophy, and his own project as continuing the effort of post-Kantian German idealism to carry forward a recognizable form of the spirit of Kant's position. In other words, for Hegel, who rejects the letter of Kant's position, post-Kantian German philosophy represents the correct development of the spirit of the critical philosophy with which he identifies in his own position.

Fichte, Hegel, and the Spirit of the Critical Philosophy

Hegel's interest in separating the spirit from the letter of the critical philosophy gives him room to develop Kant's position in ways very different from anything Kant could have approved. Even in his early writings, before he composed the *Phenomenology*, Hegel understood philosophy as progressing through a dialectical interaction among different thinkers against the background of a common project. In the *Differenzschrift*, he regards his contemporaries, Fichte, Schelling, and Reinhold, as carrying the critical philosophy beyond Kant. And he comprehends the position he formulates in reacting to their positions as belonging to this general effort.

To carry forward the spirit of the critical philosophy, one must identify its spirit. Kant, who seems oblivious to the practical difficulty this poses, indicates, in appealing to a kind of interpretive holism, that it is easy to grasp the spirit from the "idea of the whole."[38] Yet this is obviously difficult, since, as he also points out, at least initially, few observers are capable of this synoptic vision for the obvious reason that they have not yet mastered the overall position. And, as he also notes, the very few original thinkers, such as Kant himself, can use, but rarely cogently describe, their own basic insights.[39] The difficulty in identifying the spirit of the critical philosophy is further indicated by the inability after more than two centuries of intensive discussion to agree on how to interpret it.

As the Kant debate attests, there is obviously more than one possibility, more than one way to identify the spirit or central thrust of the critical philosophy. In the *Differenzschrift*, Hegel points to the "principle of the deduction of the categories," which, he claims, "Fichte extracted in a purer, stricter form and called the spirit of Kantian philosophy."[40] Hegel criticizes the letter of the critical philosophy on the grounds that Kant allegedly "turns this identity . . . which is Reason, into an object of philosophical reflection."[41] From the perspective of speculative reason as the philosophical instrument, Hegel objects to Kant's dependence on categories situated in the understanding.[42] Yet this is an "external" criticism, since it presupposes the correctness of Hegel's own position.

Hegel's identification of the deduction of the categories as the spirit of the critical philosophy is also problematic in several ways. It runs the metaphysical and the transcendental deductions together, which Kant scholarship is concerned to distinguish, in simply referring to them as the deduction.[43] It further silently conflates the spirit of the critical philosophy with its letter in identifying the former as the deduction of the categories. And it incorrectly appeals to Fichte as the source of this approach. Yet Fichte reads the critical philosophy differently. In identifying its basic principle, he points not to the deduction of the categories but to the principle of identity, which it illustrates. "That our proposition [The I originally and absolutely posits its own being—T. R.] is the absolutely basic principle of all knowledge was pointed out by *Kant* in his deduction of the categories; but he never laid it down specifically *as* the basic principle."[44]

From the vantage point that Hegel shares with Fichte, the basic problem is not the deduction of the categories, which still continues to occupy students of Kant after several hundred years, but the problem of speculative identity that is central to "authentic" idealism and is only illustrated by, but does not in any way depend on, Kant's famous deduction. In Kant's wake, as for Fichte, so for Hegel, the deeper question is the problem of identity that Fichte and then Hegel correctly identify as central also to the critical philosophy.

Under Fichte's influence, Hegel's reaction to the "authentic" idealism of the critical philosophy disregards its letter in considering its spirit. Following Fichte's lead, Hegel, like the other post-Kantian idealists, perhaps even like Kant, though that is unclear, simply gives up the difficult concept of things in themselves. Kant introduces this concept as the basis of the theory of the representational approach to knowledge as early as the Herz letter. Hence all those who continue to work within any detectible form of the Kantian framework, but who abandon the concept of things in themselves, including Hegel, also turn away from representationalism and toward constructivism. Hence, like Fichte, who sharply rejects the thing in itself, Hegel turns toward a second, deeper Kantian form of epistemological identity in his Copernican revolution.

The Transition of Reinhold, Fichte, and Hegel to Phenomenology

Hegel was not a phenomenologist when he composed the *Differenzschrift*, and the term *phenomenology* does not occur in this text. He only later turned to phenomenology in the course of working out his own position. The turn to phenomenology is determined not only by Kant, Reinhold, and perhaps Lambert, but also, above all, by Fichte, the most important post-Kantian influence on the formulation of Hegel's position. Fichte's turn away from the thing in itself while continuing to work out the Kantian approach to knowledge leads him toward phenomenology in his early writings before he even mentions the term.

Phenomenology was in the air at the turn of the nineteenth century, so there are many possible influences on Hegel's interest in this theme. One, which has not so far been mentioned, is Kant's former student, Johann Gottfried Herder.[45] The latter, who was interested in Lambert's form of phenomenology, points, in a book that only appeared after Hegel's death, to an aesthetic phenomenology, which, he suggests, requires a second Lambert.[46]

Hegel's view of Reinhold as a leading nonphilosopher is strongly negative, but some observers believe Hegel relies on him in turning to phenomenology. Reinhold's view of phenomenology was influenced by Christoph Gottfried Bardili. Today, Bardili is nearly unknown, and he was certainly of little influence on the contemporary discussion. But he was well known to, although not better thought of by, Hegel in his capacity as preceptor in the Tübinger Stift during Hegel's student years there, prior to a later appointment to a professorship in Stuttgart.

Reinhold, who was a disciple of Fichte, "converted" in spring 1799 to Bardili's conception of philosophy as a system of "rational realism" based purely upon "thinking *qua* thinking."[47] According to Reinhold, Bardili's position fell between the views of Fichte and Jacobi and superseded the *Wissenschaftslehre*.[48] In his study of the situation of philosophy at the turn of the new century, which attracted Hegel's attention and served as the pretext for the *Differenzschrift*, Reinhold entitles the fourth part "Elements of Phenomenology, or the Explanation of Rational Rationalism through Its Application to True Appearances" ("Elemente der Phänomenologie oder Erläuterung des rationalen Rationalismus durch seine Anwendung auf die Erscheinungen").[49] Reinhold is distantly following such predecessors as Lambert. Like Lambert, Reinhold here describes phenomenology, whose task consists in explaining so-called rational realism, his position at the time, through the application of its principles to true appearances as distinguished from false appearances. In the preliminary statement preceding this text, he defines phenomenology with respect to so-called rational realism as follows: "[Phenomenology] completes the exposition of rational realism through the application of its principles to the phenomena, which it teaches us, with the help of these principles, to distinguish and separate from mere appearance."⁵⁰ The role of phenomenology consists in providing the criteria for the distinction of real appearances from mere false appearances. Experience is basically experience of nature. Phenomenology must return to the ground of nature in order to state the pure principles of the general theory of nature (*Naturlehre*). It follows that, for Reinhold, phenomenology is pure philosophy of nature.⁵¹

It is plausible to think that Hegel, who was unusually well informed, was familiar with Lambert and probably with Herder, as well as with Reinhold's book, and was aware of the latter's view of phenomenology when he composed the *Differenzschrift*. Yet since he also had a very negative opinion of Reinhold, the latter's influence on Hegel's later development, including his turn to and conception of phenomenology, is probably very minor. Hegel thought much more highly of Fichte, who also turned to phenomenology in the course of working through Kant's approach to the problem of knowledge. It is hence plausible to infer that Fichte's turn to phenomenology influenced Hegel's own phenomenological turn.

The term *phenomenology* does not appear either in Fichte's initial version of the *Wissenschaftslehre*, nor, to the best of my knowledge, in his other Jena writings. Yet one can argue that this concept, though not under that name, is important even in this text, in which, though continuing to proclaim his fidelity, Fichte has already taken his leave from Kant in working out an original position of his own.

Fichte's turn toward phenomenology can be described in terms of his close link to Kant. It directly derives from his turn away from the thing in itself, at least as Kant understands it and hence away from Kantian representationalism toward a form of Kantian constructivism. Like many of Kant's contemporaries, Fichte opposes the concept of the thing in itself. According to Fichte, the thing in itself is a pure invention with no reality whatsoever. His claim that to be committed to the thing in itself is to be a dogmatist is a veiled suggestion that Kant's critical philosophy does not escape from but falls back into the very dogmatism it officially rejects.⁵² Fichte takes a different line in suggesting that one can reject the thing in itself and remain a Kantian. One way to put the point is to say that he reconstructs the critical philosophy without the thing in itself.

This leads immediately to a new ontology that differs from the one advanced in the Kantian position. Fichte, who takes the subject as basic, understands objects in terms of the negation of, or opposition to, the subject. Though Fichte is sometimes interpreted as a Cartesian,⁵³ his position differs from that of Descartes' in most, perhaps all main points. This includes his rejection of epistemological foundationalism, as well the well-known Cartesian substance ontology, including the basic distinction between thinking being, extended being and infinite being. Fichte, like Kant, rejects any assimilation of the subject to a thing, for which he substitutes a conception of the subject as fundamentally active or activity.

Fichte is, of course, not the only Kantian contemporary to reject the thing in itself. F. H. Jacobi famously claimed that without the thing in itself, which he also found unacceptable, one could not be a Kantian. He wrote, "Without the presupposition [of the "thing in itself,"] I was unable to enter into [Kant's] system, but with it I was unable to stay within it."[54] This implies that it is not possible to be a Kantian, and the critical philosophy cannot be saved, since it cannot survive the loss of the thing in itself. Fichte, on the contrary, who believes the critical philosophy cannot survive if it holds on to the thing in itself, rejects this concept, at least as Kant formulates it,[55] while still claiming to be a Kantian. According to Fichte, authentic Kantianism, or what Hegel identifies as genuine speculative philosophy, which Fichte further defends against the author of the critical philosophy, necessarily rejects the thing in itself.

The rejection of the thing in itself entails the rejection of Kantian representationalism and representationalism of all kinds in favor of a constructivist approach to knowledge. Without ever mentioning Kant's Copernican revolution, Fichte works out a form of it in the section entitled "Deduction of Representation" in his *Foundations of the Entire Science of Knowledge*.[56] This work is divided into three parts, including remarks on the fundamental principles of the entire *Wissenschaftslehre*, followed by exposition of the foundations of theoretical knowledge and then by exposition of the foundations of practical knowledge. In his analysis of the fundamental principles (*Grundsätze*) of the entire *Wissenschaftslehre*, Fichte further develops and reformulates Kant's view of the transcendental unity of apperception in the form of three principles. These include the assertion of the subject, then of its "negation" by an object defined as that which is not the subject, and finally of the interaction between subject and object. The third basic principle, or the claim that self and not-self stand in a relation of reciprocal interdetermination, is analyzed by Fichte as two separate claims that form the content of the theoretical and practical portions of the work.

The discussion in the theoretical part of the work reaches a high point in "Deduction of Representation." Kant's deduction of the categories is motivated by his effort to understand the relation between appearances, or objects given in experience, and what can be thought but does not appear.[57] Fichte's rival deduction of representation is justified by his complaint that Kant fails to prove his theory, since he fails to prove that representations possess objective validity. Fichte's deduction presupposes *inter alia* three points: there is nothing higher than the subject or self (*das Ich*); in philosophy we start from the self that cannot be deduced; and deduction is a direct, genetic demonstration focused on the self.[58] In short, in abandoning the conception of the thing in itself, or the mind-independent world as a presupposition, he gives up the Kantian aim of analyzing the relation of ideas in the mind to the world in favor of a "deduction" of knowledge from the point of view of the subject.

Fichte's deduction is a complex argument in no less than eleven steps. Suffice it to say that, starting from the hypothesis that the self, or subject, is active, he maintains that we can understand the subject as what is left when all objects have been eliminated by the power of abstraction, and the not-self as that from which abstraction can be made. Either can be considered as determined by the other, and conversely. The deduction concludes with the claim that the subject is in fact either finite, or determined, or, on the contrary, infinite and hence determining, and that in both cases it is reciprocally related merely to itself. According to Fichte, theoretical philosophy can go no further. In summarizing his deduction, Fichte concludes that the subject and object mutually determine each other.

This is a turn toward phenomenology, even before he uses the term, since Fichte is committed here to an explanation of knowledge, in this case in the misnamed "Deduction of Representation," through the activity of the subject, not through the causal activity of the object on the subject.[59] However, the "Deduction" is misnamed, since Kantian representation presupposes a mind-independent object, which Fichte, in giving up the thing in itself, abandons as an explanatory concept.

In writings after the Jena period, Fichte continues to move in a phenomenological direction in developing his version of the constructivist claim that the subject only knows what it in some sense constructs. Certain features of the new method that Fichte experimented with in 1800–1801, and which were incorporated in the 1801–1802 *Darstellung*, such as the terms *Konstruktion* and *Nachkonstruktion*, became distinctive features of his later attempts to characterize the activity of the transcendental philosopher.[60]

In the 1804 *Wissenschaftslehre*, which was not published during Hegel's lifetime and hence probably did not influence his position, Fichte reworks the Kantian distinction between false appearance and true appearance. According to his son and editor, Fichte called the second part of his 1804 *Wissenschaftslehre* "Erscheinungs- und Scheinlehre."[61] At the beginning of the second set of lectures, Fichte announced his intention to argue for the intrinsic unity of being and thinking. Yet he continues to subordinate this view to faith while adducing phenomenological dimensions. In the tenth lecture, he provides a short overview of his present science of knowing (*Wissenschaftslehre*) at this point in his development. This science, which turns on consciousness, is, Fichte notes, both "a doctrine of truth and reason" as well as "a *phenomenology*, a doctrine of appearance [*Erscheinungslehre*] and illusion [*Schein*]."[62] Understood in this way, phenomenology is, for Fichte, a theory of true appearance and false appearance as distinguished from the theory of being (*Seynslehre*), which attracted Heidegger and which Fichte understands as a "theory of reason *and* of truth."[63] Unlike Lambert and the early Kant, for whom phenomenology concerns false appearance, Fichte here uses the term in a positive sense.[64] In anticipating Hegel, Fichte defines phenomenology as the science of true appearing (*Erscheinungslehre*). Unlike Lambert, he asserts that true appearing (*Erscheinen*) is never the mere appearance of illusion (*Schein*). Since truth is phenomenal, phenomena are not false, or false appearances, but true. Fichte, who depicts phenomenology as a description of the field of true appearing, here anticipates later efforts by Hegel and Husserl to understand philosophy as science of the phenomenological approach to truth.[65]

Kant's, Fichte's and Hegel's Phenomenological Turns

Phenomenology, which is not yet present in Hegel's *Differenzschrift*, emerges in the *Phenomenology of Spirit*, where Hegel presents his mature approach to the problem of knowledge as it comes to him in German idealism. Hegel draws on a wide variety of contemporary thinkers, especially Kant and Fichte, in presenting an explicitly phenomenological solution to the problem of knowledge. His own view of phenomenology can be understood in the first instance as correcting and carrying forward Kant's Copernican revolution, as amended by Fichte.

To understand Hegel's phenomenological reformulation of Kant's and Hegel's positions, one must grasp his diagnosis of their faults. Kant's representational approach fails since it relies on a causal analysis of the relation of representations to the unknown and unknowable mind independent world, which he theorizes under the heading of the thing in itself. Hegel follows Fichte, Jacobi, and many others in turning away from Kant's thing in itself, but not from the mind-independent world.

For Hegel, Fichte's revision of the Kantian subject is promising but insufficient. Kant, who "reduces" the subject, which is not a human being, to its epistemological capacities, employs an epistemological approach to subjectivity. His famous description of the subject as the "I think" that can always accompany any representation[66] fails because he is unable, as noted, to describe the activity through which it allegedly constructs the object of experience and knowledge. Fichte corrects Kant on this point in stressing (even overstressing) the cognitive role of human activity and hence of the subject's activity.

For Hegel, Fichte's approach fails because in eliminating the thing in itself he can be understood as relying exclusively on the subject to explain knowledge. The difficulty can be described with respect to Fichte's view of positing (*setzen*). This term is sometimes understood as "to be aware of," "to reflect upon," or "to be conscious of"—definitions that suppose there is an object of which one is conscious. Yet if this were the case, then positing would not be creative but similar to Kantian representation of what already is independent of the knower. If we recall that Fichte invokes philosophical theory to explain human practice, a more sober assessment is that he is claiming that we are forced, as a condition of knowledge, to the inference that, through positing, the subject constructs the world as its epistemological object. Thus he writes, "The absolute self must therefore be the cause of the not-self, insofar as the latter is the ultimate ground of all representation; and the not-self must to that extent be its effect."[67]

It is unclear how to interpret Fichte's view of positing. Some observers draw attention to a distinction between finite human being and Fichte's view of the self.[68] Yet the suspicion that Fichte went too far in stressing the role of the subject is illustrated by the German Romantic poet Schiller's suggestion that, for the Fichtean subject, reality is nothing more than itself.[69] Fichte's statements about positing are ambiguous. The confident view that the subject literally constructs the world is tempered by a more cautious, epistemologically agnostic claim that he advances elsewhere in acknowledging the limits of his theory "in that it shows how neither does the mere activity of the self provide the ground of the reality of the not-self, nor the mere activity of the not-self provide the ground of passivity in the self."[70]

Hegel's approach turns away from the claim to know the world as it is and hence from the thing in itself, while maintaining an interaction between it and the subject to explain experience and knowledge as the construction of phenomena. Early in the nineteenth century, he gives up cognitive reference to the mind-independent world beyond appearance, which cannot be known, while maintaining the difference between what appears and what is, not in itself but, as Aristotle would say, for us. Hegel participates in the post-Kantian shift away from a transcendental analysis of the a priori conditions of knowledge toward a description of knowledge as resulting from an a posteriori process that plays out in the social and historical context.

From Kant he takes over the seminal idea, whose proximal origin he does not acknowledge, but on which his own position clearly depends, that we "construct" what we know, and from Fichte he borrows the view that a grasp of the cognitive object crucially depends not on a merely logical epistemological subject but on the finite subject's activity. Hegel rehabilitates phenomenology, which, for Kant, was earlier confined to false appearance, hence mere appearance, as distinguished from truth. What for Kant is a mere prolegomenal stage prior to and apart from the process leading to truth becomes its main and indeed only source. Kant distinguishes sharply between noumena and phenomena, between what is true but cannot appear and what appears and is not true. In response, Hegel relativizes the distinctions between falsity, appearance, and truth in calling attention to appearance as a stage on the way to truth. Mere falsity, which is not truth, is replaced by a conception of appearance (*Schein*) that, under the right circumstances, becomes true appearance (*Erscheinung*), or truth.

Hegelian phenomenology provides an account of how through their cognitive activity human beings progressively come to know their surroundings and themselves. It has been suggested that Hegel's achievement finally lies in assembling ideas, all of which are due to others, in a grand synthesis.[71] Since the philosophical discussion never begins again without precedent, any or almost any philosophical claim is in some sense anticipated somewhere by earlier writers. With sufficient ingenuity, one can always find some kind of precedent. Yet in pointing, arguably for the first time, to the way in which finite human beings in fact transform imperfect claims to know into progressively better and hence relatively more acceptable epistemological claims, Hegel invents a strikingly novel phenomenological approach to the problem of knowledge.

Consciousness and Hegel's Phenomenological Turn

Hegel's phenomenology emerges as an alternative to theories of knowledge based on a causal theory of perception. If his attacks on such theories fail, then there is no reason to turn to his proposed alternative. The causal theory of perception, or new way of ideas, includes what is usually designated as rationalism, or theories running from ideas to the mind-independent world, and empiricism, or theories deriving from experience of the world. Rationalism and empiricism have in common a causal relation between ideas and the world—between the world, which causes ideas, and the ideas through which we know the world. Both further rely on the reverse inference from ideas, taken as an effect, to the world, taken as their cause.

It has repeatedly been pointed out that Kant, in his representationalist phase, restates this view in holding that representations can be understood as caused by and hence as effects of, the world, thing in itself, or noumenon, which appears. He denies a causal approach to perception by denying a reverse inference from ideas to the world. In Kant's theory, this denial, which is adumbrated but never worked out, takes the form of pointing to a series of well-known, related difficulties. They include the impossibility of knowing the world, or thing in itself, which cannot be experienced; the difficulty of understanding a causal connection to a world that is not in space and time; and the inconsistency in extending causality beyond the level of perception, in short, the inability to provide a cognitive grasp of an independent object to which there is no epistemological connection.

Hegel again attacks Kantian representationalism and any form of the causal theory of perception in criticizing causal theories of perception in detail in two main places: in the *Encyclopedia of the Philosophical Sciences* in opposing empiricism, and in the *Phenomenology of Spirit* in criticizing consciousness.[72] In both places, Hegel depicts Kant as if he were committed to representation alone, without acknowledging the latter's commitment to constructivism. He further treats Kant as if he were only in principle a critical thinker, but was in fact a dogmatist. In the *Encyclopedia*, Hegel's account in the section entitled "Preliminary Conception" is subdivided into three "Positions of Thought with Respect to Objectivity," including metaphysics, empiricism, and the critical philosophy, as well as, finally, immediate knowing.

Hegel's critiques of metaphysics and immediate knowing follow and develop further Kant's own rejections of precritical, or dogmatic metaphysics, or theory of knowledge that fails to criticize its cognitive instrument as well as claims for direct, or immediate knowledge. In his remarks on metaphysics, Hegel describes, interprets, and criticizes pre-Kantian dogmatic, hence unjustified, claims to know, such as those featured in Christian Wolff, the dogmatist whom most Kant admires.[73] The account of immediate knowing similarly reviews contemporary forms of the direct, or naive realist, approach to knowledge, implicitly featuring Jacobi and perhaps Descartes.[74] The "Second Position of Thought with Respect to Objectivity" studies in succession empiricism and then the critical philosophy as a form of empiricism. Hegel's short remark specifically on empiricism usefully places it in the historical context while setting the stage for a longer, critical series of remarks on Kant. Empiricism goes beyond (dogmatic) metaphysics, which is abstract and universal, in providing concrete, determinate, or so-called finite content. Empiricism further differs from metaphysics, which proceeds from the specific to the abstract and universal and not conversely. Hegel's critique of empiricism here loosely follows Hume. Empiricism, which begins with what is real, or "actual," cannot detect necessary connections in experience.

Hegel extends his critique of empiricism in remarks on Kant. In the "Second Position of Thought with Respect to Objectivity" he contrasts the critical philosophy, which he considers to be a form of empiricism, with ordinary empiricism. Kant, who holds that all knowledge begins with experience as the sole source of cognition, introduces a seminal distinction between appearances and things in themselves, between what is as it is and what appears to us in the guise of representations of the mind-independent external world. His view differs from ordinary empiricism in two ways: we have cognition of appearances only, and universality and necessity are in fact present in experience.[75]

Kant's approach results in a contrast between the subjective and the objective. According to Hegel, he argues for objective knowledge in a psychological-historical analysis that depends on conceptions of the cognitive subject and of the categories. Hegel follows Fichte's claim that Kant fails to deduce the categories with the requisite necessity (sec. 42, 84) while pretending they elevate mere perception into objectivity, or into experience (sec. 43, 86–87). The categories cannot give knowledge of the absolute, or things in themselves (sec. 44, 87). And Kant has no other means to arrive at knowledge understood as a grasp of specific content (sec. 46, 89). Kant's improvement on ordinary empiricism is, as Salomon Maimon holds, a sophisticated form of skepticism that fails as a theory of cognition.[76] Maimon believes the critical philosophy cannot be improved. But Hegel, like other post-Kantian German idealists, thinks the critical philosophy can be carried beyond the point at which Kant left it.

In discussing the critical philosophy, Hegel never mentions constructivism, the Copernican revolution, or similar terms. For Hegel, the critical philosophy illustrates epistemological representationalism, all forms of which fail. The discussion of representationalism, which is presupposed but not provided in the *Encyclopedia*, is provided earlier in often bewildering detail in the *Phenomenology* in the context of an analysis of consciousness. Consciousness includes empiricism and rationalism, the main forms of the modern causal theory of perception. Hegel mounts a devastating attack on any approach to the problem of knowledge through mere consciousness of the world, with special attention to representationalism. Kant, who initially favors representationalism, later rejects it for constructivism without discussing other positions. Hegel, who is better grounded than Kant in the philosophical tradition, rejects any form of the modern causal theory of perception, and hence any form of the modern claim to grasp the mind-independent world as it is, through a series of references to a long list of positions.

Hegel's analysis of consciousness is exceedingly complex, approaching in some passages, even by elastic Hegelian standards, utter impenetrability. The analysis, which loosely follows the critical philosophy, is divided into three moments: sense-certainty (*sinnliche Anschauung*), or sensation; perception (*Wahrnehmung*); and force (*Kraft*) and understanding (*Verstand*). Since this part of the *Phenomenology* has been studied in detail, we can go quickly here.[77]

Ancient Greek philosophy, which does not distinguish sensation and perception, refers to them both through the single term *aisthesis*. Kant is the first important thinker to draw this distinction clearly. Though many observers run sensation and perception together, Hegel studies them separately. The account of sensation attacks the possibility of immediate knowledge, which is often thought to be the richest kind of knowledge. But, since language, which is universal or at least general, cannot identify the particular object, sensation yields only the immediate knowledge that something is but not what it is.

Hegel analyzes perception as a distinct approach to knowledge of the thing with many qualities. Perception consists in saying what something is by identifying its qualities or predicates. In identifying the various predicates, the unity of the cognitive object, which is present for sensation, disappears in perception. As a result, perception, which belongs to the process of knowledge, cannot function as its sole source. The inability of either sensation or perception to provide a satisfactory resolution of the problem of knowledge leads to the third and final stage of consciousness in which theories are advanced to understand the unity and diversity of the cognitive object, or, in Hegelian language, the unity of unity and diversity. This means that a cognitive object must exhibit both the unity of a single object as well as the diversity due to its various properties within the overall framework of its particularity.

The account in the section entitled "Force and Understanding" focuses on specific thinkers. It studies efforts by Newton to base theory of knowledge on the invisible force of gravitation and by Kant to found Newtonian science in the critical philosophy, which he bases on the understanding. When Hegel was writing, Newton was the leading modern natural scientist, and Kant was an enthusiastic Newtonian. Newton's main achievement is the formulation of Newtonian mechanics to explain the laws of planetary motion. Hegel studies the consequences of his approach for theory of knowledge in general. He considers Newton and Kant together with respect to a single conceptual model loosely echoing the Kantian distinction between appearance and reality. In criticizing Newton, he rejects force as an explanatory concept as well as modern scientific explanation. Scientific explanation relies on a conception of scientific law that fails to account for each individual thing. It is arguable that Hegel sets the standard higher than can reasonably be met on a scientific basis.[78] In modern natural science, laws that, like the law of gravitation, unify or combine other laws are regarded as stronger than those other laws. Yet Hegel, who may be following Socrates' view in the *Phaedo* that natural scientific causality fails to explain the individual object and hence justifies a turn to the theory of forms, considers such laws as bereft of content, as expressing no more than the mere notion of law (sec. 150, 91). According to Hegel, the concept of force derives from mathematics instead of, as Newton falsely claims, from experience. Hegel identifies a series of confusions due, in his opinion, to the fact that force lies in the understanding but not in the world.

Hegel treats the Kantian concept of understanding as the analogue of the Newtonian concept of force. He rejects the Kantian concept of the understanding, which functions, in his interpretation of the critical philosophy, as the middle term between the extremes of reality, or the object in itself, and its appearance. For Hegel, the understanding, like force, is an abstract concept that simply fails to grasp its object (sec. 155, 95). In restating contemporary objections to the thing in itself, he contends that Kant fails to show that reality appears. This point amounts to the obvious claim that things in themselves do not and cannot appear. In working through the Kantian analysis, Hegel comes to the conclusion that when we penetrate beyond appearance to the object in itself, what we find there is only ourselves. In an important passage, which sums up his critique while pointing to his solution, he writes, "This curtain . . . hanging before the inner world is therefore drawn away, and we have the inner being [the I] gazing into the inner world—the vision of the undifferentiated selfsame being, which repels itself from itself, posits itself as an inner being containing different moments, but for which equally these moments are immediately *not* different—*self-consciousness*" (sec. 165, 103).

This passage makes two important points. On the one hand, we cannot know on the basis of consciousness. For if what we seek to know is the mind-independent world, we cannot reliably make out this claim. In other words, neither Kantian representationalism nor any causal theory of perception suffices to go from appearance to reality. In fact, what we mistakenly take to be reality is not the world as it is beyond mere appearance. On the contrary, when we go there, we find no more than ourselves. For there is nothing there, nothing in consciousness, unless we put it there. Hence, consciousness fails in all its many forms as an appropriate strategy for knowledge. On the other hand, self-consciousness potentially succeeds as an epistemological approach, though this remains to be shown.

Hegel's assertion that when we attempt to surpass mere appearance, what we find is only ourselves is a version of the constructivist thesis, illustrated in Kant's view that we can know only what we construct.[79] Hegel formulates this insight as early as the *Differenzschrift* as the identity of knowing and being. This can be paraphrased as the claim that the condition of knowledge is that the view of the object and the object of the view about it coincide. In the *Phenomenology*, Hegel restates this constructivist insight from a phenomenological perspective in suggesting that knowledge is based on self-consciousness.

We can reconstruct the argument as follows. We know only what we construct. If in knowing we know only ourselves, then we do not know noumena. Hence, we do not know the world in itself, but only the world as it occurs for us within conscious experience. Since we construct phenomena, in knowing we know only phenomena. But since we know only phenomena, and what we know is constructed by us as a condition of knowing it, knowledge is self-knowledge or self-consciousness. We need then to turn away from claims to know through mere consciousness in acknowledging that we do not know a mind-independent object. "For this knowledge of what is the truth of appearance as ordinarily conceived, and of its inner being, is itself only a result of a complex movement whereby the modes of consciousness 'meaning,' perceiving, and the Understanding, vanish; and it will be equally evident that the cognition of *what consciousness knows in knowing itself*, requires a still more complex movement" (sec. 165, 103).

Hegel summarizes his claim in his account of the truth of self-certainty. From the perspective of consciousness, or a causal theory of perception, what is true is other than itself. Yet what we take to be an object other than ourselves is no more than the object as it is for us. In other words, there is a difference between what we take the object to be and what it turns out to be. From his constructivist perspective, Hegel enigmatically claims, in reaction, say, to the Cartesian version of the causal theory of knowledge, that "certainty gives place to truth" (sec. 166, 104). This means that the cognitive relation of the subject to the object as mere consciousness of the object, which yields no more than certainty, is replaced on the level of self-consciousness by the identity of subject and the object in the form of externality. In other words, knowledge is not consciousness, but self-consciousness. For in knowing, we know only ourselves or, as Hegel says, "the certainty is to itself its own object, and consciousness is to itself the truth" (sec. 166, 104). In other words, the concept of the object and the object of the concept coincide, or are identical.

Self-Consciousness and Knowledge as Phenomenological

The remainder of the book consists in an elaborate argument for a theory of cognition as self-consciousness. This argument is rarely studied in detail since the phenomenological nature of Hegel's approach to knowledge is only rarely acknowledged. Constructivist thinkers like Hobbes, Vico, Kant, and Hegel need to explain what it means to "construct" the cognitive object. A key to Hegel's position lies in his ability to provide a plausible account of what it means to construct what one knows and hence to construct phenomena.

It is surprising, in view of the enormous dimensions of the Hegel discussion, that little attention seems to have been directed to his specifically phenomenological contribution to knowledge.[80] The widespread inattention to phenomenology in the Hegel discussion can be explained by several factors. One is the Husserlian claim, which is frequently reiterated but never justified, that Husserl invented phenomenology worthy of the name. This claim incorrectly suggests that he had no predecessors. Another is that, as already noted, Hegel, in the *Phenomenology*, never employs the term *phenomenology* and hence never employs this term to designate his own position.[81] Thus Hegel's readers are obliged literally to reconstruct the outlines of his view of phenomenology as well as its link to the problem of knowledge.

Hegelian phenomenology features a dialectical interaction between theories and cognitive objects in an analysis of knowledge as arising within the limits of conscious experience. Hegel distinguishes between what is and what we experience in describing an approach, remarkably similar to how human beings seek to know the world and themselves, to how we can reliably claim to know what is given in experience. Unlike Kant, who analyzes the preconditions of consciousness, and such later writers as Freud, and perhaps also Nietzsche and Marx, depending on how they are interpreted, he makes no claim to know what lies beyond the plane of consciousness.

Hegel's phenomenological approach to knowledge is presented in outline form in the introduction and developed throughout the book. His specifically phenomenological approach restricts cognitive claims to the contents of consciousness understood as mere phenomena, which do not refer beyond themselves either to noumena, to the thing in itself or things in themselves, or to the mind-independent external world.

At the dawn of the modern era, Montaigne and Descartes draw attention to subjectivity as the unavoidable path to objectivity. Hegel follows Fichte in grasping objectivity from the perspective of the subject, in Hegel's case through a distinction between subject and object within consciousness.[82] As for Kant, and as for all correspondence theories of knowledge since Parmenides, the criterion of knowledge is the identity of subject and object, knower and known. Yet Hegel parts company with Kant's a priorism in basing his view of theory on the contents of conscious experience. Hegel's empirical commitment is visible in his attention to empirical phenomena as prior to theories about them, that is, to the subordination of theory to practice.

For Hegel, knowledge is not the result of a simple "constatation," or determination of what is, for instance, an identification of what is as it is at a given temporal instant. It is rather the result of a cognitive process in which theories are formulated on the basis of experience and then compared (and contrasted) with further experience. A theory is a claim for knowledge, formulated on the basis of experience, that can be validated or confirmed, or undermined or disconfirmed by testing it in further experience.

This point can be generalized. In discussing knowledge, Hegel is not working out a theory of what must be the case but describing everyday epistemological practice. There is no reliable knowledge of the mind-independent external world. We know and can know only what is constructed by us and further appears within conscious experience. In constructing phenomena, we literally construct our world. Yet phenomena are not constructed freely, without limit, as the result of mere fantasy; rather, they emerge in the process of working out a particular theory by comparing our view of the matter at any given point in time to what is given in experience.

Wilfrid Sellars criticizes the supposed commitment by Hegel and others to the myth of the given.[83] But this objection seems unrelated to Hegel. In the *Phenomenology*, what we call the cognitive object, or the world is never a mere given but depends on theories about the world. Claims to know are adjudicated through simple comparison between the concept of the object and the object of the concept within consciousness (sec. 84, 53). Talk about truth does not discover, uncover, or otherwise cognize a mind-independent external object. It rather concerns no more than the construction of phenomena given in consciousness, which in turn function as the standard in terms of which to construct further theories about it (sec. 84, 53).

According to Hegel, we test the relation of our concept or theory about the cognitive object within conscious experience. In simplest terms, conscious experience includes a concept of the object and the object of the concept, both of which are contained within consciousness, within which we distinguish and compare them (sec. 85, 54). Hegel hence leaves behind any velleity to know, grasp, or otherwise cognize the mind-independent world as it is. Now there are only two possible outcomes of an examination of the relation of concepts and experience. Either the result agrees with our expectations, since the theory describes, or corresponds to, what we find in experience, or it does not.

Hegel's conception of phenomena is clearly paradoxical. Phenomena in Hegel's position have a dual status both within and outside consciousness. In the first instance, they are clearly "within" consciousness, where they depend on the construction of conceptual schemes, or theories, to cognize conscious experience. But they are also in a sense "outside" consciousness in that theories are tested in confronting them with the external world as given in the contents of conscious experience, that is, in the form of contents that either agree or correspond with, or disagree with in failing to correspond to (and hence resist) our theories about it. Everyone is familiar with theories that, when confronted with experience, fail the test and must be reformulated. In the latter sense, what we seek to know acts as an external, empirical standard for evaluating our theories about it.

Kant is representative of philosophers who believe there is unmodifiable knowledge, independent of time and place. Yet we rarely if ever knowingly arrive at a result of this kind, that is, at a theory that does not, now or ever, conceivably need to be modified. In most cases, the theory, or working concept of the cognitive object, is refuted by experience that reveals a distinction between what, on the basis of our theory, we expect and what in practice we find. This is the case for all kinds of epistemological investigation from astronomy to zoology, in which our conjectures can always fail the test of experience.

Sometimes the theory provisionally adopted appears to accord with experience, or at least initially appears to do so before other, more stringent tests are devised. This suggests that what we presently take to be knowledge and truth coincide, since our view of what is the case in fact correctly identifies the character of future experience. Although this need not ever occur, if this happened, the cognitive process would reach its end, or epistemological closure.[84]

If, as is more often the case, our expectations are thwarted in some way, if there is a discernable difference between what the theory itself seems to suggest and what we find, then the theory must be altered to "fit" what we encounter in experience. There is nothing novel about Hegel's insistence that our views must be altered if they are refuted in practice. Most observers, including all empiricists, insist on the importance of respecting the verdict of experience. Kant, who thinks it is possible to work out a theory of knowledge that is a priori and hence immune to experience, is an exception. If he is an empiricist, then he is an empiricist who believes that claims for knowledge initially depend on experience but later become independent of further experience. The novel aspect in Hegel's approach lies in his conviction that, when we alter the theory by adjusting it to "fit" experience, then the cognitive object, which depends on the theoretical framework, is also altered. In effect Hegel denies that there is a single, determinate way the mind-independent world is, to which we adjust our theories. He rather believes that what we mean by "world" depends on the theory about it. If cognitive objects are not independent of, but dependent on, the theories about them, then a change in the theory results in a corresponding change in the cognitive object. In other words, a new cognitive object, or new phenomenon, is literally constructed as a result of the change in the theory (sec. 85, 54).

FOUR

Husserl's Phenomenological Epistemology

Husserl is a phenomenologist in the Kantian tradition with further debts to Descartes, Franz Brentano, and others. Husserl's phenomenology has attracted attention from an astonishing roster of important thinkers running from Heidegger through Sartre, Merleau-Ponty, and Derrida, as well as Carnap and even Wittgenstein.[1] Like Hegel's, Husserl's phenomenological epistemology can be assessed in relation to Kantian epistemology. Husserl, who came to philosophy from mathematics, never attained more than a highly selective grasp of the philosophical tradition. He was not well versed in either Descartes or Kant,[2] both of whom influenced him, and he was largely unaware of prior phenomenology. He believed that he invented phenomenology and that earlier efforts, notably in Hegel, whom he seems to have known little about, but whom he criticized, were not significant.

Though he did not know Kant well, the critical philosophy is crucial for his own position. Husserl depends on Kant in a number of ways: for example, his concern with philosophy as a rigorous science, his conception of phenomenology as transcendental idealism, the relation of transcendental phenomenology to the life-world, and, above all, the problem of psychologism. This problem, which arises in Kant's criticism of Lockean so-called physiology, leads to a conception of the subject as a later version of the Kantian transcendental unity of apperception running throughout Husserl's position from beginning to end. It further shapes his view of phenomenology as epistemology. Through his response to the problem of psychologism, which Husserl constantly tries to overcome, his position is in constant dialogue with Kant's critical philosophy, to which he comes increasingly closer through the evolution of his position from descriptive phenomenology to transcendental idealism.

Husserl, who, like Fichte, spent his entire career in attempting to state his basic themes, never produced what he regarded as an adequate statement of his position. He published a number of books during his lifetime, and left an enormous *Nachlass*, some forty-five thousand pages, much of it in shorthand, which some observers consider as even more important than the works published during his lifetime. Since, unlike other figures discussed here (Kant, Hegel, Heidegger, and Merleau-Ponty), Husserl produced no single central statement of his position, it will be necessary to draw on a selection of his texts to reconstruct the main outlines of that position. This chapter is based on the published writings, with little attention to the still enormous unpublished corpus.

It is important to note the distinction between Husserl and his students with respect to epistemology. Husserl continually insists on the epistemological thrust of his view of phenomenology, which Heidegger later rejects. Husserl's followers often give little attention, even none at all, to the epistemological dimension of his position. Yet Husserl constantly returns to the claim for the relation of phenomenology to epistemology. Thus in the introduction to the second volume of his *Logical Investigations*, he entitles section 1 as "The Necessity of Phenomenological Investigations as a Preliminary to the Epistemological Criticism and Clarification of Pure Logic," which accords phenomenology a status prior to epistemology, and he entitles his sixth investigation "Elements of a Phenomenological Elucidation of Knowledge."

Husserl initially reacted to a number of prior and contemporary thinkers but later increasingly worked out his position with little regard to the earlier discussion.[3] Yet any evaluation of the nature and importance of his contribution to a generally phenomenological approach to epistemology benefits from studying it in the wider phenomenological context. In what follows, I reconstruct his position from a broadly Kantian perspective. Husserl initially stresses Kant in *Logical Investigations* but later moves increasingly toward Descartes, culminating in *Cartesian Meditations* (1929). In this way, he perhaps unintentionally but usefully calls attention not only to the differences but also to the strong link between Kant and Descartes, which is often covered up by Kant in the disproportionate attention he accords to Hume.

In focusing on Kant, I concentrate more on the result of his position than on its genesis. It is widely believed that Husserl's position emerges out of his critical reception of Brentano and hence only indirectly, if at all, through his reaction to Kant.[4] Husserl shares a large number of themes with Brentano, which he reworks in his own distinctive way. These include the conception of philosophy as rigorous science, the theory of mind as scientific psychology based in the "science of mental phenomena,"[5] the conception of intentionality,[6] and the analysis of time-consciousness. Yet he disagrees fundamentally with Brentano on other issues. An instance is Brentano's "traditional" view of logic as a *Kunstlehre*, which Husserl rejects in favor of a rival view of logic as a pure a priori science of ideal truths and ideal laws. Brentano, who was aware of this disagreement, and is arguably guilty of what Husserl understands as psychologism,[7] answered his erstwhile student. He refers dismissively to Husserl's effort to establish phenomenology as independent of psychology.[8] Another disagreement concerns the theory of intentionality, which Husserl appropriated and transformed. To put the difference simply, Brentano is always concerned with the relation to real, mind-independent, intentional objects as distinguished from merely mental objects (*entia rationis*). In his later thought, beginning early in the twentieth century, after Husserl's period as a student, he rejects a relation to purely mental objects through his view of "reism." Under the influence of his mathematical background, Husserl took a wider view of intentionality, which included both real and nonexistent intentional objects.[9]

From early in the phenomenological period, beginning with the *Logical Investigations*, which he regarded as his breakthrough to phenomenology, Husserl continually insists on the epistemological thrust of phenomenology.[10] The second volume is entitled *Investigations in Phenomenology and Theory of Knowledge*. The sixth of the studies it includes is entitled "Elements of a Phenomenological Elucidation of Knowledge." And the 1907 series of lectures, entitled *The Idea of Phenomenology* is explicitly focused on a single central question: How is knowledge possible?[11]

Phenomenology and psychologism are inseparably conjoined in Husserl's position. Husserlian phenomenology arises out of his initial response to psychologism.[12] His later position features a series of further efforts to overcome this difficulty. A reading of Husserl in terms of the problem of psychologism has a number of advantages. Since this problem is already featured, though not under that name, in the critical philosophy, it provides a way to link Husserl to Kant and the surrounding discussion. Paul Natorp, for instance, correctly thought as early as 1901 that as Husserl's theory developed it would be forced in an increasingly Kantian direction.[13] A focus on psychologism further provides a way to grasp the evolution of Husserl's position through its multiple avatars.[14] Many of the problems with which Husserl is concerned, as well as others that arise in his position, are due in one way or another to his concern with psychologism. This theme further offers a way to understand Husserl's relation to later forms of phenomenology. For after psychologism came to Husserl's attention, it remained a central focus in his thinking over decades, even after he stopped discussing it at length.[15]

I emphasize the development of Husserl's position as a continuing effort to resolve difficulties, particularly as concerns psychologism, arising in his effort to work out a phenomenological approach to knowledge. Husserl advances related, but genuinely different approaches in *Logical Investigations* (1900–1901), self-described as his initial breakthrough to phenomenology, and in his later writings, which react to perceived difficulties in this work, all the while continuing to develop the basic view. Though at different times he stresses different themes, as early as the *Idea of Phenomenology* (1907) he seems to have arrived at a coherent approach, which, through its many twists and turns and despite its incessant adoption of different terminology, remains basically the same.

Husserl became aware of the importance of psychologism early in his phenomenological phase. He states in a letter written in 1900 that the critique of psychologism is central to his phenomenology of knowledge in general.[16] The continual effort to counter the danger of psychologism is integral to his phenomenological position from its initial statement in *Logical Investigations* until his final texts. Though his position cannot be reduced to the problem of psychologism, it also cannot be understood without it. Concentrating on this theme is useful on several levels. It provides us with a way to understand the later evolution of his position as a related series of efforts to deal with difficulties that continue to arise in his refutation of psychologism. His initial, very detailed attack on psychologism in *Logical Investigations*, where he devotes an entire volume to this theme,[17] is followed by a long period in which he continues to come to grips with a series of related issues. Second, it offers, as noted, a convenient way to understand the increasing convergence of Husserl's position with the critical philosophy. Third, this theme helps us to understand, in response to those who believe that Husserl later turned away from his most significant insights, that his understanding of the problems of phenomenology, above all the theme of psychologism, led him from descriptive psychology to transcendental idealism. In turning to idealism, Husserl does not, as is often objected, abandon his early emphasis on objectivity. He rather clarifies and strengthens it in claiming to be the first to put idealism on a scientific basis.

Phenomenology, Epistemology, and the Problem of Psychologism

Logical Investigations is a lengthy treatise—roughly seven hundred and fifty pages in German and seven hundred pages in English translation—composed of two volumes. Though he later went on to write many more books, many, including Heidegger, consider this to be Husserl's most important philosophical contribution. The first volume contains a lengthy attack on psychologism, and the second features a series of six separate studies, or investigations. Scholars disagree about the degree of unity of the two volumes, particularly the contents of the second volume. In highly simplified terms, the overall aim of this treatise can be described as a defense and development of a modified version of, in Husserl's view, Bolzano's unparalleled systematic sketch of a pure logic against prevailing psychologistic interpretations.[18] In his *Wissenschaftslehre*, in extending earlier work on the philosophy of mathematics, Bolzano tries to provide the logical foundations for all sciences by justifying fundamental truths. In this text, Husserl similarly works out a view of logic as a pure a priori science, or *mathesis universalis*, roughly in the sense pioneered by Leibniz.[19] Although deeply impressed by Leibniz, Husserl, who is sparing in his compliments, goes so far as to claim that "Logic as a science must . . . be built upon Bolzano's work."[20]

The theme of psychologism, which interests both Husserl and Frege, is central in the emergence of both twentieth-century phenomenology and Anglo-American analytic philosophy. The philosophical pendulum swings widely from side to side over the centuries. It is hardly surprising that themes that earlier attracted rapt attention later slowly fade from sight or at least reach a point in which they appear insignificant, hardly worth the trouble to debate, certainly not focal points around which to build an entire theory. Something like this has happened to psychologism. The discussion of psychologism was a battleground from the time of Kant until early in the twentieth century. During this period even the staunchest opponents of psychologism, such as the author of the critical philosophy, were regularly accused of falling victim to it. Over the recent decades, this accusation has largely lost its hold on the philosophical debate. Few philosophers devote more than cursory attention to psychologism or its consequences at present. Many more are interested in ideas that earlier appeared to be excluded by the possible suspicion of psychologism. One indication among others is the strong, ongoing turn to naturalism, perhaps most strongly identified with Quine. Naturalism was earlier closely linked, for instance by Husserl, to the whole series of difficulties due to psychologism, a point to which I return later.

The theme of psychologism finds a series of important thinkers arrayed on different sides. Depending on how the term *psychologism* is interpreted, it is widely represented, even pandemic, in the tradition. All the British empiricists understand knowledge as human knowledge and hence tend in this direction. The accusation of psychologism is raised against the continental rationalists, especially Descartes and, with lesser frequency, Leibniz. Among Kant's main modern predecessors, perhaps only Spinoza is not clearly associated with psychologism.

Though he does not use the term, which only emerged later, Kant opposed psychologism. *Psychologism* is understood in many different ways. If it means basing logical and mathematical theories, and knowledge of all kinds, on psychology, hence on empiricism, then Kant is an anti-psychologist, committed to denying that knowledge of any kind, hence logic, can be based on psychological premises. In featuring a conception of knowledge as universal and necessary, hence a priori, he rejects in principle any effort to base knowledge on experience. His commitment to anti-psychologism is evident in his argument in favor of an a priori conception of knowledge and in his critique of Locke, who is sometimes identified as the original source of psychologism. In rejecting his so-called physiological approach, Kant rejects in advance what later became known as psychologism.

Kant distinguishes strictly between a transcendental analysis of the general conditions of knowledge and a psychological analysis in rejecting this approach. He famously distinguishes between the *quaestio facti* and the *quaestio juris* in rejecting the former for the latter, which he interprets as requiring a wholly a priori deduction of the categories.[21] Kant's position comes to a peak in his conception of the epistemological subject as a transcendental unity of apperception.[22] This conception enables Kant to justify the use of the understanding, which synthesizes the sensory input in working up objects of experience and knowledge, the entire field of logic, as well as the transcendental approach, in order to analyze the general conditions of knowledge.

In Kant's wake, the problem recurs in such thinkers as Fichte and Hegel. Fichte's most important innovation arguably consists in rethinking the Kantian subject as finite human being. He helps to inaugurate the crucially important historical turning that he does not undertake and that only later reaches full force in Hegel and Marx, as well as in such contemporaries as Herder, all of whom can be considered as running afoul of psychologism. Fichte offers a particularly blatant example of this difficulty in his famous claim that the type of philosophy one chooses depends on who one is.[23] Yet philosophy, which depends on who one is, loses its scientific status in becoming philosophical anthropology. In Fichte's wake, Hegel rejects psychologism. Fries and Beneke later defend psychologism against the Hegelians in advocating views of philosophy based solely on self-observation. According to Beneke, "With all of the concepts of the philosophical disciplines, only what is formed in the human soul according to the laws of its development can be thought; if these laws are understood with certainty and clarity, then a certain and clear knowledge of those disciplines is likewise achieved."[24] In effect, Fries and Beneke reject the Kantian view that philosophy must be worked out independently of and prior to experience. From the point of view of introspection, psychology becomes the basis of philosophy, including theory of knowledge. Philosophy is, hence, no longer thought of as the basis of a transcendental analysis of experience, from which it is rather inseparable.

The controversy concerning psychologism continues throughout the entire nineteenth century. It recurs toward the middle of the century in the opposition between Lotze and Mill. Lotze rejects the very idea of founding philosophy on logic. Controversy about the proper interpretation of Mill's position continues.[25] He is often thought, and was thought by Husserl, to be a paradigmatic defender of psychologism. Lotze distinguishes sharply between psychological acts, for instance, the act of thinking, and the content of thought. He explicitly denies that philosophy could be founded on psychology. Mill, however, apparently denies a distinction between philosophy and psychology. In *A System of Logic*, he proposes to ground the axioms of mathematics and the principles of logic on introspection. According to Mill, logic is a "science of reasoning, as well as an art, founded on that science."[26] Mill, who gives different accounts of the relation of psychology to logic, goes so far as to assert that logic is justified by psychology: "Its [the science of logic's—T. R.] theoretic grounds are wholly borrowed from Psychology, and include as much of that science as is required to justify the rules of the art."[27] In his *Examination of William Hamilton's Philosophy* he influentially depicts logic as belonging to psychology. In his argument with Hamilton, Mill maintains that the fundamental logical principles apply not to things in themselves but only to the objects of our experience. For the laws of logic are "laws of all Phænomena.[28]

Others involved in this controversy include Hermann von Helmholtz, F. A. Lange, and the German neo-Kantians. Helmholtz and Lange both believe that an appeal to physiological psychology is compatible with at least the spirit of the critical philosophy. Starting in the 1880s, the Marburg neo-Kantians, including Hermann Cohen and Paul Natorp, who later influenced Husserl, began to object to psychologism. Natorp in particular points out that psychologistic approaches to knowledge, which are subjective, are therefore incompatible with claims for objective knowledge. According to Natorp, since Kant relies on a so-called "act of spontaneity" (B129) in the transcendental deduction, he falls back into psychologism.[29] Heidegger later raised a similar objection against Husserl.

On the contrary, the Baden, or southwest-German, school of neo-Kantians criticized Husserl's claim that the normative-practical discipline of logic must be based on logic as a theoretical science. Richard Kroner defended the view that logical laws are imperatives founded on values.[30] According to Kroner, only hypothetical imperatives and their cognate ought-sentences fit Husserl's scheme.

Husserl's Early View of Psychologism

Husserl's phenomenological breakthrough occurred in the midst of the ongoing dispute about psychologism, to which he strongly contributed. He later came to regard his initial position as highly problematic. Yet positive reception of the initial statement of his position was strongly influenced by the vigor and depth of his treatment of this theme. His defense of anti-psychologism through a multidimensional attack on psychologism was directed against psychologistic thinkers, against certain Kantians, and even against Kant. Yet Husserl clearly belongs in the general Kantian camp with respect to many themes, including his anti-psychologism, which, through his criticism of Locke, Kant also opposes.

When Husserl attacked psychologism, it was a central theme in the debate. His analysis of this topic was immediately regarded as a major contribution, even as authoritative. It helped to shift attention away from this issue, which continued, however, to occupy Husserl. A decade later, when the debate had largely shifted to other matters, Husserl, who exhibited great continuity in his thinking, was still engaged in dealing with a long series of difficulties concerning the overall question of psychologism.

Volume 1 of the *Logical Investigations* contains an elaborate attack on psychologism. The term is not due to Husserl. Benno Erdmann apparently initially used it in 1870 to criticize Friedrich Eduard Beneke.[31] Carl Stumpf, who directed Husserl's *Habilitationsschrift*, employed it again in 1891 to refer to the reduction of philosophical and epistemological issues to psychological ones, which he opposed. He used it as well to refer to the anti-psychological attitude of the neo-Kantians, which he also opposed.[32] According to Spiegelberg, the term appears earlier in writings by Johann Eduard Erdmann and Orestes Brownson.[33]

Husserl's sharp turn against psychologism in the *Logical Investigations* constitutes a basic change in his initial position. He now unmercifully attacks what he formally defended. In the *Philosophy of Arithmetic* (1891), his first book, Husserl took a psychologistic approach to mathematics. Husserl's mathematical psychologism was later famously and sharply criticized by Gottlob Frege.[34] The interaction between Frege and Husserl has been studied in detail. It remains unclear whether Husserl later turned against psychologism, especially mathematical psychologism, because of the evolution of his position, in reaction to Frege's critique, or for a combination of factors.[35] What is clear is that the most elaborate critique of psychologism by any thinker occurs strategically in the *Prolegomena to Pure Logic*, immediately prior to the initial statement of his phenomenological position.

The *Logical Investigations* exists in no less than three editions. Its main themes continue to percolate in Husserl's mind throughout his career. Thus in *Formal and Transcendental Logic* (1929), when he returned to the investigation of logic that occupied him in his initial phenomenological treatise, he also comes back to psychologism.[36] In the meantime, his initial conception of phenomenology as descriptive psychology has been transformed through further reflection into a conception of phenomenology as transcendental idealism.

In the foreword to the first edition of *Logical Investigations*, Husserl states that his interest in a philosophical clarification of pure mathematics led to a universal theory of formal deductive systems, on the one hand, and the view that logic in general and the logic of the deductive sciences could be clarified on the basis of logic, on the other. Further research on epistemology and logic as a science pointed him toward what he describes as "*a new foundation [Neubegründung] of pure logic and epistemology.*"[37] In the foreword to the second edition, written after *Ideas* (1913) and hence after the shift to a new conception of phenomenology as transcendental idealism, Husserl indicates a number of reservations about his original position. He mentions the need to provide a sketch of the main structures of pure consciousness, regrets his supposedly misleading account of phenomenology as descriptive psychology in identifying fundamental differences between the description of internal events and external events (1:6), and refers to a lack of attention to the distinction and parallelism between the noetic and the noematic. We return to these differences below.

When Husserl composed the *Prolegomena to Pure Logic*, the philosophical debate was dominated by various forms of psychologism. In reacting against this theme, Husserl argues for a generally Kantian conception of philosophy as science. He detects psychologism in a long list of contemporary and near contemporary thinkers, including J. S. Mill, Sigwart, Lipps, Spencer, Lange, Kroman, Heymans, Liebmann, Bergmann, Bain, Wundt, and others. In echoing Kant's approach in the B preface to the *Critique of Pure Reason*, but in denying the latter's claim that logic had already become a rigorous science in ancient Greek philosophy, Husserl stresses the need to set logic on the secure path of a science.

Husserl's appeal to a broadly Kantian vision of logic points to a twofold relation to Kant. On the one hand, he partly accepts the end in view. Different domains provide different kinds of knowledge that, in all cases, require a basic methodological innovation to set them on the secure road of science. On the other, he disagrees with Kant's claim that logic has been a completed science since the time of Aristotle. Husserl held this view until the end of his career. In *Formal and Transcendental Logic*, whose title echoes Kant's approach, he returns almost three decades later to the idea of pure logic that he studied in *Logical Investigations*, once again indicating that after thousands of years, logic has not yet become an a priori science.[38] Yet he remains close to Kant in other ways, such as his view that logic is a normative discipline. He further rejects the idea that it is an empirical *Kunstlehre*, or a mere technique, an idea favored by some contemporary neo-Kantians, for a conception of logic as an a priori, independent discipline.

In arguing against psychologism, Husserl objects to contemporary efforts to found logic, which he understands as an a priori science, in psychology, an empirical science. Following Kant, he notes that the laws of logic are not contingent, but necessary. Since no logical law implies matters of fact, pure logic is necessarily independent of psychology. There is a basic distinction between the psychological and logical presuppositions of logical laws. He devotes an entire chapter (chapter 5) to allegedly psychologistic interpretations of the law of noncontradiction in Mill, Spencer, and others. He repeats his view that the logical is necessarily exact, whereas psychologism leads to an inexact, vague, and general view of logic. He devotes another chapter (chapter 6) to the effort to interpret syllogistic inference in Heymans and others. In summarizing his view, Husserl strikes a Kantian note. Knowledge worthy of the name, including logic, is necessarily a priori and hence cannot be based in empirical psychology or in any other form of empiricism: "Logical truths must lose their *a priori* guarantee, and their wholly exact, purely conceptual character, and must become more or less vague probabilities resting on experience and induction, concerned with matters of fact in the life of man—all this, if we ignore its emphasis on vagueness, is what empiricism expressly teaches" (1:56).

In chapter 7, Husserl studies the association of psychologism with skeptical relativism. He later returns to this theme on a number of occasions, particularly in the programmatic article entitled "Philosophy as Rigorous Science."[39] According to Husserl, skepticism results from going against the general conditions of theory. He distinguishes subjective and objective forms of skeptical relativism as arising on psychologistic soil. Subjectivist relativism results when there is no mechanism to validate truth claims, not in reality, but in an ideal, or, in Husserl's terminology, noetic sense. Objectivist skepticism occurs if one denies the so-called objective unity of truth or propositions, such as laws, on which the theory depends. Husserl's basic insight seems to be that psychologism has the effect of denying an ideal conception of theory, which in turn ineluctably leads to epistemological skepticism.

Husserl thinks skepticism can only be defeated in affirming the validity of self-evident, universal claims. This ideal view of knowledge is undermined by any effort whatsoever to link cognitive claims to the nature of the subject. He considers in passing so-called individual relativism, a view that, he concedes, no modern thinker holds. According to Husserl, few modern thinkers are free of what he calls specific relativism, or the doctrine that what is true for a given species is true, especially anthropologism. Husserl contends that the meaning of the words *true* and *false* is not species-relative and hence does not depend on the nature of a given species, such as the nature of human beings. The central insight is that cognitive claims are not relative, but "irrelative." The relativity of truth claims implies the absurdity that the existence of the world is itself relative, so that there is, as Husserl says, "no world 'in itself,' but only a world for us" (1:81) This point commits Husserl to a form of the standard empiricist view that knowledge concerns the mind-independent external world as it is. Since claims for truth are not relative, but claims based on facts can only be relative, it would be absurd to attempt to deduce logical principles, or indeed logic itself, from facts.

Husserl's attack on psychologism is clearly motivated by a prior commitment to a conception of knowledge as independent of the nature of the subject, as well of time and place. If knowledge claims are intrinsically "irrelative," any effort to limit them must be resisted. Psychologism is pernicious because it ties epistemology to psychology, hence to the empirical world. It leads unavoidably to epistemological relativism, which is merely a form of skepticism. Husserl implicitly follows Hume and Kant, who believe that universal and necessary knowledge cannot be a posteriori. Any claim to know that falls short of universality and necessity, hence endorses relativism, is merely skepticism. Husserl draws this conclusion in identifying psychologism and relativism. "Psychologism in all its subvarieties and individual elaborations is in fact the same as relativism" (1:82).

There is a distinction between relativism and psychologism. Since all forms of relativism are not psychologistic, he seems to mean that psychologism is an important species of relativism. Husserl's claim for the "irrelativity" of logic counts against psychologism and hence against attempts to treat the pure laws of logic as empirical, or psychological, or as deduced from the nature of the human mind. In the latter case, he seems to have in mind not only Locke, whose empiricist theory depends on "the psychophysical constitution of man," but also the Kantians and even Kant, whose a priori theory depends on "an innate (generally human) disposition" prior to "all thought and experience" (1:83).

In the last two chapters, Husserl sums up his critical treatment of psychologism (chapter 10) and discusses the idea of pure logic (chapter 11) that it presupposes. Husserl thinks he has established that logic cannot be either empiristic or psychologistic. He now turns to his conception of a pure logic as independent of the empirical world, hence of psychology, which also makes possible logic as a *Kunstlehre*. He agrees in general with Kant's distinction between pure and applied logic, while rejecting much of the rest of his position. He feels closer to Herbart, who, despite certain confusions concerning the relation of concepts to experience, treats logical concepts as purely objective. Among the great philosophers, he feels closest to Leibniz, whose view of pure logic he wishes to extend as central to epistemology, which precedes metaphysics, psychology, and the other disciplines. The general impression is that epistemology founds the other philosophical disciplines and is itself based in pure logic. And among recent thinkers, as noted above, he regards himself as building on Bolzano.

In the final chapter, Husserl sets forth the idea of pure logic that he has constantly presupposed in his critique of psychologism. He turns first to the question, What makes science science? He finds the answer in the unity of science. The Vienna Circle theorists also appeal to this term,[40] which they generally link to physicalism, including a reduction of psychology to physics, to extensionalism, and to the empirical criterion of meaning. On the contrary, in Husserl's lexicon the unity of science implies the a priori, inseparable "*interconnection of the things* to which our thought-experiences (actual or possible) are intentionally directed" as well as "an *interconnection of truths*, in which this unity of things comes to count objectively as being what it is" (1:145; Husserl's emphases). His view resembles the standard approach to knowledge in terms of the relation of truth claims to objects, with a single crucial difference. For Husserl, what "counts" as an object of knowledge can either be real or ideal. It follows that, epistemologically, Husserl is as concerned with real states of affairs as well as with relations that are merely logical and hence are not exemplified.

As concerns the unity of science, Husserl is close to Kant's influential view of systematic science. We recall Kant's famous view of a scientific system as unifying different cognitions under a single idea.[41] This alone separates it from what Kant, in reference to Aristotle, identifies as a mere rhapsody.[42] According to Husserl, who seems determined to avoid a mere rhapsody through a Kantian strategy, the unity of science means that it follows rigorously, hence necessarily, from a ground (*aus dem Grunde*). The result is a universal science, such as universal arithmetic, which initially interested Husserl. On the basis of these reflections, he now answers his basic question: What makes science science? According to Husserl, science provides unity of explanation in a theoretical unity of its explanatory principles. The sciences are further divided into two types. They include the abstract, theoretical, or nomological sciences, which count as theories, and the practical or normative sciences, which depend on an external unity, or the unity of the thing in a single empirical genus. Instances might include such descriptive sciences as geography, history, astronomy, and so on, which are directed toward the description of whatever empirical unity falls under their object.

Husserl next turns to the general question of the very possibility of science, or theory, which is understood as the deductive interrelation of truths. This question can be understood subjectively or objectively. In the former case, it means the general conditions of the possibility of theoretical knowledge. If the conditions are ideal, there are again two possibilities. They refer either to "*noetic* conditions," grounded in the "Idea of Knowledge as such," or, on the contrary, they are purely *logical* conditions, in which case they are grounded in the content of knowledge (1:149–50). In both cases, they are a priori. Systematic theories are rooted in the ideal constituents of theory in general, and finally in the essence of theory, also known as the theory of theory.

With this in mind, Husserl now delimits the tasks assigned to pure logic. These include three main areas. First, pure logic must identify and study primitive concepts with respect to their phenomenological origin, or essence, through intuitive representation. Second, there is the search for laws. Third, there is the study of possible forms of theory. In the latter respect, Husserl believes there is a clear analogy with the mathematical theory of the pure manifold. The difference is that the mathematician constructs theories, but the philosopher studies the essence of theory, including its possibility. Husserl concludes by stating that pure logic concerns the ideal conditions of science in general, which is different from determining the true element in empirical facts. The objective sciences of fact follow from an ideal norm. This is also the case in empirical thinking. In other words, there must be what Husserl calls an "idea of the Empirical Unity of Explanation," which, since it concerns the empirical realm and hence cannot yield certainty, is "the Idea of Probability" (1:161).

Husserl's lengthy and detailed attack on psychologism is finally elusive, difficult to grasp or to summarize, and not obviously convincing. This may explain the fact that secondary works on Husserl, which exist in profusion, rarely provide more than a cursory account of the overall argument. A further reason is that numerous Husserl students, including Heidegger and Merleau-Ponty, believe that, despite his opposition to psychologism, Husserl fell back into it.[43]

One difficulty is that Husserl seems to be working with different views of the term *psychologism*, whose core meaning arguably lies in the difference between his ideal conception of pure logic and all other alternatives.[44] In *Logical Investigations*, psychologism refers to any appeal to psychology to provide the theoretical foundations for logic. At this point, Husserl has in mind Mill's view of logic as well as Lipps's empathy theory. If Husserl falls back into psychologism, it cannot be transcendental psychologism, since he has not yet embarked on a transcendental reinterpretation of phenomenology. It is rather a form of psychologism that is, as Heidegger reports, linked to Husserl's vision of phenomenology as beginning with the description of the acts of consciousness related to knowledge.[45] In later lectures on phenomenological psychology, after the transcendental turn, he seems to have fallen into another form of psychologism due to conflating "philosophical-transcendental phenomenology" and "psychological phenomenology."[46] Later, he gave psychologism still another, more extended meaning in *Formal and Transcendental Logic*, where it refers to any attempt to convert objects of any type, including objects situated in the conceptual space beyond logic, into psychological experiences.[47]

With respect to psychologism, he seems to have a twofold aim in view. On the one hand, he is concerned to show that a psychologistic interpretation of logic is self-defeating and hence that any and all efforts to base logic in psychology are self-stultifying. He is especially opposed to the intimate connection between psychologism and subjectivist relativism. In this respect, he points to difficulties arising from any effort to interpret logical laws, such as the law on noncontradiction, in psychological terms, with particular attention to the problem of skeptical relativism. On the other, he is concerned to work out, very much in a mathematical manner, a theory of theory in general, with a view to answering the question, What makes science science? ultimately with the aim of expanding and clarifying epistemology, in which logic plays a key role. Like Frege, Husserl believes logic is a purely formal, a priori science, which says nothing about the real world. But unlike Frege, he thinks the study of logic has a crucial epistemological consequence in elucidating essential correlations between acts of knowing and the objects known. In this way, Husserl comes close to Kant's view that the study of logic, in this case transcendental logic, is a necessary means to reach the epistemological goal.

Long after he composed the *Prolegomena to Pure Logic*, the problem of psychologism continued to remain central to the success of Husserlian phenomenology. Husserl's many-sided attack on psychologism is arguably unsuccessful. Difficulties in his effort to overcome this problem begin with his inability to arrive at a single view of the term *psychologism*. Since it is clear he changed his mind, it is unclear which, if any, conception of psychologism Husserl can fairly be said to overcome. Is it logical psychologism? Is it mathematical psychologism, to which Frege objected? Is it transcendental psychologism, which derives from the later transcendental idealist turn in his position? Competent Husserl scholars, who are familiar with his enormous corpus, believe he never succeeded in banishing the problem. That is tantamount to conceding that, if his position depends on vanquishing psychologism, then it fails.

There is a further difficulty with respect to epistemology. In attacking psychologism, Husserl is not only concerned with the inadequacy of contemporary psychologistic forms of logic. He raises specifically epistemological claims for phenomenology. In his attack on psychologism, he is wearing both logical and epistemological hats. A pure logic is important not only in itself but also as a prerequisite to an adequate theory of knowledge. Yet it is at this very point that Husserl's argument becomes obscure. This difficulty can be focused through a remark on psychologism. It is unclear why, even if Husserl could satisfactorily deal with the difficulty of logical psychologism, this would clear the way to an adequate approach to phenomenological epistemology. Here the difference between Husserl and Kant with respect to psychologism is crucial. Kant's objection to Locke, already mentioned above, is twofold. It includes his rejection of Locke's supposed reduction of the conditions of knowledge to the psychological conditions of knowledge. It further includes his rejection of Locke's view that knowledge consists in a direct, intuitive grasp of ideas that supposedly stand in a one-to-one relation to what is as it is. Since things in themselves cannot be known, from Kant's perspective they cannot be grasped through ideas, whose epistemological relation to the way the mind-independent world is cannot be analyzed.

Kant's and Husserl's ways of understanding psychologism, hence its remedy, clearly diverge. In the critical philosophy, the problem of psychologism cannot simply be resolved through objecting to the reduction of the logical process of knowledge to a psychological process. For Kant, a further, central dimension of the problem of psychologism concerns what, for want of a better name, we can call *epistemological psychologism*. Its treatment lies in identifying, refuting, and finding an adequate substitute for the standard empiricist claim, already full-blown in Locke, to grasp the mind-independent world through a one-to-one relation between ideas and objects. This view, which cannot be supported through argument, is a variation on the general theme of what Husserl also claims. For Husserl as for Locke, there is intuitive knowledge of cognitive objects—for Husserl, through directly grasping their essences; for Locke, in grasping ideas, which stand in a one-to-one relation to the world. According to Kant, we cannot reliably claim to grasp the world as it is through epistemological intuition or in any other way. It is because psychologism also concerns the unwarranted claim to know the mind-independent world as it is that Kant argues in favor of his complex theory of the subject's constitution of the cognitive object. Husserl, on the contrary, parts company with Kant on this specific point in claiming, as we shall see in his conception of phenomenology, that to know is to grasp directly through intuition.

The first volume of the *Logical Investigations* launches a concerted, many-sided attack on psychologism in order to rescue logic from psychology. Yet the impression remains that, even after an impressive series of analyses, Husserl finally fails to clarify, perhaps even to address, the link between logic, psychology, and epistemology. He focuses more clearly on epistemology in his account of phenomenology in the second volume. Yet it is arguable that in this work, perhaps even later, Husserl is finally unable to clarify his basic claim for the relation of phenomenology to epistemology.

Phenomenology as Descriptive, or to the Things Themselves

In the remainder of the work, Husserl plays the intuitive card separating his theory from Kant's in tying his conception of phenomenology to intuition. The title of volume 2 of the *Logical Investigations, Investigations into Phenomenology and the Theory of Knowledge*, focuses attention on Husserl's conception of phenomenology as the way into epistemology. This volume, which is divided arbitrarily into two parts in the German edition, consists of an introduction and six investigations, whose interrelation and relation to the attack on psychologism in the service of pure logic in the first volume remains unclear. Some observers regard the relation between the two volumes as loose, whereas others detect a close connection.

In the introduction, Husserl immediately focuses on forging a link between phenomenology and epistemology. He begins by calling for a continuation of the process of clarification, which here and elsewhere he seems to rely on as a substitute for the formulation of theoretical alternatives. He immediately turns to the connection between "objective theory of knowledge" and "the pure phenomenology of the experiences of thinking and knowing," in short between phenomenology and epistemology. The epistemological die is cast very rapidly in Husserl's account of phenomenology. His phenomenological approach to theory of knowledge is firmly rooted in essentialism. By *phenomenology* he means "experiences [*Erlebnisse*] intuitively seizable and analyzable in the generality of their essence, not experiences empirically perceived and treated as real facts . . . as experiences . . . that we posit [*gesetzten*] as an empirical fact" (2:166). He specifically detaches meaning from a single object in generalizing it to all possible objects, in effect making use of the generality of language signaled by Hegel in the section on sense-certainty and thus making an epistemological virtue of what, for Hegel, since language does not pick out the individual object, is a defect.

This general approach goes back in the tradition at least to Aristotelian essentialism. Essentialism is one of the central themes in Husserl's phenomenological theory. Husserl, who later gave different descriptions of phenomenology, sometimes defined it in terms of essentialism, or the search for essences. In "Philosophy as Rigorous Science," he says phenomenology can only be an investigation into essences.[48] In *Ideas*, he states that phenomenology is a theory of essences based on pure intuition.[49]

In the first edition of the *Logical Investigations*, Husserl understands *phenomenology* as "descriptive psychology," which later gives way, in the second edition (1913), to the so-called necessary basis of scientific psychology. Phenomenology, as Husserl expounds it here, is descriptive, concerned with the description of essences. The epistemological tradition consists in an effort to cognize the real, often in some version of the claim to cognize metaphysical reality. Husserl turns away from this task in characterizing phenomenology. Its task lies in describing essences in total independence from any presupposed claim to the existence of its contents. There is a reciprocal link between phenomenology, which describes essences as intuited, and essences, which supposedly make themselves known directly in intuition. Heidegger later makes the Husserlian claim that things show themselves to us central to his understanding of phenomenology. I will come back to this point.

Husserl fleshes out his conception of phenomenology in depicting it as the common root of such other scientific disciplines as empirical psychology. It further discloses the sources of pure logic, from which its basic concepts and ideal laws spring, and to which they can be traced. Described in this way, phenomenology is deeper than either empirical psychology or logic. In other words, analysis of pure logic as well as the psychological penchant underlying psychologism necessarily lead in the direction of phenomenology.

According to Husserl, the description of essences is not a posteriori but a priori. In describing essences, the phenomenologist is not describing anything one takes as existing, since existence is not itself a relevant part of the phenomenological conception of its task. If, as for Kant, existence is a posteriori, then it is consistent to claim, as Husserl asserts, that statements about essence are a priori. Yet this claim is also problematic, in that it assumes the relevance of existence, which it claims not to take into account.

Husserl stresses the essentialist character of phenomenology. The obvious predecessor for an essentialist analysis is Aristotle. His influence on Brentano, Husserl's teacher, is well known. It is also known that Brentano's dissertation, "On the Manifold Meaning of Being since Aristotle" (1862) influenced Heidegger's interest in phenomenology.[50] Aristotle's distinction between form and matter provides an early anticipation of Husserl's theory of essence. Aristotle believes that though substances exist as particulars, we perceive only universals.

Husserl further links his conception of phenomenology to the problem of meaning (*Bedeutung*) or, perhaps better, reference. Semantics is often thought of as the study of the relation of signs, including words, to what they represent. Frege, who, as noted, famously distinguishes between meaning (*Sinn*) and reference (*Bedeutung*), thinks that meaning determines reference. Philosophers have traditionally insisted on various ways that claims about objects correctly pick out their characteristics. Husserl gives up any form of the claim to grasp the mind-independent object as it is in giving up existence as a criterion. He falls back on a view of what is meant or intended. All theoretical research consists in statements (*Aussagen*) given in terms of meaning-intention (*Bedeutungsintention*) or meaning-fulfillment (*Bedeutungserfüllung*) of verbal expressions.

Pure logic concerns logical, not psychological, judgments. Phenomenology, which does not belong to pure logic, is indispensable to it in bringing logical concepts and laws to epistemological clarity. Logical concepts arise through intuition in experience and can be indefinitely reconfirmed as identical. Husserl insists here and elsewhere that we cannot rely on mere words but must go to things themselves (*die Sachen selbst*).[51] This term, which should not be conflated with Kant's term *thing in itself*, which is not and cannot be given in experience, refers to what is directly given in the natural attitude, or experience of the natural world, what Husserl later calls the lifeworld (*Lebenswelt*). The *thing itself* does not designate a mind-independent object but a state of affairs and hence, by extension, a context. In claiming to go to things themselves, Husserl believes he can arrive at fixed meanings, hence at clarity with respect to logical propositions. By the same token, according to Husserl, psychologism can only be overcome through pure phenomenology. It follows that the account in the first volume of *Logical Investigations* is merely prolegomenal.

Pure logic and psychologism are two basic epistemological concerns. More generally, thought and knowledge concern objects or states of affairs (*Sachverhalte*) with respect to their "being in itself" (*An-sich-sein*) as an identifiable unity in multiplicity as actual or possible acts of thought (*Denkakte*). Before Husserl, efforts to come to grips with the problem of knowledge often turn on an analysis of the relation between an idea in the mind and an external object. Analysis by different thinkers shows the difficulty of this enterprise. Husserl, who identifies the epistemological difficulty, insists on the stable identification of an intuitable, essential core of meaning or act of thought. He points to a series of epistemological themes, or the "in itself" of the relation of objectivity to "representation" (*Vorstellung*), as avoiding the relapse into subjectivity.

This problem can be put more generally. Husserl, who brackets existence, is concerned with forms in things; hence, he is closer to Aristotle, who puts forms into things, than to Plato, who, on most interpretations, separates them. Since Husserl claims to know essences, a version of the Aristotelian difficulty recurs in Husserlian phenomenology. The point can be restated in terms of the difference between Husserlian and Kantian terminology. Husserl's central thesis concerns things themselves, not things in themselves, though the precise relation between them is unclear. In proposing to go to things themselves, he is not proposing to go to, nor to have knowledge of, things in themselves. Hence, he is not proposing to analyze the relation of ideas in the mind to mind-external objects, which remains an enigma. If he could answer this enigma, he could provide a credible phenomenological response to the problem of knowledge. The difficulty is how, for an essentialist, one can claim to grasp the really existing external object. Husserl, who does not respond either to this theme or to the questions he raises, insists that the clarification of logical ideas necessarily leads to these queries. In this way he issues a promissory note, which, to make out the epistemological claim for phenomenology, he needs later to redeem. It is as if he thinks that in pursuing his own path he will unavoidably elucidate the classical problems of epistemology.

Instead of responding, he turns to a series of difficulties in his conception of pure phenomenological analysis, difficulties that only obscure the underlying epistemological issues. Psychology rests on a false antithesis between inner and outer perception. According to Husserl, rather than focusing on naively posited objects, we should focus on the acts themselves and their *Sinnesgehalt*. In this way, Husserl turns away from the usual objective stance, which attributes perceived properties to really existing objects in concentrating on appearances and meanings in mental acts.

In leaving behind naive assumptions about existence, phenomenology gives up naturalistic interpretations and assumptions. In this way, Husserl opens a basic distinction between what, in the natural attitude, is "naively" only believed but not known to be really given and what is really given in the phenomenological elements of representations. Yet in evoking "representations," Husserl appears to suppose the very existence that should no longer be naively assumed.

His assertion that analytic phenomenology is primarily concerned with "representations" is problematic (2:172). It suggests that, beyond meaning-intentions and meaning-fulfillment, as Kant thinks, something in fact appears. Clarifying the relation between expressions and meaning can arguably improve the linguistic precision required to state results. But it cannot help to make out the claim to *represent* if, as for Kant, this term refers to a relation between an appearance and an object.

Husserl either does not grasp or is not concerned with this theme. He turns instead to clarification of the basic ideas of pure, or formal, logic. As suggested by his essentialism, such investigation centers on logical form, for instance, as concerns the connection between meaning-experiences and expressions, to determine the significance of talk about "expressing" (*Ausdrücken*) and reference (*Bedeuten*). Husserl, who thinks that such clarification precedes further clarification of logic, claims that the psychological, epistemological, and logical aspects of "representation" are confused. Yet it remains unclear what, in the phenomenological attitude, representation amounts to.

Similar difficulties arise with respect to the relation of intentional subject-matter and the object, to which Husserl also refers through the expressions *objectivity* (*Gegestandlichkeit*) and *objectlessness* (*Gegestandlosigkeit*).

Husserl adds three notes to this statement. First, the investigations in the second volume will inevitably go beyond the theme of pure logic. Second, a phenomenological analysis of logic is necessarily circular, since it relies on concepts that it must also clarify. Third, in anticipating the objection that phenomenology is also prey to psychologism, Husserl asserts that it is not descriptive psychology and hence not part of natural science. The difference lies in the phenomenological focus on pure description of pure essence, which, as pure, is not at all empirical. For this reason, he claims that phenomenology is the basis for psychology as a science as well as pure mathematics and exact natural science. In other words, phenomenology is only possible by leaving the natural attitude behind.

This assertion calls for two remarks. On the one hand, Husserl merely claims but does not show that phenomenology is the foundational science of all the other sciences. On the other hand, at this point, in a passage added in the second edition of his work, he gives up his initial conception of phenomenology as descriptive psychology (2:176). He later abandoned this conception when he saw that it opened the door to the charge of psychologism, a charge that, despite enormous further labor, he was arguably never able to allay.

Husserl ends the introduction to the second volume with an implausible comment about the alleged freedom of phenomenology from presuppositions. He later repeats but fails to demonstrate this claim in the introduction to the English translation of *Ideas*.[52] This aim, which goes back to early in the tradition, is on the horizon at least as early as Plato's description of philosophical dialectic as beyond hypothesis. By "freedom from presuppositions," Husserl has in mind completed phenomenological analysis, that is, so-called pure intuition of essences on the basis of experience concerning thinking and knowing. The putative result is intuitive knowledge (*einsichtiges Wissen*).

Theory of knowledge, as Husserl understands it, must deal with questions about "real" things or transcendent objects. But it will not aim at such knowledge, which is an empirical question. Theory of knowledge is neither deductive nor subordinated to deductive theories. For instance, his reflections on pure logic were carried out a priori, hence prior to empirical knowledge. The aim of a phenomenological theory of knowledge lies in clarifying the very idea of knowledge directed to fulfillment in intuition. Since a phenomenological epistemology makes no claims at all about real existence, it is wholly unrelated to metaphysical, scientific, or psychological premises.

According to Husserl, a pure phenomenological "theory" of knowledge is applicable to all the naive sciences, which it transforms in this way into "philosophical" sciences. The result is knowledge that is both clarified and sure (or secure). Husserl is claiming that theory of knowledge worthy of the name can only be based on phenomenology. Real premises are clarified through adequate phenomenological demonstration, that is, in rigorous fulfillment through evidence (*Erfüllung durch Evidenz*).

A claim of this kind is not unusual. A number of modern philosophers propose to formulate theories free from presuppositions. The Cartesian cogito is arguably the most widely known instance of a supposedly presuppositionless theory. Kant further aspires to this ideal. He insists on the conception of system as demanding unity with respect to a single idea in basing his position on a hypothesis. According to Kant, both the astronomical and the philosophical Copernican revolutions are mere hypotheses, though they are allegedly also demonstrable.[53] If this were correct, it would have the effect of freeing the critical theory from its hypothetical status.

Husserl's comment about freedom from presuppositions conflates at least three themes: (1) the phenomenological claim to found any and all other forms of cognition, (2) the phenomenological claim to justify itself through clarification of basic concepts and principles, and (3) a supposed freedom from presuppositions. He claims, but does not, as noted, argue, that phenomenology founds other forms of cognition. Hence, this assertion is sustained by no more than his phenomenological faith, or faith in the epistemological power of phenomenology. It is further unclear that, as Husserl asserts here and later, phenomenology can legitimately assert its freedom from presuppositions.[54] Husserl seems to rely on examining the theory, which he also presupposes. Yet this is a clearly circular, hence unsatisfactory, procedure. It follows that there is no reason to infer that phenomenology is in fact free from presuppositions.

Logical Investigations touches on a number of themes, including psychologism, pure logic, and the relation of phenomenology to epistemology, as well as a series of special investigations. It would take us too far from our central theme of phenomenology and epistemology to discuss in detail the six investigations that round out this work. But I return to Husserl's view of categorial intuition in the next chapter when I discuss Heidegger. Instead, I conclude the discussion of this book with a short remark about Husserl's relation to Kant. What Husserl calls "phenomenology" in the *Logi-*

cal Investigations and perhaps in later works as well is mainly a restatement of the representational approach to the problem of knowledge of a mind-independent, external object—in contemporary language so-called externalism—as it runs throughout modern philosophy and peaks in Kant's critical philosophy. Accordingly, as concerns epistemology, Husserl's phenomenology can be understood with respect to Brentano's variation on the Kantian representative approach to knowledge. My claim is that Husserl's approach to epistemology develops as a series of modifications of the basic approach fixed as early as *Logical Investigations*, a basic approach that commits him to knowing the mind-independent object from the first-person perspective and hence to a form of Kantian representationalism, from which it descends. To justify his continued adherence to a view that Kant advances but later abandons, Husserl would need to argue the point. Yet Husserl's reaction to Kant is limited by the limits of his grasp of the critical philosophy, which is never more than superficial; hence, he never discusses it in detail. As early as *Logical Investigations*, Husserl returns behind Kant's Copernican turn to a semantic approach that depends on the relation of words to objects of intuition (2:204). As concerns perception, Husserl retreats behind Kant, who denies direct intuitive apprehension, on which Husserl insists. According to Husserl, perception is perception of thinghood, of the object itself (2:220). Categorial intuition is always founded on sensuous intuition (2:306). Knowledge refers to a relationship between acts of thought and the fulfillment of intuitions (2:323). According to Husserl, in epistemology the thing is not merely meant but is also given. He specifically claims that the intentional object of a presentation is the same as its actual object and, on occasion, as its external object (sec. 21, 2:127).

Between *Logical Investigations* and *Ideas*: The Idea of Phenomenology

Husserl later regarded his initial position as problematic. He took steps to correct it in ways that many of his followers found increasingly problematic, while clearly affirming his interest in a phenomenological solution to the problem of knowledge. An extremely prolific writer, he composed a number of texts between the second volume of *Logical Investigations* and *Ideas* in the course of the transition from an initial descriptive view of phenomenology to a later view of phenomenology as transcendental idealism. These texts include two series of lectures, *Einleitung in die Logik und Erkenntnistheorie* (1906–7) and especially *The Idea of Phenomenology* (1907), where Husserl focuses on the relation between phenomenology and epistemology.

In the former set of lectures, Husserl distinguishes logic from psychology in differentiating types of logic as a theory of science. Husserl now begins to distance himself from the thesis that meaning (*Sinn*) is instantiated in individual acts. Instead he introduces the view of a correlation between *Sinn*, or *Bedeutung*, terms that Frege distinguishes but Husserl apparently uses interchangeably, and the objectivity to which the latter term refers. Like Kant, he regards the correlation between meaning and an object as a priori. Yet Husserl, who applies the term *Gegenstand* in an extended sense to any and all objects,[55] differs in his usage from Kant's restriction of the term *Gegenstand* to refer only to a real cognitive object.

In the later series of lectures entitled *The Idea of Phenomenology*, Husserl develops a phenomenological approach to theory of knowledge in terms of a method he attributes to Descartes. This points toward the Cartesianism he later develops in *Cartesian Meditations*.[56] Yet he has not left Kant behind, since here and later he continues to wrestle with the theme of psychologism in the problem of knowledge. It remains to be shown whether in these lectures Husserl makes progress toward a solution of the epistemological problem.

In his lecture series *The Idea of Phenomenology*, Husserl introduces the conception of the phenomenological reduction, which can be taken as delimiting the difference between his early period, prior to the reduction, and his later, or mature, period, which dates from that moment. This conception, which is only briefly adumbrated here, concerns the reduction of an appearance to a mere phenomenon since the reality of the object is explicitly suspended. Someone who was unfamiliar with Husserl's later development would be surprised to find that this conception, which is barely mentioned here, later becomes central to Husserl's position in a way that leads eventually to a split between his followers. On one side, there are those who remain committed to some version of the descriptive phenomenology expounded in the *Logical Investigations*. On the other, there are those who follow the reformulation of the position as the transcendental idealist form of phenomenology that he proposed, starting with *Ideas*. The latter is made possible by the phenomenological reduction.

The phenomenological reduction, which is intended to solve an important difficulty, creates another equally important one. Husserl, who is still concerned with the problem of psychologism, distinguishes sharply between the psychological and the logical subject. Like Kant, he believes the problem of knowledge is a logical but not a psychological problem. Hence, also like Kant, he thinks the subject must be a logical and not a psychological concept. The reduction enables Husserl to call attention to the difference between the psychological subject and the logical subject. Yet the cost of this innovation lies in no longer being able to solve the difficulty of how to go from the subject to the object. If, as in a descriptive view of phenomenology, the subject is in the world, it is relatively simple to claim that knowledge consists in a careful description of what is really given. If, on the contrary, the subject is no longer a finite human being in context, then how to go from the subject to the cognitive object becomes a central enigma, which Husserl is never able to resolve. In other words, Husserl's continued efforts, after *Logical Investigations*, to overcome psychologism through the reduction lead to a deep difficulty to which he was unable to respond.[57]

Husserl's effort to grasp the relation of subjectivity to objectivity after the introduction of the reduction is comparable to Kant's turn away from representationalism and toward constructivism. Kant's constructivism replaces the problem of the correspondence of the representation to the mind-independent object, that is, the relation of appearance to reality, by a single phenomenon at the cost of eliminating, or at least turning away from, the real, but unknown and unknowable mind-independent world. Husserl, who does not comment on this difficulty in these lectures, addresses instead a second series of difficulties in linking *The Idea of Phenomenology* to *Logical Investigations*. According to Husserl, Kant, who lacks the concepts of phenomenology as well as the phenomenological reduction, was guilty of psychologism and anthropologism.[58] The first point is false. At most Kant lacks the Husserlian theory of phenomenology, but not a theory of phenomenology. Kantian constructivism is a theory of the construction of phenomena as a condition of knowledge, hence a phenomenology. It remains to be seen whether, as Husserl charges, Kant lapses into psychologism or such other variants as anthropologism or biologism.

Kant's constructivism allows him to answer the problem Husserl raises at the end of his lectures about *"the relation between subjective psychological experience and the actuality grasped therein"* (60; Husserl's emphasis), that is, the relation of the cognitive subject to the cognitive object. Husserl, who is also unable to solve the problem on the basis of the classical modern causal theory of perception, appeals to a different strategy. Through the phenomenological reduction, he puts the question of the relation of the subject to the transcendent object out of play in opting for a phenomenological explanation of the alleged correspondence between the contents of consciousness and the cognitive object.

This ingenious solution brings into play conceptions of phenomenological reduction, essential seeing, and intentionality, as well as a suggested correspondence (or correlation) between noesis and noema. In this way,

Husserl works out his alternative to the classical causal theory of perception as well as to Kantian constructivism in reaction to Descartes. Following the French thinker, he describes cogitations as knowledge without doubt, or absolute data.

At this point in the analysis, Husserl distinguishes three different levels. On the first level, he claims that "the 'seeing' cognition of the *cogitatio* is immanent" (2). On the second level, he asserts that the Cartesian *cogitatio* already requires the phenomenological reduction. He criticizes Descartes for stopping short of the reduction as well as for insisting that in the pure phenomenon, or absolute datum, we reach an absolute given, which cannot be doubted. On the third level, Husserl affirms that the object constitutes itself within cognition. Husserl, who takes the term *appearance* as equivalent to *phenomenon*, appeals in this respect to the familiar distinction between the appearance and what appears (11). I take him to be suggesting that after Kant the problem of knowledge should be approached through the relation between what appears in consciousness and the mind-independent object. In other words, Husserl parts company with Kant, who later abandons representationalism for constructivism, in his steadfast commitment, even after Kant's Copernican turn, to solving the problem of knowledge on a representationalist basis.

The key difficulty lies, in Husserlian terms, in reaching objectivity (20). Kant, who regarded this difficulty as insuperable, reformulated the problem in terms of the phenomenon, abandoning the familiar distinction between appearance, or representation, and reality. Husserl, who does not know the critical philosophy well, and who never indicates an awareness of the details of Kant's approach to knowledge, works out his new formulation by abandoning any claim to know reality as it is while maintaining a basic dualism between appearance and reality. He begins by asserting that, in order to avoid psychologism as well as anthropologism and biologism, cognition requires a phenomenological reduction.

Husserl's explanation at this point appears confused. His claim that the data of the cogitations are absolutely immanent, that is, independent of any external object (33), severs any causal connection to a mind-independent external object. He differs on this point from Descartes, who appears staunchly committed to a causal theory of perception. The phenomenological reduction has several functions in Husserl's theory. On the one hand, it serves to justify the claim for access to a so-called absolute datum, or absolute data grasped through phenomenological "seeing." On the other hand, in going further, Husserl asserts that through the reduction, we give up transcendental presuppositions (38), such as, presumably, the familiar causal theory of perception allegedly linking perception to the mind-independent external world. If the theory no longer relies on a causal relation to the mind-independent world, then the familiar presupposition that the world "causes" ideas in the mind can be abandoned. If that were the case, then, as Husserl insists, reality, or the existence of the mind-independent world, could be bracketed.

Husserl's conception of a phenomenological reduction remains basically unclear. It is unclear, for instance how to "reduce" the contents of consciousness, as well as how to know when this has been successfully carried out. Merleau-Ponty's objection that this is an infinite and hence never fully realized task has been very influential, even among those close to Husserl's view of phenomenology.[59] I return to this point in the last chapter.

Husserl, who brackets the reality of the transcendent world, inconsistently makes use of it in various ways in his phenomenological epistemology. He develops his claim of absolute immanence both with respect to essences and with respect to transcendent objectivity. The theme of essence remains unclear. In line with his refusal of Kantian constructivism, Husserl insists that we identify and hence, reveal, uncover, or discover essences, which we do not make, create, produce, or construct.

According to Husserl, cognitive mental processes are intentional; hence they refer to something, such as an object, that may or may not be present and that is given through appearance, whether or not it is really given (43). This amounts to the indemonstrable claim that, even after the reduction, there is a correspondence between mental processes and things. As concerns essences, Husserl holds, in a way that brings him close to certain forms of Platonism, that every cognitive phenomenon is both particular and general, or universal. In the phenomenon the observer detects not only the particular shade of red, but also red as such (45). Since in phenomenological "seeing" essences are by definition directly given, Husserl claims that doubt is not possible. This argument develops his form of Cartesianism as a basic phenomenological evidentiary claim. Questions about the meaning, say, of redness would, hence, be pointless. Phenomenology proceeds by "seeing" in abstracting essences within the limits of phenomenological reduction (46) Naturally, such claims are limited to what one "sees" in bracketing any claims that go beyond it (50).

Husserl, who so far argues that through the *cogitatio* universals are given, now supplements this result through comments on what he calls "constitution." This concept presupposes a distinction between the object, which is not part of the reduced phenomenon, namely, what is directly, or immanently given, and what is given—roughly, a distinction between appearance and mind-independent external object. The object appears, or is constituted within, the phenomenon (53), that is, the object for us, or again, as Husserl also says, the thing itself as distinguished from the Kantian thing in itself. Husserl goes on to distinguish different senses concerning the "constitution" of objectivity through the ego's mental acts.

The difficulty lies in grasping the link between what is constituted in and hence present in mind and the world, or, as Husserl puts it, the "correlation of cognition and the object of cognition" (60). Husserl seems to be caught in a bind from which there is no escape. If he limits himself merely to the reduced object, which omits all reference to transcendence, then he cannot depict the required correlation. Yet if he goes beyond the self-imposed limit of subjective psychological experience in referring to the real object supposedly self-given within experience, then he falls back into the causal theory of perception that he is at pains to escape. In either case, his phenomenological alternative to Kantian constructivism through a reformulation of the representationalist strategy that Kant later rejects simply fails. Brave talk about immanence in transcendence, claims that objects are experienced as transcendent to appearances, cannot be demonstrated.[60]

The difficulty, which arguably cannot be resolved from Husserl's phenomenological perspective, compromises his ability to work out a phenomenological form of epistemology. In order to make out his epistemological theory, Husserl needs to demonstrate knowledge of objects. His chosen approach runs through the phenomenological reduction. He clearly has not solved the difficulty in this version of his position, which occurs in the interim between its initial descriptive formulation and its later idealist reformation. And it is unclear whether he later solves this difficulty on the idealist plane. Phenomenology, which begins with research into the essence of phenomena, later turns to the constitution of objectivities. But that does not suffice to overcome the problem of knowledge. For after Husserl introduces the reduction, there is no longer any plausible way to comprehend the relation of psychologically immanent experiences [*Erlebnisse*] to a transcendent reality.[61]

Phenomenology as Transcendental Idealism

After *The Idea of Phenomenology*, Husserl remains committed to the phenomenological reduction. In the important programmatic article "Philosophy as Rigorous Science" (1911) and in *Ideas* (1913), he continues to work out a phenomenological theory of knowledge on the basis of a solution to the problem of psychologism. This effort took various forms, whose arguably most important element, which takes shape after the phenomenological reduction, lies in the supposed correspondence between immanent consciousness and transcendent objects.

The programmatic article originated as a response to Dilthey, who published an account of metaphysics as *Weltanschauungsphilosophie*.[62] In answering Dilthey, Husserl extends the earlier attack on psychologism in a robust critique of naturalism, historicism, and *Weltanschauungsphilosophie*. Husserl, who believes that naturalism, which is currently much favored by analytic thinkers,[63] leads to the naturalizing of consciousness and all absolute ideas and norms, criticizes that approach. He is especially concerned with the naturalization of consciousness in rigorous, scientific forms of psychology. Since theory of knowledge cannot be based on empirical science, psychology cannot ground the other disciplines. With respect to knowledge, Husserl recommends study of the relation of consciousness and being, which are correlated in the relation between consciousness and something intended.[64] In pursuing his familiar, anti-psychologistic critique of contemporary nonphenomenological approaches to theory of knowledge, Husserl once again states his basic phenomenological thesis: The possibility of knowledge turns on a correlation between subjective experiences and what they intend.

Husserl later wrote numerous books, but *Ideas* arguably already provides as close to an authoritative statement of Husserl's mature position as we possess. In his preface to the English edition (1931), which was written later, we find a short, clear presentation of a new science called transcendental subjectivity. This is described as an absolutely independent realm of direct experience that results through the phenomenological reduction.[65] Transcendental subjectivity is a nonempirical, a priori science that provides an original and pure description of psychic life and also preserves a parallelism between phenomenological psychology and transcendental phenomenology. In a typical statement of this point, which recurs obsessively in related ways, Husserl contends that "to each eidetic or empirical determination on the one side there must correspond a parallel feature on the other."[66]

In this study, Husserl continues to work out a viable form of phenomenology, after rejecting psychologism and after the phenomenological reduction, in now abandoning description for transcendental idealism. Here as before, his grasp of the history of philosophy remains limited. His background in idealism is especially weak, limited to an elementary grasp of Kant, mainly filtered through Natorp, and a still weaker grasp of Berkeley, Fichte, and other idealists. An instance is his sharp objection in the programmatic article that, as he puts it, with Hegel and the Romantic School, any critique of reason was lost.[67] He is apparently unaware that, under the heading of spirit (*Geist*), the critique of reason is central to Hegel's position.⁶⁸

Husserl's tenuous grasp of idealism weakens his turn to idealism in *Ideas*. Uninformed opponents of idealism, including Marxists, analytic philosophers, and such phenomenologists as Sartre and Merleau-Ponty, routinely regard it as opposed to and incompatible with realism. In fact, many of those said to belong to the idealist camp, such as Plato, Kant, and Fichte, believe that idealism and realism are compatible. The former, who is often understood to be committed to the theory of forms or ideas, and in that sense an idealist, notoriously suggests in the *Republic* that under proper conditions at least some individuals can literally "see" the mind-independent real. Kant, who opposes "bad" idealism but not idealism as such, argues that a mind-independent real "affects" the cognitive subject. He further works out a theory of knowledge of empirical reality. Fichte should arguably be read as holding a position combining idealism and realism.

In working out the new version of his position, Husserl follows the uninformed, anti-idealist view that idealism is incompatible with realism. In now espousing idealism, he turns against realism, which he formerly defended (for instance, in the realist commitment in his original account of categorial intuition), as in principle absurd.⁶⁹ The supposed incompatibility of idealism with realism seems further to inspire Merleau-Ponty's rejection of idealism in any form, which he specifically directs against Husserlian idealism. I return to this point below. Though there are obviously many different forms of idealism, and though he is critical of Kant, Husserl's model of idealism seems to be the critical philosophy. He understands idealism as transcendental idealism, and phenomenology as transcendental phenomenology. In that sense, Husserl belongs to the illustrious group of post-Kantians who believe it is both possible and necessary to take the critical philosophy beyond Kant. Transcendental phenomenology is idealism worked out as a science, in short, as Husserl explicitly says, "the promised land" (21).

In the leap from descriptive to transcendental phenomenology, Husserl draws the consequences of his initial critique of psychologism for the problem of knowledge. In restating phenomenology as transcendental idealism, he approaches epistemology through two key moves already adumbrated in *The Idea of Phenomenology*: the phenomenological reduction through which he claims to arrive at pure immanence in consciousness, and the supposed correspondence between transcendental phenomenology and empirical psychology, or between subjective experiences and objectivity. These two moves are closely related in the progression from the critique of psychologism to the phenomenological reduction, and from the phenomenological reduction to a parallelism between subjective experience and objectivity.

In *Logical Investigations*, where Husserl combines his critique of psychologism with a descriptive approach to knowledge, he does not avoid psychologism. Psychologism there takes the form of descriptive phenomenology on the psychological plane. He later introduces the phenomenological reduction for two reasons: to avoid the persistent problem of psychologism, which he arguably never succeeds in overcoming, by leaving behind psychology, on the one hand, and, on the other, the Cartesian insistence on pure immanence as necessarily true beyond any hint of skepticism. Yet there is a heavy price to pay for cutting the link between the observer and the real world. Husserl, who can no longer claim to grasp the cognitive object directly, claims to know it indirectly through a supposed parallel between subjective experience and objectivity. Hence, the solution to the problem of knowledge, which earlier lay in the careful description of the object, now turns, after the phenomenological reduction and the reformulation of phenomenology as transcendental phenomenology, on the ability to make out the parallel in question.

The account of phenomenological reduction, which is crucial to Husserl's later thought, but which he barely touches on in *The Idea of Phenomenology*, is surprisingly superficial. The treatment of (phenomenological) reduction to a mere phenomenon, which is now called bracketing, as in bracketing the natural standpoint, is brief and unsatisfactory. The discussion of the supposed parallelism is extremely detailed but also unsatisfactory.

The general topic of the phenomenological reduction is mainly handled in two numbered sections (secs. 31–32) and more briefly in other passages. Husserl refers to a general thesis, or natural thesis, about the existence of the spatiotemporal "fact-world," which is normally taken for granted. Though it is normally assumed that there is something to be known, this belief can be suspended, "disconnected" or "bracketed," as in Cartesian doubt, which Husserl, in turning to the vocabulary of ancient skepticism, which recommended the theoretical suspension of judgment, hence the cessation of action, as in Pyrrhonism, also calls *epoche* (abstention).

In ancient skepticism (e.g., Pyrrhonism), *epoche* functioned to support skepticism in introducing systematic doubt. Descartes introduces systematic doubt to overcome the problem of the possibility of skepticism. Husserl brings in bracketing less to avoid skepticism than to gain a new scientific domain of immediate experience. Phenomenological *epoche* justifies a transition from the natural standpoint, which relies on the natural attitude, or "unthematized" assumption of the reality of the world, in order to concentrate on what is given. Husserl detects a parallel here between the ordinary person and the scientist. Both the ordinary person and the scientist assume the existence of the mind-independent external world. On the level of scientific research, there is no alternative to assuming the factual existence of what scientists investigate.[70] Husserl believes that this natural assumption is misguided, or at least unnecessary, and in any case incompatible with philosophy understood as rigorous science, which is wholly lacking in presuppositions of any kind. In introducing the phenomenological reduction, Husserl intends to go back behind the sciences, which rely on assumptions, in gaining access to a directly immanent given without presuppositions.

In this and other texts from his mature period, Husserl stresses his relation to Descartes and, to a lesser degree, to Kant, who, Husserl believes, was the first to point to what later becomes phenomenology, which, he claims, is no less than "the secret longing of the whole philosophy of modern times" (sec. 62, 166). Husserl asserts that Kant is "the first to perceive it [i.e., phenomenology—T. R.] truly," but cannot be said to "have brought the distinctive features of the phenomenological field into the focus of full consciousness" (sec. 62, 166). Yet if Kant's constructivism is already a form of phenomenology, then he does more than merely anticipate Husserl's position. In that case, the parallel is deeper than Husserl suspects. There is a further parallel with respect to the claims Kant and Husserl make for their positions. We have already noted that Kant implies more than once that philosophy in his specific sense did not exist before him and that, since he has definitively solved the main questions, in a real sense he can be said to have brought the tradition to an end. Husserl makes a similar point in suggesting that all of modern philosophy is concerned with a problem that in his form of phenomenology reaches a peak and an end.

The simplicity with which Husserl treats the phenomenological reduction contrasts with the complexity of his account of the supposed parallelism. The latter begins with an Aristotelian distinction between sensible *hyle* and intentional *morphe*. The former, also called hyletic or material data, or sensile or again sensory materials, refers to the input, what Kant calls the content of the sensory manifold. Husserl's point is that consciousness is consciousness of something, which is intended, on the basis of sensory materials. The terms *noesis* or *noetic phase*, from *Nous* (mind, spirit) refer back to cogitations. According to Husserl, the contents of consciousness, which are given in the form of a phenomenological stream, are both material and noetic (sec. 85, 230).

Husserl's enigmatic distinction between noema and noesis is difficult but crucial to his transcendental idealist epistemology. The distinction becomes clearer, if not clear, if we relate it to Brentano and Bolzano. In his *Wissenschaftslehre,* the latter distinguished between subjective and objective ideas or representations (*Vorstellungen*). For Bolzano, logic is concerned with objective ideas, and psychology considers subjective ideas, such as the mental activities in a particular mind at a given time and place. Husserl transforms this distinction in his view of phenomenology as the study of phenomena, or the objective intentional contents, or again the intentional objects of consciousness, which is subjective. He employs the Greek terms *noesis* to refer to the intentional character of consciousness, and *noema* to refer to its ideal content.

Presumably, Husserl has in mind the difference between an "input" of some kind, say from the physical pole, often called mind-independent reality, or the world, as a result of which the contents of consciousness are "constituted," and the role of the mental pole, that is, mind or consciousness, in this process. Phenomenology, understood in this way, is transcendental, or concerned with problems arising from an approach to experience as intentional, hence "consciousness-of," with respect to eidetic essence (sec. 86, 232–33); it is the only possible solution of the problem of knowledge (sec. 97, 263).

Husserl begins his account with what he calls the proper components of the intentional experiences, in other words with what is directly given after the phenomenological reduction, and their so-called intentional correlates, or what they point toward. Intentional experience is noetic, or harbors "meaning." Another way to put this point is to say that there is a correlation between pure intuition and the noematic contents, or the noematic correlate, or again between the mental acts through which objects are constituted in the mind and the object as meant, as distinguished from the real object as it is prior to the phenomenological reduction. In insisting on a parallelism, Husserl is concerned to preserve the claim to objective knowledge after the phenomenological reduction, which severs the link between the immanent contents of consciousness and the world. From this perspective, knowledge is only possible if there is a parallel between subjective experiences and objectivity, between the contents of consciousness and the world.

Now one might argue for an analogous point in developing Kant's so-called double aspect thesis, according to which the object can be taken as both a thing in itself and as an appearance. Kant's view rests on a causal impact of the thing in itself on the subject.[71] Yet Husserl, who turns away from causality as a result of the reduction, does not have this move available.

Husserl's "argument" consists in insisting on a correspondence between the contents of consciousness and the world. In sticking to his view of a basic correlation, he claims that there is no noetic phase without a specifically correlated noematic phase (sec. 93, 250). But this assertion, which rests on a prior claim about the relation of purely immanent contents of consciousness after the reduction, seems questionable. The origin of the supposed parallel perhaps lies in the old scholastic view of intentionality. The suggested parallel is Husserl's way of rendering the old scholastic distinction between "mental," "intentional" or "immanent" objects and "real" objects (sec. 90, 242). Yet it is insufficient for his epistemological purposes to invoke intentionality. It is not enough to say that consciousness is directed toward an object of some kind if, as is the case for Husserl, the problem consists in explaining under what conditions the subject can know the object on that grounds that the contents of consciousness supposedly match up with, or correspond to, objectivity.

Husserl goes on to work out a theory of the noetic-noematic structures, starting from the point that phenomenologically pure experience has real components. He contends that in starting with the real, after the phenomenological reduction the "residue" consists in a parallelism between the noetic and the noematic, or between experience and its correlative, or noematic, content (sec. 97, 263–64). This phenomenological view is idealist in that, as for Berkeley, the being of the object consists in its being perceived, with the obvious difference that, in virtue of the reduction, the object perceived is not real (sec. 98, 264–65). But Husserl differs from Berkeley in that phenomenological "apprehension" is not real "apprehension" (sec. 113, 291). Husserl nails down this claim in a series of repeated assertions, never demonstrated and arguably indemonstrable, to the effect that there is always a counterpart, or noema, that corresponds to each cogito (sec. 114, 294). In other words, in virtue of the distinction between noesis and noema, there is always a correlate of consciousness that is not contained in it (sec. 128, 331).

The difficulty lies not in asserting but in demonstrating the parallel between the contents of consciousness and objectivity. Husserl is at least aware of the problem, even if, after the reduction, if to know means to cognize the mind-independent real, there is arguably no phenomenological solution in sight. He raises the problem against himself in asking a crucial question: "But what then does this 'real' mean for objects which are indeed given to consciousness, yet only through meanings and positions?" (sec. 135, 348).

One way to put the difficulty concerns the distinction between the noesis and the noema. Husserl insists that every noema has a unified content or meaning. The difficulty lies in the sense in which one can claim, on the basis of Husserl's analysis, that there is objective knowledge, or that one reaches objectivity. According to Husserl, in principle the appearance of any thing is inadequate (sec. 138, 355). Husserl here seems to follow Kant's view that appearances are appearances of a transcendental object = X. Husserl goes on to claim, that, at least in principle, there is always a way in which every object can be grasped primordially and perfectly adequately (sec. 142, 365). Yet this is a kind of promissory note that cannot be redeemed. The result is, as he notes, that the adequate presentation of a thing is merely an idea in the Kantian sense (sec. 143, 366–67). But unless Husserl can make out the claim to knowledge, his phenomenological form of epistemology fails.

Phenomenological Epistemology and the Subject in Husserl's Selected Later Writings

The transition from descriptive to transcendental forms of phenomenology establishes the main lines of Husserl's mature position. In writings after *Ideas*, Husserl builds on his shift to transcendental idealism in continuing to work out a mature version of his phenomenological theory. Husserl's position later develops in many ways but does not basically change. His later writings expand the position he initially expounds in *Ideas* while addressing a series of related difficulties. If, for present purposes, we limit ourselves merely to the published writings, then three of the most important later texts are *Cartesian Meditations: An Introduction to Phenomenology* and *Formal and Transcendental Logic*, both of which appeared in 1929, and his last, unfinished work, *The Crisis of European Sciences and Transcendental Phenomenology*, which appeared posthumously.

Of these three works, the most interesting for the theme of phenomenology and epistemology is arguably *Cartesian Meditations*. *Formal and Transcendental Logic* returns to a series of themes initially broached in *Logical Investigations* from the transcendental idealist perspective that Husserl had meantime adopted. It sharpens the initial treatment of many themes mentioned then. Once again, Husserl focuses on the theme, already central in *Logical Investigations*, of logic as a theory of science, now under the guise of an intentional explication of formal logic. In the meantime, since the appearance of Heidegger's *Being and Time* in 1927, Husserl feels called upon to defend his own view of phenomenology. He does so in part by coming back to formal ontology, which as he notes, was already introduced in *Logical Investigations*.[72] Returning once again to the theme of logic, Husserl now contends that only a transcendental logic can be a theory of science in an ultimate sense that comes to us from Plato—indeed, a universal theory of the principles and norms of science.[73]

The Crisis, Husserl's last, unfinished work, which is once again intended as an introduction to transcendental phenomenology, obsessively goes over a series of familiar themes. Yet it breaks new ground in several ways. There is a lengthy account of the relation between *objectivism*, Husserl's term for a positivistic approach to science, and transcendentalism, which, according to Husserl, is realized only in transcendental phenomenology. In this account, which takes up all of part 2,[74] Husserl clarifies his relation to modern pre-Kantian philosophy, especially to Descartes. Husserl argues here that the rise of modern science is based on the successful application of mathematics to nature. This analysis can be read as a counternarrative refuting Kant's suggestion of the key role of Copernican astronomy. This discussion of the rise of modern science is followed by a lengthy account of the way into phenomenological transcendental philosophy from psychology, which takes up the whole of part 3. The account of the life-world works out for the first time Husserl's understanding of what is left behind in the phenomenological reduction. Interesting here is Husserl's critique of Kant for supposedly taking the life-world for granted as an unexamined presupposition.[75] The account of the way into transcendental phenomenology from psychology once again goes over the ground Husserl has covered earlier, from slightly different perspectives, in a series of works.

In the same year in which he brought out his last work on logic, Husserl gave a series of lectures again intended as an introduction to phenomenology under the title *Cartesian Meditations*. This work has long attracted attention for Husserl's effort, unavailing in the eyes of most commentators, to respond to the problem of solipsism deriving from the phenomenological reduction and, as a result, to address such crucial questions as intersubjectivity.[76] But for present purposes, this text is even more important for the light it sheds on Husserl's conception of the subject.

It has already been mentioned that the Kantian view of the subject is the conceptual coping stone of the critical philosophy. In *Cartesian Meditations*, Husserl begins with the comment that transcendental phenomenology is in a sense neo-Cartesian before adding that it opposes nearly all the main Cartesian doctrines.[77] Husserl here formulates a conception of the phenomenological subject, which brings him closer to Kant. It has been noted above that in responding to what later comes to be called psychologism, Kant introduces a conception of the subject as enduring and hence not a mere transitory bundle of perceptions, as in Hume, but also not reducible to mere physiology, as in Locke. In *Cartesian Meditations*, as elsewhere after *Ideas*, Husserl against insists on his view of phenomenology as a transcendental theory of knowledge (sec. 40, 81). Unlike Kant, who takes a constructivist approach, what Husserl means by "transcendental idealism" is phenomenology understood as the explication of the ego cogito, for which all that exists is constituted by it. For, as he again contends, genuine theory of knowledge is possible only as transcendental phenomenology (sec. 41, 83).

Once again, Husserl insists that psychologism can only be overcome through the reduction. According to Husserl, the reduction transforms the ego into an ego cogito. The ego cogito, or transcendental-phenomenological ego, is not an existing human being. After the reduction, and as in the early Wittgenstein, for whom the subject is the limit of the world, the ego does not belong to the world, and the world does not belong to the ego (sec. 11, 25–26). In clarifying the reduction, Husserl suggests that it shifts the "weight" of transcendental evidence from the identical ego to the manifold cogitations, while introducing (one might add, in a Kantian manner) a basic distinction between the psychological and the transcendental dimensions of subjectivity (sec. 14, 31–33).

This distinction points to a key difficulty in the Kantian view of the subject. Kant's formulation of a conception of subjectivity reduced to its epistemological role obscures the relation between the epistemological subject and finite human being.[78] Roughly the same difficulty recurs in Husserl. Husserl clearly asserts continuity between the transcendental ego and finite human being in insisting that the transcendental ego is inseparable from life (sec. 30, 65–66). In virtue of his claim to go to things themselves, Husserl cannot follow Kant's constructivism about the object. He contends, however, that both subject and object are constituted, in insisting that the ego or identical pole of the subjective processes is continuously self-constituting (secs. 31 and 33). According to Husserl, this ego, one can say almost magically, retains many, perhaps all, of its human capacities, such as the capacity to make decisions (sec. 32). As a result, Husserl breaks ranks with Kant, for whom the subject "constructs" its object, in claiming that transcendental idealism, or phenomenological epistemology, is a genuine explanation of the ego cogito (sec. 41, 83–88).

FIVE

Heidegger's Phenomenological Ontology

Husserlians, like Husserl, tend not to acknowledge pre-Husserlian phenomenology. Heidegger is in that specific sense Husserlian, though he can also be read as interpreting Aristotle as a very early phenomenologist, as someone who does the same kind of things that Husserl does but does them better. Certainly with Heidegger, the very idea of a phenomenological movement that is Husserlian in character is called into doubt.

Though Husserl was clearly enormously influential, and though there were a number of more or less "orthodox" Husserlians, such as Fink, Pfander, Stein, Cairns, and, further afield, Shpet, Farber, and so on, the most significant post-Husserlian phenomenologists usually (perhaps always) adopt less hierophantic and more critical stances. Rather than anything so grand as a "phenomenological movement," which suggests a wave of support for a series of basic insights by a group of workers in the great phenomenological vineyard, or, to vary the metaphor, by thinkers engaged in mining the phenomenological vein of ore, later phenomenologists, including Heidegger, seem to have quickly but decisively abandoned many, indeed most of Husserl's basic insights. In short, Husserl did not begin but strongly stimulated work in phenomenology, which through his influence became a movement. Yet this movement was never Husserlian but was largely anti-Husserlian.

Except for Husserl, in discussing the epistemological views of the main phenomenological thinkers, it is possible to concentrate on a single main text. Heidegger's position took shape in a single early book, *Being and Time*, in which he expounded the main elements of his phenomenological position, and on which we can focus the discussion.

It is important, since this study is tightly focused on the relation of phenomenology and epistemology, to justify devoting a chapter to Heidegger. Though he claims to be a phenomenologist, his stress is not basically epistemological, not basically centered on knowing, but focused on what he calls *being*. In *Being and Time*, he argues, since he believes that ontology is always presupposed in other philosophical studies, including ethics, aesthetics, logic, and epistemology, for the priority of ontology over all other philosophical investigations. Yet being and knowing, ontology and epistemology, are "indissociably" linked, hence inseparable. It is only in modern times that epistemology emerges as a distinct field. *Epistemology* means different things to different observers. If by this term one has recent epistemology in mind, then obviously neither Heidegger nor Aristotle, on whom he often relies, qualifies as an epistemologist. Yet if *epistemology* relates to *knowledge* understood broadly, then this consideration is widely present in Aristotle's writings. Though he does not use that term, he is often concerned with themes, problems, and difficulties that would now belong to the general heading of epistemology. Many of his treatises raise questions of methodology,[1] questions that, say, for Kant, who is routinely understood as an epistemologist, belong to the problem of knowledge.

Aristotle, who raises the canonical form of the problem of being, clearly addresses a subset of the wider epistemological problem. He was already aware of what is now called epistemology or theory of knowledge. His critique of Plato's theory of forms addresses an approach to the problem of knowledge that he attributes to his teacher. In the *Metaphysics*, where he discusses the relation between ontology and epistemology, he does not propose a general theory of knowledge. Rather, he proposes a restricted theory of knowledge of the many ways in which being is said. From Aristotle's angle of vision, ontology cannot be divorced from epistemology, since any theory of being is also inevitably a theory of knowing, or the knowing of being. Roughly the same project recurs in Husserl, who is sometimes interpreted as wrestling with the general problem of being.[2] He explicitly states that epistemology, or the critique of natural cognition, is the precondition for a science of being.[3] In this sense, for Husserl, the Heideggerian program of bypassing epistemology to go directly to ontology is problematic.

Heidegger's main interest lies in what he calls the problem of the meaning of being, which dominates his early work. This theme points toward an aspect of knowing being in general, as distinguished from knowing beings, or things, which is a restricted form of the general problem of knowledge. In modern philosophy, the problem of meaning, in Heidegger's case the meaning of being, is studied under the headings of semantics and reference by a large number of thinkers, including such Heideggerian contemporaries as Frege and those influenced by him. Though Heidegger claims to be uninterested in the wider problem of knowledge, it is at least arguable that he did not know enough about the modern epistemological debate to assess the relation of his interests to what is now called epistemology. Certainly a number of aspects of his position, including his views of interpretation, his theory of truth, and his analysis of the hermeneutical circle, have important epistemological implications. At the end of the day, and despite Heidegger's explicit denial, it looks very much as if in exploiting the opening provided by Husserlian phenomenology, Heidegger does not simply give up phenomenological epistemology for phenomenological ontology. Instead, he proposes a new form of phenomenology; for instance, as concerns truth, and also interpretation, and so on, he often, in effect, substitutes a different form of phenomenological epistemology, under the guise of phenomenological ontology, for a Cartesian alternative exemplified by Husserl that he is at pains to discredit. If this is correct, then Heidegger, who never identifies with epistemology, is at least covertly an epistemological thinker.

This point can be sharpened. In spite of Heidegger's claim to abandon epistemology for phenomenology, it is arguable that his position, which has clear epistemological aspects, is in some ways directly intended as an epistemological replacement for the kind of epistemology that, under the cover of ontological debate, Heidegger rejects. There are different forms of epistemology, for instance, the effort to formulate a theory of knowing a particular thing, as in Descartes, or of knowing being in general, which is an ontological pursuit but has a strong epistemological component. In not even mentioning consciousness in *Being and Time*, Heidegger distances his approach from German idealism in perhaps intentionally obviating an epistemological reading of his position. But in denying that he is concerned with epistemology by ostensibly closing the door to it, he brings it in through the window, so to speak. Since he explicitly claims that being lies beyond the possibility of representation,[4] one way to describe his position is as a nonrepresentational form of epistemology.

This claim is sometimes made by qualified observers. For instance, Gadamer, who studied with and was strongly influenced by Heidegger, argues in detail that (Heideggerian) phenomenology overcomes the epistemological problem.[5] Accordingly, this chapter identifies and discusses selected aspects of Heidegger's wider phenomenological theory that seem closely related to epistemological concerns.

On the Philosophical Relation between Heidegger and Husserl

The relations between Heidegger, who was a student of Husserlian phenomenology, as well as Husserl's assistant and successor, are complex and have never been satisfactorily clarified. It is clear that the personal relations between them were difficult.[6] For our purposes, the philosophical relation is more significant. Like Hegel, who responds to Kant on virtually every page of his corpus, Heidegger needs to be understood primarily through his reaction to Husserl and only afterward in terms of his reactions to an exceptionally broad span of other thinkers ranging widely over the entire Western tradition.[7] Heidegger's ambivalent philosophical relation to Husserl is crucial to his own view of phenomenology. He dedicated *Being and Time* to Husserl. He further indicates that his own work was made possible by the latter's discovery of phenomenology.[8] The parallels extend further to Brentano, Husserl's teacher, who also influenced Heidegger. The latter indicates that his concern with philosophy was awakened by Brentano's dissertation, "On the Manifold Meaning of Being since Aristotle" (1862). Further like Husserl, Heidegger's effort to work out his phenomenology depends on his reading of and reaction to Descartes and Kant. Yet despite these and other forms of similarity, Heidegger's overall relation to Husserl is extremely critical.

Hegel's critical reaction to Kant can be described in terms of the Kantian revival of the ancient Pauline distinction between the spirit and the letter. Hegel defends and develops the spirit of the critical philosophy, by disregarding, if necessary, its letter. Heidegger's complex reaction to Husserl is both personal and philosophical. On the personal plane, Heidegger seems to have been skeptical, even contemptuous of Husserl's claim to invent phenomenology,[9] the very assertion that Heidegger himself publicly accepts. In a letter to Jaspers, he sarcastically remarks that Husserl is wholly taken up with his mission as the inventor of phenomenology, though no one can say what that is.[10] It is also known that Husserl and Heidegger were unable to cooperate to write an article on phenomenology for the *Encyclopedia Britannica*. In his official role as rector of the University of Freiburg, Heidegger may or may not have forbidden Husserl, who was born into a Jewish family but later converted to Lutheranism, to use the university library. It is further known that Heidegger did not attend Husserl's funeral.

Though he identified with phenomenology, the extent of Heidegger's allegiance to Husserlian phenomenology was limited, even very limited. In the same passage in which he records his dependence on Husserl's supposed invention of phenomenology, he indicates that his interest does not lie in the actuality of the phenomenological movement but in its possibility, in what it could yet become.[11] One can take him to be suggesting that Husserl points to a possibility that is not attained in his writings and hence remains to be realized. Yet Heidegger was also concerned with specific aspects of Husserl's corpus. He records his fascination with *Logical Investigations*,[12] and he edited Husserl's lectures on internal time-consciousness.[13]

Heidegger's conception of phenomenology differs from Husserl's in a number of ways, beginning with its "official" orientation to ontology rather than epistemology. Husserl consistently identifies phenomenology with epistemology. Heidegger abandons Husserl's single-minded phenomenological focus on epistemology for an equally single-minded, even obsessive, focus on phenomenological ontology. Husserl, who understands *phenomenology* in many different ways, uses this term to refer to virtually anything he is interested in at the time. A similar comment describes Heidegger, who employs *ontology* with respect to an exceedingly wide range of phenomena, often where one might expect another term. A cardinal example is his celebrated reading of Kant not as an epistemologist but as an ontologist. I will come back to this point.

Husserl's position develops in a complex evolution from an early descriptive to a later transcendental idealist form of phenomenology. Heidegger, like most other post-Husserlian phenomenologists, including Ingarden, Sartre, Merleau-Ponty, and many others, as well as non-phenomenologists such as Findlay, strongly prefers Husserl's earlier, descriptive approach to phenomenology.

Heidegger and the Problem of Psychologism

Heidegger's deep ambivalence with respect to Husserl extends to psychologism, which interested him at least mildly early on,[14] but later seems to fade from view. Heidegger's view of this complex theme changes as his conception of the subject changes. Anti-psychologism, which is a central component in Husserlian phenomenology, is at most a secondary theme for Heidegger, whose complex view of psychologism is unclear. Unlike Husserl, who defended a form of psychologism in his early work on *The Philosophy of Arithmetic*, Heidegger did not go through a psychologistic period. Like many contemporaries, such as Schlick and Natorp, Heidegger thought Husserl later fell back into psychologism

There is, to the best of my knowledge, only a single mention of psychologism in *Being and Time*. In a discussion of truth, Heidegger notes the difference between the act of judging and its ideal content. He then writes, "Is not psychologism correct in holding out against this separation," adding that this distinction does not advance the theory of truth.[15] In this passage,

Heidegger appears to be reopening the question of psychologism as well as indicating that it is not directly relevant to his present concern. This marks a change in attitude.

Heidegger initially opposed psychologism. His first published article, "The Reality Problem in Modern Philosophy," criticizes Kantian and Machian forms of phenomenalism from the general perspective of Husserl's anti-psychologism.[16] His dissertation, written on a then trendy topic, was entitled "The Doctrine of Judgment in Psychologism: A Critical-Positive Contribution to Logic" (1913).[17] Heidegger here studies four "psychologistic" theories of judgment (Wundt, Meier, Brentano, Lipps) before presenting his own "purely logical" view of judgment. He follows the Husserlian view, in reaction against Mill and other psychologistic thinkers, in insisting that the act of judging is not to be conflated with the meaning of what the judgment is about.[18]

Yet Heidegger's view of psychologism is more complex than this seeming opposition implies. For one thing, he claims at the beginning of his dissertation that is not possible to say what psychology is. This suggests the difficulty of identifying and opposing psychologism. Further, the conception of the subject is crucial for an anti-psychologistic approach. Very much like Kant, Husserl later worked out a theory of transcendental subjectivity based on a difference in kind between the philosophical and the psychological subject. Heidegger's view of the subject as *Dasein*, hence as always already in the world, appears to undo, or at least to complicate, the basic anti-psychologistic distinction between cognitive and psychological dimensions of subjectivity.

Being and Time is a highly structured work. Heidegger formally introduces the theme of Dasein in section 5 of the treatise, after delineating the main lines of his approach to being in general in prior sections. He describes an ontological approach to the subject linked to being but not founded on the problems of consciousness (and self-consciousness) and hence not tied to the problem of knowledge.[19] According to Heidegger, Dasein understands being with respect to time (*BT*, 39). It follows that the task of interpreting being requires an understanding of its temporality (*BT*, 40). Divisions one and two of *Being and Time* are devoted to the analysis of Dasein. The former takes up its so-called fundamental analysis, and the latter considers its relation to time. Heidegger goes on to describe a series of characteristics of the subject, or Dasein, understood as always in context, culminating in care (*Sorge*). This is followed by detailed discussion of Dasein's being-toward-death, authentic potentiality-for-being, resoluteness, and everydayness.

Heidegger's analysis of Dasein sounds very much like a contribution to social science. He specifically warns against conflating his view with anthropology, psychology, or biology (*BT*, 71–77). He seems to have two main reasons in mind. One is related to Dilthey's interest in life (*Lebensphilosophie*). This is, together with Scheler's view, one of the inspirations of Heidegger's conception of Dasein. Heidegger, who objects that a "personalistic" approach is too narrow, nonetheless concedes that it provides a clue to Dasein's being (*BT*, 72–73). The other reason, which is a kind of plea *pro domo suo*, amounts to the view that one cannot base a theory on a traditional anthropological approach, which comes either from ancient Greek philosophy or Christian theology, since Heidegger's question of the meaning of being is forgotten (*BT*, 75). Indeed, Heidegger goes further in claiming that Dasein is not and cannot be founded on the various human sciences, which, since they take being for granted, are not capable of grasping life. Since only Dasein interrogates being, the human sciences are based on Dasein.

Heidegger is claiming that Dasein is a concept of the subject, which, since it clarifies being, goes beyond all other available concepts, which merely presuppose it as their basis. He appears to identify Dasein with human being, for instance, in writing, "As ways in which man behaves, sciences have the manner of Being which this entity—man himself—possesses. This entity we denote by the term *'Dasein'*" (*BT*, 32; Heidegger's emphasis). This suggests that Heidegger is concerned with philosophical anthropology, which he later rejects as a misreading. An anthropological interpretation of Heidegger was especially prominent in the French discussion. The typically French anthropological approach to Heidegger was influenced by such factors as the persistent French interest in humanism, hence in the subject, at least since Montaigne and Descartes; by French existentialism; and by the relatively late translation of *Being and Time*, which was only finally fully translated in the 1980s. This French reading of Heidegger culminates, so to speak, in Jean-Paul Sartre's *Being and Nothingness* (1943). Here, under the influence of his reading of what the French call the three Hs (Hegel, Husserl, Heidegger), Sartre produced a psychological analysis of interpersonal relations under the heading of existentialism. It is no accident that Sartre, who insisted on total freedom in occupied France, rapidly emerged as the leading French thinker.

At the close of the Second World War, Sartre came into disfavor for his increasingly close relation to the French Communist Party, which prefigured his brief turn to Marxism. In *The Search for a Method* (1957), Sartre claimed that Marxism lacked a conception of the subject and offered existentialism to shore it up. Marxism, which he described as the philosophy of our time, was supposedly in danger of collapse. This text later became the preface to *Critique of Dialectical Reason* (1960), in which he reformulated his originally ahistorical existentialism on a historical basis influenced by his passing interest in Marx and Marxism. As an existentialist, Sartre supported a novel conception of humanism according to which each person is always responsible for everyone. Though he was never a member of the Communist Party, he was attacked nearly immediately after the end of the war as the author of an atheistic position with close links to communism. Sartre publicly defended his position in a famous lecture, "Existentialism Is a Humanism" (1946). In this lecture, and as part of his public defense of existentialism, he drew attention to the relation between his position and Heidegger's.

This defense helped to create an opportunity for Heidegger. The latter was at that point in disfavor because of his collaboration with National Socialism. He was in danger of being dismissed from the university, of losing his pension, and of losing his role in German intellectual life. Freiburg, where Heidegger taught, and where he had briefly served as rector during the Nazi period (1932–33), was in the French occupation zone. It was therefore strategically important for Heidegger to make an intellectual appeal to French public opinion. Heidegger did so in a brief philosophical text, the famous *Letter on Humanism*. The text was addressed to Jean Beaufret, at the time a young, little-known French philosopher and member of the French resistance. Beaufret, who at the time was interested in Sartre, later transferred his allegiance to Heidegger in becoming his single most important proselytizer in the French context. Beaufret wrote to Heidegger and posed a series of questions. Heidegger's answers attracted widespread attention in the French intellectual context, in which he gradually but steadily displaced Sartre as the French "master thinker."

In the *Letter on Humanism*, Heidegger carefully distinguishes between Sartre's position and his own, while seeking to curry political favor with his French readers through a new, rival form of humanism based on the "nearness to being."[20] According to Heidegger, who proposes a new view of human being keyed to his interest in ontology, "man is the shepherd of being" (*LH*, 210). Sartre's position is a form of metaphysics that Heidegger has meanwhile left behind. For Sartre, it is not essence that precedes existence, but rather existence that precedes essence (*LH*, 210). The result is to reverse the order of the terms *essence* and *existence*, an order going back in the tradition at least to Plato. Yet, as Heidegger points out, the reversal of metaphysics is still metaphysics (*LH*, 208). Although existentialism is the correct name for this position, it is incorrect as a name for Heidegger's position, which is not metaphysics, and which has nothing in common either with it or with Sartre's existentialism (*LH*, 209).

It is a deep mistake to ignore the relation of the thinker to the context, to interpret Heidegger's philosophical evolution in wholly immanent terms without reference to his implication in the politics of the day.[21] In the *Letter on Humanism*, Heidegger, who was in difficult straits because of his turn to Nazism during the war, has mixed philosophical and personal motives. In attacking Sartre on the philosophical plane, he is at the same time clearly also seeking to defend himself on the political plane. As concerns the *Letter on Humanism*, it is important to distinguish between the circumstances of its composition and Heidegger's need to defend his person (and his family) in difficult circumstances, on the one hand, from its philosophical message, on the other. This text turns on the rejection of an anthropological tendency allegedly illustrated by French humanism. Heidegger's argument in the *Letter on Humanism*, which is already adumbrated in section 10 of *Being and Time*, claims that there are true and false forms of humanism. Sartre illustrates traditional philosophical humanism, which, since it falls below the level of the true humanism in the service of being, must be rejected.

The *Letter on Humanism* includes both a text and a subtext. The reader comes away with the impression that whatever Heidegger may have earlier thought and done, including putting his position in the service of National Socialism, he has now left philosophy and hence Nazism, to which he may or may not have turned because of his philosophy, behind. Yet this is less than clear. He has, for instance, not left behind his veneration of the Nazi view of sacrifice for the state, foreshadowed prior to Hitler's rise to power in *Being and Time* (*BT*, 434–39),[22] as evidenced by his approving remark in this text about young Germans "confronted with death" (*LH*, 219). And he has not left behind, as he signals in an infamous remark about "the philosophy of National Socialism," his attachment to "the inner truth and greatness of this movement."[23]

The supposed transformation of his position is linked to a mysterious, so-called turning (*Kehre*) in his thought to which Heidegger strategically alludes in a number of places,[24] including the *Letter on Humanism* (*LH*, 207–8), after he resigned his post as Hitler's rector in Nazi Germany. In this text, he refers to the turning from the theme of being and time to the further theme of time and being as a turning that is not a change of standpoint but a deepening.[25] Heidegger believes that we experience what he enigmatically calls the "forgetfulness of being." He explicitly links the allegedly true, or deeper, humanity of human being—beyond the shallowness of humanism—and the truth of being (*LH*, 231). His position, which is supposedly now no longer philosophy but thinking (*Denken*), should be understood as a new, deeper, authentic humanism, which, though no longer philosophy, achieves a central philosophical goal since it is indispensable for the good life (*LH*, 235–42). In this respect there is an obvious parallel to the view of Marx, who supposedly leaves philosophy behind while solving its problems.

In *Being and Time*, Heidegger took the view that the road to being runs through Dasein and hence, since *Dasein* refers to human being, through human being as well. In later writings, Heidegger weakens the role of the subject in rejecting any velleity to approach being through human being. In reacting against Sartre, Heidegger reacts against the typically French anthropological interpretation of Dasein. In writings after *Being and Time*, Heidegger reaffirms his rejection of an anthropological reading of the subject in a number of places. In section 10 of *Being and Time*, he refers briefly to Descartes in noting that the latter's account of the *cogito sum* leaves the *sum* completely undiscussed (*BT*, 71). This is tantamount to accusing Descartes, who is widely known for importing a conception of the subject into the epicenter of modern philosophy, of failing to comprehend it. For Heidegger, the Cartesian subject that later became crucial to the modern debate remains to be thought. In his essay on "The Age of the World-Picture" (1938), Heidegger inveighs against the anthropological element that, since Descartes, increasingly dominates the modern discussion.[26] In *Contributions to Philosophy*, which was composed at about the same time (1936–38), he "deconstructs" Dasein, which is now written as Da-seyn, in increasingly adopting a view of being that, since it no longer depends on human being, is self-manifesting.[27]

How does it stand with respect to psychologism? The answer, after this survey, is unclear. Psychologism concerns the reduction of the logical to the psychological. If the relation of the logical to the psychological runs through the subject, then the subject is central to the problem of psychologism. Over time, Heidegger seems to have several different, contrasting views of the subject: as the active, non-anthropological subject that is the clue to being in *Being and Time*; and as the passive, non-anthropological subject in the *Letter on Humanism*, in which being is self-manifesting and hence independent of subjectivity. The constant element in the different views of subjectivity lies in the steadfast refusal to define the subject in anthropological terms while relating it to being. It is difficult to reconcile Heidegger's early defense of anti-psychologism with his later depiction of Dasein in *Being and Time* and other writings as always already in the world and hence as the clue to being. And it is difficult to grasp a view of being as self-manifesting. If by Dasein Heidegger has in mind finite human being as the subject, then it would seem that he falls into psychologism into which he believes Husserl also relapsed. If by Dasein he does not have in mind finite human being, then he does not fall into psychologism, but his view of subjectivity remains basically unclear. In the latter case, everything happens as if Heidegger, who is intent on guarding against the supposed anthropological misreading of the subject, has finally, despite his awareness of the conceptual pitfalls, been unable to formulate an adequate conception of it.

Heidegger and Husserl's Categorial Intuition

In turning now to Heidegger's reading of Husserl's view of categorial intuition, we need to address two questions: How does Heidegger's reading of this concept relate to its role in Husserl's position? What is its epistemological payoff in Heidegger's position?

Heidegger, who, like many others, refused Husserl's later transcendental turn, remains on the descriptive level in developing a version of Husserl's theory of categorial intuition, taking it beyond the place where Husserl left it. This points to an enduring concern with Husserl's early phenomenological breakthrough as distinguished from its later transcendental idealist development.

Heidegger reports in a short essay his fascination with Husserl's *Logical Investigations*, which he read again and again. This fascination continued even after the publication of *Ideas*, that is, after Husserl had moved away from his earlier descriptive form of phenomenology. He was especially taken with Husserl's view of categorial intuition in the sixth and final investigation in volume 2 of the *Logical Investigations*.[28] Husserl thinks that his phenomenology needs to reach the level of what he later calls rigorous science (*strenge Wissenschaft*), which was, he believes, the common goal of all philosophy. Heidegger, on the contrary, understands phenomenology as providing an important clue to earlier positions, in particular for his reading of Aristotle and other early Greek thinkers.[29] He notes that at a time when Husserl had turned away from this work, he continued to study it in special courses on phenomenological seeing.[30] In effect, like the post-Kantian reaction to Kant, which began to develop with the initial reception of the *Critique of Pure Reason*, Heidegger was already committed to carrying the spirit of Husserlian phenomenology beyond Husserl.

Heidegger reports that when Husserl came to Freiburg in 1916, his teaching took the form of what he called "phenomenological 'seeing,'" which "relinquish[ed] the untested use of philosophical knowledge," namely, simply taking over ideas and theories dogmatically, as well as any appeal to "the authority of great philosophers."[31] Unlike Husserl, whose interests lay in realizing goals he believed were aimed at but not reached by earlier thinkers, Heidegger was concerned to reinterpret earlier positions in new ways to disclose their potential for further development. In working through Husserlian phenomenology, Heidegger also in effect worked his way out of it. He reports that he arrived at the conclusion that Husserl's effort to grasp "the acts of consciousness as the self-manifestation of thought," which is close to the central thrust of his version of phenomenology, was "thought more originally by Aristotle and in all Greek thinking and existence as *aletheia*, as the unconcealment of what is present, in being revealed, its showing itself."[32]

The theory of truth as *aletheia* is put forward in *Being and Time*. It follows that even in *Being and Time*, when Heidegger is still claiming allegiance to Husserl, he is no longer (and indeed probably has never been) a phenomenologist in the Husserlian mode. For through the process of thinking out the Husserlian approach, he has supposedly gone beyond it in a qualified return to ancient Greek philosophy. From Heidegger's perspective, Husserl's whole effort is finally not decisive—not, as Husserl believes, a breakthrough to a new domain, but only a pale reflection of what, on a deeper level, has already gone before. From Heidegger's angle of vision, Husserl, who was largely unschooled in the history of philosophy, is unaware of the riches of early Greek philosophy and hence, in comparison, a superficial thinker. For the effort to understand the self-manifestation of phenomena through the acts of consciousness, which Husserl believes he has discovered, is basic to Aristotle, to Greek thought, and perhaps even to philosophy itself. Hence, and even though some commentators discern a perfect continuity between them,[33] at the very moment when he seemed closest to Husserlian phenomenology, Heidegger, who was striving to return beyond Husserl and modern philosophy to ancient Greek philosophy, had already gone beyond it.[34]

The sixth and final investigation in *Logical Investigations*, entitled "Elements of a Phenomenological Elucidation of Knowledge," attracted a special following among Husserl's initial readers. He revised the *Logical Investigations* in 1913 at the time *Ideas* was published to bring it in line with his new views. But, since in the meantime his interests had changed, he waited until 1922 to republish the sixth investigation with some changes but without the deep revision he believed necessary.

In the foreword for the republication of the sixth investigation, Husserl indicates that he revised the second section on sensibility and understanding, and that he is especially concerned with the chapter on sensuous and categorial intuition, which, with the arguments of preceding chapters, opens the way for "a phenomenological clarification of *logical* self-evidence."[35] The theory of logical self-evidence is built on the relation between meaning-intention and meaning-fulfillment. This is a restatement of the familiar distinction between concept, or thought, taken as mere meaning, which has no meaning-fulfillment, and corresponding intuition, that is, intuition of a cognitive object.[36]

Husserl develops this theme in his partially revised republication of the sixth investigation, including the chapter on intuition, which attracted Heidegger's attention. It has long been understood that Husserl's theory of intuition is central to his position.[37] In his revised version of the sixth investigation, Husserl takes up the problem of the fulfillment of *categorial meaning-forms*, his terminology for what is traditionally known as the problem of knowledge.[38] He is at pains here to understand the relation between the meaning and the perception. According to Husserl, we see that the parallelism between the meaning-intention of expressions and their corresponding percepts can be restated as a parallelism between meaning-intentions and what he now calls "perceptually founded" acts, or acts that are based in actual perceptions.[39]

Heidegger implicitly rejects this later improvement of the theory as well as Husserl's claim not to relapse into psychologism. He was, as noted, not interested in the partially revised version but in the original version of the sixth investigation in the first edition of the work. According to Heidegger, who reads Husserl against his intentions, the latter version disclosed an essential clue for the problem of the meaning of being, which is Heidegger's "official" concern.

Since this is not a study of the evolution of Husserl's position, we do not need to discuss the differences between the original and the later versions of the sixth investigation. For present purposes, it suffices to recall some main lines of the version of Husserl's view of categorial intuition that interests Heidegger. Husserl begins his initial account in "Sensuous and Categorial Intuitions" with remarks on the problem of the fulfillment of categorial meaning forms (sec. 40), followed by a distinction between sensuous stuff, what is given in sense perception, or phenomenological seeing, and categorial form (sec. 42), before stressing that "the objective correlates of categorial forms are not 'real' [*realen*] moments (sec. 43). He explicitly says that "*being is absolutely imperceptible,*"[40] indicating that it cannot be an object of phenomenological seeing. If this were the case, then Heidegger's investigation of the meaning of being would clearly be compromised. But Heidegger, who does not feel bound by Husserl's intention, immediately reinterprets his view so that being becomes an object of phenomenological seeing.

Heidegger's interest in categorial intuition is clear around the time he was writing *Being and Time* and in later texts. In the lecture series entitled *History of the Concept of Time* (1925), he claims that Husserlian phenomenology is not a solution of or even a new approach to theory of knowledge, as Husserl thinks. The subtitle of the second volume of *Logical Investigations* is *Investigations into the Phenomenology and Theory of Knowledge*. The sixth investigation is, as noted, entitled "Elements of a Phenomenological Elucidation of Knowledge." The simplest interpretation, which is corroborated by passages throughout Husserl's later writings, some of which have been cited above, is that Husserl intends to solve the problem of knowledge on a phenomenological basis. Heidegger simply denies this obvious point in claiming the subtitle was chosen in deference to the tradition, since, as he says, "theory of knowledge is not a theory at all"[41] before citing Husserl's own statement about "reflection which comes to an evident understanding of what thinking and knowing as such are in their generally pure essence."[42]

The Heideggerian and Husserlian approaches to intuition, hence to categorial intuition, are incompatible, fundamentally different, and basically opposed. Heidegger, who turns Husserl's theory of categorial intuition against the intentions of Husserlian phenomenology, asserts that Husserlian intuition is not a form of intuitionism. It is nothing more than a claim about "seeing" something. In his lectures on the *History of the Concept of Time* (1925), where he devotes a lengthy section to categorial intuition, he notes that categorial acts are founded, or based, on sense intuition. This offers what Heidegger calls "a specific *sense of being, being in the sense of being-true*,"[43] since being is itself present in such cases. According to Heidegger, this claim is merely a restatement of the Aristotelian view that the soul can presume nothing and apprehend nothing objective without experience. Heidegger views this approach, which relies on evidence actually given in experience through sense intuition, or phenomenological seeing, as an antidote to the "mythological" view of "an intellect which glues and rigs together the world's matter with its own forms."[44] In effect, he is here siding with Husserl against Kant. For Heidegger, Husserl's "discovery" of categorial intuition for the first time demonstrates the categories. He sees Husserl as finally resolving the old dispute about the problem of universals.[45] In other words, through this insight, phenomenology in fact finally attains the objectivity sought in vain by ancient ontology. Yet Heidegger explicitly denies, as he will shortly do in *Being and Time*, any difference between phenomenology and ontology, since, as he writes, *"scientific ontology is nothing but phenomenology."*[46]

Heidegger's rereading of categorial intuition turns it against Husserl. There are three main differences. First, Husserl's interest is formal, concerned with the form underlying his essentialism, but Heidegger's concern is factual, concerned with the specific clue permitting a phenomenological approach to ontology. Second, for Heidegger, categories are not superimposed on the contents of consciousness but already immanent to them. Third, Heidegger rejects a so-called idealist approach in refuting the view that we in some way make, produce, or construct what we experience and know. We see already in this lecture series, prior to *Being and Time*, what will later motivate Heidegger in that treatise. He is implying here what he later says explicitly: through phenomenological intuition, we grasp directly what is given as it is given, and in phenomenological intuition, being is given as the basis for an analysis of the meaning of being. In a 1973 seminar at Zähringen, he returns to this point in asserting that "in order to be able to unfold the question concerning the meaning of being, being had to be given, so that one could inquire its meaning from it."[47] It is, however, not clear that a phenomenological interpretation of experience suffices to claim that we experience being in the way that Husserl denies but Heidegger affirms.

Heidegger's interest in so-called facticity, hence in a particular form of realism, is a constant theme in his writings virtually from the beginning;[48] witness his early interest in epistemological realism, which he interprets as opposed to idealism. Realism is one of the earliest themes in Heidegger's writings. In his early essay "The Problem of Realism in Modern Philosophy" (1912), he defends the critical realism that he attributes to ancient Greek philosophy and scholasticism against recent idealism, especially Kant's.[49] In this essay, Heidegger rejects Kant's view that the understanding modifies what we perceive, experience, and know. In arguing for critical realism against Kant, he straightforwardly insists that it is not possible to justify the presupposition that categories modify or otherwise change what is given in experience. And he further affirms that it is possible to think without categories.[50] At this point, Heidegger is close to what is often called naive realism. His aim is to establish the familiar view that there is a mind-independent, real, external world, which, under suitable conditions, we can reliably claim to experience and know as it is.

In *Being and Time*, Heidegger takes up this problem in a lengthy section on the existence of the external world (*BT*, 244–56). This is also a theme, as we will see below, in his specific interpretation of Kant, which defends the latter's early representationalist approach to knowledge against the later constructivist approach.[51] The simplistic opposition between realism and idealism, on which Heidegger apparently relies, is often employed to justify rejecting idealism.[52] Yet this distinction, which is routinely rejected even by idealist thinkers such as Fichte,[53] cannot be accepted as a fair characterization of idealism. This raises questions about the relation of Heidegger to Kantian idealism, which may or may not be affected by his consistent stress on realism. Observers are divided on this point,[54] to which I return below. Heidegger's approach here consists in asserting that, from his phenomenological perspective, realism does not present a problem. Hence, it cannot be discussed from the epistemological perspective, but only through his theory of Dasein.

According to Heidegger, it is only possible to ask the question about the meaning of being if there is an understanding of being, which belongs to Dasein. This means that Dasein understands being in general, or the real. Yet the question of the existence of the transcendent world cannot be raised by Dasein, or the subject in the world, without contradicting itself. Kant, who is concerned with this theme, uncritically bases himself on Descartes in failing to clarify "the *phenomenon of the world* as such," which in turn presupposes Heidegger's theory of Dasein (BT, 247; Heidegger's emphases). It follows that in allaying the celebrated scandal of philosophy that fails to prove the existence of the external world, Kant does not reach the level of what Heidegger calls being in the world. For he has not correctly understood the subject, which, like Descartes, he takes as an isolated being. For Heidegger, on the contrary, it is not necessary to prove the existence of the world but to understand it from the perspective of Dasein and hence to overcome the inadequacies of earlier epistemological efforts through a so-called "existential analytic of Dasein," leading to a "well secured phenomenal problematic" (*BT*, 250).

Heidegger's account of what he earlier called critical realism is composed of a plea for his position as conceptually prior as well as an assertion, which he does not justify or even examine, concerning the question of the real that allegedly cannot be asked. Yet with respect to his own inquiry into the problem of the meaning of being, Heidegger's treatment of realism is doubly insufficient. On the one hand, even if he could establish critical realism, he would still need to show that phenomenological seeing "reaches" being. Heidegger neither shows nor even argues for this point. On the other hand, he also does not prove the prior point, namely, that critical realism is correct. He limits himself to asserting that this is not a problem and hence need not be demonstrated, since Dasein is always already in the world. Yet this assertion does not establish the existence of the mind-independent external world, which Kant famously regards as a scandal of philosophy, but Heidegger believes is no problem at all.

At issue is whether in rereading Husserl's categorial intuition, or phenomenological seeing, as a way to encounter being Heidegger has detected a clue to the problem of the meaning of being. This question is complicated by another factor not mentioned so far concerning Heidegger's understanding of his ontological approach. He distinguishes between beings, say tables or chairs, and being in general, which he understands as the being of beings; to take one of many possible examples, he does so in the assertion that "Being is always the Being of an entity" (*BT*, 29). Yet it does not follow that if, as Heidegger thinks, everyone always has a vague, average understanding of being in general (*BT*, 25); or if Dasein essentially asks about or can be understood in terms of asking about being (*BT*, 36–49); or if the theme of Dasein is different from anthropology, psychology, and biology (*BT*, 71–77), then phenomenologically we directly "see" or otherwise detect being in experience.

Heidegger's Ontological Reading of Descartes

Descartes and Kant are both relevant to understanding Heidegger's phenomenological approach to knowledge. Descartes is important in Heidegger's position for two main reasons. On the one hand, Heidegger rejects the related Cartesian (and Kantian) views of the subject as well as the Cartesian view of the object in working out his view of Dasein. On the other hand, Descartes is important for Heidegger's reading of Kant since, like Husserl, he thinks that in many ways the positions of Kant and Descartes are continuous.

Cartesian epistemology derives from the familiar three-substance ontology grounded in the ontological distinction between God (infinite being), human being (thinking being), and the object or world (extended being). For Descartes, the subject, or thinking substance, knows extended substance through a causal theory of perception. The object is implicitly understood to be the cause of ideas, which are understood as effects situated in the mind of the subject. In the Cartesian theory, the solution to the problem of knowledge consists in the familiar reverse inference, disallowed by Plato but rehabilitated in modern philosophy, from subject to object, or mind-independent world. Heidegger's reading of Descartes is perspicacious, but very unsympathetic, even hostile. He formulates an "external" critique of

Descartes from the perspective of Dasein, his own rival view of subjectivity, whose correctness he assumes in rejecting the ontological distinctions subtending Cartesian epistemology. Since he thinks that in many respects Kant uncritically takes over the Cartesian position, in criticizing Descartes he points beyond him to Kant, whose position he further criticizes in detail.

Heidegger's interest in and critique of Descartes begins early,[55] and it continues throughout his career.[56] In *Being and Time*, he studies two of the three Cartesian substances: the Cartesian cogito (*res cogitans*) and the associated concept of the object or world (*res extensa*), but not God, or infinite substance. Since Heidegger's direct remarks on the cogito are very brief, it is worth noting that there are two Cartesian views of subjectivity. One is the widely known, "official," spectator view of the subject, which depicts the subject theoretically as the source of knowledge by appropriate inference from the contents of consciousness to the mind-independent world. The other is the lesser known, less developed, "unofficial," practical view of the subject not as a spectator but as an actor. The former view is stated in a number of places, but the latter is no more than hinted at.

The problem of knowledge in modern times is often posed in terms of different variations on the Cartesian spectator view of subjectivity. According to this view, the subject is situated outside a mind-independent transcendent world to which it relates through thinking, its epistemological capacity. A straight line runs from Descartes, who provided a powerful formulation for this widely influential approach, through a great many intervening thinkers to, say, John McDowell, a recent "Cartesian."[57] Heidegger, however, summarily rejects both the Cartesian view of the subject as a cogito, or thinking being, and the associated view of the object, or world, as extended substance.

His astonishingly brief statement and critique of the Cartesian view of subjectivity is formulated as a series of unsupported assertions. Heidegger, who points out that Descartes takes the subject as a *fundamentum inconcussum* in defining the subject ontologically as a *res cogitans*, that is as an *ens*, or being, claims that Descartes fails to provide an ontology of Dasein (*BT*, 46). Kant, who takes over the Cartesian approach, allegedly reproduces this error. Heidegger opposes the views of subjectivity in both Descartes and Kant on the "external" ground that the only way to get at the problem of Greek ontology is through Dasein, that is, through his own rival view of subjectivity (*BT*, 47). Put in different words, Heidegger is complaining that as concerns the subject Descartes considers thinking (*cogitare*) but completely omits its existence (*sum*) (*BT*, 71–72). In invoking Dasein as his standard, Heidegger seems to calling for the kind of philosophical anthropology of

Dasein that he is often read as laying out in this work, but which he rejects as an incorrect reading of his position. Yet he does not indicate why this omission, or this alleged failure to think the *sum*, is relevant to Descartes' problem.

One can speculate that Heidegger criticizes Descartes for overemphasizing cognition, which, from his rival perspective, is merely a secondary aspect in a full or at least fuller account of finite human being in a social and historical context. Yet if one worked out a corresponding anthropological account of the subject, which Heidegger appears to be pointing to, one would be going down the anthropological path that he later rejects in "The Age of the World Picture" (1938), mentioned above, and in subsequent writings. In this particular essay, Heidegger claims that the cogito belongs to the modern metaphysical period in which truth is the truth of beings, which in turn entails the forgetfulness of being in general. The understanding of truth on a representational model commits this entire age to representationalism with respect to particular things. Though Heidegger's own position is opposed to Kantian and later forms of constructivism and hence is broadly representational,[58] he rejects representationalism in favor of phenomenological seeing from the perspective of Dasein, which is concerned with the wider problem of being.

Yet if this is what Heidegger has in mind, then the difficulty with the Cartesian view of the subject is not that it is depicted in terms of knowledge but that it is not depicted in terms of Heidegger's favorite kind of knowledge, which concerns the question of the meaning of being. In other words, in criticizing the Cartesian concept of the subject Heidegger seems to be rejecting one form of epistemology that he finds in Descartes and throughout the modern tradition in favor of a different kind of epistemology that he finds in Husserl and appropriates for his own concern with being. We see this, for instance, in the way he abandons the correspondence view of truth, used by Descartes and other modern thinkers who rely on a causal theory of perception and hence on a representational approach to cognition, in favor of a phenomenological theory of truth as disclosure. I return to this point below.

In *Being and Time*, after his critique of the Cartesian understanding of the cogito's *sum*, or existence, or the failure to provide an ontology of Dasein, Heidegger provides a long passage on the Cartesian conception of the world as extended being. Heidegger's aim here is to contrast the Cartesian view of the world with his own phenomenological analysis of it.

This account occurs in chapter 3 of part 1, which is entitled "The Worldhood of the World." According to Heidegger, Dasein is always already in the world. He criticizes the Cartesian view of the world in redescribing the world as a phenomenon. According to Heidegger, the phenomenon of the world cannot be reached through depicting beings or interpreting their being (*BT*, 40). In his rival account, *world* designates that in which a particular person, or Dasein, lives as well as what he calls the "ontologico-existential concept of worldhood" (*BT*, 93). His overall point seems to be that what it means to exist as a human being in the world must be understood from the angle of vision of the subject, or Dasein. Hence, if the world is the context of human beings, their *environment*, or what we mean by this term from a phenomenological point of view, depends on its appearance to human individuals.

Heidegger's account includes three parts: A: "Analysis of Environmentality and Worldhood in General"; B: "A Contrast between Our Analysis of Worldhood and Descartes' Interpretation of the World"; and C: "The Aroundness of the Environment and Dasein's Spatiality." In part B, Heidegger turns to Descartes' ontology of the world and systematically discusses the definition of the world as *res extensa* (sec. 19); the foundations of this definition (sec. 20); and, finally, the Cartesian ontology of the "world" (sec. 21).

In the first section, devoted to Descartes' conception of the *res extensa*, Heidegger begins by noting the distinction between the ego cogito, or spirit, and the *res corporea*, or nature. He studies the original Latin text of the *Principles of Philosophy* before coming to the anodyne conclusion that the being of the *res corporea* is its extension, or *substantia*. He next studies the Cartesian understanding of *substantia*. Descartes, since he evades the question of substantiality, fails to raise the question of the meaning of being. On that basis, Heidegger accuses the French philosopher of failing to master the question of being. Yet it is again unclear why Descartes should have taken up this theme, which seems to lie outside his sphere of interests. In the hermeneutical discussion of the Cartesian ontology of the "world," Heidegger claims that Descartes neither provides a phenomenology of the world nor enables us to comprehend it from his grasp of things in the world. We can note in passing that Heidegger's suggestion that Descartes has no redeeming phenomenological value contrasts with Husserl's effort to locate his own phenomenological position as a successor of Descartes' position.

Heidegger contrasts Cartesian and phenomenological approaches. The former is linked to knowing in mathematics and physics, a form of knowing which in Heidegger's opinion fails to get at the real being of things. For instance, the famous account of the wax in the "Second Meditation" fails to pay attention to sensation. Heidegger seems to be complaining that in uncritically taking over ideas from preceding thinkers, Descartes fails to bring Dasein into the ontological investigation. In taking extension as the central characteristic of substance, he is unable to reach the so-called being of substance (*BT*, 133). Heidegger's complaint derives from his reading of Husserl's categorial intuition, which he takes as providing phenomenological access to what is otherwise not available, that is, the being of things in the world. Yet the fact remains that Heidegger's critique of Descartes on the basis of his own theory of being is utterly "external" and hence not obviously relevant to Descartes' project. And one wonders if some of the harshness of Heidegger's treatment of Descartes is not due to his importance for Husserl's rival position.

Heidegger's "Ontological" Reading of Kant

Kant is a touchstone for many of the later phenomenologists, especially Hegel, Husserl, and Heidegger, and to a lesser extent for Merleau-Ponty, each of whom defines his position in whole or in part in reference to the critical philosophy. To a much greater degree than Descartes, Heidegger's reading of Kant is central to his position. With the exception of Heidegger, most (perhaps all) other important observers consider Kant to be a paradigmatic epistemologist, centrally concerned with the problem of knowledge. This approach is flatly rejected by Heidegger, who presents himself as a nonstandard Kantian who takes Kant to be, like himself, an ontological thinker.[59] In implausibly claiming that Kant incompletely anticipates his own phenomenological ontology, Heidegger disputes the post-Kantian German idealist claim to develop the critical philosophy beyond Kant, or the German neo-Kantian claim to return behind post-Kantian German idealism to Kant. In effect, Heidegger is suggesting that post-Kantian German idealism does not carry the critical philosophy further in an "authentic" way and that German neo-Kantianism is not worthy of Kant, whose position lives on in phenomenological ontology, which alone assumes its legitimate mantle.

Heidegger's link to and interest in Kant is unusually strong and highly significant for his phenomenological ontology. He differs from other phenomenologists influenced by Kant in that he is also an important Kant scholar. He lectured and wrote on Kant frequently. It is known that he was writing *Kant and the Problem of Metaphysics* at the same time as he was writing *Being and Time*. The two books emerged nearly simultaneously—*Being and Time* in 1927 and the Kant book in 1929—and presuppose each other. Heidegger's account of the meaning of being in *Being and Time* depends his "ontological" reading of Kant.

Heidegger's interpretation of Kant is extremely original but also controversial. A number of observers think Heidegger's interpretation of Kant is "external" in that it is based on the views he develops in *Being and Time*, which have little or nothing in common with the problems motivating Kant.[60] It is widely thought to distort, even to do "violence" to Kant's views.[61] Kant, of course claims to be concerned with metaphysics. The term *metaphysics* has been employed in different ways since Aristotle: in respect to Aristotle's theory of metaphysics, as expounded in the *Metaphysics* and other writings, and in modern philosophy since Descartes as a synonym for theory of knowledge or epistemology. Heidegger depicts Kant as beginning, but finally failing, to work out a theory of metaphysics understood not as epistemology but as ontology, and in that respect as a predecessor of his own position. In *Being and Time*, he describes Kant as partially anticipating his own position but as failing to go further, even, as it were, "shrinking back" before something that, according to Heidegger, must be brought out to conduct his own inquiry into being (*BT*, 45).

Heidegger's book on Kant raises two series of questions: as concerns Kant interpretation and as concerns his own position. Kant interpretation is a large and interesting domain, which lies beyond the focus of the present discussion. I concentrate here on Heidegger's Kant interpretation as it affects the relation of phenomenology and epistemology.

Heidegger's ontological interpretation is developed in a number of places, including *Being and Time*, *Kant and the Problem of Metaphysics*, a famous debate with Ernst Cassirer in Davos (1929), which has been seen as leading to the split between continental and analytic philosophy,[62] and in various essays and lecture courses.[63] An obvious reason why Kant, who is so important for Heidegger, is not discussed in more than cursory fashion in *Being and Time* is that he is discussed in great detail in *Kant and the Problem of Metaphysics*. In *Being and Time*, Heidegger's cursory treatment of Kant includes the claim that "the positive outcome of Kant's *Critique of Pure Reason* lies in what it has contributed toward [the] working out of what belongs to any Nature whatsoever, not in a 'theory' of knowledge. His transcendental logic is an *a priori* logic for the subject-matter of that area of Being called 'Nature'" (*BT*, 31).

At stake is what Heidegger means by *ontology* and *epistemology*. He may be saying that the critical philosophy, as an a priori theory, is not directed toward knowledge of a single object, say a chair, but at any and all objects of experience and knowledge. If this is what Heidegger means, then the difference between epistemological and ontological interpretations of Kant is mainly a question of emphasis, especially if, as I believe, ontology and epistemology are inseparable. This point is relevant to Heidegger's reading of Kant, who combines both epistemological and ontological dimensions in the critical philosophy. Kant's epistemology is widely understood as based on an analysis of the conditions of the possibility of objects of experience and knowledge, where knowledge depends on the account of the construction of the cognitive objects.

Heidegger, who concedes he is less interested in historical philology than dialogue between thinkers,[64] indicates in the first sentence of *Kant and the Problem of Metaphysics* his intention to read the *Critique of Pure Reason* (arguably disregarding the reason for which it was written) as if it were a treatise in fundamental ontology: "The task of the following investigation is to explicate Kant's *Critique of Pure Reason* as a laying of the foundation of metaphysics in order thus to present the problem of metaphysics as the problem of a fundamental ontology" (*KPM*, 3). In picking out "fundamental ontology," Heidegger is drawing attention away from the traditional interpretation of the critical philosophy as epistemology and toward the suggestion that he and Kant are engaged in the same project. He is also indicating his intention to understand *metaphysics* against the Aristotelian ontological background by simply setting aside the comprehension of this term in modern philosophy as referring to epistemology. Kant very obviously follows Descartes on this point. For instance, Kant's *Prolegomena to Any Future Metaphysics* is widely understood as directed toward preparing the ground of any possible future epistemology as distinguished from a possible future ontology. In adding that "fundamental ontology" means "the ontological analytic of man's finite essence" in order to "prepare the foundation of metaphysics" lodged in human nature, Heidegger points squarely to his own concern to analyze ontology through Dasein (*KPM*, 3–4). Yet it is exceedingly unlikely that Kant intends to base his position on Heidegger's specific conception of Dasein or even, more broadly, on a conception of finite human being.

Heidegger, who never considers Kant's conception of the subject, makes his case in studying five stages for "realizing" ontology, which he relates to the transcendental imagination as its supposed Kantian root. In passing, he explains why Kant never works out a similar reading of the transcendental imagination, from which he allegedly "recoiled," through a failure to work out a theory of Dasein (*KPM*, 167). According to Heidegger, there is a difference between a proof that man is a finite being, and a determination of this finitude (*KPM*, 226). The latter requires determining its being, which in turn depends on being in general (*KPM*, 230). The relation of the comprehension of being and the Dasein in man lies in the fact that we always have a preconceptual view of being in general. Indeed, the finitude of Dasein is deeper than man (*KPM*, 237). Though this is not an anthropology, which cannot found metaphysics (*KPM*, 239), Heidegger believes that only the structure of the being of Dasein makes possible the idea of a fundamental ontology (*KPM*, 240). He brings his argument to a close in asserting that fundamental ontology and the critical philosophy converge around the insight that being must be understood as relative to time (*KPM*, 252).

The differences between the two conceptions of the subject are striking. Kant's concern with the conditions of experience and knowledge of objects is at most tangentially related to the problem of the meaning of being. The two projects further diverge concerning basically different views of objects, which for Kant is the *terminus ad quem* of objective knowledge and for Heidegger the *terminus a quo* of the problem of the meaning of being. Another way to put the point is to say that Kant is concerned with knowledge of beings and Heidegger is interested in knowledge of the being of beings.

Heidegger, like Kant, is interested in man, or what man is, what is now called human being, which is for Kant the most interesting of all questions. Yet the two theories of the subject, which agree in disclaiming any effort at philosophical anthropology, differ sharply. The Heideggerian theory of Dasein is about man, or finite human being, or about something in man that allegedly refers beyond man to being in general. Through his theory of Dasein he specifies that fundamental ontology consists in certain specific assumptions about man. In the critical philosophy, Kant distinguishes between his own conception of the subject and finite human being. The Kantian theory of the subject concerns the conditions of the general possibility of knowledge through the description of the synthetic unity of apperception, the highest principle of transcendental philosophy.[65] The transcendental unity of apperception is a specific epistemological function lodged in the framework of Kant's transcendental epistemological analysis. Since he rejects any "reduction" of the logical conditions of knowledge to their psychological conditions, his epistemological conception of the subject is unrelated to finite human being.

Heidegger and the History of Ontology

Heidegger's interest in the problem of the meaning of being concerns the interpretation of specific historical phenomena. *Being and Time* includes an important section entitled "The Task of Destroying the History of Ontology" (sec. 6). His effort to return to the problem of the meaning of being as it was allegedly authentically raised in early Greek philosophy by going back behind the tradition to which it led raises deep questions about interpretation that I address here with respect to the prior history of the tradition and below in remarks on interpretation in general.

It is sobering to realize, since so much in philosophy depends on interpreting written texts—those of our contemporaries as well as those written by philosophers who lived long ago—that, after some two and a half thousand years of debate in the Western tradition, there is still no generally accepted view about how to read and to appropriate philosophical writings. We can distinguish rival claims about textual interpretation as subjective or objective, according to whether it is believed that we can get it right, as it were, about what the text in fact says. Those who think that textual interpretation is subjective hold that there is no hope of making an objective claim, since meanings are not discovered, uncovered, or revealed in the text but "imported" into it; that interpretation and the interpretive disciplines do not yield knowledge, or at least not rigorous knowledge; that there is no such thing as valid interpretation, since all interpretations are "valid"; and that there is no way to bring the open-ended interpretive debate to an end.[66] On the contrary, those who think interpretation is objective believe that objective claims for interpretation can be and are routinely made; that meanings are discovered, uncovered, or revealed in the text but not "imported" into it; that under proper conditions interpretation and the interpretive disciplines do yield (rigorous) knowledge; that there are valid (and invalid) interpretations; and that the interpretive debate can be and in practice normally is brought to an end.[67]

The view that interpretation yields or can yield knowledge beyond the endless interpretive debate is widely held in the cognitive disciplines, including the sciences, and even in aesthetics. This issue cuts across the doctrinal boundaries separating, for instance, continental and analytic philosophers. Within analytic philosophy, this can be illustrated by the difference between W. V. O. Quine and Donald Davidson. Quine's view of the indeterminacy of translation yields the inference that interpretation is always indeterminate, hence never determinate.[68] It is opposed by Davidson's idea that through a process of triangulation we come ever closer to what is really there.[69]

Those who hold that interpretation yields (rigorous) knowledge often favor strong forms of realism. The term *realism* is used in many different ways. By *metaphysical realism* I mean the view, widespread in the modern discussion and rooted in early Greek philosophy, that there is a mind-independent external world that, under appropriate conditions, can be known as it is.[70] Steven Weinberg, for instance, thinks that unless science uncovers the structure of the real world, it is not worth doing.[71] Similarly,

Monroe Beardsley holds that the aesthetic features of an artwork are independent of our perception of them.[72]

Heidegger defends a version of metaphysical realism with regard to textual interpretation, which separates him from his disciples Jacques Derrida and Hans-Georg Gadamer. Derrida holds the extreme antisemantic view that, since any reference can always be "deconstructed," definite reference is never possible. Gadamer, who is more moderate, believes that interpretation is intrinsically perspectival and hence depends on the views that prevail at a given time and place, or in the historical moment. We read texts differently at different times, but can never discover what is there beyond interpretation. In Heidegger's extreme view, under appropriate conditions we can and indeed must go beyond whatever view is in the air in a given historical moment to determine meanings in a text that do not depend on what different readers say about it.

According to the early Heidegger, we return behind the later Western philosophical tradition to grasp the problem of the meaning of being as it was originally raised in ancient Greek philosophy. Yet it is not clear that we can reliably claim to grasp meanings that are in the text that are independent of interpretation, nor that we can go back "behind" the interpretive tradition, nor even that we can recover problems, doctrines, theories, or ideas as they were supposedly originally raised at some earlier time.

From the perspective of text interpretation, Heidegger is a remarkable philosophical figure. He stands out, even among German philosophers, through his deep grasp of selected portions of the Western philosophical tradition and through his complicated interweaving of systematic and historical themes in his writings. Few philosophers demonstrate as wide and as deep a grasp of the philosophical tradition as Heidegger, and even fewer are as arbitrary in proposing textual interpretations. In Germany during the period in which he was active, others with a similarly detailed grasp of the philosophical tradition might be Cassirer and Gadamer. Yet more than anyone since Hegel, it would seem that Heidegger makes his philosophical theories depend on his reading of the history of the philosophical tradition. Hence, much is at stake in his readings of philosophical problems and figures as concerns his own ideas and theories.

The very short passage preceding the introduction to *Being and Time* begins with a citation from a speech by the Eleatic stranger in the *Sophist*. The Eleatic stranger, who appears in the dialogue, is a pupil and critic of Parmenides as well as a pupil of Zeno. The passage Heidegger cites occurs in the midst of detailed criticism of Eleatic doctrine,[73] where the theme of nonbeing is examined. The Eleatic stranger suggests that the general question of specifying the meaning of *nonbeing* requires us to make sense of the terms we use, including the conceptually prior question of the meaning of being.[74] He then indicates problems in the use of the term in pointing to the difficulty of the question.

Heidegger begins the discussion by citing a passage where the stranger states that no one knows precisely what *being* signifies,[75] before continuing on to direct criticism of Parmenides. Heidegger takes this passage as the "official" excuse for *Being and Time* in citing Plato's Greek before providing a German "translation," or paraphrase—the difference, which is not always clear, is compounded in translations of Heidegger's own "translation"—before observing that we are no closer to an answer now. This remark allows Heidegger, some two and a half millennia later, to again raise the question of the meaning of being.

In citing this passage, Heidegger is not interested in grasping any particular Platonic doctrine nor in Plato's general theories, but in identifying the problem of the meaning of being that, he contends, runs as a leading thread throughout early Greek philosophy and the entire later Western philosophical tradition. According to Heidegger, this problem has persisted unchanged over many centuries, has still not yet been adequately studied, and in the meantime has receded into oblivion, where it has been forgotten. Heidegger believes that over the centuries this problem has engaged some of the most important philosophical minds, that the prevailing view from Plato and Aristotle to Hegel has remained the same, and that the same problem that stimulated Plato and Aristotle remains even today unchanged as the main problem of Western philosophy. Heidegger, who takes it as a given that this problem concerns a struggle among giants, implicitly suggests that in taking it up he now takes his place as a true philosophical giant.

Philosophy is a historical discipline, which can never be isolated from the history of philosophy. Heidegger insists on so-called authentic historicity (*Geschichtlichkeit*). Yet this way of raising the question appears to be insensitive to the historical nature of the philosophical tradition. He seems to be suggesting that views come and go, but the problem that interests him, which is intrinsically timeless, has remained the same beyond the meanders of the philosophical debate over millennia. Yet if this problem, indeed any problem, depends on the positions, theories, debates, or other contexts in which they arise, then it is implausible to suggest that it remains unchanged or could be taken up as it originally arose. It would, for instance, be incorrect to believe that the problem of knowledge in Kant is the "same" as in Descartes. Kant was aware of, influenced by, and reacted against the views of Descartes. For Descartes, to know is to know the mind-independent external world as it is. But the author of the critical philosophy contends that we cannot claim to know cognitive objects that we do not in some manner "construct." It follows that problems do not remain stable but change over time. Heidegger later makes an analogous point in pointing to the difference between *energeia* in Greek and *actus* in Latin to support a claim for the utter difference between earlier and later Western philosophy.[76] It is further unclear that the distinction Heidegger makes between beings and being as such is ever made in ancient Greek texts in the same or in an analogous way. It as if Heidegger, who is a twentieth-century German thinker and not an ancient Greek, were reading his modern concern into texts clearly written for other purposes. It is finally even unclear that the Greek term *to be* (*einai*) functions in the same way the German word *to be* (*sein*) or its close relatives does in German or in other modern European languages.[77]

This point can be generalized. Heidegger correctly calls attention to the need to think historically, or against the background of the historical tradition. But, perhaps because of his negative treatment of tradition as a central obstacle in getting clear about the problems in the texts, he does not seem to be sensitive to it in his interpretive practice. His treatment of the problem of being as a single problem from ancient Greek philosophy to Hegel presupposes that there is one and only one problem, not more than one. This way of raising the question presupposes that any differences between, say, Hegel, Plato, and Aristotle are finally not significant. Perhaps for that reason, here and elsewhere in his early writings, for instance, in his lectures on Plato's *Sophist* during the winter semester of 1924–25,[78] Heidegger typically runs Plato and Aristotle together as if they were concerned with precisely the same themes or questions, as if there were no important differences between them, as if there were in fact a single, identifiable ancient Greek approach to the problem of being. Heidegger further implausibly claims in *Being and Time* that Hegel has the same basic view of time as Plato and Aristotle (*BT*, 480–86). Yet, if for no other reason, in virtue of his historical perspective Hegel obviously differs from the great Greek philosophers, who further differ among themselves.

Above I suggested that Heidegger employs a recognizably realist approach to reading the texts of the history of philosophy. Heidegger's realism about texts derives from his realist view of interpretation. This view is illustrated in his famous (Nietzschean) example of the hammer. According to Heidegger, we understand things we encounter or come in contact with in terms of their possible uses, uses that they objectively possess and that can be uncovered. In understanding, we do not "import" a specific use but rather find, uncover, or discover it as already there. For instance, we do not attribute the property of being useful for hammering to the hammer, which only functions in that way because it objectively possesses that particular property. "The hammering itself uncovers the specific 'manipulability' of the hammer. The kind of Being which equipment possesses—in which it manifests itself in its own right—we call *'readiness-to-hand'"* (BT, 98; his emphasis).

I take Heidegger to be claiming in this and in similar passages that the hammer in fact "contains" or possesses a specific use, a use that is not projected onto it and that can only be uncovered because it is objectively possessed. Hammers are for hammering, and nothing else (e.g., the heel of a shoe) will do. Yet it seems fairly obvious that any claim about a hammer and the uses to which it can be put depends on the fact that Heidegger contingently happened to live in a society in which there were such things as hammers. In a society in which there were no hammers, it seems unlikely that one could uncover this single, allegedly correct usage when confronted with such an object. It further seems improbable that the ordinary or even the unusual observer, one without contact with a society in which hammers were a usual or even an unusual occurrence, would accept the claim that hammers are for hammering and nothing else, for instance, to use as doorstops, paperweights, or for other purposes.

Husserlian reduction is a methodological device to focus in principle on what is directly given as it is given. In bracketing existence, Husserl brackets, or puts out of play, any claims about the reality of what is given. As a direct result of dropping Husserlian reduction, there is for Heidegger no difference between essentialism and realism. Heideggerian essentialism is a form of the traditional epistemological claim that to know requires a grasp of the mind-independent real as it is, but without the justification for this claim, a justification that Husserl derives from the phenomenological reduction.

Heidegger deploys his essentialist realism in claiming to grasp the intrinsic meaning of particular objects, like hammers, in analyzing the average structures of Dasein, and in reading philosophical texts. The chief instance of Heidegger's textual interpretation is his sustained effort in *Being and Time* and in many later writings to analyze the problem of the meaning of being. He contends that the problem was correctly posed, but incorrectly analyzed, in ancient Greek philosophy and in the entire later Western philosophical tradition. According to Heidegger, a necessary precondition to making progress with the problem is to recover it as it was originally and supposedly authentically raised. In this way, Heidegger is proposing to participate as at least an equal member in what he, following Plato, ironically also describes as the *gigantomachia peri tes ousias* (BT, 2).

This description is ironic since, in virtue of his distinction between beings and being as such, for Heidegger the problem of the meaning of being is hopelessly miscast as a question about things. The Greeks were not concerned with being as such as Heidegger understands it, but with beings, or at most the unity of a being. Thus, in the *Metaphysics*, when Aristotle remarks that no one has spoken about what it means to be something or about what constitutes the being of things,[79] and that there is a science which concerns only being as such,[80] and when he surveys four main meanings of *being*,[81] he has in mind beings, not being in general. Heidegger's professed aim is to go back behind the philosophical tradition to take up the problem as it was originally posed in ancient Greek philosophy. But we must ask, What sense can we make of the idea that problems can be recovered as they were originally raised? And even if this were possible, why is the original way authentic, whereas other, later ways of raising the problem are inauthentic? Would it make sense to claim to read Hamlet in the way that Shakespeare intended it? Is a way of reading Hamlet that could be reliably attributed to Shakespeare the only authentic way to read this play? And we must further ask, Can we approach the history of philosophy in a way that reveals what is really there as opposed to what appears to be there to different observers in different ways in different times and places?

Heidegger's demonstration of his claim comports successive accounts of Dasein, of destroying the history of ontology, and of the phenomenological method of investigation. The excuse for studying Dasein, or his situated conception of the subject, is that it is the "official" clue to the question of the meaning of being. Heidegger claims that Dasein must be investigated to begin with, since it possesses a pre-ontological understanding of being (*BT*, 24–28). In section 5, the analytic of Dasein, he asserts that we need to bring out the being of Dasein in a preparatory fashion in its average everydayness in order to work out the meaning of being. He further claims that time is the horizon to understanding being as well as Dasein that understands being (*BT*, 39).

It is not clear how this general assertion about implicit knowledge of being could be demonstrated. Heidegger's complex philosophical distinction between beings and being as such is certainly wholly unknown to the average person. It scarcely follows that ordinary people use the term to allude, in even the most extended sense, to being as Heidegger understands it, nor that the analysis of the ordinary use of language can bring us closer to the goal of grasping being in general. In section 6, "The Task of Destroying the History of Ontology," he asserts that Dasein is its past, which may be hidden to it, but which can also be discovered and studied (*BT*, 41). The relation to the past, which can be either positive or negative, is negative when what the past transmits is concealed, hence inaccessible (*BT*, 43). If this occurs, "Dasein no longer understands the most elementary conditions which would alone enable it to go back to the past in a positive manner and make it productively its own" (*BT*, 43). Heidegger illustrates his claim through key references to Descartes, Kant, and the general problem of recovering the philosophical tradition.

His remarks on Descartes and Kant are intended to illustrate the more general claim that theories, concepts, problems, and ideas can be seamlessly later recovered as they were when they initially came into the discussion. In effect, this is to take the later discussion as a kind of false appearance, even as a curtain that can be withdrawn to reveal the truth about what is incorrectly depicted. If this is correct, then the problem of recovering the past, for instance the original formulation of a philosophical concept, problem, or theory, consists in penetrating behind a false appearance—what for Marxism is a merely ideological representation—to the essence, or to what really is.

Heidegger says that the problem of the meaning of being was inadequately formulated and later forgotten in pointing to Descartes and to Kant. According to Heidegger, Descartes conflates the problem with the world in failing to question the being of the cogito, or subject (*BT*, 44), and Kant, who was influenced by Descartes, lacks an ontological analysis of the subject (*BT*, 45). These specific interpretations of Descartes and Kant raise highly specialized issues that cannot be pursued here. Suffice it to say that Heidegger is right to note that Kant was influenced by Descartes. Yet Heidegger's reading of the Cartesian cogito both here and in later writings, including the famous 1938 lecture, "The Age of the World Picture," which is overly reductive; insensitive to the full view of the subject as both passive and active, spectator and actor; and arguably misrepresents his French predecessor's view.

For present purposes, the more important issue is not whether Heidegger provides a plausible reading of Descartes, Kant, or any other figure, but whether, in seeking to understand the question of being, he can "loosen up its history," so to speak, in order to "arrive at those primordial experiences in which we achieved our first ways of determining the nature of Being" (*BT*, 44). Ancient Greek ontology is oriented toward the world or nature in the sense of presence, which points toward the grammatical present (*BT*, 47). According to Heidegger, the high point in the ancient Greek study of ontology is reached in Aristotle, who, in abandoning Plato's dialectic, provides the first detailed interpretation of the temporal structure of being (*BT*, 48), which we can only understand after "destroying" the ontological tradition (*BT*, 49).

Heidegger's account here passes rapidly over three ideas that he simply runs together: the specific interpretation of particular theories, for instance, those of Descartes or Kant; then the so-called destruction of the history of ontology, which is carried out through criticizing particular theories; and, finally, the problem of returning to allegedly primordial experiences through such criticism or in other ways. In one sense, it looks very much as if Heidegger intends to disqualify later views of being in order to call attention to the merits of Aristotle's view. It is plausible that numerous ideas in the tradition, which did not earlier receive the attention they deserved, would look better if obvious alternatives were criticized. Yet it does not follow that in criticizing selected positions (in order to exhibit the merits of a prior alternative) we can ever return to what Heidegger, more than two thousand years later, takes to be "primordial experiences" in ancient Greek philosophy.

Heidegger's view of destroying the ontological tradition picks out two themes that can be stated as questions: How should we go about interpreting philosophical texts? How, as a result, can we recover the tradition, where *recover* means to uncover the tradition as it originally was before it was later covered up through the ensuing discussion? These themes are related, since it is only through textual interpretation, if at all, that we can "recover" the tradition. Heidegger offers two views of interpretation as yielding phenomenological truth.

How do we know when we know? Heidegger makes everything depend on the subject and the object: on the subject since, he claims, perhaps following Kant's view of the transcendental unity of apperception, that there is only truth when there is a subject; and on the object, since a claim for truth does not depend on a judgment about correspondence, but on the fact that the object is discovered as it is. But how does the subject know when it knows the object? Heidegger's way of responding only postpones but does not resolve the question of error, which arises in this account in the injunction to accept only authentic disclosure that avoids, for instance, such obvious pitfalls as semblance and disguise, in brief, taking mere appearance for what is.

Heidegger needs to have a reliable way, other than a mere injunction, to avoid conflating gold with fool's gold. He contends that since the time of ancient Greek philosophy, commentators have been led astray in suggesting there is an original, better, in fact correct view consisting in the way the problem was originally posed. Perhaps. Yet how, on the basis of Heidegger's theories of interpretation, can we know this if there is no way to distinguish between what appears to be the case and what is the case, between an apparently correct interpretation of a text and a correct interpretation, between still another reading and Heidegger's?

Heidegger has no way to justify his effort to provide the correct reading of the problem of the meaning of being by going back behind the tradition. He has no way to justify the very idea of getting it right about a particular text, idea, theory, or doctrine in independence of the discussion of it. His enthusiastic claim for the relative virtues of Aristotle's theory of time over rival views cannot be adjudicated through the supposed destruction of the history of ontology. It can only be adjudicated through the effort to show that this particular view, or this reading of a particular view, is more promising than the available alternatives. But Heidegger precisely wants to avoid opening a discussion of the issue on its merits, which is likely to lead to an endless debate. Yet there is no way to bring the debate to an end by allegedly grasping the correct, or authentic interpretation of Aristotle's view of time, of the problem of the meaning of being as it was originally raised, or of any particular text. In a word, there is no way to make sense of the very idea of authenticity as concerns interpretation.

We always approach texts through conceptual frameworks or categorial schemes, rooted in the forms of life or historical moments that we contingently happen to inhabit, and on whose basis we work out views about texts that we later test and develop through further textual study. Interpretation is an ongoing process, which can never be brought to an end, which can hence never claim to arrive at interpretive bedrock, the so-called primal experiences of ancient Greek philosophy. In fact, even that can only be a construction of what we, from the vantage point of our own particular historical moment, believe ancient Greek philosophy to be as the result of an interpretive process lasting centuries. It makes eminent good sense to intend to go behind later distortions to uncover or discover the text in its pristine newness unsullied by later misreadings or other accretions. But even this idea is no more than a rational construction, a regulative ideal that can never be constitutive. If, as Heidegger suggests through his conception of Dasein, we comprehend the subject as rooted in the surrounding social context, we understand that the very idea of somehow going back behind the historical tradition is merely another form of the self-delusion that knowledge means surpassing what we ourselves construct through the desirable but impossible task of finally knowing mind-independent reality as it really is.

Heideggerian Phenomenology; or, To the Things Themselves

Heidegger, who shares Husserl's concern to go to things themselves (*BT*, 50), says the maxim of "phenomenology" can be formulated as "To the things themselves!" (*BT*, 50, 58). Yet he comprehends *phenomenology* in a basically different way from Husserl. One difference concerns the conception of intentionality, which Husserl adapted from Brentano. Husserl initially held that the world could be described and later, after the reduction, that it could at least be intended, or meant. Heidegger transforms intentionality, which for Husserl is an attitude or way of being toward objects, into a way of being toward the world. It is sometimes claimed that Heidegger generalizes Husserlian intentionality from consciousness to Dasein's entire being in the world.[82]

Heidegger understands phenomenology primarily as a methodological conception about things themselves (*die Sachen selbst*) in order to highlight the being of beings. Though he is unusually well informed about the history of philosophy, he ignores the prior history of phenomenology, which, he suggests, is not significant for understanding it. Instead he pursues an etymological approach in noting that the term is composed of *phenomenon* and *logos*. The remainder of the section is subdivided into accounts of (A) the concept of the phenomenon, (B) the concept of the logos, and (C) the preliminary conception of phenomenology. Heidegger does not pause to discuss or otherwise legitimate this strategy. It is, hence, useful to recall that phenomenology has an interesting pre-Husserlian history that, if Heidegger is correct, includes Aristotle. Yet everything happens as if ignoring modern practice in favor of grasping the way terms were allegedly used long ago in ancient Greece is sufficient to orient us in contemporary phenomenology.

Heidegger's etymological reconstructions, which are scattered throughout his writings, are crucial here. Yet they are suspect for two reasons. First, since it is not possible to determine with certainty what words actually signified in ancient Greece, Heidegger can offer nothing more than interpretations, whose exact value cannot be determined. Second, it appears that, as he concedes in his dialogues with important thinkers, Heidegger deliberately "forces" the interpretation to make the points he has in mind on the grounds that this is useful.[83]

Heidegger's approach to *phenomenology* is intended to cut through the conceptual thicket posed by such terms as *phenomenon, semblance, appearance,* and so on. He presupposes two historical references, which are not named but on which he relies: Kant's general understanding of the distinction between phenomena and noumena,[84] and Hegel's specific conception of phenomena. Since for Kant in an appearance something appears, there is a distinction between the appearance and what it refers to. But for Hegel phenomena do not refer, or at least do not refer to the mind-independent world. These distinctions reappear in Heidegger's interpretation of *phainomenon*, the Greek predecessor of *phenomenon*, as distinguished from semblance, or false appearance, and as further distinguished from (true) appearance (*Erscheinung*). Through an unclear argument, Heidegger arrives at the Kantian view that in appearing something shows itself, or announces itself. This leads to the view that "phenomena are *never* appearances . . . though every appearance is dependent on phenomena" (*BT*, 53; his emphasis). I take this to be a restatement of Kant's point that all appearances are phenomena, but only some phenomena are appearances. The distinction lies in referring to something—in Heidegger's terminology, to something that shows itself. This view is amplified in Hegel's conception of phenomena as self-developing in consciousness. Heidegger supports this Hegelian reading in distinguishing between *appearance*, which refers to an entity, and *phenomenon* as self-showing.

Heidegger, of course, favors a phenomenological approach and hence phenomena over appearances, or even, on this crucial point, Hegel over Kant. His unannounced turn to a Hegelian approach derives from his conception of phenomenology. He turns away from Kant in accepting the Husserlian view that we can go no further than what is directly given. It follows that he cannot accept an approach based on the supposed appearance of mind-independent reality, which Kant denotes as things in themselves. This is one of the ways in which he, like Husserl, understands the Husserlian slogan "To the things themselves!" Yet the extent of his Husserlian allegiance is very limited, hence easy to overestimate. In eschewing the phenomenological reduction, thus in cutting the link to transcendental phenomenology, he obviously turns away from Husserl. In turning away from Kant and Husserl, Heidegger partly turns toward Hegel in understanding phenomena in independence of appearances as, to use his term, *self-showing*. By dint of a series of allusions to the various forms of *logos*, Heidegger suggests that the primary function of *logos* is in apophantical discourse (*BT*, 58), or linguistic propositions, which can be true or false.

In calling attention to the cognitive function of speech, Heidegger also parts company with Hegel. The latter attacks the capacity of language, which is intrinsically universal or general (*allgemein*), as unsuited to identify particulars.[85] Despite his focus on being in general, Heidegger contends, though without argument, that, in virtue of the supposed meaning of the relevant terms in ancient Greek philosophy, language functions to reveal individual things. The problem with this inference is twofold. On the one hand, there is no reason to believe that because an earlier thinker held one or another view, it is therefore true. At best this is an unacceptable argument from authority, in this case the authority of ancient Greek thinkers over the moderns, who have supposedly lost their way as the later tradition diverged from its earlier and allegedly "authentic" inspiration. On the other hand, Heidegger fails to meet or even to consider Hegel's objections, considered above, to claims to grasp particulars through language.

Heidegger, who does not stop for such considerations, sketches his preliminary conception of phenomenology in translating the relevant terms into Greek. He contends that since *legein* means *apophainesthai*, then *phenomenology* or *legein ta phainomena* means "to let that which shows itself be seen from itself in the very way in which it shows itself from itself" (*BT*, 58). This provides "official" status to his reading of *phenomenology*. In suggesting that this is the meaning of the Husserlian slogan, "To the things themselves!" he reinterprets Husserl's position in a way closer to its earlier, pre-reduction avatar than to its later, post-reduction formulation. Certainly after he introduced the reduction, Husserl could not accept any claim to approach the being of beings through particular entities, since the aim of the reduction is to bracket their existence.

Though Heidegger at least partly follows Husserl in claiming that, as a science of phenomena, phenomenology grasps its objects directly, it needs to be seen what this amounts to. Unlike Husserl, Heidegger is not concerned with beings but with being in general. Lacking, however, is an account of the transition from beings to being in general. In this crucial respect, Heidegger is not helpful, and his account remains merely prolegomenal. He points to situations in which something remains hidden, or is covered up, or shows itself in disguise (*BT*, 59). These different situations are arguably plausible about beings but not about being in general without an account that he never supplies and that remains an unredeemed promissory note. Heidegger's claim that phenomenology is possible only as ontology must be supported to be credible (*BT*, 60). Heidegger usefully distinguishes various ways in which phenomena can be covered up, so to speak. They might, for instance, be undiscovered or buried either accidentally or deliberately (*BT*, 60–61). This general approach, which influenced Habermas's effort to reconstruct historical materialism,[86] does not explain how we can "rise" from the phenomenology of beings to being in general.

At this point, there seems to be a break in the argument. Heidegger, who has just introduced the conception of interpretation, turns now to *being*, which he describes as *"transcendens pure and simple"* (*BT*, 62; his emphasis).

His view of being in general as transcendent is apparently based on Kant's conception, which Husserl applies to objects, or beings, and Heidegger apparently extends to being in general.

Heidegger further says that phenomenological truth, which he defines as the disclosure of being in general, is *veritas transcendentalis* (*BT*, 62). Yet he only muddies the conceptual waters in talking about transcendental truth. He runs together the view that description of any kind is always and necessarily interpretive, and the very different view that claims to know are transcendental. Since Kant, transcendental claims are usually understood as universal and necessary, unrevisable, beyond debate, hence beyond interpretation. In short, a transcendental claim is not interpretive, and an interpretive claim is never transcendental. Applied to the problem of the meaning of being, this suggests that we could recover the original problem by returning behind the succeeding discussion, that is, behind the ensuing tradition. Heidegger's claim that phenomenological truth discloses transcendent being seems to mean that every being also points beyond itself to transcendent being. If, in knowing any particular thing, one also knows the being of beings, or being in general, then knowing any particular thing also provides access to transcendent being. It is difficult to grasp what Heidegger could be affirming here. His claim sounds almost Platonic, as if each individual thing, which can be known as it is, also shed light on being in general, in which it "participates." Yet it does not follow that in knowing any particular thing, one therefore knows the proper response to the problem of the meaning of being as it was supposedly originally posed.

This claim calls for four remarks. First, it is unclear from a Husserlian perspective how one could claim to know a transcendent object. If it is transcendent, it is not immanent, not given in intuition, and hence, for Husserl at least, uncognizable. In other words, in Husserl's position we can intend but not cognize transcendent objects. And it is further unclear how in Heidegger's position this is possible. Second, unlike beings, which are "visible" and hence can be given in intuition, being in general is neither "visible" nor in any other way a possible object of intuition. Unlike a Husserlian phenomenology of the visible, Heidegger features a phenomenology of the invisible. He understands *phenomenology* as the interpretation of what shows itself. Beings show themselves in human experience, but it is at least arguable that being in general does not show itself. Hence, it is difficult to understand how what clearly looks like a phenomenology of the invisible is possible. Third, since the being of entities cannot be directly given nor evaluated with respect to evidence, Heidegger can insist when it suits him that any particular instance of phenomenological seeing is incomplete.

Certainly, one would not want to claim that each and every experience has been exhaustively "mined," that nothing further could possibly be learned by further experience of the same object. Yet Heidegger's suggestion would be more interesting if there were a way of distinguishing between full and incomplete forms of phenomenological seeing. Fourth, if *transcendental* is taken in a Kantian sense as unrevisable, then it is incompatible with interpretation. Since interpretation is an intrinsically endless process, it is inconsistent to suggest that it ends in transcendental truth.

At the close of this section, Heidegger respectfully says that Husserl, who discovered phenomenology, made his own work possible. Yet in also suggesting that possibility is higher than actuality, Heidegger points beyond Husserl to his own phenomenological approach, which is clearly inspired by but basically different in numerous ways from Husserl's phenomenology. Though Heidegger is especially interested in Husserl's initial form of phenomenology, it would be erroneous to think that even here he more than distantly follows Husserl. For the latter is always and only concerned to know beings, but Heidegger, on the contrary, is at least "officially" always and only concerned to know being in general.

Interpretation and the Hermeneutical Circle

Heidegger, who devotes an important section to interpretation, proposes a theory of interpretation with epistemological intent. His theory of interpretation undermines the Husserlian view that knowledge is based on immediate intuition of the given. In its place, Heidegger suggests that knowledge is based on immediate intuition plus its interpretation. Unlike Husserl, Heidegger does not employ a specifiable method to justify interpretive claims. He tells us how he understands interpretation, but not how to engage in interpretation in a way that must, or is even likely to, produce reliable results, for instance, what can be regarded as a "correct" interpretation in a specific situation.

His normative view of phenomenology as interpretive is insufficient for his announced "official" goal of recovering the problem of the meaning of being as originally raised. Interpretation can promote one reading among others in weighing the advantages or disadvantages of a particular reading of one or more texts. One might, for instance, come to be convinced that Heidegger's innovative concept of truth as disclosure enables us to grasp a basic insight about truth in ancient Greek philosophy. In that case, one could say that Heidegger's insight is not only seminal for his own position but also for understanding ancient Greek philosophy, which is "transformed" when viewed from this new perspective. But, for Heidegger's purposes, that would be insufficient, since no interpretation of the ancient tradition that anyone can put forward can ever guarantee that we have finally reached the so-called primordial experience in which the problem that interests Heidegger was raised, or originally raised, or even authentically raised in ancient Greece.

In a detailed, but unusually complex account, complex even by elastic Heideggerian standards, provided in "Understanding and Interpretation" (sec. 32), he usefully notes that interpretation always arises on the basis of a prior understanding (*BT*, 188). It follows that there is not and cannot be anything like a "pure" interpretive given, say in the Husserlian sense in which the subject is wholly passive in grasping the given as it is given. Variations on the theme that there is no unadulterated, pure given are frequently urged in the debate, for instance, in Neurath's objection to Carnap's idea of (pure) protocols,[87] in Sellars's critique of the so-called myth of the given,[88] and in Davidson's rejection of the empiricist distinction between form and content.[89] In different ways, the denial of the very idea of pure givenness goes back at least to Kant's conviction that interpretation is always based on a prior understanding, which inevitably shapes the interpretive process. This amounts to saying that interpretation, which is never "innocent," always depends on the interpreter.

Heidegger works out the consequences of his view of the link of interpretation to a prior understanding in making theory depend on practice. Interpretation, which depends in the first instance on a use to which something might be "put," features a purpose, an "in order to," in which "something [is interpreted] as something" (*BT*, 189). This approach yields the "as" that belongs to the understanding of what is to be interpreted, as in, for instance, Heidegger's example of a hammer as a tool for hammering, which we encounter in this way.

There appear to be two difficulties in this view. It could be objected that "neutral" interpretation is impossible because the subject always interprets things in terms of their possible use. It could also be objected that interpretation is merely arbitrary, hence without constraints. In other words, in Heidegger's approach objectivity "dissolves" in subjectivity. For there is no way of reaching objectivity in interpretation if anything can be interpreted as any other thing. So a hammer can be interpreted as a hammer in the sense in which this term is ordinarily used, but a handy stone can also serve the same purpose and hence be interpreted similarly.

Heidegger concedes the first but not the second point. "Neutral" interpretation is possible if and only if it is possible to abstract from the implication of the interpreter as a finite human being in the surrounding world. Yet Heidegger contests any implication that for this reason the putative objectivity of interpretation is compromised. According to Heidegger, we do not freely attach or otherwise link a particular significance to a particular object without constraint, or "throw a 'signification' over some naked thing" devoid of it; on the contrary, each thing is already in relation to other things, or in a relation that is identified, or "laid out by the interpretation" (*BT*, 190–91). In other words, interpretation is not free-floating, or unconstrained, since it is always constrained by context.

Heidegger's suggestion that interpretation requires reference to context, or the surroundings, however interpreted, raises numerous further difficulties. Like Kant, who believes it is possible to designate a single, correct interpretation of the critical philosophy, Heidegger seems to think that there is one and only one correct interpretation, which he provides in his study of Kant. Further, like Kant, Heidegger simply overlooks many difficulties in understanding the relation of an object to its surroundings. There is no reason to infer that because a thing is in some sense "involved with" other things, hence in "context," that this relation will be "correctly" picked up in interpretation. It is further doubtful, unlikely in most cases, that a single interpretation can be identified as "correct" to the exclusion of all other possibilities. In most cases certain readings can be excluded on the grounds of insufficient evidence, but a single, correct interpretation cannot be identified. It follows that it is usually not sufficient to identify the relation of the object to the context to validate more than one among different ways to interpret it. Further, since what counts as the web of involvement itself also depends on interpretation, this line of argument is suspect and, in practice, simply inapplicable.

Heidegger, who is apparently unaware of such obvious objections, simply identifies a set of terms to frame his analysis: *fore-having, fore-sight,* and *fore-conception.* I infer that his intention is to provide the conceptual background to show how objective interpretation is practically possible. Fore-having is having something one has in advance, and which, Heidegger claims, we in fact "see in advance" (*BT*, 191). I take this to mean that in all cases the interpreter "possesses" at least an initial "reading" of the object in context. Obviously this will not always be the case and will depend on the degree of experience of the interpreter. One can be and frequently is confronted with wholly unprecedented situations, or at least situations that are largely unrelated to whatever one has been confronted with in the past. In such circumstances, there is no prior conception on which to rely. Yet, according to Heidegger, whatever we take to be an interpretation is always grounded in a so-called fore-conception, which is the basis from which all interpretation begins.

Heidegger, who does not take experience into account, sums up his point in saying there never is anything like presuppositionless apprehension (*BT*, 191–92). He appears to conflate direct givenness, on which Husserl appears to rely, and interpretation, which interests him. Direct givenness, which specifically refers to an immediate grasp of what is as it is, is prior to interpretation, which takes direct givenness as the text, so to speak.

The entire view of interpretation depends on the conception of the fore-structure of interpretation. Heidegger turns here to meaning, which depends on Dasein, or the interpreter, not on the thing being interpreted, since things do not have any intrinsic meaning (*BT*, 193). In suggesting that any instance of understanding refers to Dasein, who in turn refers to the context in working out an interpretation, Heidegger contends that all interpretation is intrinsically circular. As part of his analysis, he assumes that interpretation is historiological. He distinguishes between interpretation and other, non-historiological, allegedly more rigorous forms of knowledge. Yet unless one adopts epistemological foundationalism, I see no way to avoid this conclusion. Theories of all types are always and inherently circular, since they rely on presuppositions from which they derive. This is the case for all theories and does not pertain only in particular cases of interpretation. It follows, as Heidegger emphasizes, that circularity is not itself a defect, since it belongs to the nature of theory (*BT*, 194). Heidegger, on the contrary, attributes circularity to the fore-structure of Dasein, which belongs to the so-called structure of meaning of any interpretation (*BT*, 195). Yet this point fails to acknowledge the overlap between the fact that theory of all kinds depends on presuppositions it cannot demonstrate, hence is circular, and the way Dasein's alleged prior understanding of being structures the analysis of the meaning of being.

Heidegger and the Theory of Truth as *Aletheia*

Heidegger's theory of truth, the capstone of his position in *Being and Time*, is interrelated with his conceptions of interpretation; going to things themselves; the destruction of the history of ontology; his readings of Husserl, Descartes, and Kant; and other elements in his investigation of the problem of the meaning of being. In *Being and Time*, Heidegger seems to hold at least three different views of truth: first, the object can be directly grasped in what amounts to *veritas transcendentalis*; second, the object can be intuited in grasping its essence; and, third, the intuited object must be interpreted. The first view, which presupposes direct givenness, is close to the later Husserl's turn to transcendental idealism, which depends on the phenomenological reduction that Heidegger rejects. The second view is obviously related to Husserlian essentialism, which assumes that mind-independent objects possess essences, which are given but not constructed by the observer and which, under specifiable conditions, can be intuited. The third view is formulated in a lengthy account: "Dasein, Disclosedness, and Truth" (*BT*, sec. 44).

Heidegger's analysis of truth has two main goals, which frame the discussion. On the one hand, and as a precondition to introducing his ontological conception of truth, Heidegger needs to refute traditional alternatives. On the other hand, he must demonstrate that the new ontological conception of truth provides an adequate basis to answer the question of the meaning of being.

Heidegger begins by invoking the authority of Parmenides and Aristotle for the claim that, since ancient Greece, Western philosophy has always associated truth and being. According to Heidegger, since truth is associated with being, and Dasein is associated with being, Dasein "goes together" with the truth of being. Heidegger's analysis divides into three parts: (a) the traditional conception of truth and its ontological foundations, (b) the primordial phenomenon of truth and the derivative character of the traditional conception of truth, and (c) the kind of being that truth possesses and the presupposition of truth.

The claims about ancient philosophy depend on interpretation as well as on the ontological theory of truth Heidegger is introducing. In this passage, Heidegger's spare references to Parmenides outweigh the more ample references to Aristotle. He credits the latter with carrying out research concerning truth but the former with a theory of truth. Heidegger's attribution of a specific theory of truth to Parmenides is obviously crucial to his argument. Yet his straightforward assertion that Parmenides discovered the being of entities and hence being in Heidegger's specific sense of being is deeply problematic. It would obviously be helpful to Heidegger's argument if he could show that the problem he is dealing with is anticipated in the same or closely similar fashion in ancient Greek philosophy. In that case, he could plausibly claim to be taking up the ancient Greek theme as it was already raised at the onset of the Western philosophical tradition. In order to make this point, it would need to be shown that Parmenides and Heidegger hold recognizably similar views of being. Heidegger credits Parmenides with having "'identified' Being with the perceptive understanding of Being" in the statement that "to gar auto noein estin te kai einai" (*BT*, 256). He repeats this controversial claim elsewhere in very similar fashion, again without any effort to substantiate his view.[90] Yet his claim is uncertain, since this text, as well as the translation and interpretation of it that Heidegger advances, is acceptable only on the basis of the very tradition he finds untrustworthy.[91] Thus the specific Parmenidean fragment (B3) that interests Heidegger is only preserved in "citations" by Simplicius (commentary on Aristotle's *Physics*), Clement (*Strom*. 6) and Plotinus (*Enneads* 5),[92] which we cannot compare to the original that has not come down to us. Heidegger, who claims to go back behind the later tradition to capture ancient thought as it initially appeared, needs to rely on later writers, since we do not possess Parmenides' original text. Thus Hegel, who was very well versed in ancient Greek thought, including the pre-Socratics, and who relies on Simplicius, thinks the main idea is that thought is self-producing and that thought is identical with being.[93] Yet even the main outlines of Parmenides' view of the relation of thought and being remain controversial and basically unclear.[94] In sum, Heidegger's ontological view of truth undercuts his effort to reintroduce it as the "authentic" successor to a previous view, which, since it cannot invoke the authority of Parmenides, must be introduced for the first time on its merits.

Heidegger, who casts his net narrowly, immediately turns to three views that allegedly characterize the essence of truth: truth as assertion or judgment, truth as the agreement of the judgment with its object, and the Aristotelian view of truth as agreement. It appears that by *agreement* he means correspondence. Heidegger is concerned with variations on the theme of the correspondence theory of truth, which he refers to through the scholastic formulation of *adaequatio intellectus et rei*. He thereby infers that Aristotle's view is adequately captured in these terms. He never mentions any of the many other conceptions of truth, such as the coherence theory, the semantic conception, the constructivist view, the pragmatic theory, the deflationary theory of truth, the consensus theory of truth, and so on. According to Heidegger, who ignores the main alternatives and may not even be aware of other conceptions of truth, the correspondence view comes down to us from Aristotle through a long series of later thinkers, some of whom Heidegger mentions. Yet even if Heidegger were correct that the modern form of the correspondence theory is not only influenced by Aristotle but also essentially unchanged since its inception, that would be insufficient to overcome the traditional conception of truth. For the latter exists in various forms arguably unrelated, or at most only distantly related, to Aristotelian correspondence. Hence decisive criticism of Aristotle's approach would not in any way contribute to opening the way for Heidegger's proposed alternative view of truth.

As concerns truth, Heidegger stresses an ontological conception against an epistemological approach. He asks rhetorically if he must bring up the epistemological problematic of the subject-object relation or rather restrict himself to interpreting what he calls the "immanent consciousness of truth" (*BT*, 259). Yet this formulation does not appear to identify a real choice. On an average reading, through his phenomenology of the experience of consciousness, Hegel is, for instance, committed both to a subject-object relation and to the so-called immanent consciousness of truth.

In discussing truth, Heidegger is closer to Kant than to Hegel. He follows the author of the critical philosophy in describing knowledge as judging, in which there is a distinction between the psychical process, which is real, and the object of judgment, which is "an *ideal* content," hence ideal (*BT*, 259; Heidegger's emphasis). Heidegger asserts that claims of truth are made about the cognitive object. "It will be said of the latter [i.e., an ideal content—T. R.] that it is 'true'" (*BT*, 259). That is mistaken because truth claims concern a relation between something and something else. According to Heidegger, there is a distinction between the psychical process, or judging, which is real, and the ideal content. Now it is unclear what is ideal about the content. One possibility might be that in predication, the predicate is general, or universal, and hence ideal. In saying that something is red, one is bringing the thing, or subject, under the nonspecific, "ideal" color predicate. Be that as it may, this short reflection does not excuse Heidegger from taking the "epistemological" problematic into account.

Heidegger now turns to the relation between an ideal entity and a real thing. He asserts that we make no progress in remaining on the level of the distinction between the content and the act of judgment. The difficulty lies in bringing out the so-called phenomenon of truth, in which "agreement must become visible" (*BT*, 260). Agreement does not become visible because a representation is compared to a thing but because the thing in question, what is to be known, is revealed as it is. Heidegger articulates this claim in two points. First, the object must be made visible as it is, hence revealed as what it is. Second, we know that we have knowledge, or receive a "confirmation," if and only if the thing is made visible. It follows that "true" means no more and no less than to "uncover" a thing "as it is in itself" (*BT*, 261).

I understand Heidegger to be saying that to go to things themselves, which he takes as the phenomenological slogan, means to grasp them as they supposedly really are beyond the way in which they merely appear.

Heidegger is here taking aim at both Kant and Husserl. We can parse this surprising claim as follows. What he calls being true, or the way a thing really is, depends on being in a context, hence in the world. Being true has the operational meaning of uncovering, which consists in grasping something as it is in whatever way. But that depends on interpretation leading to a judgment that the self-identical thing has been grasped.

This view is problematic because, though things are or are not, judgment consists in a claim about them. Heidegger apparently believes that what we mean by truth is in practice immediately evident in the experience of the thing as it really is. His use of the term *in itself* signals his disagreements with Kant, who denies we can ever experience, or grasp, things in themselves, and with Husserl, who, in bracketing existence, focuses on what is given in consciousness as distinguished, after the phenomenological reduction, from what really is. The difficulty lies in making out the explicit claim to grasp, or cognize, a thing not merely as it appears but as it really is. How is one to know that one knows anything as it really is beyond mere appearance? And as Hegel points out, the only access to what something really is, however construed, lies in its appearance in consciousness.

This theme, which is not unprecedented, has attracted attention from a number of important thinkers. According to Hegel, in cognitive process the distinction between appearance and reality is gradually overcome, since the real—that is, the real for us as distinguished from the real in itself—can be said to appear. Peirce offers an operational conception of truth in the "long run" in his pragmatic theory of the real. His position amounts to claiming that we accept the results of the scientific process of inquiry as what we mean by *real*. Heidegger, who may have Plato in mind, who claims that exceptional individuals can literally see the real but offers no guidelines for how to do this, suggests that such cognition is immediately evident. Yet he provides no guidance for this suggestion, and the case remains to be made.

Heidegger supposes he has clinched the argument. He immediately turns to showing that the traditional conception of truth as correspondence depends on, hence derives from, his ontological view of truth. His view equates truth not with a judgment about an object, but with the object, or being. Heidegger, who is impatient with the idea of examining and weighing rival theories, contends that his view is not the product of so-called word mysticism but follows as the *"necessary* Interpretation" of the ancient view, which in this way is *"appropriated . . . primordially"* (*BT*, 262; his emphasis). Difficulties arise with respect to the force of "necessary" and "appropriated primordially." If the former means anything like "the interpretation is necessarily correct," then Heidegger has not shown this. If the latter means something like "taken up again as it originally occurred in successfully bypassing the later debate," then he has not shown this either.

Heidegger's view, which attributes the capacity of "uncovering" beings, or grasping things as they are, to Dasein, can be paraphrased as follows. Truth depends on grasping things as they are, which depends on the subject interpreting what is given. With this in mind, he makes four points, which we can further paraphrase. First, Dasein, or the subject, possesses the cognitive capacity to know objects; second, the subject is always already in context; third, cognition is based on projection with respect to individual human potentials; and, fourth, for the most part, truth claims are false because a human subject seeks to know in a way that neglects its own potentials.

Heidegger's ontological conception of truth exaggerates the subjective component in cognition. According to Heidegger, "To Dasein's state of Being belongs *projection*—disclosive Being towards its potentiality-for-Being" (*BT*, 264). It would be as mistaken to leave the subject out of truth claims as it would be to reduce them merely to subjective factors. The concern to link truth claims to the capacities of finite human beings situated in context is more persuasive than the further effort to make such truth claims dependent on the realization of individual human capacities. In passing, as part of the analysis, Heidegger remarks that perhaps psychologism is correct to refuse the separation of knowing and judging (*BT*, 259). Yet in implying that truth or falsity depend on whether the subject is "authentically" judging with respect to itself, Heidegger appears to fall into a particularly egregious form of psychologism, in which truth claims depend not merely on subjectivity but also on personal characteristics.

Heidegger's attention is directed less toward objective cognition than toward the relation between the ancient view of truth that he wishes to renew and the modern correspondence view. According to Heidegger, in abstracting from oneself, the result is a superficial, familiar view of truth as agreement (*BT*, 267–68). He regards the latter as a derivative, deficient result of the former, which is allegedly "primordial" and which further belongs to the structure, or nature, of Dasein. "Primordial" suggests two meanings: older, or prior to, but also better, in the sense of not only the first, or earliest, but also the only "authentic" view. According to Heidegger, the ontological view of truth is primordial. He contends that this view is already put forward by Aristotle, who never appeals to the (Kantian) thesis that truth depends on judgment (*BT*, 269).

The correspondence view of truth, which Heidegger rejects, is often traced back to Aristotle (and Plato). In *Metaphysics*, he famously says, "To say of what is that it is not, or of what is not that it is, is false, while to say of what is that it is, and of what is not that it is not, is true."[95] Scholars point out that Plato provides highly similar formulations,[96] and Aristotle gives a more robust version of the correspondence theory in *Categories*.[97] Further, in *De Interpretatione* he states that thoughts are "likenesses" (*homoiosis*) of things.[98] Hence, to justify his claim, Heidegger needs to deal with the scholarly discussion that presents another, incompatible reading. Further, even if Heidegger were able to make out his interpretation of Aristotle, it would not suffice to abandon the correspondence view in favor of his rival ontological view, which also needs to be argued.

In the final section, Heidegger sums up his account in relating truth claims to Dasein. His view that truth depends on Dasein stresses the subject's role in uncovering things. According to Heidegger, all truths, including the law of noncontradiction and Newton's laws, depend on the subject (*BT*, 269). But if, as he also holds, truth depends on the way things are, and if the mind independent-world is in fact independent of human beings, it is implausible to contend that, for instance, Newton's laws would not hold in independence of human beings. It is rather because the things to which they refer stand in relations that do not depend on the subject that the such laws hold whether or not they are formulated and without regard to the existence of human beings. What would it mean, say, to claim that before Newton the inverse square law did not hold? It is more plausible to say that Newton's laws were true but not recognized as such prior to Newton, who formulated them for the first time. Yet this point should not be taken as authorizing claims for timeless truth, which depends on other considerations.

Heidegger effectively ends the exposition of his ontological theory of truth by once again addressing the possible objection that his approach is merely subjective. He responds that the subject is brought face to face as it were with things themselves. Yet there is no indication that the claim to know things themselves needs be made out in practice. Husserl can make this claim because he brackets existence, but Heidegger cannot, because any such claim relies on interpretation as correct. Heidegger's solution lies in affirming that we must presuppose subjects capable of reaching truth, since skepticism cannot be refuted (*BT*, 271) This amounts to a simple, unsupported claim that truth is possible as opposed to a demonstration of its theoretical or its practical possibility.

A Concluding Remark on Being and Knowledge

Relatively little attention is directed to the link between epistemology and phenomenology in the immense Heidegger literature. Students of Heidegger often take him to be correctly avoiding epistemology in favor of ontology. I take him on the contrary to be making repeated "surreptitious" but for the most part invalid epistemological claims in the context of his attention to being in general. It might be objected that I have unfairly expounded and evaluated Heidegger's phenomenological ontology from an epistemological perspective that he rejects. Yet one cannot isolate ontology from epistemology, since an answer to the question of the meaning of being must take up related epistemological aspects of this question.

I have argued that Heidegger cannot separate his concern to know being from theory of knowledge and pointed to various difficulties in specific claims. Despite Heidegger's interest in the history of philosophy, he does not seem to have studied the problem of knowledge in any detail. He may be supposing that epistemology derives from the Cartesian theory he rejects and hence that in rejecting Cartesianism he has also overcome the problem of knowledge as well. Though Descartes is a strong influence in the epistemological tradition, there are numerous non-Cartesian forms of epistemology. Heidegger's ontology is broadly neo-Aristotelian. Ontology as Heidegger understands it from his generally Aristotelian perspective is a restricted form of the problem of knowledge focused on being only. In that specific sense, Heidegger's form of ontology is also epistemology, and can be judged by normal standards of the epistemological debate.

SIX

Kant, Merleau-Ponty's Descriptive Phenomenology, and the Primacy of Perception

In the present context, Maurice Merleau-Ponty is important for two reasons: he belongs to the group of phenomenologists who associate phenomenology and epistemology, and he also belongs to the effort, after Heidegger, to continue a recognizably "Husserlian" form of phenomenology in drawing on both Husserl and Heidegger.

Husserl restates a version of the Platonic claim, stated in the famous passage on the divided line, that science and mathematics must be justified or grounded in philosophy, which is self-grounding. Though he criticizes the inability of science to reflect on its presuppositions, he never "impugns" but seeks to understand its cognitive claims.[1] Even Heidegger suggests that historiology, or rigorous knowledge—roughly phenomenology and science—are different, without rejecting science.[2] Merleau-Ponty's view of the relation of phenomenology to other cognitive approaches, including natural science, is more extreme, since he rejects science in favor of phenomenology as a privileged source of knowledge. Though he was familiar with modern psychology, on which he draws in his phenomenological theories, he prefigures a new form of romanticism, especially common among later French figures, who reprise the early nineteenth-century revolt against reason. This new romanticism, which is known as postmodernism, is characterized by unsupported claims for a new, deeper form of direct knowledge (e.g., in Alan Sokal's famous article "Transgressing the Boundaries: Towards a Transformative Hermeneutics of Quantum Gravity"),[3] a distrust of science, and a series of vague, general, often uninformed claims about other forms of philosophy.[4]

Merleau-Ponty's most distinctive epistemological thesis concerns the primacy of perception. He further draws attention to the historical relativity of claims to know. This chapter focuses on these two related claims. I give special attention to his important presentation to the Société française de philosophie (1947), where he focuses perhaps better than elsewhere on what he regards as the epistemological consequences of his distinctive phenomenological approach.

Since Merleau-Ponty's writing style is often ambiguous, much of the discussion consists in reconstructing the outlines of his overall position. He intends his position as a refutation of idealism. But I contend that he misunderstands idealism and hence the relation of his position to idealism. I argue further that in reaction to the supposed idealist tendency to detach the subject from the world, he mistakenly reduces the world to the subject's perceptual world.

Some Influences on Merleau-Ponty

Merleau-Ponty's form of phenomenology is multiply determined by an unusually wide range of influences, including German idealism, the Husserlian phenomenological tradition, French phenomenology, the French philosophical tradition, so-called French idealism, and his well-known interest in modern psychology.

In a sense, the French phenomenological debate began as early as the first third of the nineteenth century in the interaction between Hegel and Victor Cousin. Cousin, who met Hegel in Heidelberg in 1817 and 1818, became interested in his work and remained in correspondence with him.[5] He discusses Hegel's *Phenomenology of Spirit* in his courses at the Collège de France in 1828.[6] Yet in another sense, it only began more than a century later, around 1930, with Levinas's book on Husserl's concept of intuition,[7] the initial translations of Heidegger, and Alexandre Kojève's famous lectures on Hegel. In the latter respect, it includes the reaction in the French discussion to Hegel, Husserl, and Heidegger by Levinas, Kojève, Hippolyte, Wahl, Sartre, Ricoeur, Derrida, Henry, Marion, and many others.

French phenomenology has a number of specifically French characteristics. To begin with, French phenomenology is, like French philosophy in general, strongly dependent on foreign, mainly German models. There is a measure of truth in Heidegger's boast that, when the French begin to think, they think in German.[8] French philosophy in the twentieth century was largely dominated by the reception of Kant, Hegel, Heidegger, Nietzsche, Freud, and others. When Merleau-Ponty was a student, German idealism was strongly represented in France by the Kantians Léon Brunschvicg and Pierre Lachièze-Rey.[9] It has been insightfully argued that French philosophy since the early 1930s consists in a series of reactions to Hegel.[10] In the second half of the twentieth century, when he displaced Sartre, Heidegger became for many observers the undisputed "French master thinker."[11]

Second, it should be noted that in French phenomenology, like French philosophy itself, translation has long played a key role. The enormous influence of Kojève's vision of Hegel is partly due to the fact that, having studied in Germany before he emigrated to France, he had access to the original text at a time when Hegel's *Phenomenology* was not yet available in French, and few French philosophers knew German. In the French context, Merleau-Ponty was an exception in that his command of German was sufficient to enable him to read untranslated texts, while most other French thinkers depended on translations.

Translation was also critical to Heidegger's emergence as a French master thinker after the war. *Being and Time* was only translated into French relatively late, several decades after the French discussion began and long after Heidegger had already become central in the French debate. The French tradition of Heidegger studies emerged before his central work was widely known in France. *Humanism*, which is understood differently by different observers, always refers in some way to human being. This is a central concern throughout French philosophy as early as Montaigne and Descartes and as late as Sartre. Montaigne's focus on himself as the author of his work, Descartes' concern with the cogito as the subject, and Sartre's interest in the humanistic claim for existentialism comprise a single tradition. Though Heidegger was not concerned with this theme, his intervention in the French debate after the war through the *Letter on Humanism* at a time when there was still no full translation of *Being and Time* was enormously successful. His claim that his concern with being was deeper than Sartre's metaphysical humanism helped call attention to Heidegger's position as supposedly humanist in a new and deeper sense.[12]

Third, there is the way that foreign models, when they are adopted into a different tradition, are transformed by local philosophical commitments. British idealism, which bears only a distant relation to German idealism, is transformed by its contact with the British philosophical context. For hundreds of years, Descartes has been the central thinker in French philosophy. Since Descartes emphasizes method, it is hardly surprising that French philosophers often claim to detect a single phenomenological method shared by Hegel, Husserl, and Heidegger.[13] A claim of this kind is not only useful, in calling attention to other kinds of phenomenology, other thinkers outside the narrow Husserlian fold, but also harmful in suggesting that phenomenology can be understood through an identifiable method. Since there does not seem to be any such method, it is arguably erroneous to suppose the main phenomenologists share such a commitment.

The uneasy relation between Husserl and Heidegger is central to the later development of phenomenology. The so-called phenomenological movement, a conception invented by Spiegelberg[14] that implies a continuous development starting in Husserl and continuing in his disciples, is misleading, even false. After Heidegger, who is basically opposed to a series of central Husserlian doctrines, twentieth-century phenomenology diverges from its Husserlian inspiration in an increasingly Heideggerian direction. Heidegger's position has long been dominant in French phenomenological circles. With the exceptions of Sartre, Ricoeur, and Dufrenne, the most important "phenomenologists," including Merleau-Ponty, Henry, Derrida, and, in the younger generation, Courtine and Marion, are all decisively influenced by encounters with Heidegger and hence opposed to basic Husserlian doctrines. In this respect, Merleau-Ponty stands out as someone interested in Hegel, who interprets Husserl and Heidegger as closely related thinkers, and who borrows from both while formulating his own original position.

Husserl is a central phenomenological figure for both Sartre and his younger colleague Merleau-Ponty, more for the former than the latter. Merleau-Ponty's grasp of phenomenology, like that of Sartre, is shaped by his very imperfect views of Husserl, Heidegger, and the relation between them, as well as by the peculiarly French understanding of idealism toward the end of the war as his own position was taking shape. Sartre's conception of phenomenology emerged from intensive study of Husserl before he turned to Heidegger and, to a lesser extent, to Hegel. Merleau-Ponty's view of Husserl includes his reading of (1) Heidegger, (2) the relation of phenomenology to other forms of philosophy, and (3) the relation of philosophy to science, particularly psychology.

Even Heidegger scholars, who know Husserl's thought well, approach Heidegger's thought with little or no recourse to Husserl's position. In a classic presentation of Heidegger's thought prepared under Heidegger's direction, Otto Pöggeler typically devotes comparatively little attention to Husserl. Pöggeler accepts Husserl's view that Heidegger failed to build upon the Husserlian basis.[15]

Pöggeler's reading of Husserl and Heidegger as discontinuous is implicitly disputed by Merleau-Ponty, who draws on both positions while stressing, perhaps overstressing, their continuity. According to Merleau-Ponty, who minimizes differences between Husserl and Heidegger that are more important than he is willing to concede, Heidegger merely prolongs Husserl's thought, from which he does not basically depart. He maintains that Heidegger's own main text can fairly be understood as the "explication" (*explicitation*) of Husserl's idea of the life world [*Lebenwelt*].[16] Few French philosophers go as far as Merleau-Ponty in stressing the continuity between Husserl and Heidegger. Yet his concern to understand Heidegger against the Husserlian background is typical of the French discussion.

Merleau-Ponty is further distinguished among French phenomenologists by his interest in Hegel. Husserl, who knew very little about Hegel, never acknowledges the phenomenological dimension of the latter's position and mistakenly accuses him of failing to criticize reason.[17] Heidegger, who concedes Hegel's importance, contends that the condition of continuing philosophy mandates a dialogue with Hegel, which he never undertook.[18] With the possible exception of Derrida, who wrote extensively on Hegel,[19] Merleau-Ponty goes further than other phenomenologists down the Hegelian path. In a famous passage, Merleau-Ponty resists the idea that all phenomenology worthy of the name is Husserlian, as well as the related idea that phenomenology, which he does not mention, is the single road, so to speak. According to Merleau-Ponty,

> All the great philosophical ideas of the past century—the philosophies of Marx and Nietzsche, phenomenology, German existentialism, and psychoanalysis—had their beginnings in Hegel; it was he who started the attempt to explore the irrational and integrate it into an expanded reason which remains the task of our century. He is the inventor of that Reason, broader than the understanding, which can respect the variety and singularity of individual consciousnesses, civilizations, ways of thinking, and historical contingency but which nevertheless does not give up the attempt to master them in order to guide them to their own truth. But, as it turns out, Hegel's successors have placed more emphasis on what they reject of his heritage than on what they owe to him.[20]

Merleau-Ponty's Descriptive Conception of Phenomenology

Husserl's unconvincing claim to have invented *phenomenology*,[21] which he struggles to define in a long series of texts, leaves both the meaning of the term, the genesis of this approach, and its import unresolved. Merleau-Ponty opens his most important work, the *Phenomenology of Perception*, with the still unanswered question: What is phenomenology?

Merleau-Ponty's answer, based on his rereading of Husserl and Heidegger in mid-1940s France under the influence of Sartre and others, culminates in a phenomenological approach to epistemology. Merleau-Ponty stresses a view of phenomenology as descriptive, as distinguished from explanatory or interpretive. "It is," he says, "a matter of describing, not of explaining or analyzing."[22] He can be read as claiming that there is a mind-independent reality, which is always already there prior to analytic reflection and scientific explanation (PP, x), a reality that can be, as he says, "described, not constructed or formed" (PP, xi).

Merleau-Ponty, who links description to the problem of epistemology, understands his descriptive conception of phenomenology as excluding science, or what he also calls analytical reflection, and scientific explanation. It further excludes any version of the idealist constructivist approach in favor of a conception of the world as always already there, a view that is supposedly denied by transcendental idealism. Science presupposes experience by human beings, which cannot be accounted for on a strictly scientific basis. This is a form of the familiar claim that science presupposes the prescientific realm, which Husserl calls the life-world, including direct human experience of the world. This explicit claim is conjoined with a further implicit claim amounting to the denial of any form of reductionistic explanation of human beings, which is now widely familiar in contemporary philosophy of mind. Merleau-Ponty similarly insists on the irreducible status of the world as given, or "the world as directly experienced" (PP, ix), which is further analyzed, on a secondary level, in science. Phenomenological experience precedes and in a sense "founds" the possibility of science as a "second-order expression" (PP, ix). Analytical reflection and scientific explanation only arise on the prior phenomenological basis. The world, which is always already there, and which is neither constructed nor formed (PP, xi), has an "opacity and transcendence" (PP, xiii), which we experience but which is or would be "destroyed" by transcendental idealism. An instance might be if the reduction, which is an infinite task,[23] could ever be completed (PP, xv).

In adopting a descriptive conception of phenomenology, Merleau-Ponty follows Husserl, perhaps Heidegger, and, closer to home, Bergson in committing to an idea of unadulterated experiential givenness. Unlike Neurath and Sellars, who oppose what the latter calls givenness, he accepts the view that the experiential given can in fact be identified and described.

What would it mean to describe experience as it is given on a prescientific, pre-reflective level? The general idea seems to be that one can attend to what is really "there" as opposed to what merely seems to there. In different ways, givenness goes back at least to Descartes' concern to identify indubitable ideas in the mind in order to ground knowledge. Unlike his French colleague, Merleau-Ponty, who is not an epistemological foundationalist, is not committed to building on an epistemological foundation. He needs, however, to justify his conception of description as opposed to reflection and explanation.

This point can be generalized. Merleau-Ponty insists on concrete description. But this is problematic. For the very idea of, say, the pure given of experience prior to explanation and interpretation is itself a mere construction, since so-called pure givenness is no more than a myth. Or, to put the same point differently, we never go directly to experience, but always do so on the basis of our prior experience, which is, hence, always already in that sense "constructed" by us as a condition of its apprehension. For the "uninterpreted" given, which is described, but not analyzed or explained, is no more than the product of interpretation.

On Idealism, Kantian Idealism, and Perception

Merleau-Ponty's claim about the epistemological importance of phenomenology rests on his critique of idealism and his assertion of the primacy of perception. Yet, like many other observers, he does not seem to have an adequate grasp of the history of phenomenology. The later Husserl insists on the intrinsic link between phenomenology and idealism, which such self-described "Husserlians" as Heidegger, Sartre, and Ingarden are concerned to distinguish. Heidegger, who does not claim to be a Husserlian, also rejects Husserl's later idealism. Perhaps because he was persuaded by Husserl's claim to invent phenomenology, Merleau-Ponty seems to believe it was invented after idealism, or at least after it had ceased to be a conceptual force. Idealism is a favorite whipping boy, which is rarely studied, hence less often understood, but routinely rejected. Like Sartre and many others (and as in Marxism and Anglo-American analytic philosophy), Merleau-Ponty seems not to know much about idealism, which he refutes without adequately characterizing it. Thus there is no idealism in general, no single shared conceptual commitment that is common to all those who claim or are claimed to be idealists and that further distinguishes idealists from adherents to other philosophical approaches. His suggestion, for instance, that one must "leave idealism without reverting to the naïveté of realism"[24] echoes Sartre's attack on Husserlian idealism[25] but fails to notice that all forms of idealism are committed to forms of realism.

Merleau-Ponty cannot consistently reject idealism as such, since his own position is similar to, in fact indistinguishable from, various forms of idealism. He is especially close in various ways to Berkeley and to Hegel. He explicitly accepts Berkeley's view that in the last analysis things, which are not in themselves, are inseparable from a perceiver.[26] This thesis is reflected in the further claim that any statement about the world as in some way independent of human beings presupposes prescientific experience of it.[27] He is also close to Hegel's view of knowledge as intrinsically historical, hence limited. I return to this point below.

His refutation of idealism is directed against Kantian idealism, which distinguishes form and matter while maintaining a transcendental concept of the subject. Kant's transcendental argument, which is based on the idea of elucidating general conditions of the possibility of knowledge, attempts to solve the problem of knowledge along Aristotelian lines. Kant initially stresses an analysis of the relation of representations to mind-independent objects before adopting the alternative strategy that we know only what we in some sense "construct."

In adopting a descriptive conception of phenomenology, Merleau-Ponty rejects Kantian constructivism, which undermines phenomenological claims to go to things themselves. For his strategy to be successful, Merleau-Ponty must show that he can capture things themselves merely through description. In stressing perceptual experience as the ultimate source of knowledge, Merleau-Ponty "collapses" the basic Kantian distinction between sensation, perception, and experience. Sensation, which is prior to and presupposed as a condition of perception, is inferred, not perceived or experienced in any way. Hence a claim not to perceive sensation, the denial that it is part of experience, does not count against it.

Kant's distinction between perception and experience is roughly the difference between cognition from the perspective of the individual and from that of the group. Individual experience, based on the report of the individual, is not yet knowledge, or experience in Kant's technical sense, which requires a universal and necessary law.[28] For that reason, experience but not perception must yield the same result for all observers. Merleau-Ponty, who conflates this crucial distinction, leaves unresolved the difficult problem of how perceptual experience, which is individual, can lead to objective knowledge, which is universal or at least general.

On Kantian Idealism and the Traditional Approach to Perception

Merleau-Ponty's attack on transcendental idealism aims at three main targets: the later Husserl, who abandoned his initial conception of phenomenology as descriptive psychology in favor of phenomenology as transcendental idealism; Kant; and the French view of idealism. As Merleau-Ponty was emerging, French idealism was exemplified by two Kantians: Brunschvicg, Merleau-Ponty's teacher at the Ecole normale supérieure, and Lachièze-Rey, a leading contemporary Kant scholar. Both were strong proponents of Kantian idealism, against which Merleau-Ponty later rebelled. In his so-called critical idealism, Brunschvicg developed a theory of judgment leading to universal reason allegedly exhibited in philosophy and the natural sciences.[29] Lachièze-Rey defended a version of Kantian idealism.[30] Merleau-Ponty thinks that Brunschvicg's neo-Kantian view that knowledge depends on judgment demonstrates his own Husserlian counterview that natural science always presupposes prescientific experience.

Merleau-Ponty's critique of the later Husserl and Kant focuses on *idealism*, which they understand in radically different ways. In general terms, Kant comprehends this term from a constructivist angle of vision, whereas Husserl takes a nonconstructivist, representational approach. In his last, unfinished book, *The Crisis of European Sciences and Transcendental Phenomenology*, Husserl distinguishes objectivism, which seeks truth on the basis of the world as taken for granted, and transcendentalism, which holds that meaning is a subjective structure based on prescientific experience and thought. Husserl, who favors transcendental phenomenology, further distinguishes psychological idealism, which he opposes, and transcendental idealism, which he defends.[31]

In part under Heidegger's influence, Merleau-Ponty in effect defends Husserl against Husserl in espousing one theme but rejecting another. He defends Husserl's conception of the life-world against Husserl's later transcendental perspective.[32] For Merleau-Ponty, an account of the life-world needs to begin from immediate experience, which, he believes, is closed off by Husserl's later transcendental analysis. The latter illustrates so-called intellectualism, which supposedly substitutes a concept of the subject for human being in the world. Merleau-Ponty is equally opposed to what, partly following Husserl,[33] he refers to as objectivism, and which he associates with reductive approaches to subjectivity, such as philosophical naturalism, psychological behaviorism, and biological mechanism.

According to Merleau-Ponty, who does not grasp the relation between idealism and phenomenology, phenomenology refutes idealism, or at least the idealist view of perception, through the view of the subject as finite human being. His rival view of the subject is presupposed in his critique of Sartre's Cartesian conception of subjectivity, leading to a supposedly post-Cartesian subject.[34] His conception of subjectivity arises out of his reinterpretation of the Cartesian cogito. Merleau-Ponty, who identifies three readings of the cogito, argues that the only adequate view is a conception of the subject as incarnate and hence as an embodied being in the world, not transcendent to it. His conception of subjectivity, in breaking with the views of Kant and the later Husserl, resembles a widespread, but arguably mistaken humanist reading of Heidegger that was prevalent at the time in French circles. According to Merleau-Ponty, the "true" cogito parts company with the familiar Cartesian epistemological approach to the subject in terms of its thoughts, indubitability, and so on in revealing the subject as "being-in-the-world" (*PP*, xiv).

In this context, three points come to mind. First, it is difficult to say whether what Merleau-Ponty calls the "true" cogito merits this name. Through the mysterious term *Dasein*, Heidegger, who is a strong critic of Descartes, stresses against the latter that existence is prior to epistemological theory. Merleau-Ponty similarly emphasizes the priority of the finite human being in the social and historical context over idealist approaches to subjectivity through consciousness (Descartes) or epistemological function (Kant).

Second, Merleau-Ponty's view of subjectivity is misleading as concerns both Descartes and Heidegger. Though he appears to defuse Heidegger's attack on Descartes, his suggestion that being-in-the-world is the correct interpretation of the Cartesian cogito, which appears to undermine Heidegger's attack on Descartes, is questionable. It is more accurate to say that in his conception of the subject he offers an alternative to some views of the Cartesian cogito. Suffice it to say that Heidegger misreads Descartes in suggesting that the cogito, which is transcendent to the world, is instead immanent to it. It is a further misreading to conceive of the Heideggerean subject, which can be understood as deriving from denying the Cartesian cogito, as compatible with it. Since Heidegger's intention is not to develop but rather to deny any form of the Cartesian cogito, it would indeed be ironic if he had restated the Cartesian view in different words. Whatever he is, Heidegger is not and does not consider himself to be a Cartesian. Since he is arguably the most important recent anti-Cartesian, Heidegger's conception of Dasein should not be conflated with even the most ingenious reading of the Cartesian cogito.

The third point concerns Merleau-Ponty's phenomenological refutation of Kant. It is incorrect to regard phenomenology and idealism as incompatible. Since there are only types of phenomenology and types of idealism, then, strictly speaking, neither phenomenology as such nor idealism as such exists. At most, the view of the subject as directly in the world is incompatible with forms of idealism but not with idealism as such. Types of idealism compatible with his view of the subject as being-in-the-world include the view of Descartes, who relies on ideas and is sometimes classed as an idealist, as well the theories of Fichte, Hegel, and, if he is an idealist, Marx.

In presenting his view of the subject as immanent as a refutation of idealism, Merleau-Ponty overlooks the many links between Descartes and Kant while implicitly misreading post-Kantian German idealism. On the one hand, there is a deep, obvious continuity between the Cartesian concept of the cogito (*je pense*) and the Kantian view of the transcendental unity of apperception (*ich denke*). Both approach the subject through its cognitive capacities. Both also replace a conception of finite human being in the world with an abstract analysis of its capacity for knowledge. According to Merleau-Ponty, the idealist concept of the subject reduces the subject to its thinking and the world to the thought of the world. Yet, as Kant points out in his "Refutation of Idealism," a thought of the world is possible only because there is a mind-independent world, which differs from, hence is not reduced to, a thought of it.[35] The post-Kantian idealist reaction to the critical philosophy, which parts company with Kant as concerns subjectivity, turns on a novel conception of the subject as finite human being, both immanent in as well as transcendent to the world. This view, which is initially worked out by Fichte and reformulated by others, including Hegel and Marx, is generally compatible with Merleau-Ponty's phenomenological view of the subject in the social and historical context.

A Note about Psychologism

Merleau-Ponty's reinterpretation of the true Cartesian cogito as being-in-the-world, or as finite human being in context, raises again the complex theme of psychologism. This term is used in different ways, whose relation is unclear and whose core meaning is sometimes described as a conflation of logical with psychological entities and hence the conflation of the logical with the psychological,[36] or even as the naturalization of consciousness.[37]

Merleau-Ponty's conception of the subject as immanent is difficult to distinguish from psychologism as Husserl understands it. Husserl's approach to this difficulty is inconsistent. He believes that Kantian epistemology mainly falls prey to psychologism.[38] Yet his proposed solution drives him in the Kantian direction, hence toward transcendental idealism, in his revised conception of the subject as a transcendental subject and of phenomenology as transcendental phenomenology. From Merleau-Ponty's perspective, Husserl tries but fails to discover a remedy for psychologism. He agrees with Heidegger's suggestion that Husserl falls back into psychologism. According to Merleau-Ponty, the reduction puts the "naive" causal view of perception out of play at the cost of adopting an "idealist" perspective in which the world is reduced to a correlation of the contents of consciousness to the world as meant but not as experienced (*PP*, xi), in short, to the world as reduced to the thought of the world. Yet Merleau-Ponty's appeal to a view of the subject as always already in context as well as his appeal to psychology as the basis of philosophical claims is itself a form of psychologism from Husserl's point of view.

There are many different approaches to the problem posed by psychologism. Kant draws a rigorous distinction between the subject of the critical philosophy and finite human being, thereby opening a gap he cannot later close. Frege takes flight into mathematical Platonism. Husserl moves closer to Kant at the cost of being unable to recapture the life-world from the transcendental plane,[39] for instance, in his inability to retain the historicity of history.[40] Merleau-Ponty seeks an immanent approach based on a view of the subject as paradoxically both within as well as transcendent to the world.

The contrast between Husserl and Merleau-Ponty on this point is important. For Husserl, psychologism with regard to logic and mathematics undermines any claim to knowledge in these domains. One way to put the point is that mathematics and logic are a priori, and psychology is a posteriori. Hence psychology cannot ground either mathematics or logic. For Merleau-Ponty, on the contrary, Husserl, in rethinking phenomenology as transcendental idealism in order to overcome psychologism, simply undermines claims to knowledge.

In sum, Merleau-Ponty's relation to psychologism is difficult to summarize. His basic principle is a steadfast refusal to separate epistemological claims from the experience of human subjects. By implication, he follows Fichte, Marx, perhaps Heidegger, and others in closing up the "gap" opened by Kant between the epistemological subject and finite human being. According to Merleau-Ponty, the experience of embodied human subjects leads to the constitution of meaning from the individual perspective (*PP*, 170). On this prescientific level, the experience of the embodied subject is organized around and by its incarnate status (*PP*, 239). For Merleau-Ponty, all cognitive claims of whatever kind ultimately refer to the experience of embodied human subjects situated in the prescientific life-world. Hence, there is always and necessarily an ineliminable psychological component.

Phenomenology and Psychology

With the exception of Kant and Heidegger, a number of phenomenologists, especially Hegel, Husserl, and Merleau-Ponty, are knowledgeable about psychology. Kant is an exception. Though he made important contributions to modern science, he was not knowledgeable about modern psychology, which had not yet emerged. Hegel was deeply concerned with psychological phenomena, which he studies in detail.[41] It has been suggested that Hegel anticipates Freudian psychoanalysis.[42] Merleau-Ponty shares with Husserl an approach to phenomenology that is dependent on psychology.

Husserl's relation to psychology is complex. He initially studied astronomy, then later mathematics, physics, and philosophy. He was a student in the philosophy lectures of Wilhelm Wundt, who founded the first institute of experimental psychology. After earning a Ph.D. in mathematics, he studied with Brentano, who published *Psychology from an Empirical Standpoint* (1874), and then with the latter's student, Carl Stumpf, who is perhaps best known for his *Psychology of Tone* (two volumes, 1883/90). Husserl wrote his habilitation *On the Concept of Number* (1887) with Stumpf. This later became the basis of *Philosophy of Arithmetic* (1891), where Husserl drew on his mathematical, psychological, and philosophical competencies in providing a psychological foundation of arithmetic. Though he later reacted against psychologism, psychology remained a permanent dimension of his phenomenology. His position turns on the supposed parallelism between phenomenology and psychology. He was especially concerned in later writings with transcendental phenomenological psychology. And even in his last writings he continued to believe that the way into transcendental phenomenology must begin in psychology.[43]

Merleau-Ponty had an even deeper grounding in psychology. As a sometime professor of psychology at the Sorbonne (1949–52), Merleau-Ponty was very well versed in the discipline. He argued with behaviorism against a causal approach to psychology rooted in a Lockean atomistic theory of perception, and against behaviorism, which he thinks is still a causal approach. His interest in human action emerges very early. The first sentence of *The Structure of Behavior*, his dissertation, which became his initial book, reads, "Our goal is to understand the relationship of consciousness and nature: organic, psychological or even social."[44] His strategy here is to appropriate the Gestaltist critique of classical behaviorism, which he then criticized.

Classical behaviorism presupposes a Lockean psychology rooted in a causal approach and a view of perception as deriving from atomic perceptions. In reacting against classical behaviorism, Merleau-Ponty follows such theorists as Koehler and Koffka, who deny the stimulus-response model in favor of irreducible structures. Merleau-Ponty accepts the Gestaltist view that so-called atomic units of perception are not basic, or elementary, but derived. But, like Husserl, who rejects naturalism, Merleau-Ponty rejects the Gestaltist understanding of Gestalt psychology in terms of naturalist ontology. For Merleau-Ponty, this is a relapse into a causal theory of perception in which structures take the place of such putative atomic units of perception as sense data and the reflex arc. "The integration of matter, life and mind is obtained by this reduction to a common denominator of physical form."[45] In rejecting behaviorist psychology, he identifies an inconsistency within behaviorism in pointing toward the phenomenology of perception that he will shortly develop.

> That in the final analysis form cannot be defined in terms of reality but in terms of knowledge, not a thing of the physical world but as a perceived whole, is explicitly recognized by Koehler when he writes that the order in a form "rests . . . on the fact that each local event, one could almost say 'dynamically knows' others." It is not an accident that, in order to express this presence of each moment to the other, Koehler comes up with the term "knowledge." A unity of this type can be found only in an object of knowledge. Taken as a being of nature, existing in space, the form would always be dispersed in several places and distributed in local events, even if these events mutually determine each other; to say that it does not suffer this division amounts to saying that it is not spread out in space, that it does not exist in the same manner as a thing, that it is the idea under which what happens in several places is brought together and resumed. This unity is the unity of perceived objects. A colored circle, which I look at, is completely modified in its physiognomy by an irregularity, which removes something of its circular character and makes it an imperfect circle.[46]

In effect, he argues that psychological data suffice to refute a certain philosophical approach to perception but not to construct an adequate replacement theory. Yet psychology is not and cannot be adequate to formulate a theory of perception. Like the other sciences, it presupposes the prescientific level of personal experience, hence phenomenology. He makes a similar claim about philosophy. He begins "The Primacy of Perception and Its Philosophical Consequences" by claiming that psychological study of perception reveals that the classical philosophical approach is false.[47] As in psychology, so in philosophy Merleau-Ponty relies principally on a critical reading of Gestalt psychology in contradicting the Kantian idealist theory of perception. According to Merleau-Ponty, the classical distinctions of form and matter and the view of the subject as ordering sensory content are false. The correct alternative lies in acknowledging three points. First, all perception takes the form of practical experience within a horizon; second, the perceptual subject is both immanent and transcendent; and, third, all cognitive claims, which are limited by experience, are indexed to history.[48]

Merleau-Ponty's phenomenological appeal to psychology is problematic. It runs the risk of falling back into another, more important type of psychologism: the philosophical reliance on psychological science. It is unclear how to base phenomenology on or otherwise take into account a specifically psychological approach to perception without this consequence.

More specific difficulties arise with respect to the appeal to psychology from a phenomenological perspective, which relies on science as a privileged source of knowledge about perception. One form of psychology can serve to criticize another form of psychology, but, from a phenomenological point of view, psychology cannot determine the truth about perception. In appropriating but also rejecting Gestalt psychology, Merleau-Ponty implicitly rejects scientism. Scientism is the view that science is the only reliable source of knowledge. According to Sellars, it is the only reliable form of the "logical space of reasons."[49] Yet others, for instance Bergson, deny that science offers an even potentially acceptable approach.[50] If this is correct, then an argument needs to be made that at most a certain kind of science, hence a subset of psychology, is acceptable.

Merleau-Ponty is clearly inconsistent in this regard. His position begins by disavowing science in adopting a view of phenomenology as descriptive, but not as explanatory or interpretive. Yet, as Dilthey points out, natural science in all its forms is basically explanatory. This view of science is very old. It is inconsistent to rely on science in order to adopt phenomenology as opposed to Kantian idealism since, from the perspective of the type of phenomenological perspective that Merleau-Ponty espouses, science depends on, hence does not precede, phenomenology. For these reasons, it seems questionable to invoke psychology in working out a phenomenological theory of perception.

Descriptive Phenomenology and the Primacy of Perception

Merleau-Ponty's theory of the primacy of perception bears at least a superficial similarity to Heidegger's distinction between the ready-to-hand (*Zuhandenheit*) and the present-to-hand (*Vorhandenheit*). For Heidegger, the practical dimension subtends and makes possible more abstract theoretical analysis. Yet, unlike Heidegger, Merleau-Ponty does not further subordinate cognitive claims to individual self-fulfillment. He merely contends that phenomenology could only arise after rationalism and modern science. His thesis of the primacy of perception is intended to suggest that phenomenology is in practice prior to all other cognitive approaches.

The modern epistemological debate can be described as a series of variations on the theme of a causal theory of perception, whose most important philosophical representative is arguably Kant. Merleau-Ponty's epistemological thesis about the primacy of perception is a nonstandard form of the empiricist claim familiar in Kant's view that knowledge of any kind begins in experience.[51] This Kantian view returns in Merleau-Ponty's thesis that knowledge of any kind begins in perception. In examining the perceptual phenomena of the life-world, he redescribes perception in a way that is inconsistent with so-called classical accounts. Classical accounts of sense perception presuppose a distinction between consciousness and its contents. Typically there is an assertion of consciousness of something and hence a complex relation between the thing, the subject, and the subject's consciousness of it. Locke, for instance, influentially defines *consciousness* as "the perception of what passes in a man's own mind."[52] A form of this dualism recurs in Husserl's distinction between noesis (acts of thought) and noema (intentional acts of thought providing determinate semantic reference).

In refusing any dualism between consciousness and nature, Merleau-Ponty reacts against ordinary empiricism. Empiricist thinkers typically reduce knowledge claims to claims about sensation. Unlike British empiricists and their analytic successors, Merleau-Ponty denies empiricist efforts to reduce sensory perception to its supposed origin in sense data, qualia, sensibilia, and so on. In that sense, he usefully anticipates the later analytic critique and rejection of empiricism (e.g., in the later Wittgenstein, Sellars, Rorty, Putnam, Quine, and Davidson).

In denying that consciousness is consciousness of something, Merleau-Ponty further reacts against the concept of the thing in itself, which Kant introduced to account for the contents of consciousness through a causal analysis. For Kant, we are causally impacted by a world we cannot know in arriving at cognitive claims whose relation to the world remains unknown. Perception, which is private, differs from experience and knowledge, which respect universal and public laws.

Already in Kant and even more clearly after him, there are increasing efforts to think about knowledge in terms of phenomena that do not relate to anything beyond themselves; hence they are neither appearances, nor do they represent the mind-independent world. For Kant, who distinguishes between phenomena and appearances, all appearances are phenomena, but only some phenomena, namely, those that refer beyond themselves, are appearances. Merleau-Ponty belongs to the widespread effort after Kant to abandon the thing in itself in focusing on things in the world. His thesis of the primacy of perception belongs to the ongoing effort to work out a theory of knowledge in terms of phenomena.

Merleau-Ponty is better at indicating what he rejects than at describing his positive view of knowledge. Claims to know of all kinds routinely refer to the *real*, or *reality*, which is understood in many different ways. Though he is often said to reject realism, Merleau-Ponty in fact favors a form of empirical realism. Like many others, too numerous to name, he limits claims to know the world as given in experience, in his case through perception. He holds that the world is what we perceive (*PP*, xviii). And he relates his view of the world to truth, intentionality, rationality, being, and consciousness.

In refusing to go beyond what is given in perception, Merleau-Ponty typically denies any distinction between the world as given and as perceived. *The Structure of Behavior* ends with a call for a philosophy that "inverts the natural movement of consciousness" in describing how the world is constituted in perception.[53] He responds to that call in his phenomenological description of perception, in which, as in Husserl, constitution replaces causality. Instead of the familiar causal analysis of perception in terms of the step-by-step analysis of claims to know through sensory experience of a preexisting external world, he insists that things are constituted for us. He writes that by the "primacy of perception,"

> we mean that the experience of perception is our presence at the moment when things, truths, values are constituted for us [*se constituent pour nous*]; that perception is a nascent *logos*; that it teaches us, outside all dogmatism, the true conditions of objectivity itself; that it summons us to the tasks of knowledge and action. It is not a question of reducing human knowledge to sensation, but of assisting at the birth of this knowledge, to make it as sensible as the sensible, to recover the consciousness of rationality. This experience of rationality is lost when we take it for granted as self-evident, but is, on the contrary, rediscovered when it is made to appear against the background of non-human nature. (*PP*, 25)

In this crucial passage, as elsewhere in his writings, Merleau-Ponty's view is stated in typically ambiguous language. It is not clear what is being claimed and hence not clear what Merleau-Ponty's new view amounts to. It was noted above that the term *constitution* is never successfully clarified by Husserl.[54] It is also not clarified in Merleau-Ponty's restatement of it. Left unclear is how to understand the idea that the subject in some sense can be said to constitute the object. Since *constitution* is central to the thesis of the primacy of perception, there is a basic unclarity at the center of Merleau-Ponty's theoretical innovation.

The Primacy of Perception and Theory of Perception

In turning from a causal to a descriptive analysis, Merleau-Ponty turns from a transitive to an intransitive conception of perception. In his view we do not become conscious of a mind-independent world; rather, we become conscious at the same moment as we perceive the world. In breaking with the view that consciousness is consciousness of something, Merleau-Ponty breaks with Kant's critical philosophy, Sartre, and the later Husserl, each of whom presupposes a dualism between noesis (acts of thought) and noema (intentional acts of thought).

The suggestion that perception is no longer presumed to be true, or true perception of something, points to a specific conception of intentionality. Merleau-Ponty denies the Kantian view that the unity of the object is due to the subject. He employs a widened conception of intentionality to distinguish phenomenological description from traditional "intellection" (*PP*, xx). Merleau-Ponty is pointing to a different theory of rationality that is not isolated from but depends on experience and that does not explicate a preexisting world (*PP*, xxii).

Merleau-Ponty's view of the primacy of perception can be clarified in relation to other theories of perception. The seventeenth-century search for primary qualities by Galileo, Descartes, and others led in the twentieth century to successor claims to know in various forms of empiricism, which Merleau-Ponty opposes. Such claims are based on sense data, description and acquaintance, protocol statements, and so on. Claims to know based on primary qualities are variations on the theme of direct perception of things in the world. The introduction of sense-data theory in the twentieth century led to different formulations of the general view that there are mind-independent objects, that we are directly aware of them in perception, and that they have exactly the properties they appear to have. Russell, a proponent of this approach, famously called attention to a distinction between knowledge by acquaintance, which is direct, and knowledge by description, which is by definition indirect. According to Russell, knowledge by acquaintance is obtained through a direct causal (experience-based) interaction between a person and the object that person perceives. Like Locke,

Russell holds that we are only directly acquainted with sense data but not with the physical objects to which they refer.[55]

Merleau-Ponty's view differs from Russell's in affirming direct knowledge of phenomena but denying a causal relation to the world. His position is closer to Ayer's early conception of perception. Ayer espoused but later rejected phenomenalism, which he defined as "a reduction of the way things are to the way they seem."[56] For a phenomenalist like Ayer, to talk about verification is ultimately to talk about sense data and hence about private experience.

Ayer's view further entails a so-called translatability requirement. He defends the claim that statements about physical objects are always translatable into statements about sense data. This much is arguably acceptable to Merleau-Ponty, who denies a central premise that Ayer for a time also defended, namely, that unperceived physical objects continue to exist. Yet Ayer eventually came to reject phenomenalism. He thought that for it to succeed, the existence of the object must stand in a deductive relation to sense data, and conversely, and that neither of these conditions could be satisfied.[57]

Merleau-Ponty does not consider the relation between perception and science other than to argue for the priority of the former. Yet a similar difficulty arises in his position. If he bases knowledge on phenomenological perception, he needs to show how immediate experience can lead to objective knowledge. In other words, like other thinkers who claim that science originates in or at least is continuous with ordinary science, for instance, Carnap, in his protocol theory phase, he must show how, on this basis, he can maintain a belief in the objectivity of modern science. I will come back to this point.

Phenomenological Perception and the Limits of Knowledge

Merleau-Ponty's first main epistemological thesis concerns the primacy of perception. As a result of this thesis, Merleau-Ponty parts company with the traditional Kantian claim that we sense mind-independent objects that we transform into perceptual objects. In its place, Merleau-Ponty substitutes an alternative model based on individual experience, in which objects emerge whole as it were, already constituted, without a contribution from the side of the perceiver. This is a descriptive revision of a theory Kant arrives at through considering the general conditions of knowledge on a causal basis.

Merleau-Ponty's second main epistemological thesis concerns the historical limitations of knowledge. In a preliminary summary of the argument, he describes perception as an original modality of consciousness, and then, in generalizing his results, states that ideas, which derive from perception, are only valid for a period. He writes, "Evidence is never apodictic, nor is thought timeless, though there is some progress in objectification and thought is always valid for more than an instant."[58]

Merleau-Ponty does not argue for this complex claim, which he merely states. Yet there are indications of how he might support his claim. We can reconstruct the line of reasoning leading to his claim about the historical relativity of cognitive statements as follows. According to Merleau-Ponty, all rationality, all value, and all existence are based on the perceived world. Thus, one might claim from this perspective that the Pythagorean theorem is not final, since it is indexed to a particular historical period, and is not, hence, a timeless truth that can never be contradicted nor later modified. It follows that the mathematical claim formulated in the Pythagorean theorem is like any inductive claim, for instance, a perceptual claim that can at least in principle always be contradicted by a further perceptual claim. According to Merleau-Ponty, all thought will later need to be taken up in a so-called "new unity."[59] More generally, thought and perception are inscribed within a temporal horizon and are hence temporal. We do not go straight to the truth, or the essence of things; rather, we proceed through clarification and further experience. In consequence, rationality is not destroyed but is preserved in linking it to experience.[60]

We need to distinguish between the claim and the argument in its favor. This general epistemological thesis is familiar, for instance, in Hegel, who, as a contextualist, also considers epistemological assertions in relation to the surrounding world. These versions of the general claim for the historical relativity of cognition arise in reaction to well-known Cartesian and Kantian claims for epistemological apodicticity. This general claim contradicts all forms of anti-psychologism. Heidegger's obscure suggestion that Newton's laws were not true before they were discovered further suggests, despite his opposition to any form of Cartesian subjectivity, that truth depends in some unclarified way on human being.[61] If this is true, then, as Descartes suggests in placing subjectivity at the epicenter of his analysis, any and all claims for objective cognition have to be made out from within subjectivity to speak. Yet this approach is no more than a minority view, which is contradicted by the well-known thesis that truth is independent of the observer. Thus according to Frege, the Pythagorean theorem is simply independent of what any person thinks and hence independent with respect to time and place.[62] It follows that this and other mathematical theorems are not in any way historical but rather ahistorical.

In its present, fragmentary formulation Merleau-Ponty's argument is insufficient to justify his conclusion that all knowledge is indexed to the historical context. He bases his claim for the relativity of perception on its unexamined relation to culture and history.[63] Hegel, on the contrary, bases his version of a similar claim on two points: the historical character of human being and hence of a conception of philosophy that cannot jump over its shadow since it always belongs to the historical moment,[64] and a description of the relation of theories to cognitive objects.[65] He differs from Merleau-Ponty in relating the development of claims to know to the historical and intellectual context in which they emerge.

Merleau-Ponty's argument for the historical relativity of cognitive claims is comparable to but weaker than Hegel's. To strengthen his argument, he would need at least to sketch the relation of cognitive claims to culture and history. Since he never wrote his book on truth, he never made out this part of the argument. He would further need to show that, as Hegel shows through detailed criticism of Descartes, Kant, and others, stronger claims to know, which would preempt his own weaker claim, in fact fail. In other words, he would need to provide the same detailed, concrete examination of other philosophical theories that he accords elsewhere in his writings to contemporary psychological theories.

Merleau-Ponty on Phenomenology, Idealism, and Epistemology

Merleau-Ponty's insight about the primacy of perception should be grasped as a response to idealism. This is associated in his mind not with Hegel, whom he approves but whose idealism he seems to overlook, but with Descartes and Kant, two thinkers whom he believes "detach" the conscious subject from the world as given in experience. For an approach to knowledge based on a transcendent subject, or a subject that supposedly knows a mind-independent world, he substitutes a subject that is paradoxically both immanent in as well as transcendent to the world.

His project for an approach to knowledge through a descriptive phenomenology of perception remains, because of his untimely death, very rough, no more than an unrealized project. He claims, but does not demonstrate, that knowledge begins in the experience of immanent subjects. To be taken seriously as an epistemological thesis, this claim must be defended and expanded. It must be shown that all claims for knowledge, or, to take his example, all forms of science, ultimately originate in individual perceptual experience. This appears difficult to sustain with respect, say, to

Newtonian mechanics or relativistic theories about space-time based on abstract analysis arguably unrelated to individual experience. To rephrase the point, individual theoreticians, for instance Newton and Einstein, on occasion formulate theories that seem wholly unrelated to individual perception. It is further difficult to show, if all one means by *world* is what arises in perception, how one can test claims to know against experience. The "world," which is always more than one perceives, is paradoxically both immanent in and transcendent to perception. There is no alternative to assuming an independent world against which we test our claims to know. It follows that we must acknowledge, for instance, both the object, say, a house, that we perceive as well as something else we do not perceive that lies beyond my experience. In other words, even though we cannot claim to perceive the world as it is and hence cannot reduce perception to sensation of that world, we must nonetheless presuppose it in theory of knowledge.

CONCLUSION

On Overcoming the Epistemological Problem through Phenomenology

It is widely believed that phenomenology worthy of the name arises with Husserl, who forges a link to epistemology that Heidegger dissolves in turning to ontology. This book argues that, on the contrary, Kant is already concerned to work out a phenomenological approach to epistemology, which in his wake is rethought by his main phenomenological successors: Fichte, Hegel, Husserl, Heidegger, and Merleau-Ponty. I conclude with some rapid remarks about a phenomenological approach to epistemology. These remarks should not be taken as an argument but as an indication of what an argument might look like as concerns the epistemological interest of phenomenology.

Phenomenology arguably appears in a bewildering variety of recognizable forms well before the term was invented. It is ascribed to thinkers whose positions, on even a charitable reading, seem to have little in common, such as Aristotle and Peirce.[1] It is not widely known that the latter was interested in both phenomenology[2] and what, in coining a neologism to refer to what is usually referred to as phenomenology, he calls *phaneroscopy*, from *phaneron*. Further, like Hegel, he understands phaneroscopy, his own form of phenomenology, to be concerned with what is given to consciousness without regard to a possible relation to the real or mind-independent world as it is.[3]

Claims about the epistemological value of phenomenology are often imprecise. Gadamer, who seems to have Heidegger in mind, proposes to overcome the epistemological problem through phenomenology. If this claim is restated as going to things themselves, then it is implausible in either the original Husserlian or the later Heideggerian formulations.

A claim for a phenomenological approach to epistemology needs to be formulated carefully. If Kant's critical philosophy is the criterion, we must distinguish between phenomena, which need not refer, or do not necessarily refer, and appearances, which always refer to something beyond themselves. It follows that all appearances are phenomena, but only some phenomena are appearances. We further need to be attentive to the difference between a representational approach to knowledge, in which a mind-independent object appears, which Kant initially espouses but later rejects, and constructivism, to which he turns, and in which the subject is said to "construct" its cognitive object. With this in mind, we can reconstruct constructivist phenomenology as the twofold Kantian claim that the subject must construct its cognitive object, which is composed of one or more phenomena, as distinguished from appearances.

Kant's later view of knowledge as resulting from the construction of phenomena provides the basis for a phenomenological approach to knowledge. Though representationalism remains popular, it arguably reaches a high point in the critical philosophy, where Kant shows the inability to demonstrate the usefulness of this strategy, the inability to show that through representation one in fact knows the mind-independent world not as it appears but as it is.[4] Kant's criticism of representationalism has never been answered. Kant, who accepts a correspondence approach to truth, in effect argues that it cannot be shown that we can reliably claim to represent and hence know a mind-independent object, but we can reliably claim to know an object that we can be said to "construct."

If we accept Kantian constructivism as the criterion of a phenomenological approach to knowledge, then we must turn away from Husserl, Heidegger, and Merleau-Ponty, who, each in his own way, eschew constructivism. Husserl and Heidegger share the well-known but mysterious Husserlian concern to go to things themselves. There is a deep similarity between "things in themselves" and the later formulation "things themselves." The difference seems to be that things in themselves do not and cannot appear and hence cannot be known; but things themselves supposedly can appear and hence can be known, according to Heidegger, since they show themselves.

The difficulty lies in making out this claim under Kant's influence but after his turn away from representationalism. Husserl, Heidegger, and Merleau-Ponty employ different strategies, all of which can be seen to fail. Husserl presents a complex choice between two forms of phenomenology, which are separated by the phenomenological reduction: an initial, descriptive form, and a later transcendental idealist form. The descriptive form expounded in *Logical Investigations* potentially suffices if and only if there is naive, or direct apprehension of what is as it is. This approach rests on the implicit commitment to a naive, or direct, realism, for which Husserl does not argue, but which is later assumed without argument by Heidegger and Merleau-Ponty, and which is apparently denied by Kant's clear-cut assertion that our cognitive access to experience is never direct but always mediated by a categorial framework.

The situation is not ameliorated in Heidegger's phenomenological ontology. The position he expounds in *Being and Time* counts as an effort to improve on Husserl's early, nontranscendental, pre-reductionistic phenomenology for his own ontological purposes. Heidegger's main innovation lies in inventing a theory of truth in which objects allegedly show themselves to the phenomenological observer. Yet this theory rests on the dubious, phenomenologically unverifiable premise, for which Heidegger never argues, that objects in fact show themselves to us as a condition of knowledge.

Husserl's later view derives from the distinction that, through the transcendental reduction, he introduces between the life-world, or ordinary experience, and the transcendental plane. Yet, like Descartes, who, once he leaves the world behind can never later return to it, Husserl, cannot resolve this difficulty. Since he cannot exhibit the parallel on which he relies between the transcendental and immanent views of the world and hence cannot show that on the transcendental plane he is able to go to things themselves in reaching phenomenological bedrock, he cannot demonstrate the parallel on which he relies between the transcendental and immanent views of the world.

The situation is similar for Merleau-Ponty, whose thesis of the primacy of perception closes up the crucial Kantian distinction between sensation and perception. In virtue of his rejection of the phenomenological reduction, Merleau-Ponty's phenomenological approach to knowledge belongs to the line pioneered by the early Husserl and carried further by Heidegger. The insuperable difficulty lies in showing that perception, which is individual, can, under suitable conditions, lead to experience and knowledge. To put the same point differently: Merleau-Ponty is apparently unable to demonstrate that perception, which is subjective, can function as the basis of a theory of objective knowledge.

Husserl, Heidegger, and Merleau-Ponty, three of the most important twentieth-century phenomenologists, share a nonconstructivist or anticonstructivist phenomenological approach to knowledge. This rapid review of twentieth-century phenomenology tends to confirm the Kantian point that, after Kant, who excludes direct realism and criticizes representationalism, efforts to make out either a direct realist or a representational approach to knowledge fail. It remains to examine the constructivist approach that Kant brings into German idealism and that is carried further by Hegel.

The central insight in Kant's constructivist epistemology is that knowledge consists in knowing phenomena that cognitive subjects construct. *Construction* is not as such a problem. The term is widely present in the twentieth century outside German idealism, for instance in Locke, and then in later empiricist movements in twentieth-century thought, including the writings of sense-datum empiricists such as Russell, C. D. Broad, H. H. Price, and others. Russell for a time favored logical construction.[5] Others committed in various ways to logical construction out of sense data include Ayer, Carnap, and Goodman.

The difficulty consists in understanding how to construe *construction* in claiming that in the process of knowledge we in some sense construct what we know. Kant, who illustrates his own suggestion that an important thinker is able to utilize an idea he often does not fully understand, and which is articulated by his successors,[6] does not answer this question. In the *Critique of Pure Reason*, the transcendental deduction supposedly sets forth the categories as the so-called "principles of the possibility of experience."[7] The deduction suggests that there is closure, and hence an identifiable set of categories,[8] which functions in a particular way in constituting the objects of perception on the one hand and experience and knowledge on the other. But Kant does not ask how perception becomes experience and knowledge in the *Critique of Pure Reason*; and when he does raise this question in the *Prolegomena*, he is unable to answer it. We have already cited his remark that "this schematism of our understanding with regard to appearances and their mere form is a hidden art in the depths of the human soul, whose true operations we can divine from nature and lay unveiled before our eyes only with difficulty."[9] This statement only points to the problem. Kant's inability to explain how we in fact construct cognitive objects suggests that he identifies a theoretical requirement of knowledge, or the claim that we must construct what we know, that he cannot explain in practice.

Hegel's contribution to what it means for the subject to construct the cognitive object is routinely overlooked for two reasons. In German idealism construction is phenomenological. Yet since there is little discussion of the phenomenological dimension of his position, it is not often noted, despite the title of his treatise, that his *Phenomenology of Spirit* is in fact phenomenological. There is also an unfortunate tendency to overemphasize the distance separating Hegel from Kant. Since Hegel participates in the post-Kantian German idealist project of working out and completing Kant's

Copernican revolution, his criticism of Kant on nearly every page of his writings is not incompatible but compatible with his own Kantianism. The interest of Hegel's phenomenology lies in its suggestion of how to construe the basic epistemological claim at the heart of Kant's Copernican revolution: We construct what we know and only know what we in some sense construct.

Hegel, who goes beyond Kant down the path that the latter opens, does not go far enough. Unlike Kant, who believes that constructivism is a priori, Hegel holds that it is a posteriori, arising within the epistemological process in which we seek to know the world and ourselves. Hegel's view of knowledge is constructivist in three senses: first, knowledge arises in an ongoing historical process in which we construct conceptual frameworks based on prior experience that we test against later experience. Second, we routinely alter these frameworks when they fail to fit experience; and to alter the framework alters the conceptual object. Third, since cognitive objects depend on the conceptual framework, a change in the framework results in a change in the object.

As Hegel puts it, "in the alteration of the knowledge [i.e., the conceptual framework—T. R.], the object itself alters for it too, for the knowledge that was present was essentially a knowledge of the object: as the knowledge changes, so too does the object, for it essentially belonged to this knowledge."[10] A simple example might be the difference between water, which is an object in everyday experience, as distinguished from H_2O, which depends on a chemical framework. The two conceptual frameworks are irreducibly different because the chemical framework, which arises to respond to conceptual problems that emerge in ordinary experience, cannot be reduced to or otherwise understood as a further form of the explanatory framework of everyday experience.

Kant calls for but does not develop a phenomenological epistemology. Hegel, who reformulates Kantian constructivism as a posteriori, applies it to an a posteriori construction of phenomena. His constructivist strategy, which is routinely overlooked in phenomenological circles, is arguably the best such approach we currently possess. Hegel points out that knowledge emerges, not in a relation between the mind and the world, but rather in an ongoing process within consciousness.

Hegel's view is most helpful in pointing out that knowledge, which is not the result of an instantaneous determination, emerges within an ongoing historical process. His view is weakest at the point where he pretends that our contribution in the knowledge process is simply superfluous since the process takes place without our contribution: "But not only is a contribution by us superfluous, since concept and object, the criterion and what is to be tested, are present in consciousness itself, but we are also spared the trouble of comparing and really *testing* them, so that, since what consciousness examines is its own self, all that is left for us to do is simply to look on."[11]

The difficulty lies in combining the human role in the cognitive process with claims for objective cognition. Kant stresses objective cognition at the expense of subjectivity. After Kant, Fichte's reformulation of the conception of the subject as finite human being is sometimes seen as reintroducing subjectivity at the expense of objectivity.[12] Writing after Fichte, Hegel adopts the former's conception of finite human subjectivity, to which he adds plural and historical dimensions. Yet, perhaps to maintain claims to objective cognition, he also diminishes the human role in human knowledge and hence scants the historical dimension on which he otherwise insists.

We can supplement Hegel's account in drawing attention to the distinction between the general conceptual framework in any cognitive discipline at a given time and the specific theories formulated within that framework. Hegel is correct that "consciousness provides its own criterion from within itself, so that the investigation becomes a comparison of consciousness with itself."[13] Yet it is wrong to believe that one simply looks on. What we take to be knowledge is rather based on a conscious decision and other factors too numerous even to list. In other words, finite human beings intervene at every step of the cognitive process. Specific cognitive claims are routinely formulated against the background of more general views, which hold sway at different times in different cognitive domains. The more general views derive from negotiations among the participants in a given cognitive domain about currently acceptable standards. The results of such negotiations, which are always subject to further debate, furnish the general criteria of acceptable theory in terms of which particular theories are formulated and evaluated. Since one can never knowingly claim to have reached the end of the cognitive process, changes in the normative views about knowledge as well as the formulation of particular theories are continually played out in the interpersonal domain.

There is an obvious relation between the interpersonal formulation and the testing of knowledge claims, between constructivism and phenomenology. Constructivism and phenomenology are two sides of the same cognitive process, which, according to Hegel, unfolds through the experience of phenomena and the formulation, or construction, of theories in the ongoing process of human cognition. Theories about experience do not arise in a void but in the mind of the cognitive subject, who does not merely look on but plays an active role in interpreting and carrying forward the cognitive process. The difficulty, which is real, lies in acknowledging the role of finite human beings in the cognitive process while comprehending the conditions of objective cognition, which can never successfully be disjoined from the social dimension.

Aristotle points out we do not aim toward the good in itself but toward the good for us.[14] Hegel similarly notes that knowledge does not concern the world in itself but the world for us, which we only know through conscious phenomena. Hegel sides with Fichte in rejecting the Kantian abstract cognitive subject. He points away from Kant's effort to elucidate the conditions of knowledge in general toward knowledge for finite human beings caught up in human history. Now as in Kant's time, the problem of knowledge lies in understanding how we "construct" phenomena in the interaction between human beings situated within the historical process in which we come to know the world and ourselves.

NOTES

INTRODUCTION

1. See Michael B. Gil, "Moral Phenomenology in Hutcheson and Hume," *Journal of the History of Philosophy* 47 (October 2009): 569–94.
2. For recent discussion emphasizing the relation of phenomenalism to physicalism, see *Phenomenal Concepts and Phenomenal Knowledge: New Essays on Consciousness and Physicalism*, ed. Torin Alter and Sven Walter (New York: Oxford University Press, 2007).
3. See Michael Williams, *Problems of Knowledge: A Critical Introduction to Epistemology* (Oxford: Oxford University Press, 2001), 107. A. J. Ayer, a main proponent of phenomenalism, described it as a reductionist position that refutes skepticism in holding that things are what they seem to be; see *The Problem of Knowledge* (Baltimore, MD: Penguin, 1969), 118–29. Husserl thought it failed to distinguish between the appearance, understood as an intentional object, and the apparent object and hence conflated sensation with objective reality. See Edmund Husserl, *Logical Investigations*, 2 vols., trans. J. N. Findlay, revised by Dermot Moran (London: Routledge, 2001), 2:90.
4. He refers, for example, to phenomenology that "die ich [i.e., Husserl—T. R.] de facto in die Geschichte eingeführt habe." See Edmund Husserl, *Die Krisis der europäischen Wissenschaften und die transzendentale Phänomenologie. Eine Einleitung in die phänomenologische Philosophie*, ed. Walter Biemel, Husserliana 6 (The Hague: Martinus Nijhoff, 1954), 440.
5. See, for example, on realism, Dallas Willard, "A World Well Won: Husserl's Epistemic Realism One Hundred Years Later," in *One Hundred Years of Phenomenology: Husserl's Logical Investigations Revisited*, ed. D. Zahavi and F. Stjernfelt (Dordrecht: Kluwer Academic Publishers, 2002), 69–73.
6. See, for an exception, Charles Guignon, *Heidegger and the Problem of Knowledge* (Indianapolis, IN: Hackett, 1983). Guignon sees Heidegger as presenting an alternative to Cartesian epistemology. He argues that *Being and Time* fails because Heidegger is still caught in the same kind of calculative-rational thinking used in the tradition he wishes to overcome.
7. Cassirer specifically claims allegiance to Hegelian phenomenology. See Ernst Cassirer, *Philosophy of Symbolic Forms*, vol. 3, *The Phenomenology of Knowledge*, trans. Ralph Manheim (New Haven, CT: Yale University Press, 1965), xiv.

8. See, for example, David Woodruff Smith, "Intentionality Naturalized?" in *Naturalizing Phenomenology: Issues in Contemporary Phenomenology and Cognitive Science*, ed. Jean Petitot, Francisco Varela, Bernard Pachoud, and Jean-Michel Roy (Stanford, CA: Stanford University Press, 1999), 83–110.
9. See, on the naturalist movement in analytic philosophy, Georg Gasser, ed., *How Successful Is Naturalism?* (Frankfurt: Ontos, 2007).
10. See Michael Wheeler, *Reconstructing the Cognitive World: The Next Step* (Cambridge, MA: MIT Press, 2005).
11. See Evan Thompson, *Mind in Life: Biology, Phenomenology, and the Sciences of Mind* (Cambridge, MA: Harvard University Press, 2007).
12. This is especially true of his recent study of music. See Oliver Sacks, *Musicophilia: Tales of Music and the Brain* (New York: Vintage, 2008).
13. See Carl F. Craver, *Explaining the Brain: Mechanisms and the Mosaic Unity of Neuroscience* (New York: Oxford University Press, 2007).
14. See Henry Pietersma, *Phenomenological Epistemology* (New York: Oxford University Press, 2000).
15. Henry E. Allison makes this point in his review of Strawson; see "Transcendental Idealism and Descriptive Metaphysics," *Kant-Studien (1969)* 60, no.2 (1969): 216–33.
16. The question of the Kantian distinction between appearances and phenomena is complex and unclear. Kant's view changed over time. In the first edition, he wrote, "Erscheinungen, sofern sie als Gegenstände nach der Einheit der Kategorien gedacht werden, heissen Phänomena" (Immanuel Kant, *Kritik der reinen Vernunft*, ed. Raymund Schmidt [Hamburg: Felix Meiner Verlag, 1976], A249, 298). The interpretation of this passage is uncertain but could suggest that phenomena are appearances. In that case, all phenomena would be appearances, and there would be no distinction between phenomena and appearances. His view later evolved. His critique of representationalism as well as his later Copernican turn arguably commit him to denying this point, since in phenomena mind-independent reality does not appear. This way of reading the distinction between appearances and phenomena is arguably further consistent with Hegel's as well as Husserl's and Heidegger's views of phenomena and hence of a phenomenological approach to knowledge.
17. See Immanuel Kant, *Critique of Pure Reason*, trans. Paul Guyer and Allen W. Wood (New York: Cambridge University Press, 1998), chap. 3: "On the grounds of the distinction of all objects in general into *phenomena* and *noumena*" (B295–315, 354–65).
18. See Aristotle, *Metaphysics*, trans. Richard Hope, with an analytical index of technical terms (Ann Arbor: University of Michigan Press, 1968), 1:6, 19–21.
19. See *Plato's Theory of Knowledge: The Theaetetus and the Sophist of Plato*, translated, with commentary, by Francis M. Cornford (Indianapolis, IN: LLA, 1957), 151D, 29.
20. See Plato *Republic*, bk. 10, 596, in *Complete Works*, ed. John M. Cooper (Indianapolis, IN: Hackett, 1997), 1200.
21. See *Plato's Theory of Knowledge*, 242C–E, 216–17.
22. See Plato *Phaedo* 99A–100E, in *Complete Works*, 85–86.
23. This view that ideas cause things is repeated after the *Phaedo* in other dialogues. Instances include *Republic* 508E and *Timaeus* 29A–30B.
24. Hegel seems to support this view. See G. W. F. Hegel, *Phenomenology of Spirit*, trans. A. V. Miller (New York: Oxford University Press, 1977), sec. 150, 91–92.
25. See, for example, Lee Smolin, *The Trouble with Physics: The Rise of String Theory, the Fall of a Science, and What Comes Next* (Boston: Houghton Mifflin, 2007).
26. See *Plato's Theory of Knowledge*, 151E, 29.

27. See, for example, Nelson Goodman, *Ways of Worldmaking* (Indianapolis, IN: Hackett, 1978), 130–40.
28. See Kant, *Critique of Pure Reason*, B370, 396.
29. The idea that Kant is a Platonist is sometimes rehearsed in the discussion. This was more common in the nineteenth and early twentieth centuries than at present. See, for example, Julius Heidemann, *Platonis de ideis doctrinam quomodo Kantius et intellexerit et excoluerit* (Berolini, Germany: Schade, 1858); Karl Fuchs, *Die Idee bei Plato und Kant* (Wiener-Neustadt, Germany: Klinger, 1886); Theodor Valentiner, *Kant und die platonische Philosophie* (Heidelberg: Winter, 1904).
30. The key text, which echoes through the later discussion, is Augustine, *On the Free Choice of the Will*, trans. Thomas Williams (Indianapolis, IN: Hackett, 1993). There is an extensive literature on the relation of the subject in Augustine and Descartes. See, for example, Etienne Gilson, *La Liberté chez Descartes et la théologie* (Paris: Alcan, 1913).
31. See Thomas Nagel, *The Last Word* (New York: Oxford University Press, 1997).
32. See Paul Boghossian, *Fear of Knowledge: Against Relativism and Constructivism* (Oxford: Clarendon Press, 2006).
33. See Kant, *Critique of Pure Reason*, B1, 136.
34. See Jean-Louis Le Moigne, *Les Epistémologies constructivistes* (Paris: Presses universitaires de France, 1995).
35. For a general survey of constructivism, see Bernard Taureck, *Das Schicksal der philosophischen Konstruktion* (Wien/München: Oldenbourg, 1975). For a survey of constructivism limited to German idealism, see Helga Ende, *Der Konstruktionsbegriff im Umkreiss des Deutschen Idealismus* (Meisenheim am Glan, Germany: Anton Hain, 1973).
36. Edmund Husserl, *Ideas: General Introduction to Pure Phenomenology*, trans. W. R. Boyce Gibson (New York: Collier Books, 1962). This book, which appeared during his lifetime, is often cited as *Ideas* 1 to avoid confusion with the other two volumes, which appeared after his death. In citing it as *Ideas*, I am always referring to this specific volume. See also Edmund Husserl, *The Idea of Phenomenology*, trans. William P. Alston and George Nakhnikian, introduction by George Nakhnikian (The Hague: Martinus Nijhoff, 1964).

CHAPTER ONE

1. See Karin de Boer, *Thinking in the Light of Time: Heidegger's Encounter with Hegel* (Albany: State University of New York Press, 2000).
2. See, on scientism, Joseph Margolis, *The Unraveling of Scientism: American Philosophy at the End of the Twentieth Century* (Ithaca, NY: Cornell University Press, 2003).
3. See "What Is Pragmatism?" in *The Essential Peirce*, ed. Nathan Houser and Christian Kloesel (Bloomington: Indiana University Press, 1998), 2:338.
4. See G. S. Kirk and J. E. Raven, *The Presocratic Philosophers* (Cambridge: Cambridge University Press, 1957), 269–70.
5. Ibid., 273–78.
6. Plato *Sophist* 246C, in *Complete Works*, ed. John M. Cooper (Indianapolis, IN: Hackett, 1997), 268, 248A, 269–70.
7. Plato *Phaedo* 96a, in *Complete Works*, 83.
8. Ibid., 100C.3–7, 86: "Consider then, he said, whether you share my opinion as to what follows, for I think that, if there is anything else beautiful besides the Beautiful itself, it is beautiful for no other reason than because it shares in that Beautiful, and I say so with everything. Do you recognize this sort of cause?—I do."

9. Ibid., 101C, 87: "You do not know how else each thing can come to be except by sharing in the particular reality in which it shares." Cf. 102 B, 88: "It was agreed that each of the Forms existed, and that the other things acquired their name by having a share in them."
10. Russell, who follows Hume's skepticism in causal matters, regards causal laws as outmoded. "The law of causality, I believe, like much that passes muster among philosophers, is a relic of a bygone age, surviving, like the monarchy, only because it is erroneously supposed to do no harm." Bertrand Russell, "On the Notion of Cause," *Proceedings of the Aristotelian Society* 13, no. 1 (1913): 1–26.
11. See Martin Heidegger, *Being and Time*, trans. John Macquarrie and Edward Robinson (New York: Harper and Row, 1962), 435–44.
12. See Plato *Republic*, bk. 10, 596B, in *Complete Works*, 1200.
13. See Immanuel Kant, *Prolegomena to Any Future Metaphysics, and the Letter to Marcus Hertz, February 1772*, trans. James W. Ellington (Indianapolis, IN: Hackett, 2001), sec. 38, pp. 58–59.
14. See G. W. F. Hegel, *Hegel's Phenomenology of Spirit*, trans. A. V. Miller (New York: Oxford University Press, 1977), sec. 150, 91.
15. See Karl Marx, "Introduction," in *Grundrisse: Foundations of the Critique of Political Economy (Rough Draft)*, trans. Martin Nicolaus (Harmondsworth, UK: Penguin, 1973), pt. 3: "The Method of Political Economy": "Human anatomy contains a key to the anatomy of the ape" (105).
16. See Michel Foucault, *The Order of Things*, trans. Ben Brewster (New York: Vintage, 1973).
17. For an influential study, see Eric Auerbach, *Mimesis: The Representation of Reality in Western Literature*, trans. Willard Trask (Princeton, NJ: Princeton University Press, 1968).
18. This is an early form of the reflection theory of knowledge later discussed by many thinkers, including Francis Bacon, Engels, Lenin, and the early Wittgenstein, all of whom are epistemological anti-Platonists.
19. See Iris Murdoch, *The Fire and the Sun: Why Plato Banished the Artists* (Oxford: Clarendon Press, 1971), 31.
20. See Stephen Halliwell, "Aristotelian Mimesis Re-evaluated," *Journal of the History of Philosophy* 28 (1990): 487–510.
21. "A poet, then, is an *imitator* in so far as he is a *maker*, viz. of plots. The paradox is obvious. Aristotle has developed and changed the bearing of a concept which originally meant a faithful *copying* of preexistent things, to make it a *creation* of things which have never existed, or whose existence, if they did exist, is accidental to the poetic process. Copying is after the fact; Aristotle's *mimesis* creates the fact. It is clear that his use of the word in such a way can only be accounted for historically: that is, that such a redefinition of a simple concept can only be understood as the end-product of a long, gradual development. Without Plato especially, and a considerable development of the idea in him, Aristotle's use of *mimesis* would be inconceivable" (Gerard Else, *Aristotle's Poetics: The Argument* [Cambridge, MA: Harvard University Press, 1957], 322).
22. See Aristotle, *Physics*, in *The Complete Works of Aristotle*, 2 vols., ed. Jonathan Barnes (Princeton, NJ: Princeton University Press, 1984), 2.2, 2:330–32, and 2.8, 2:339–41.
23. See Aristotle, *Poetics* 25, in *Complete Works*, 2:2237–2339.
24. See Auerbach, *Mimesis*.

25. See Ernst Gombrich, *Art and Illusion: A Study in the Psychology of Pictorial Representation* (Oxford: Phaidon, 1982).
26. See Nelson Goodman, *Languages of Art: An Approach to the Theory of Symbols* (Indianapolis, IN: Hackett, 1988).
27. "Je vous dois la vérité en peinture, et je vous la dirai." Letter from Paul Cezanne to Emile Bernard, 25 October 1905, cited in Jacques Derrida, *La Vérite en peinture* (Paris: Flammarion, 1978), 6.
28. For an account of the controversy between Locke and Stillingfleet, see "Prolegomena: Biographical, Critical, and Historical," in *An Essay Concerning Human Understanding*, by John Locke, 2 vols., collated and annotated by A. C. Fraser (New York: Dover, 1959), 1:xli–xlii.
29. The Cambridge Platonists (e.g., Henry More, Ralph Cudworth, and others), who were influenced by Plato, Plotinus, and Aristotle, and repudiated scholasticism, were associated in the mid-seventeenth century with the University of Cambridge.
30. See Kant, *Critique of Pure Reason*, trans. Paul Guyer and Allen W. Wood (New York: Cambridge University Press, 1998), B377, 399.
31. See Plato *Parmenides* 132A1–B2, in *Complete Works*, 365–66.
32. This term was invented by Aristotle, who appears to discuss Plato's argument in various places. See, for example, *Metaphysics* 1.9.990b23–991a8, 1566; 7.13.10339a2, 1640; 11.1.1059b8, 1674.
33. See, for discussion, "Plato's 'Third Man' Argument (*Parm.* I 32 a1–b2): Text and Logic," in *Platonic Studies*, by Gregory Vlastos (Princeton, NJ: Princeton University Press, 1982), 342–65. For a different view, which casts doubt on the supposed link between Aristotle's comments and Plato's criticism of the theory of ideas in Parmenides, see Gail Fine, "Owen, Aristotle, and the Third Man," *Phronesis* 27 (1982): 13–33.
34. See Plato *Phaedo* 65E, in *Complete Works*, 57.
35. See Aristotle *Metaphysics* 987b.1–7, in *Complete Works*, 2:1560.
36. See, for a recent discussion, David Clemenson, *Descartes' Theory of Ideas* (London: Continuum, 2007).
37. For a general account, see Roger Ariew, "Descartes and Scholasticism: The Intellectual Background to Descartes' Thought," in *Cambridge Companion to Descartes*, ed. John Cottingham (New York: Cambridge University Press, 1992), 58–91.
38. See, for example, Etienne Gilson, *Index scolastico-cartésien* (New York: Burt Franklin, 1963).
39. See Richard H. Popkin, *The History of Skepticism: From Savonarola to Bayle* (New York: Oxford University Press, 2003).
40. See, for example, Etienne Gilson, *Etude sur le role de la pensée médiévale dans la formation du système cartésien* (Paris: Vrin, 1930); and Daniel Garber, *Descartes' Metaphysical Physics* (Chicago: University of Chicago Press, 1992).
41. This has been widely studied. See, for example, George J. Ryan, "Plato's Ideas in the Light of Early Scholasticism," in *Transactions and Proceedings of the American Philological Association* (Baltimore, MD: Johns Hopkins University Press, 1937).
42. Augustine, "On Eighty-Three Different Questions," q. 46.2, in *Five Texts on the Mediaeval Problem of Universals: Porphyry, Boethius, Abelard, Duns Scotus, Ockham*, trans. P. V. Spade (Indianapolis, IN: Hackett, 1994): "In Latin we can call the Ideas 'forms' or 'species,' in order to appear to translate word for word. But if we call them 'reasons,' we depart to be sure from a proper translation—for reasons are called 'logoi' in Greek, not Ideas—but nevertheless, whoever wants to use this word will not be in

conflict with the fact. For Ideas are certain principal, stable and immutable forms or reasons of things. They are not themselves formed, and hence they are eternal and always stand in the same relations, and they are contained in the divine understanding" (383).

43. Thomas Aquinas *Summa Theologica* 1.84.a5.427: "Whenever Augustine, who was imbued with the doctrines of the Platonists, found in their teaching anything consistent with faith, he adopted it: and those things which he found contrary to faith he amended.... But since it seems contrary to faith that forms of things should subsist of themselves, outside the things themselves and apart from matter, as the Platonists held ... Augustine ... substituted the types of all creatures existing in the Divine mind, according to which types all things are made in themselves."

44. Aquinas *Summa Theologica* 1.84.a5.427: "The human soul knows all things in the eternal types, since by participation of these types we know all things. For the intellectual light itself which is in us, is nothing else than a participated likeness of the uncreated light, in which are contained the eternal types.... But since besides the intellectual light which is in us, intelligible species, which are derived from things, are required in order for us to have knowledge of material things; therefore this same knowledge is not due merely to a participation of the eternal types, as the Platonists held."

45. "Third Replies," in *The Philosophical Writings of Descartes*, vols. 1 and 2 trans. J. Cottingham, R. Stoothoff, and D. Murdoch; vol. 3, trans. J. Cottingham, R. Stoothoff, D. Murdoch, and A. Kenny (Cambridge: Cambridge University Press, 1984, 1985, 1991), 2:127.

46. See Plato *Phaedrus* 265E, in *Complete Works*, 542.

47. René Descartes, *The Philosophical Works of Descartes*, 2 vols., trans. Elizabeth S. Haldane and G. R. T. Ross (New York: Cambridge University Press, 1970), 1:160, 159.

48. Anthony Kenny, "Descartes on Ideas," in *Descartes*, ed. Willis Doney (New York: Doubleday, 1967), 229. Kenny refers to L. J. Beck, *The Metaphysics of Descartes* (New York: Oxford University Press, 1965), 152.

49. René Descartes, *Meditations on First Philosophy*, in *Philosophical Works*, 1:159 ("Third Meditation").

50. See René Descartes, *Objections with Replies*, in *Philosophical Works*, 2:66–67 ("Objections Three," no. 5).

51. Descartes, *Philosophical Works*, 1:138.

52. See Richard A. Watson, *Representational Ideas: From Plato to Patricia Churchland* (Dordrecht: Kluwer, 1995), 47.

53. See Descartes, *Philosophical Works*, 1:161.

54. Ibid., 2:70.

55. Descartes, "Sixth Meditation," in *Philosophical Works*, 1:187.

56. Ibid., 191.

57. See Kant, *Critique of Pure Reason*, B274–80, B326–29.

58. See Spinoza, *Works of Spinoza*, translated from the Latin, with an introduction, by R. H. M. Elwes (New York: Dover, 1951), 82 (*The Ethics*, pt. 2, definition 3).

59. Ibid., 86 (pt. 2, prop. 7).

60. See G. W. Leibniz, "Monadology," secs. 62, 63, 78, in *Leibniz: Basic Writings*, trans. George R. Montgomery, with an introduction by Paul Janet (Chicago: Open Court, 1957), 265, 268–69.

61. See Leibniz, "Discourse on Metaphysics," in *Basic Writings*, sec. 26, 44–45.

62. Difficulties in the Cartesian program and rationalism in general extend over hundreds of years and are an important factor in the transition from rationalism to al-

ternative epistemological strategies. Watson, who is a close student of Descartes, condemns the entire movement of thought he engenders. See Richard A. Watson, *The Breakdown of Cartesian Metaphysics* (Indianapolis, IN: Hackett, 1998). This book is a straightforward attack on Cartesian metaphysics leading to the conclusion that, as he claims, Cartesian science is nescience and cannot be saved. Watson's main argument is that " if every representation must be like the object it represents, and if every cause must be in some way like its effect, then the Cartesian metaphysical system incorporates an unbridgeable gap between mind and matter" (22). On this basis, he contends that rather than apodictic claims to knowledge, Descartes can know nothing at all. See chapter 14, "Descartes Knows Nothing" (193–204).

63. Locke, *Human Understanding*, bk. 1, chap. 8, pt. 47.
64. Ibid., bk. 4, chap. 4, pt. 3, 563, and bk. 4, chap. 21, pt.4, 721.
65. The interpretation of Locke's position is delicate. A commitment to the view that we directly know only our own ideas is seen as favoring skepticism by Reid in answering Locke, by Kant in replying to Descartes and Berkeley, and by Moore in answering Kant and all idealists of whatever kind, who supposedly contend that reality, understood as the mind-independent external world, is confined to the contents of our minds.
66. See Locke, *Human Understanding*, bk. 2, chap. 2, 145.
67. Ibid., bk. 2, chap. 32, 521.
68. See Otto Neurath, "Protocol Sentences," in *Logical Positivism*, ed. A. J. Ayer (New York: Free Press, 1959), 199–208.
69. See Aristotle *De Anima* 429b30–430a3, in *The Complete Works of Aristotle*, 2 vols., ed. Jonathan Barnes (Princeton, NJ: Princeton University Press, 1984).
70. In a striking passage, which deserves to be cited at length, Locke writes: "It is your opinion the ideas we perceive by our senses are not real things, but images or copies of them. Our knowledge, therefore, is no farther real than as our ideas are the true *representations of those originals*. But, as these supposed originals are in themselves unknown, it is impossible to know how far our ideas resemble them; or whether they resemble them at all. We cannot, therefore, be sure we have any real knowledge"; see "Three Dialogues between Hylas and Philonous," in *George Berkeley, Principles of Human Knowledge and Three Dialogues Between Hylas and Philonous*, ed. R. S. Woodhouse (London: Penguin, 2004), 192; Berkeley's emphasis.
71. See George Berkeley, *Principles of Human Knowledge*, in *Principles of Human Knowledge, and Three Dialogues*, ed. Howard Robinson (Oxford: Oxford University Press, 1996), secs. 85–86, 61–62.
72. See Antoine Arnauld, *L'art de penser: La Logique de Port-Royal*, ed. Bruno Baron von Freytag Löringhoff and Herbert E. Brekle (Stuttgart-Bad Cannstatt: Frommann, 1965), 1: chap. 6.
73. See the introduction to George Berkeley, *A Treatise Concerning the Principles of Human Knowledge*, in *Philosophical Works*, ed. M. R. Ayers (London: Dent, 1992), sec. 12, 69–70.
74. See *A New Theory of Vision*, in ibid., sec. 125, 45.
75. See Berkeley, *Principles*, sec. 116, in ibid., 113.
76. See Kant, *Critique of Pure Reason*, B274, 326.
77. See Berkeley, *Principles*, secs. 85–86, 61–62.
78. See Julian Offray de La Mettrie, *Machine, Man, and Other Writings*, ed. Ann Thomson (Cambridge: Cambridge University Press, 1996).
79. See Berkeley, *Principles*, sec. 4: "It is indeed an opinion strangely prevailing amongst men, that houses, mountains, rivers, and in a word all sensible objects have an

existence natural or real, distinct from their being perceived by the understanding. But with how great an assurance and acquiescence soever this principle may be entertained in the world; yet whoever shall find in his heart to call it in question, may, if I mistake not, perceive it to involve a manifest contradiction. For what are the forementioned objects but the things we perceive by sense, and what do we perceive besides our own ideas or sensations; and is it not plainly repugnant that any one of these or any combination of them should exist unperceived?"

80. Ibid., sec. 8: "But say you, though the ideas themselves do not exist without the mind, yet there may be things like them whereof they are copies or resemblances, which things exist without the mind, in an unthinking substance. I answer, an idea can be like nothing but an idea; a colour or figure can be like nothing but another colour or figure."
81. Kant's erroneous claim in his "refutation of idealism" that as an idealist Berkeley denies the reality of the external world is extended in Paul Redding's view that Berkeley is a spiritualist but not an idealist; see his *Continental Idealism: Leibniz To Nietzsche* (London: Routledge, 2009), 19.
82. See David Hume, *Enquiries Concerning the Human Understanding and Concerning the Principles of Morals*, reprinted from the 1777 edition, ed. L. A. Selby-Bigge (Oxford: Clarendon Press, 1966), 19.
83. See Hume, *Enquiries*, sec. 2, 12.
84. Ibid., 19.
85. David Hume, *Enquiries Concerning Human Understanding and Concerning the Principles of Morals*, ed. L. A. Selby-Bigge, 3rd ed., revised by P. H. Nidditch (Oxford: Clarendon Press, 1975), sec. 8, pt. 73, 95.
86. See "Of Liberty and Necessity," as first presented in David Hume, *A Treatise of Human Nature*, ed. L. A. Selby-Bigge (Oxford: Clarendon Press, 1968), bk. 2, pt., 1–2, 399–413 and, later, in a slightly amended form, in Hume, *Enquiries* (3rd ed., 1975), sec. 8, 80–103.
87. See Berkeley, *Principles*, secs. 85–86, 61–62.
88. See Thomas Reid, *Essays on the Intellectual Powers of Man* (Edinburgh: J. Bell, 1795), 128; cited in John W. Yolton, *Perceptual Acquaintance from Descartes to Reid* (Minneapolis: University of Minnesota Press, 1984), 3.
89. See Kant, *Critique of Pure Reason*, B274–79, 326–29.
90. See Thomas Reid, *Essays on the Intellectual Powers of Man*, ed. Derek Brookes (University Park: Pennsylvania State University Press, 2002), 31.
91. See Hilary Putnam, *The Threefold Cord: Mind, Body, and World* (New York: Columbia University Press, 1999).

CHAPTER TWO

1. See Tom Rockmore, *Kant and Idealism*, New Haven, CT: Yale University Press, 2007.
2. See, for example, T. K. Seung, *Kant's Platonic Revolution in Moral and Political Philosophy* (Baltimore, MD: Johns Hopkins University Press, 1994).
3. See, for a recent study, Mihaela C. Fistioc, *The Beautiful Shape of the Good: Platonic and Pythagorean Themes in Kant's Critique of the Power of Judgment* (London: Routledge, 2002). According to Fistioc, "We do not know if Kant read any of Plato's dialogues, whether in the original or in translation" (7).
4. See Johann Jakob Brucker, *Historia critica philosophiae a mundi incunabuli: ad nostram usque actatem deducts*, 4 vols. (Lipsiae [Leipzig]: Impensis Haered. Weidemanni et Reichii, 1766–67; repr., Hildesheim: G. Olms, 1975).

5. Hamann, quoted in Manfred Kuehn, *Kant: A Biography* (New York: Cambridge University Press, 2001), 253.
6. Ibid., 470, n. 19, and 193.
7. See Paul Guyer, *Kant* (London: Routledge, 2006), 34, 126.
8. See Kant, *Critique of Pure Reason*, trans. Paul Guyer and Allen W. Wood (New York: Cambridge University Press, 1998), B9, 129. This work is subsequently cited parenthetically by page number in the text.
9. See the letter to Marcus Herz, February 11, 1772, in Immanuel Kant, *Correspondence*, trans. and ed. Arnulf Zweig (New York: Cambridge University Press, 1999), 133.
10. See G. W. F. Hegel, *Elements of the Philosophy of Right*, ed. Allen W. Wood, trans. H. B. Nisbet (Cambridge: Cambridge University Press, 1991), 20.
11. Kant, letter to Herz, 11 February 1772, in *Correspondence*, 132.
12. The most important current defender of this approach is Henry E. Allison, who claims that the two aspects refer to ordinary and epistemic considerations directed to the conditions of the possibility of cognition of the same object; see *Kant's Transcendental Idealism: An Interpretation and Defense*, rev. ed. (New Haven, CT: Yale University Press, 2004).
13. See Kant, *Critique of Pure Reason*, 1st ed., chap. 3: "On the ground of the distinction of all objects in general into *phenomena* and *noumena*," A338–54: and 2nd ed., chap. 3: "On the ground of the distinction of all objects in general into *phenomena* and *noumena*," B354–66.
14. See Robert Hanna, *Kant and the Foundations of Analytic Philosophy* (Oxford: Clarendon Press, 2001), 22: "Kant's Copernican Revolution of 1781–7 is in this way an all-things-considered answer to the fundamental semantic question he raised in 1772: how can mental representations—and more specifically necessary a priori mental representations—refer to their objects. And the answer is that mental representations refer to their objects because 'objects must conform to our cognitions'; hence our true a priori judgments are necessarily true independently of all sense experience because they express just those cognitive forms or structures to which all the proper objects of human cognition automatically conform."
15. See George Berkeley, *Three Dialogues between Hylas and Philonous*, in *Philosophical Works, Including the Works on Vision*, ed. M. Ayers (London: Dent), 238.
16. See Ernst Cassirer, *The Philosophy of Symbolic Forms*, vol. 3, *The Phenomenology of Knowing*, trans. Ralph Manheim (New Haven, CT: Yale University Press, 1957), 20.
17. See G. W. F. Hegel, *Hegel's Phenomenology of Spirit*, trans. A. V. Miller (New York: Oxford University Press, 1977), sec. 73, 46–47.
18. There are other similar passages. For instance, in reference to the distinction between rain and a rainbow Kant writes, "Thus, we would certainly call a rainbow a mere appearance in a sun-shower, but would call this rain the thing in itself, and this is correct as long as we understand the latter concept in a merely physical sense" (B63, 187).
19. For a good summary, see Sebastien Gardner, "Review of Henry E. Allison, *Kant's Transcendental Idealism: An Interpretation and Defense*, Revised and Enlarged Edition, Yale University Press, 2004," in *Notre Dame Philosophical Review* (2005). Published online; no further information available.
20. See Allison, *Kant's Transcendental Idealism*, 4.
21. See J. G. Fichte, "First Introduction," in *Introductions to the Wissenschaftslehre and Other Writings (1797–1800)*, trans. and ed. Daniel Breazeale (Indianapolis, IN: Hackett, 1994), sec. 1, 6–7.

22. Ibid., sec. 6, 22.
23. "The thing in itself is a pure invention which possesses no reality whatsoever" (ibid., sec. 3, 11).
24. Ibid., sec. 7, 32.
25. Ibid., sec. 7, 34.
26. Ibid., sec. 7, 29.
27. For these criticisms and Allison's responses, see Allison, *Kant's Transcendental Idealism*.
28. See R 5554 (1778–1781, 18:229–31), cited in Kant, *Critique of Pure Reason*, B725, n. 26.
29. See Plato *Republic* 7.510A, in *Complete Works*, ed. John M. Cooper (Indianapolis, IN: Hackett, 1997), 1131.
30. Duns Scotus, Ord. 1, d. 3, pars.
31. See, for an analysis of medieval views of intentionality in relation to modern philosophy of mind, Peter King, "Rethinking Representation in the Middle Ages," in *Representation and Objects of Thought in Medieval Philosophy*, ed. Henrik Lagerlund (Burlington, VT: Ashgate, 2005), 83–102.
32. See H. Grice, "The Causal Theory of Perception," in *Perceiving, Sensing, and Knowing*, ed. Robert J. Swartz (Garden City, NY: Anchor Books, 1965), 438–72.
33. See Peter Strawson, "Causation in Perception," in *Freedom and Resentment and Other Essays* (London: Methuen, 1974), 66–84; Alvin Goldman, "A Causal Theory of Knowing," *Journal of Philosophy* 64 (December 1967): 355–72.
34. See Gottlob Frege, "On *Sinn* and *Bedeutung*," in *Frege Reader*, ed. Michael Beaney (Oxford: Blackwell, 1997), 151–71.
35. Nelson Goodman, *Of Mind and Other Matters* (Cambridge, MA: Harvard University Press, 1984), 55.
36. See, for a well-known critical account, Ernest Gellner, *Words and Things: An Examination of, and an Attack on, Linguistic Philosophy*, foreword by Bertrand Russell (London: Routledge and Kegan Paul, 1979).
37. See Bertrand Russell, "On Denoting," in *Mind* 14, no. 56 (1905): 479–93; see also Bertrand Russell, *Mysticism and Logic* (Garden City, NY: Doubleday Anchor, 1957), 202–24; Peter Strawson, "On Referring," in *Mind* 59, no. 235 (1950): 59, 320–44; Saul Kripke, *Naming and Necessity* (Cambridge, MA: Harvard University Press, 1980); and Hilary Putnam, *Mind, Language, and Reality: Philosophical Papers, Volume 2* (Cambridge: Cambridge University Press, 1975).
38. See W. V. Quine, *The Roots of Reference* (Chicago: Open Court, 1973).
39. See Robert B. Brandom, *Making It Explicit* (Cambridge, MA: Harvard University Press, 1992). He regards inferentialism as succeeding where representationalism fails since it invokes asking for and giving reasons. "The claim developed and defended here is that representational locutions should be understood as making explicit certain features of *communicating* by claiming—the *interpersonal giving and asking for reasons*" (496). Left unexplained is why, in substituting inferentialism for representationalism, giving and asking for reasons makes it possible to ascertain the nature of the mind-independent real.
40. See Anandi Hattiangadi, *Oughts and Thought: Scepticism and the Normativity of Meaning* (New York: Oxford University Press, 2007).
41. See "On the ground of the distinction of all objects in general into *phenomena* and *noumena*," in Kant, *Critique of Pure Reason*, B295–315, 354–65.
42. See, for example, the criticism of Hobbes's *De Cive* under the heading "On the Relation of Theory to Practice in the Right of a State (against Hobbes)," in the essay

entitled "On the Common Saying: 'That may be correct in theory, but it is of no use in practice,'" in Immanuel Kant, *Practical Philosophy*, trans. and ed. Mary J. Gregor (New York: Cambridge University Press, 1996), 290–304.

43. "Before [John Watt's] time, spinning machines, although very imperfect ones, had already been used, and Italy was probably the country of their first appearance. A critical history of technology would show how little any of the inventions of the 18th century are the work of a single individual. Hitherto there is no such book. Darwin has interested us in the history of Nature's Technology, i.e., in the formation of the organs of plants and animals, which organs serve as instruments of production for sustaining life. Does not the history of the productive organs of man, of organs that are the material basis of all social organisation, deserve equal attention? And would not such a history be easier to compile, since, as Vico says, human history differs from natural history in this, that we have made the former, but not the latter?" See Karl Marx, *Capital*, 3 vols., translated from the third German edition by Samuel Moore and Edward Aveling, edited by Frederick Engels (New York: International Publishers, 1975), 1:372, n. 3.

44. See Hans Blumenberg, "What Is Copernican in Kant's Turning?" in *The Genesis of the Copernican Revolution*, trans. Robert M. Wallace (Cambridge, MA: MIT Press, 1987), 595–614.

45. According to Wolff, Kant mainly knew Hume through Beattie. See Robert Paul Wolff, "Kant's Debt to Hume Via Beattie," *Journal of the History of Ideas* 21, no. 1 (1960): 117–23.

46. See Blumenberg, "What Is Copernican in Kant's Turning?" 603.

47. See Isaac Newton, *Opera omnia*, ed. S. Horsley (London: Excudebat J. Nichols, 1779–85), 2:xiv.

48. In the first letter of his "Briefe über die Kantische Philosophie," which appeared in August 1786, before the second edition of the *Kritik der reinen Vernunft*, Reinhold refers to the relation between Kant and revolution and then to Kant and Copernicus; see Karl Leonhard Reinhold, "Briefe über die Kantische Philosophie," *Teutscher Zeitschrift* 27 (August 1786): 124–25, 126.

49. In a *Nachruf* on the occasion of Kant's death, Schelling suggests that Kant intended to make a Copernican turn. "Ähnlich wie sein Landsmann Copernikus, der die Bewegung aus dem Centrum in die Peripherie verlegte, kehrte er zuerst von Grund aus der Vorstellung um, nach welcher das Subjekt unthätig und rühig empfangend, der Gegenstand aber wirksam ist: eine Umkehrung, die sich in alle Zweige des Wissens wie durch eine elektrische Wirkung fortleitete." See "Immanuel Kant" (1804), in *Schellings Werke*, ed. Manfred Schröter (Munich: Beck, 1958), 3:599.

50. Ptolemy (Claudius Ptolemaeus), *The Almagest*, trans. R. C. Taliaferro, in *Great Books of the Western World*, vol. 16, *Ptolemy, Copernicus, Kepler*, ed. R. M. Hutchins (Chicago: Encyclopedia Britannica, 1952). This work is cited parenthetically in the rest of the text paragraph.

51. See the introduction to Nikolaus Copernicus, *Three Copernican Treatises*, trans. Edward Rosen (New York: Dover, 1959), 57–59.

52. Copernicus, *Three Copernican Treatises*, 59.

53. See Nikolaus Copernicus, *On the Revolutions of the Heavenly Spheres*, trans. C. G. Wallis, in *Great Books of the Western World*, vol. 16, *Ptolemy, Copernicus, Kepler*, ed. R. M. Hutchins (Chicago: Encyclopedia Britannica, 1952), 506. This work is subsequently cited parenthetically in the text.

54. See especially Charles Peirce, "The Fixation of Belief," in *The Essential Peirce*, 2 vols., ed. Nathan Houser and Christian Kloesel (Bloomington: Indiana University Press, 1992), 1:109–23.

55. See Stephan Körner, *Categorial Frameworks* (New York: Barnes and Noble, 1970).
56. See Isaac Newton, "The General Scholium," in *The Principia: Mathematical Principles of Natural Philosophy*, trans. I. Bernard Cohen and Anne Whitman (Berkeley and Los Angeles: University of California Press, 1999), 943.
57. See Newton's letter to Cotes of March 28, 1713, in *Correspondence of Sir Isaac Newton and Professor Cotes, Including Letters of Other Eminent Men*, ed. J. Edleston (London, John W. Parker; and Cambridge, John Deighton, 1850), 154–55. See also J. E. McGuire, "Atoms and the Analogy of Nature: Newton's Third Rule of Philosophizing," *Studies in the History and Philosophy of Science* 1, no. 1 (1970): 3–58.
58. See Wolfgang Bonsiepen, "Einleitung," in G. W. F. Hegel, *Phänomenologie des Geistes* (Hamburg: Felix Meiner Verlag, 1988), ix–x. Oetinger supposedly used the term *phenomenology* arguably for the first time in an unpublished diary in 1736, where he defines it as a divine science of relations. See, on this point, Niels Bokhove, "Phenomenology," in *Handbook of Metaphysics and Ontology*, ed. Hans Burkhardt and Barry Smith (Munich: Philosophia Verlag, 1991), 2:698.
59. See J. H. Lambert, *Über die Methode, die Metaphysik, Theologie und Moral richtiger zu beweisen*, ed. K. Bopp, Kant-Studien Ergängzungshefte 42 (1762; repr. Berlin: von Reuther und Reichard, 1918).
60. See Francis Bacon, *The New Organon*, ed. Fulton H. Anderson (Indianapolis, IN: Library of Liberal Arts, 1959).
61. See Kant, letter to Johann Heinrich Lambert, September 2, 1770, in *Correspondence*, 108.
62. See Immanuel Kant, *The Metaphysical Foundations of Natural Science*, trans. Michael Friedman (New York: Cambridge University Press, 2004). In this respect, Kant writes, "At issue here is not the transformation of semblance [*Schein*] into truth, but rather of [true] appearance [*Erscheinung*] into experience; for, in the case of semblance, the understanding with its object-determining judgments is always in play, although it is in danger of taking the subjective for objective; in the [true] appearance, however, no judgment of the understanding is to be met with at all—which needs to be noted, not merely here, but in the whole of philosophy, because otherwise, when appearances are in question, and this term is taken to have the same meaning as semblance, one is always poorly understood" (Kant, letter to Johann Heinrich Lambert, September 2, 1770, in *Correspondence*, 108).
63. See, for example, Martin Heidegger, *Phenomenological Interpretation of Kant's Critique of Pure Reason*, trans. Parvis Emad and Kenneth Maly (Indianapolis: Indiana University Press, 1997).
64. See Plato *Sophist* 245E–246E, in *Complete Works*, 267–68.

CHAPTER THREE

1. See Kant, *Critique of Pure Reason*, trans. Paul Guyer and Allen W. Wood (New York: Cambridge University Press, 1998), B860, 691.
2. See Paolu Mancosu, *Philosophy of Mathematics and Mathematical Practice in the Seventeenth Century* (New York: Oxford University Press, 1996), chap. 3, "Descartes' Géométrie," 65–92.
3. See Kant, *Critique of Pure Reason*, B116, 219–20.
4. Kant, *Critique of Pure Reason*, B168, 265.
5. According to Isabelle Thomas-Fogiel, the statement of philosophy as system is German idealism; see *Le Concept et le lieu: Figures de la relation entre art et philosophie* (Paris: Editions du Cerf, 2009), 122: "Le système, comme acte de 'lier ensemble'

ou de 'poser ensemble,' n'est plus dans l'idéalisme allemand un simple mode d'exposition de la philosophie mais devient la philosophie elle-même."
6. See Kant, *Critique of Pure Reason*, B860, 691.
7. Johann Fichte, "On the Concept of the Wissenschaftslehre," in *Fichte: Early Philosophical Writings*, trans. and ed. Dan Breazeale (Ithaca, NY: Cornell University Press, 1988), 94–136.
8. See F. W. J. Schelling, *System of Transcendental Idealism*, trans. Peter Heath (Charlottesville: University Press of Virginia, 1978).
9. See G. W. F. Hegel, *The Difference between Fichte's and Schelling's System of Philosophy*, trans. H. S. Harris and Walter Cerf (Albany: State University of New York, 1977). See, for discussion, Tom Rockmore, *Hegel's Circular Epistemology* (Bloomington: Indiana University Press, 1986).
10. See Terry Pinkard, *German Philosophy 1760–1860: The Legacy of Idealism* (Cambridge: Cambridge University Press, 2002).
11. See Frederick C. Beiser, *German Idealism: The Struggle against Subjectivism, 1781–1801* (Cambridge, MA: Harvard University Press, 2002).
12. See Manfred Frank, *The Philosophical Foundations of Early German Romanticism*, trans. Elizabeth Millan-Zaibert (Albany: State University of New York Press, 1977).
13. See Paul Franks, *All or Nothing: Systematicity, Transcendental Arguments, and Skepticism in German Idealism* (Cambridge, MA: Harvard University Press, 2005).
14. See Nectarios Limnatis, *German Idealism and the Problem of Knowledge: Kant, Fichte, Schelling, and Hegel* (Dordrecht and New York: Springer Academic Publishers, 2008).
15. Opinions vary widely. For a well-known paper, see Daniel Garber, "Leibniz and Idealism," in *Leibniz: Nature and Freedom*, ed. Donald Rutherford and J. A. Cover (Oxford: Oxford University Press, 2005), 95–107. See, for a more recent discussion, Donald Rutherford, "Leibniz as Idealist," in *Oxford Studies in Early Modern Philosophy*, vol. 4, ed. Daniel Garber and Steven Nadler (New York: Oxford University Press, 2008), 141–90.
16. Paul Redding claims that German idealism begins in Leibniz, to whom Kant reacts in the critical philosophy; see *Continental Idealism: From Leibniz to Nietzsche* (New York: Routledge, 2009). Whether this is correct depends on whether Leibniz is an idealist in a Kantian sense.
17. G. W. F. Hegel, *Lectures on the History of Philosophy*, 3 vols., trans. E. S. Haldane (Nebraska: University of Nebraska Press, 1995).
18. See Immanuel Kant, *The Metaphysics of Morals*, in *The Metaphysical Principles of Virtue*, by Immanuel Kant, trans. James Ellington (Indianapolis, IN: LLA, 1964), 5.
19. G. W. F. Hegel, *Hegel's Phenomenology of Spirit*, trans. A. V. Miller (New York: Oxford University Press, 1977).
20. See 2 Corinthians, 3:6.
21. See Kant, *Critique of Pure Reason*, Bxliv, 123.
22. There is a large literature devoted to this theme. Opinions range from the idea that one should interpret a text according to discernable authorial intention to the idea that it is legitimate to interpret texts differently at different historical moments. See, for example, E. D. Hirsch, Jr., *Validity in Interpretation* (New Haven, CT: Yale University Press, 1979).
23. One could argue that in revising his account of the subject in the *Critique of the Power of Judgment* (trans. Paul Guyer and Eric Matthews [New York: Cambridge University Press, 2000]), Kant opens the way to a richer account of interpretation. This approach is quickly developed by others, including Fichte. See, for example, "Concerning the Difference between the Spirit and the Letter within Philosophy," in Breazeale, ed., *Fichte: Early Philosophical Writings*, 192–216.

24. Kant points, for example, to the stylistic gifts of Hume and Mendelssohn. See Immanuel Kant, *Prolegomena to Any Future Metaphysics*, trans., with introduction and notes, by James W. Ellington (Indianapolis, IN: Hackett, 2001), 7; and the Letter to Marcus Herz, February 11, 1772, in Immanuel Kant, *Correspondence*, trans. and ed. Arnulf Zweig (New York: Cambridge University Press, 1999), 133.
25. This is reported by Richard Rorty in *Consequences of Pragmatism* (Minneapolis: University of Minnesota Press, 1982), 211.
26. See, for example, Aristotle, *Metaphysics*, Alpha 3–10, in *The Complete Works of Aristotle*, 2 vols., ed. Jonathan Barnes (Princeton, NJ: Princeton University Press, 1984), 2: 1555–69.
27. See G. W. F. Hegel, *Hegel's Philosophy of Nature*, in *Encyclopaedia of the Philosophical Sciences* (1830), pt. 2, trans. A. V. Miller (New York: Oxford University Press, 1970).
28. See Hegel, *The Difference between Fichte's and Schelling's System of Philosophy*, 79.
29. See J. G. Fichte, *Science of Knowledge with the First and Second Introductions*, ed. and trans. Peter Heath and John Lachs (New York: Cambridge University Press, 1982), 171, n. 52. This work is subsequently cited as Fichte, *Science of Knowledge* (1794).
30. Hegel, *The Difference between Fichte's and Schelling's System of Philosophy*, 80.
31. Ibid., 81.
32. Ibid., 82.
33. Ibid., "The Historical View of Philosophical Systems," 85–89.
34. See, for a recent examination of this theme, Isabelle Thomas-Fogiel, *Reference and Self-Reference: On the "Death of Philosophy" in Contemporary Thought*, trans. Richard A. Lynch (New York: Columbia University Press, 2010).
35. See Friedrich Engels, *Ludwig Feuerbach and the Outcome of Classical German Philosophy*, ed. C. P. Dutt (New York: International Publishers, 1941).
36. See Hegel, *The Difference between Fichte's and Schelling's System of Philosophy*, 89–94.
37. In a public declaration, Kant claimed that Fichte's position was pure logic, but that it was impossible to arrive at real objects from concepts. See his "Declaration Concerning Fichte's *Wissenschaftslehre*," August 7, 1799, in Kant, *Correspondence*, 559–61. See also Kant's letter to Tieftrunk dated April 5, 1798, in ibid., 544–45. In this letter, Kant admits he has not read Fichte's *Wissenschaftslehre*, which, however, he condemns.
38. Kant, *Critique of Pure Reason*, Bxliv, 123.
39. Ibid., B862, 692.
40. Hegel, *The Difference between Fichte's and Schelling's System of Philosophy*, 79.
41. Ibid., 80.
42. See "Reflection as Instrument of Philosophizing," in ibid., 94–98.
43. See, for example, Béatrice Longuenesse, "Kant on a Priori Concepts: The Metaphysical Deduction of the Categories," in *The Cambridge Companion to Kant and Modern Philosophy*, ed. Paul Guyer (New York: Cambridge University Press, 2006), 129–68.
44. Fichte, *Science of Knowledge* (1794), 100; Fichte's emphases.
45. For an account of the influence of Herder's expressivism on Hegel, see Charles Taylor, *Hegel* (New York: Cambridge University Press, 1975), 13–27.
46. See, for this view, *Kritische Walder: Oder Betrachtungen, Die Wisschenschaft und Kunst des Schoenen*, in *Johann. Gottfried Herder Sämtliche Werke*, vol. 4, B. Suphan et al., eds. (Berlin: Weidmann, 1887–1913), 1769.
47. See C. G. Bardili *Grundrisss der ersten Logik, gereinigt von den Irrthürn bisheriger Logiker überhaupt, der kantischen insbesondere; keine Medicine mentis, brauchbar hauptsächlich für Deutschlands kritische Philosophie* (Stuttgart: Löflund, 1800).

48. See Karl Leonard Reinhold, *Sendschreiben an J. C. Lavater und. J. G. Fichte über den Glauben an Gott* (Hamburg: Friedrich Perthes, 1799).
49. Karl Leonard Reinhold, *Beyträge zur leichtern Uebersicht des Zustandes der Philosophie beym Anfang des 19. Jahrhunderts*, Heft 4 (Hamburg: Friedrich Perthes, 1802), 104.
50. Ibid., iv.
51. Ibid., 110.
52. See "First Introduction to the Science of Knowledge," in Fichte, *Science of Knowledge* (1794), 10.
53. See Reinhard Lauth, *Transzendentale Entwicklungslinien von Descartes bis zu Marx und Dostojewski* (Hamburg: Felix Meiner Verlag, 1989).
54. F. H. Jacobi, *David Hume über den Glauben, oder Idealismus und Realismus. Ein Gespräch* (Breslau: Gottlieb Löwe, 1787), 223.
55. His final attitude toward the thing in itself is complex and perhaps inconsistent. Though he elsewhere clearly rejects this concept, he also claims that the thing in itself is the indispensable presupposition of any theory of consciousness. See Fichte, *Science of Knowledge* (1794), 249.
56. See Fichte, *Science of Knowledge* (1794). The title in the text is that of the work as originally published. I have modified the translation in inserting "representation" rather than "presentation" for Fichte's term *Vorstellung*. A representation refers to what it represents, a nuance that is lost in the term *presentation*, which could merely be something in mind.
57. See Kant, *Critique of Pure Reason*, Bxxvii, 27.
58. See Fichte, *Science of Knowledge* (1794), 224, 262, 239, 269.
59. See Isabelle Thomas-Fogiel, *Critique de la représentation. Etude sur Fichte* (Paris: Vrin, 2000).
60. See Daniel Breazeale, "Towards a *Wissenschaftslehre more geometrico (1800/1)*," in *After Jena: New Essays on Fichte's Later Philosophy*, ed. Daniel Breazeale and Tom Rockmore (Evanston, IL: Northwestern University Press, 2008), 40.
61. J. G. Fichte, *Johann Gottlieb Fichtes nachgelassene Werke*, 3 vols., ed. I. H. Fichte (Bonn: Adolph-Marcus, 1834–35), 2:195.
62. J. G. Fichte, *Wissenschaftlehre 1804* (second series, 1804), in *The Science of Knowing: Fichte's 1804 Lectures on the Wissenschaftslehre*, trans. Walter E. Wright (Albany: State University of New York Press, 2005), 107. See also J. G. Fichte, *Die Wissenschaftslehre. Zweiter Vortrag im Jahre 1804*, ed. R. Lauth and J. Widmann (Hamburg: Felix Meiner Verlag, 1986), 138; hereafter cited as *WL* 1804/II.
63. Fichte, *WL* 1804/II, 150–51. Ibid.
64. See, for a detailed study of this text, Joachim Widmann, *Die Grundstruktur des transzendentalen Wissens nach Joh. Gott. Fichtes Wissenschaftslhere 1804* (Hamburg: Felix Meiner Verlag, 1977). See also Jean-François Goubet, "La phénoménologie de Fichte dans la WL-1804/II: Une approche historique," in *L'être et le phénomène. La Doctrine de la Science de 1804 de J.G. Fichte. Sein und Erscheinung. Die Wissenschaftslehre 1804 J.G. Fichtes*, ed. J.-C. Goddard and A. Schnell (Paris: Vrin, 2009).
65. The relation between Husserl and Fichte has been explored in different ways. An early effort, which remains instructive, is Jean Hyppolite, "La doctrine de la science chez Fichte et Husserl ," in *Husserl et la pensée moderne* (The Hague: Martinus Nijhoff, 1959). See also H. Tietzen, *Fichte und Husserl. Letzbegründung, Subjektivität und Praktische Vernunft im transzendentalen Idealismus* (Frankfurt am Main: Klostermann, 1980).

66. See Kant, *Critique of Pure Reason*, B132, 246.
67. Fichte, *Science of Knowledge* (1794), 22.
68. See Josiah Royce, *Lectures on Modern Idealism* (1919; repr., New Haven, CT: Yale University Press, 1964): "That this self of philosophy is not the individual man of ordinary life appears from the very outset of Fichte's discussion. The individual man of ordinary life is one of the beings to be defined by philosophy, and is certainly not the principle of philosophy" (97).
69. "According to Fichte's verbal statements, which were not mentioned in his book, the self creates through its representations, and all reality is only in the self. The world is to the self like a ball, which the self has thrown out and then caught again through reflection [*Reflexion*]." Letter from Schiller to Goethe, October 28, 1794, in Johann Christian Friedrich Schiller, *Briefwechsel zwischen Schiller und Goethe*, 2 vols., ed. H. Hauff (Stuttgart: Cotta'sche Buchhandlung, 1856), 1:26.
70. Fichte, *Science of Knowledge* (1794), 22.
71. See Beiser, *German Idealism*, 11.
72. G. W. F. Hegel, "The Encyclopaedia Logic," part 1 of the *Encyclopaedia of the Philosophical Sciences with the Zusätze*, trans. with introduction and notes by T. F. Geraets, W. A. Suchting, and H. S. Harris (Indianapolis, IN: Hackett, 1991); and Hegel, *Phenomenology of Spirit*, pp. 58–103.
73. See, for example, Kant, *Critique of Pure Reason*, Bxxxvi, 119.
74. The fact that Hegel rejects givenness, which he distinguishes from empiricism, makes it problematic to accuse him of favoring givenness in recent analytic attacks on empiricism. See Wilfrid Sellars, "Empiricism and the Philosophy of Mind," in *Science, Perception and Reality* (Atascadero, CA: Ridgeview, 1991), 127–97, esp. 127.
75. See Hegel, *Encyclopaedia Logic*, sec. 40, 80, and 81. Hereafter cited parenthetically in the text.
76. See Salomon Maimon, *Versuch über die Transzendentalphilosophie*, ed. Florian Ehrensperger (Hamburg: Felix Meiner Verlag, 2004).
77. See, for example, Charles Taylor, "The Opening Arguments of the Phenomenology," in *Hegel: A Collection of Critical Essays*, ed. Alasdair MacIntyre (Notre Dame: University of Notre Dame Press, 1972), 151–88.
78. See G. W. F. Hegel, *Hegel's Phenomenology of Spirit*, trans. A. V. Miller (New York: Oxford University Press, 1977), secs. 150–51, 91–92. Hereafter cited parenthetically in the text.
79. See Kant, *Critique of Pure Reason*, Bxviii, 111.
80. For instance, Michael Forster's detailed study of the *Phenomenology of Spirit* concerns Hegel's conception of his book, not his conception of phenomenology. See, Michael N. Forster, *Hegel's Idea of a Phenomenology of Spirit* (Chicago: University of Chicago Press, 1998).
81. The word *phenomenon* (*Phänomenon*), which does not occur either in the *Differenzschrift* nor in *Faith and Knowledge*, occurs only a total of four times in the *Phenomenology*, but it occurs each time in a way that clearly refers not to a specific doctrine but to the book of that name.
82. On Fichte's interpretation, Reinhold's basic claim is that representations are related both to subject and object, but distinguished from both. Aenesidemus, according to Fichte, objects that the relation of the representation to subject and object is different in each case. Fichte reformulates the same objection in different language as the claim that "the representation is related to the object as the effect to the cause, and to the subject as the accident to substance." See J. G. Fichte, "Aenesidemus-Rezension,"

in *Fichtes Werke*, 11 vols., ed. I. H. Fichte (Berlin: de Gruyter, 1971), 1:18. But he disagrees with—in fact finds unthinkable—Aenesidemus's assumption that the critical philosophy depends on a mind-independent thing in itself, that is, on something independent from a capacity for representation.

83. See Wilfrid Sellars, *Empiricism and the Philosophy of Mind*, (Cambridge, MA: Harvard University Press, 1997).
84. For Hegel, as for such later thinkers as Putnam, truth is a limiting, or ideal, concept. See Hilary Putnam, *Reason, Truth and History* (New York: Cambridge University Press, 1981), 216.

CHAPTER FOUR

1. On the relation of Husserl and Carnap, see Thomas Ryckman, "Carnap and Husserl," in the *Cambridge Companion to Carnap*, ed. Michael Friedman and Richard Creath (New York: Cambridge University Press, 2008), 81–105. On Husserl's influence on Carnap, see Guillermo E. Rosado Haddock, *The Young Carnap's Unknown Master: Husserl's Influence on "Der Raum" and "Der logische Aufbau der Welt,"* (Farnham [Surrey]: Ashgate, 2008). On the relation of Husserl and Wittgenstein, see Nicholas F. Gier, *Wittgenstein and Phenomenology: A Comparative Study of Wittgenstein, Husserl and Merleau-Ponty* (Albany: State University of New York Press, 1981).
2. The link to Descartes has often been analyzed. See, for example, Michael K. Shim, *Descartes and Husserl: The Philosophical Project of Radical Beginnings* (Albany: State University of New York Press, 2000). For the link to Kant, see Iso Kern, *Husserl and Kant* (The Hague, Martinus Nijhoff, 1964). In a review of this book, Robert Sokolowski begins by pointing out that Husserl's relation to Kant is ambiguous in that he sometimes credits Kant with anticipating phenomenology and sometimes criticizes him severely; see "Husserl und Kant," (review) *Philosophy and Phenomenological Research* 26, no. 1 (1965): 132–34.
3. He compared this to "criticizing traditional philosophemes." See Edmund Husserl, *Logical Investigations*, trans. J. N. Findlay, revised by Dermot Moran (London: Routledge, 2001), 2 vols., 2:187. All citations are to this edition.
4. See, for the relation between Brentano and Husserl, Robin Rollinger, "Brentano and Husserl," in *Cambridge Companion to Brentano*, ed. Dale Jacquette (New York: Cambridge University Press, 2004), 255–76. For Brentano's epistemology, see Linda McAlister, "Brentano's Epistemology," in ibid., 149–67.
5. See Franz Brentano, *Psychology from an Empirical Standpoint*, ed. Oskar Kraus, English edition ed. Linda L. McAlister, trans. Antos C. Rancurello, D. B. Terrell, and Linda L. McAlister (London: Routledge, 1995), 18.
6. Brentano reintroduced the conception of intentionality into modern philosophy. See Liliana Albertazzi, "From Kant to Brentano," in *The School of Franz Brentano*, ed. L. Albertazzi, M. Libardi, and R. Poli (The Hague: Martinus Nijhoff, 1996), 423–64.
7. Here is a passage that illustrates this point: "All judging proceeds according to psychological laws, just as physical events proceed according to the laws of nature. But this doesn't mean that the course of real events conforms to psychological laws." Franz Brentano, *On the Existence of God* (Dordrecht: Martinus Nijhoff, 1987), 78.
8. See Franz Brentano, *Psychology from an Empirical Standpoint*, 367–68.
9. See, for a thorough account of intentionality, María del Carmen Paredes Martín, *Teorías de la Intencionalidad* (Madrid: Síntesis, 2007).
10. See Husserl, *Logical Investigations*, 1:3.

11. Edmund Husserl, *The Idea of Phenomenology*, trans. William P. Alston and George Nakhnikian (The Hague: Martinus Nijhoff, 1964).
12. "From its beginning in the early twentieth century, phenomenology attacked the psychologistic interpretation of truth, reason, and the ego; psychologism was the foil against which phenomenology originally defined itself"; see Robert Sokolowski, *Introduction to Phenomenology* (New York: Cambridge University Press, 2000), 113–14.
13. See Paul Natorp, "Zur Frage der logischen Methode. Mit Beziehung auf Edmund Husserls 'Prolegomena zur reinen Logik,'" *Kant-Studien*, 6 (1901), 270–83.
14. Donn Welton depicts this theme as a continuing concern in Husserl's position; see *The Other Husserl: The Horizons of Transcendental Phenomenology* (Bloomington: Indiana University Press, 2000), 262–85.
15. A recent collection on naturalizing phenomenology, a link that Husserl would have opposed, gives almost no attention to psychologism. See Jean Pettitot, Francisco J. Varela, Bernard Pachoud, and Jean-Michel Roy, eds., *Naturalizing Epistemology: Issues in Contemporary Phenomenology and Cognitive Science* (Stanford, CA: Stanford University Press, 1999).
16. See his letter of August 27, 1900, cited in *Logische Untersuchungen*, vol. 1, *Prolegomena zur reinen Logik*, Text der 1. und der 2., Auflage Series, *Husserliana: Edmund Husserl—Gesammelte Werke*, vol. 18, ed. Elmar Holenstein (The Hague: Martinus Nijhoff, 1975), xvii.
17. A useful short description of psychologism is contained in the statement that it "'naturalizes' pure consciousness." See Edmund Husserl, *Phenomenology and the Crisis of Philosophy*, trans. Quentin Lauer (New York: Harper and Row, 1965), 92.
18. See Bernard Bolzano, *Wissenschaftslehre*, 4 vols. (repr. of 2nd ed., Sulzbach: Seidel, 1929–31; Aalen: Scientia Verlag, 1970). (Orig. pub. 1837.)
19. See Husserl, *Logical Investigations*, 1:142.
20. Ibid., 1:143.
21. See Immanuel Kant, *Critique of Pure Reason*, trans. Paul Guyer and Allen W. Wood (New York: Cambridge University Press, 1998), B116, 219–20.
22. Ibid., B133–34, 247.
23. See "First Introduction to the Science of Knowledge," in Johann Fichte, *Science of Knowledge with the First and Second Introductions*, ed. and trans. Peter Heath and John Lachs (New York: Cambridge University Press, 1982), sec. 5, 12–16.
24. Friedrich Eduard Beneke, *Die Philosophie in ihrem Verhältnis zur Erfahrung, zur Spekulation, und zum Leben* (Berlin: Ernst Siegried Mittler, 1833), xv.
25. According to D. M. Godden, Mill's view of the status of logic is equivocal, but in any case inadequate to justify deductive logic in independence of psychology. See D. M. Godden, "Psychologism in the Logic of John Stuart Mill: Mill on the Subject Matter and Foundations of Ratiocinative Logic," *Journal of the History and Philosophy of Logic* 26, no. 2 (2005): 115–43.
26. J. S. Mill, *A System of Logic Ratiocinative and Inductive: Being a Connected View of the Principles of Evidence and the Methods of Scientific Investigation* (1843), 4, in *The Collected Works of John Stuart Mill*, ed. J. M. Robson (London: Routledge, 1973; Toronto: University of Toronto Press, 1974), 7:4.
27. J. S. Mill, *An Examination of Sir William Hamilton's Philosophy* (1865), in ibid., 9:359.
28. Ibid., 381–82.
29. See, for example, Paul Natorp, *Einleitung in die Psychologie nach kritischer Methode* (Freiburg: J. C. B. Mohr, 1888). See also Paul Natorp, "Ueber objektive und sub-

jektive Begründung der Erkenntniss (Erster Aufsatz)," *Philosophische Monatshefte* 23 (1887): 257–86.
30. See Richard Kroner, "Über logische und ästhetische Allgemeingültigkeit," *Zeitschrift für Philosophie und philosophische Kritik* nos. 134 and 135 (1909): 231–66 (no. 134), 10–36, 216–57 (no. 135).
31. See J. E. Erdmann, *Grundriss der Geschichte der Philosophie*, 2nd ed., vol. 2 (Berlin: Hertz, 1870).
32. See Carl Stumpf, "Psychologie und Erkenntnistheorie," in *Abhandlungen der I. Klasse der k. Bayerischen Akademie der Wissenschaften* (München: Franz, 1891), vol. 19, pt. 2, 465–516.
33. See Herbert Spiegelberg, *The Phenomenological Movement: A Historical Introduction* (The Hague: Martinus Nijhoff, 1962), 152, n. 35.
34. See Gottlob Frege, "Review of E. G. Husserl, Philosophie der Arithmetik 1" (1894), in *The Frege Reader*, ed. Michael Beaney (Oxford: Blackwell, 1997), 224–26.
35. See Jitendra Nath Mohanty, *Husserl and Frege* (Bloomington: Indiana University Press, 1982). See also Dagfinn Føllesdall, "Husserl and Frege: A Contribution to Elucidating the Origins of Phenomenological Philosophy" (trans. Claire Hill), in *Mind, Meaning and Mathematics*, ed. Leila Haaparanta (Dordrecht: Kluwer, 1994), 3–47.
36. See Edmund Husserl, *Formal and Transcendental Logic*, trans. Dorion Cairns (The Hague: Martinus Nijhoff, 1969), 149–75.
37. Husserl, *Logical Investigations*, 1:2; Husserl's emphasis. This work is subsequently cited parenthetically in the text.
38. See Husserl, *Formal and Transcendental Logic*, 35.
39. See "Philosophy as Rigorous Science," in *Phenomenology and the Crisis of Philosophy: Philosophy as Rigorous Science, and Philosophy and the Crisis of European Man*, trans. Quentin Lauer (New York: Harper and Row, 1965).
40. See *Foundations of the Unity of Science: Toward an International Encyclopedia of Unified Science*, 2 vols., ed. Otto Neurath (Chicago: University of Chicago Press, 1971).
41. See Kant, *Critique of Pure Reason*, B860, 691.
42. See Immanuel Kant, *Prolegomena to Any Future Metaphysics, and the Letter to Marcus Hertz, February 1772*, trans. James W. Ellington (Indianapolis, IN: Hackett, 2001), 102.
43. See, for example, Welton, *The Other Husserl*, 264.
44. Mohanty, who distinguishes naturalistic and transcendental psychologism, including six kinds of naturalistic psychologism, believes that in *Logical Investigations* Husserl is concerned with the former. See Jitendra Nath Mohanty, *The Philosophy of Edmund Husserl: A Historical Development* (New Haven, CT: Yale University Press, 2008), 63.
45. See Martin Heidegger, *On Time and Being*, trans. Joan Stambaugh (Chicago: University of Chicago Press, 2002).
46. See Welton, *The Other Husserl*, 266–69.
47. See Husserl, *Formal and Transcendental Logic*, 149–75.
48. "Pure phenomenology as science . . . can only be essence investigation" (Husserl, "Philosophy as Rigorous Science," 116).
49. Husserl states in *Ideas* that the "only aim" of phenomenology "is to be a doctrine of essences in the framework of pure intuition"; see Edmund Husserl, *Ideas: General Introduction to Pure Phenomenology*, trans. W. R. Boyce Gibson (New York: Collier Books, 1962), 124. He goes on to say, "As for phenomenology, it aims only at being a descriptive theory of the essence of pure transcendental experiences in the framework of the phenomenological orientation" (139). Thus, for instance, Husserl

considers nature as the intentional correlate of empirical experience. See Edmund Husserl, *Ideen II: Phänomenologische Untersuchungen zur Konstitution*, in *Husserliana: Edmund Husserl—Gesammelte Werke* (The Hague: Martinus Nijhoff; Dordrecht: Kluwer, 1952).

50. See Franz Brentano, *On the Several Senses of Being in Aristotle* (Berkeley and Los Angeles: University of California Press, 1975).

51. On the formulation "zu den Sachen selbst," see Husserl, "Einleitung," in *Logische Untersuchungen* "Wir wollen auf die 'Sachen selbst' zurückgehen" (6). See also Edmund Husserl, "Philosophie als strenge Wissenchaft," *Logos* 1 (1910-11): 305, where he writes, "Weg mit den holhen Wortanalysen. Die Sachen selbst müssen wir befragen." See also *Husserliana: Edmund Husserl—Gesammelte Werke*, vol. 19, ed. Ursula Panzer (The Hague: Martinus Nijhoff, 1984): "Wir wollen uns schlecterdings nicht mit 'blossen Worten'... zufriedengeben... Wir wollen auf 'die Sachen selbst' zurückgehen" (10). See also Martin Heidegger, *Sein und Zeit*, in *Heidegger-Gesamtausgabe*, vol. 2, ed. Friedrich-Wilhelm von Herrmann (Frankfurt am Main: Vittorio Klostermann, 1978), 37, 46.

52. "Author's Preface to the English Edition," in Edmund Husserl, *Ideas: General Introduction to Pure Phenomenology*, trans. W. R. Boyce Gibson (New York: Collier Books, 1962), 20.

53. See Kant, *Critique of Pure Reason*, Bxxii, 113.

54. For a later claim that phenomenology is free from presuppositions, see "Author's Preface to the English Edition" (1931) in Husserl, *Ideas*, 20.,

55. See Edmund Husserl, *Einleitung in die Logik und Erkenntnistheorie: Vorlesungen 1906/7*, ed. Ulrich Melle, Husserl Gesamtausgabe (The Hague: Martinus Nijhoff, 1984), 45-46.

56. Edmund Husserl, *Cartesian Meditations: An Introduction to Phenomenology*, trans. Dorion Cairns (Dordrecht: Kluwer, 1931).

57. Some observers see Husserl as succeeding in solving the problem of knowledge on the basis of the reduction. "If the enigma of cognition... was how the psychologically immanent Erlebnis could reach out to a transcendental reality, after the reduction, we find that within the essence of an Erlebnis, as a temporal process in which both the Erlebnis and its object are being constituted. Here is the solution. We understand why phenomenology, starting with the process of research into essences of phenomena, becomes a research into the constitution of objectivities" (Mohanty, *Philosophy of Edmund Husserl*, 215).

58. Husserl, *Idea of Phenomenology*, 38. This work is hereafter cited parenthetically in the text.

59. See Maurice Merleau-Ponty, *Phenomenology of Perception*, trans. Colin Smith (London: Routledge, 2003), xv.

60. Husserl seems on occasion to take a Berkeleyan approach. See, for example, Edmund Husserl, *Analyses Concerning Passive and Active Synthesis*, trans. Anthony J. Steinbock (Dordrecht: Kluwer, 2001): "Now the *esse* (for transcendent objects) is in principle to be distinguished from the *percipi*" (55). Moran reads this view as suggesting that, as concerns *cogitationes*, which are distinguished from transcendent objects, their *esse* is *percipi*. See Dermot Moran, *Edmund Husserl: Founder of Phenomenology* (Malden, MA: Polity Press, 2005), 147

61. See Mohanty, *Philosophy of Edmund Husserl*, 215.

62. See Wilhelm Dilthey "Die Typen der Weltanschauung und ihre Ausbildung in den metaphysischen Systemen," in *Gesammelte Schriften* (Stuttgart: B. G. Teubner, 1958), 7:75-117.

63. See, for example, W. V. O. Quine, "Epistemology Naturalized," in his *Ontological Relativity and Other Essays* (New York: Columbia University Press, 1969), 69–90.
64. See "Philosophy as Rigorous Science in Edmund Husserl," in Husserl, *Phenomenology and the Crisis of Philosophy*, 89.
65. Husserl, *Ideas*.
66. Ibid., 9.
67. See Husserl, *Phenomenology and the Crisis of Philosophy*, 76–77.
68. See G. W. F. Hegel, *Hegel's Phenomenology of Spirit*, trans. A. V. Miller (New York: Oxford University Press, 1977), 263–409.
69. Husserl, *Ideas*, 12. This work is cited parenthetically in the text for the rest of this discussion.
70. See Nicholas Rescher, *A System of Pragmatic Idealism* (Princeton, NJ: Princeton University Press, 1992).
71. See "Saving Representationalism: Fichte, Allison and the Double Aspect Thesis," in chapter 2 of this book.
72. See Husserl, *Formal and Transcendental Logic*, 12; see also secs. 24–27, 76–89; secs. 43–44, 119–125; and sec. 54, 143–44.
73. Ibid., 16.
74. See Edmund Husserl, *The Crisis of European Sciences and Transcendental Phenomenology*, trans. David Carr (Evanston, IL: Northwestern University Press, 1970), secs. 8–27, 21–100.
75. See Husserl, *Crisis of European Sciences*, sec. 28, 103–10.
76. For a recent argument that Husserl solves the problem of solipsism, see Lanei M. Rodemeyer, *Intersubjective Temporality: It's About Time* (Dordrecht: Springer, 2006); and, for a recent attempt to defend Husserl's effort to develop a theory of intersubjectivity on the transcendental plane, see James Richard Mensch, *Intersubjectivity and Transcendental Idealism* (Albany: State University of New York Press, 1988).
77. See Husserl, *Cartesian Meditations*, 1. This work is hereafter cited parenthetically in text.
78. See Kant, *Critique of Pure Reason*, secs. 16–17.

CHAPTER FIVE

1. There has been much discussion about Aristotle's view of the relation of demonstration and dialectic. See, for an influential contribution, G. E. L. Owen, "Tithenai ta phainomena," in *Aristotle*, ed. J. M. Moravcsik (New York: Doubleday, 1967), 167–90.
2. See Jitendra Nath Mohanty, *The Philosophy of Edmund Husserl: A Historical Development* (New Haven, CT: Yale University Press, 2008), 398.
3. See Edmund Husserl, *The Idea of Phenomenology*, trans. William P. Alston and George Nakhnikian (The Hague: Martinus Nijhoff, 1964), 18.
4. See "The Age of the World Picture," in Martin Heidegger, *The Question Concerning Technology and Other Essays*, trans. William Lovitt (New York: Harper, 1977), 154.
5. See Hans-Georg Gadamer, "The Overcoming of the Epistemological Problem Through Phenomenological research," in *Truth and Method*, trans. Garret Barden and John Cumming (New York: Crossroads, 1975), 214–34.
6. See Toni Cassirer, *Mein Leben mit Ernst Cassirer* (Hildesheim: Gerstenberg Verlag, 1981).
7. This relation has been extensively studied. See, for example, Pierre Keller, *Husserl and Heidegger on Human Experience* (New York: Cambridge University Press, 1999).

8. See Martin Heidegger, *Being and Time*, trans. John Macquarrie and Edward Robinson (New York: Harper and Row, 1962), sec. 7, 62.
9. He says of this science that "die ich de facto in die Geschichte eingeführt habe." See Edmund Husserl, *Die Krisis der europäischen Wissenschaften und die transzendentale Phänomenologie. Eine Einleitung in die phänomenologische Philosophie*, ed. Walter Biemel, Husserliana 6 (The Hague: Martinus Nijhoff, 1954), 440.
10. See his letter of January 14, 1923, to Jaspers, in Martin Heidegger and Karl Jaspers, *Briefwechsel 1920–1963*, ed. Walter Biemel and Hans Saner (Frankfurt am Main: Vittorio Klostermann, 1990), 42: "Husserl ist gänzlich aus dem Leim gegangen—wenn er überhaupt je "drin" war—was mir in der letzten Zeit immer fraglicher geworden ist— er pendelt hin und her und sagt Trivialitäten, der er einen erbarmen möchte. Er lebt von der Mission des 'Begründers der Phänomenologie,' kein Mensch weiss, was das ist."
11. See Heidegger, *Being and Time*, 7, 62–63.
12. See Martin Heidegger, "My Way to Phenomenology," in *On Time and Being*, trans. Joan Stambaugh (New York: Harper and Row, 2002), 74.
13. See Edmund Husserl, *The Phenomenology of Internal Time-Consciousness*, ed. Martin Heidegger, trans. James S. Churchill (Bloomington: Indiana University Press, 1964).
14. See, for example, "The Idea of Philosophy and the Problem of the World View," in Martin Heidegger, *Toward the Definition of Philosophy*, trans. Ted Sadler (London: Athlone Press, 2008), 3–12 (Kriegnotssemester, 1919), English translation.
15. Heidegger, *Being and Time*, 259–60.
16. See Martin Heidegger, *Supplements: From the Earliest Essays to "Being and Time" and Beyond*, ed. John Van Buren, SUNY Series in Contemporary Continental Philosophy (Albany: State University of New York, 2002), 39–48.
17. See Martin Heidegger, "Die Lehre vom Urteil im Psychologismus. Ein kritischpositiver Beitrag zur Logik" (1913), repr. in M. Heidegger, *Frühe Schriften*, vol. 1 of *Heidegger-Gesamtausgabe*, ed. Friedrich-Wilhelm von Herrmann (Frankfurt am Main: Vittorio Klostermann, 1977), 59–188.
18. See Heidegger, *Frühe Schriften*, 110.
19. See Heidegger, *Being and Time*, 38. This work is hereafter cited parenthetically in the text as *BT*.
20. Martin Heidegger, *Letter on Humanism*, in *Basic Writings*, ed. David Farrell Krell (New York: Harper and Row, 1977), 222. This work is hereafter cited parenthetically in the text as *LH*.
21. See, for example, Jean Grondin, *Le Tournant dans la pensée de Martin Heidegger* (Paris: Presses universitaires de France, 1987).
22. For discussion of the link between this analysis and Heidegger's politics, see Johannes Fritsche, *Historical Destiny and National Socialism in Heidegger's Being and Time* (Berkeley and Los Angeles: University of California Press, 1999).
23. See Martin Heidegger, *An Introduction to Metaphysics*, trans. Ralph Manheim (New Haven, CT: Yale University Press, 1977), 199.
24. See, for a "Heideggerian" view of the turning, William J. Richardson, *Heidegger: Through Phenomenology to Thought*, 4th ed. (New York: Fordham University Press, 2003).
25. See Heidegger, *On Time and Being*.
26. See Heidegger, "Age of the World Picture," 115–54.
27. See Martin Heidegger, *Contributions to Philosophy (From Enowning)*, trans. Parvis Emad and Kenneth Maly (Bloomington: Indiana University Press, 1999).

28. See Heidegger, "My Way to Phenomenology," 78–79.
29. Ibid., 78.
30. Ibid.
31. Ibid., 78.
32. Ibid., 79.
33. See Steven Galt Crowell, *Husserl, Heidegger, and the Space of Meaning: Paths toward Transcendental Phenomenology* (Evanston, IL: Northwestern University Press, 2001). Crowell suggests that Heidegger remained faithful not just to the spirit but to the letter of Husserl's method of eidetic reduction (199–201), as well as to the corresponding concepts of categorial intuition (107) and phenomenological seeing, or the intuition of essences (227–28).
34. Husserl himself had no illusions. He remarks in a letter to Mahnke that Heidegger and other philosophers of existence praised his work but considered it not worth studying any more. See Husserl's letter of May 4–5, 1933, cited in *Becoming Heidegger: On the Trail of His Early Occasional Writings, 1910–1927*, ed. Theodore Kisiel and Thomas Sheehan (Evanston, IL: Northwestern University Press, 2007), 417.
35. See Edmund Husserl, *Logical Investigations*, 2 vols., trans. J. N. Findlay, revised by Dermot Moran (London: Routledge, 2001), 178; Husserl's emphasis.
36. Husserl, *Logical Investigations* 2:668.
37. See Emmanuel Levinas, *The Theory of Intuition in Husserl's Phenomenology* (Evanston, IL: Northwestern University Press, 1973). See also Jitendra Nath Mohanty, *Edmund Husserl's Theory of Meaning* (The Hague: Martinus Nijhoff, 1982).
38. See Husserl, *Logical Investigations* 2: sec. 40.
39. Ibid., 2:776.
40. Husserl, *Logical Investigations*, 2:781; his emphasis.
41. Martin Heidegger, *History of the Concept of Time*, trans. Theodore Kisiel (Bloomington: Indiana University Press, 1985), 25.
42. Husserl, *Logical Investigations*, 1:263; cited in Heidegger, *Concept of Time*, 25.
43. Heidegger, *Concept of Time*, 53; Heidegger's emphases.
44. Ibid., 70.
45. Ibid., 71.
46. Ibid., 72; Heidegger's emphases.
47. Martin Heidegger, *Four Seminars*, trans. Andrew Mitchell and François Raffoul (Bloomington: Indiana University Press, 2003), 67.
48. According to Sean McGrath, the most direct and vital connection exists between Scotus's account of the intuition of singularity (*haeeceitas*), Thomas of Erfurt's grammatical modes (*modi significandi*), Husserl's categorial intuition, and the young Heidegger's notion of "hermeneutical intuition" of the fore-theoretical forms of meaning that "live in life itself." See Sean J. McGrath, "Heidegger and Duns Scotus on Truth and Language," in *Review of Metaphysics*, 57, no. 22 (2003): 339–59.
49. See Kisiel and Sheehan, eds., *Becoming Heidegger*, 20–29.
50. Ibid., 25–26.
51. Heidegger later abandons representationalism when he realizes that being in general lies beyond it. See "Age of the World Picture," 254.
52. Moore influentially complains that idealists are committed to denying the existence of the external world. See, for example, G. E. Moore, "The Refutation of Idealism," in *Philosophical Studies*, by G. E. Moore (London: Routledge and Kegan Paul, 1958). (Orig. pub. 1922.)

53. See, for example, Johann Gottlieb Fichte, "First Introduction to the Science of Knowledge," in *Science of Knowledge*, ed. and trans. Peter Heath and John Lachs (New York: Cambridge University Press, 1982), 3–28.
54. On the relation of Heidegger and Kantian idealism, see especially William D. Blattner, *Heidegger's Temporal Idealism* (New York: Cambridge, 1999); see also his "Laying the Ground for Metaphysics: Heidegger's Appropriation of Kant," in *Cambridge Companion to Heidegger*, ed. Charles Guignon (New York: Cambridge University Press, 2006), 215–39; and "Is Heidegger a Kantian Idealist?" *Inquiry* 37, no. 2 (1944): 185–201; reprinted in Hubert L. Dreyfus and Mark A. Wrathall, eds., *Heidegger Reexamined* (London: Routledge, 2002). For a different view, see Hermann Philipse, *Heidegger's Philosophy of Being: A Critical Interpretation* (Princeton, NJ: Princeton University Press, 1998), 433. Philipse argues that Heidegger rejects transcendental idealism in the form of realism concerning entities.
55. It is already underway in an early course Heidegger gave in his role as a Privatdozent. See Martin Heidegger, *Phenomenological Interpretations of Aristotle: Initiation into Phenomenological Research*, trans. Richard Rojcewicz (Bloomington: Indiana University Press, 2001).
56. This relation is not often examined in detail. See Jean-Luc Marion, "Heidegger and Descartes," in *Critical Heidegger*, ed. Christopher E. Macann (London: Routledge, 2007), 67–96.
57. See John McDowell, *Mind and World* (Cambridge, MA: Harvard University Press, 1994).
58. The anticonstructivist, representational dimension of Heidegger's position is sometimes seen as consistent with artificial intelligence. See, for example, Michael Wheeler, *Reconstructing the Cognitive World: The Next Step* (Cambridge, MA: MIT Press, 2005).
59. Most Kant scholars are unimpressed by Heidegger's reading of the critical philosophy. For an example of a Kant scholar who takes Heidegger's reading of Kant seriously, see Otfried Höffe, *Immanuel Kant*, trans. Marshall Farrier (Albany: State University of New York Press, 1994). See also Otfried Höffe, *Kants Kritik der reinen Vernunft. Die Grundlegung der modernen Philosophie* (Munich: Beck, 2003).
60. See, on this point, "On the Unity of Subjectivity," in Dieter Henrich, *The Unity of Reason: Essays on Kant's Philosophy*, ed. Richard L. Velkley (Cambridge, MA: Harvard University Press, 1994), 17–54.
61. Robert Hanna, an important Kant scholar, identifies as controversial Heidegger's claims that (1) for Kant the cognitive capacity of imagination is the "common root" of the capacity of understanding (the faculty of concepts) and the capacity of sensibility (the faculty of intuitions); (2) the representational spontaneity of productive imagination is at bottom identical to the volitional spontaneity of practical freedom; and (3) Kant's transcendental theory of the imagination anticipates but still falls short of his own existential-phenomenological theory of "temporality" (roughly, human intentional agency) and "freedom" (roughly, decisive personal commitment with a view to achieving "authenticity," or psychological coherence and personal integrity over an entire finite human life). See Robert Hanna, "Review of Martin Weatherston, *Heidegger's Interpretation of Kant: Categories, Imagination, and Temporality*," in *Notre Dame Philosophical Reviews* (2003); published online, no further information available. William Blattner concludes that Heidegger simply forces the reading of the text to support what he wants to do; see "Laying the Ground for Metaphysics," 149–76.

62. See Michael Friedman, *A Parting of the Ways: Carnap, Cassirer, and Heidegger* (Chicago: University of Chicago Press, 2000).
63. See especially his lecture course entitled *Phänomenologische Interpretation von Kants Kritik der reinen Vernunft* (Wintersemester 1927/1928), published in Martin Heidegger, *Phenomenological Interpretation of Kant's Critique of Pure Reason*, trans. Parvis Emad and Kenneth Maly (Bloomington: Indiana University Press, 1997).
64. See Martin Heidegger, *Kant and the Problem of Metaphysics*, trans. James S. Churchill (Bloomington: Indiana University Press, 1962), xxv. This work is hereafter cited parenthetically in the text as *KPM*.
65. See Immanuel Kant, *Critique of Pure Reason*, trans. Paul Guyer and Allen W. Wood (New York: Cambridge University Press, 1998), B134, 247.
66. Nietzsche famously holds that there is only interpretation all the way down. In our time, the main proponents of skepticism about textual interpretation are Richard Rorty, Jacques Derrida, and Paul de Man. Rorty is skeptical about any claim to get it right. His own approach to textual interpretation reflects a cavalier attitude that illustrates this view. Derrida consistently opposes anything like definite reference, which leads to the idea that there is no way to show that words link up correctly with things. For de Man, who opposes even the distinction between history and fiction, it is not possible to separate fiction from nonfiction.
67. See, for example, E. D. Hirsch Jr., *Validity in Interpretation* (New Haven, CT: Yale University Press, 1967).
68. See Willard Van Orman Quine, *Word and Object* (Cambridge, MA: MIT Press, 1960), 72–79.
69. See Donald Davidson, "The Emergence of Thought," in *Subjective, Intersubjective, Objective* (Oxford: Clarendon Press, 2001), 123–34.
70. See Michael Devitt, *Realism and Truth* (Princeton, NJ: Princeton University Press, 1997).
71. See Steven Weinberg, "The Revolution That Didn't Happen," *New York Review of Books*, October 8, 1998, 48–52.
72. See Monroe Beardsley, *The Aesthetic Point of View*, ed. Michael Wreen and Donald Callen (Ithaca, NY: Cornell University Press, 1982).
73. See Plato *Sophist* 237B–249D, in *Complete Works*, ed. John M. Cooper (Indianapolis, IN: Hackett, 1997), 257–71.
74. Ibid., 243D, 264.
75. Ibid., 244A, 265.
76. See Heidegger, *Nietzsche*, vols. 1 and 2, trans. David Farrell Krell (New York: Harper and Row, 1984), 2:413.
77. See Charles Kahn, *The Verb "Be" in Ancient Greek* (Indianapolis, IN: Hackett, 2003).
78. See Martin Heidegger, *Plato's Sophist*, trans. Richard Rojcewicz and André Schuwer (Bloomington: University of Indiana Press, 1997).
79. See Aristotle *Metaphysics* 988b.34–35, in *The Complete Works of Aristotle*, 2 vols., ed. Jonathan Barnes (Princeton, NJ: Princeton University Press, 1984), 1563.
80. See Aristotle *Metaphysics* 1003a.21–22, in *Complete Works*, 1584.
81. See Aristotle *Metaphysics* 5.7, in *Complete Works*, 1606.
82. See Jitendra Nath Mohanty, *The Concept of Intentionality* (St. Louis, MO: Warren H. Green, 1972), 129.
83. See "Author's Preface to the Second Edition," in Heidegger, *Kant and the Problem of Metaphysics*, xv.

84. Kant considered this theme to be important. In the second edition he revised the chapter he devoted to it. See Kant, *Critique of Pure Reason*, B354-65.
85. See G. W. F. Hegel, "Sense Certainty," in *Hegel's Phenomenology of Spirit*, trans. A. V. Miller (New York: Oxford University Press, 1977), 58-66.
86. See Jürgen Habermas, "Einleitung: Historischer Materialismus und die Entwicklung normativer Strukturen," in *Zur Rekonstruktion des historischen Materialismus* (Frankfurt am Main: Suhrkamp, 1976), 9.
87. See Otto Neurath, "Protocol Sentences," in *Logical Positivism*, ed. A. J. Ayer (New York: Free Press, 1959), 199-208.
88. See Wilfrid Sellars, *Empiricism and the Philosophy of Mind* (Cambridge, MA: Harvard University Press, 1997). On the relation between Sellars and Husserl, see Gail Soffer, "Revisiting the Myth: Husserl and Sellars on the Given," in *Review of Metaphysics* 57, no. 22 (2003): 301-38.
89. See Donald Davidson, "On the Very Idea of a Conceptual Scheme," in *Inquiries into Truth and Interpretation* (New York: Oxford University Press, 1991), 183-98.
90. See, for example, Martin Heidegger, *Identity and Difference*, trans. Joan Stambaugh (Chicago: University of Chicago Press, 2002).
91. See, for recent discussion of this passage, L. Tarán, *Parmenides* (Princeton, NJ: Princeton University Press, 1964), 41-44.
92. See especially Plotinus *Enneads* 5.1.8.14-23.
93. See G. W. F. Hegel, *Vorlesungen über die Geschichte der Philosophie*, in *Werke*, ed. Eva Moldenhauer and Karl Rinus Michel (Frankfurt am Main: Suhrkamp Verlag, 1971), 18:289.
94. The discussion proceeds over many centuries. For a recent, representative sample of current thinking about Parmenides' fragment B3, see Giannis Stamatellos, Plotinus and the Presocratics: A Philosophical Study of Presocratic Influences in Plotinus' "Enneads" (Albany: State University of New York Press, 2007), 72-73.
95. Aristotle *Metaphysics* 1011b25, in *Complete Works*, 2:1597.
96. See, for example, Plato *Cratylus* 385b2, in *Complete Works*, 103; and *Sophist* 263b, ibid., 287.
97. See Aristotle *Categories* 12b11 and 14b14, in *Complete Works*, 19 and 23.
98. Aristotle *De Interpretatione* 16a3, in *Complete Works*, 25.

CHAPTER SIX

1. This is a main theme in his last, unfinished book. See Edmund Husserl, *The Crisis of European Sciences and Transcendental Phenomenology: An Introduction to Phenomenological Philosophy*, trans. David Carr (Evanston, IL: Northwestern University Press, 1970), esp. pt. 2: "Clarification of the Origin of the Modern Opposition between Physicalistic Objectivism and Transcendental Subjectivism," 23-100.
2. See Martin Heidegger, *Being and Time*, trans. John Macquarrie and Edward Robinson (New York: Harper and Row, 1962), sec. 32, 194.
3. See Alan Sokal, "Transgressing the Boundaries: Towards a Transformative Hermeneutics of Quantum Gravity," in *Social Text* 46-47 (Spring/Summer 1996): 217-52.
4. See, for the uninformed postmodern approach to science, Alan Sokal and Jean Bricmont, *Impostures intellectuelles* (Paris: Odile Jacob, 1997). See also Keith M. Ashmore and Philip S. Baringer, eds., *After the Science Wars* (London: Routledge, 2001).

5. For a discussion of the relation of Cousin to Hegel, see Jacques d'Hondt, *Hegel in His Time*, trans. John Burbidge, with Nelson Roland and Judith Levasseur (Peterborough, Ontario: Broadview, 1988), 132–61.
6. See Victor Cousin, *Cours de philosophie: Introduction à l'histoire de la philosophie* (Paris: Fayard, 1991), orig. pub. in 2 vols., 1825 and 1841. For an account of Cousin's rationalist reading of Hegel without the conception of dialectic, see Elizabeth Roudinesco and Jeffrey Mehlman, *Jacques Lacan and Co.: A History of Psychoanalysis in France, 1925–1985* (Chicago: University of Chicago Press, 1990), 136–37.
7. See Emmanuel Levinas, *Théorie de l'intuition dans la phénoménologie de Husserl* (Paris: Vrin, 1977), orig. pub. 1930; earlier eds. 1963, 1970.
8. This statement occurs in the context of a remark on the adequacy of language to philosophy: "I have in mind especially the inner relationship of the German language with the language of the Greeks and with their thought. This has been confirmed for me today again by the French. When they [i.e., the French] think, they speak German, being sure that they could not make it with their own language." See Martin Heidegger, "Only a God Can Save Us: *Der Spiegel's* Interview with Martin Heidegger," *Philosophy Today* 20, no. 4 (1976): 282.
9. See Paul Nizan, *The Watchdogs: Philosophers of the Established Order*, trans. Paul Fittingoff (New York: Monthly Review Press, 1971).
10. See Vincent Descombes, *Le Même et l'autre* (Paris: Editions de Minuit, 1979).
11. See Tom Rockmore, *Heidegger and French Philosophy: Humanism, Anti-Humanism and Being* (London: Routledge, 1995).
12. This is the main theme of the *Letter on Humanism* through which, by dint of criticizing Sartre, Heidegger displaced him as the main "French" thinker. See Martin Heidegger, *Letter on Humanism*, in *Basic Writings*, ed. David Farrell Krell (New York: Harper and Row, 1977).
13. For Derrida's view, see his long introduction to Edmund Husserl, *L'Origine de la géométrie*, trans. Jacques Derrida (Paris: Presses universitaires de France, 1974), 58n. (Orig. pub. 1962.)
14. See Herbert Spiegelberg, *The Phenomenological Movement: A Historical Introduction* (The Hague: Martinus Nijhoff, 1982).
15. See Otto Pöggeler, *Martin Heidegger's Path of Thinking*, trans. Daniel Magurshak and Sigmund Barber (Atlantic Highlands, NJ: Humanities Press International, 1989), 61. Donn Welton, who concedes that Heidegger's replacement of Husserl's conception of transcendental subjectivity by Dasein is a fundamental difference, underscores important areas of overlap; see his *The Other Husserl: The Horizons of Transcendental Phenomenology* (Bloomington: Indiana University Press, 2000), 347–70.
16. On the question of the relation of Husserl and Heidegger, Merleau-Ponty writes, "Voudra-t-on lever ces contradictions en distinguant entre la phénoménologie de Husserl et celle de Heidegger? Mais tout *Sein und Zeit* est sorti d'une indication de Husserl et n'est en somme qu'une explicitation du <<natürlichen Weltbegriff>> ou du <<Lebenswelt>> que Husserl, à la fin de sa vie donnait pour thème premier à la phénoménologie." See Maurice Merleau-Ponty, *Phénoménologie de la perception* (Paris: Gallimard, 1945), 1. In this way, Merleau-Ponty exaggerates the continuity between two very different thinkers.
17. See Edmund Husserl, "Philosophy as Rigorous Science," in *Phenomenology and the Crisis of Philosophy*, trans. Quentin Lauer (New York: Harper and Row, 1965), 76–77.

18. See Martin Heidegger, *The Basic Problems of Phenomenology*, trans. Alfred Hofstadter (Bloomington: Indiana University Press, 1982), 178.
19. Derrida published often on Hegel. See especially Jacques Derrida, *Glas* (Lincoln: University of Nebraska Press, 1986).
20. See Maurice Merleau-Ponty, "Hegel's Existentialism," in *Sense and Non-Sense*, trans. Hubert L. Dreyfus and Patricia Allen Dreyfus (Evanston, IL: Northwestern University Press, 1964), 63. This idea is later echoed by others. According to Philippe Sollers, Nietzsche, Bataille, Lacan, and Marxism-Leninism result from "l'explosion du système hégélien." See Philippe Sollers, *Bataille* (Paris: 10/18, 1973): 36; cited in Descombes, *Le Même et l'autre*, 23, n. 5.
21. See Edmund Husserl, *Phänomenologische Psychologie: Vorlesungen Sommersemester 1925*, ed. Walter Biemel (The Hague: Martinus Nijhoff, 1968): "Unter Phänomenologie versteht man eine an der Wende unseres Jahrhunderts erwachsene Bewegung" (237).
22. See Maurice Merleau-Ponty, *Phenomenology of Perception*, trans. Colin Smith (London: Routledge, 2003), ix. This work is hereafter cited parenthetically in the text as *PP*.
23. See Maurice Natanson, *Husserl, Philosopher of Infinite Tasks* (Evanston, IL: Northwestern University Press, 1973).
24. Maurice Merleau-Ponty, *Parcours: 1935–1951* (Paris: Verdier, 1997), 66.
25. See Jean-Paul Sartre, *Transcendence of the Ego*, trans. Forrest Williams and Robert Kirkpatrick (New York: Noonday Press, 1962).
26. See Maurice Merleau-Ponty, *The Primacy of Perception, and Other Essays on Phenomenological Psychology, the Philosophy of Art, History and Politics*, ed. James M. Edie (Evanston, IL: Northwestern University Press, 1964), 373.
27. Ibid., 502.
28. See Immanuel Kant, *Prolegomena to Any Future Metaphysics*, trans. James W. Ellington (Indianapolis, IN: Hackett, 1977), sec. 20, 40–42.
29. See Léon Brunschvicg, *La Modalité du jugement* (Paris: Alcan, 1897).
30. See Pierre Lachièze-Rey, *L'idéalisme kantien* (Paris: Vrin, 1931).
31. See Husserl, *Crisis of European Sciences*, sec. 14, 68–70.
32. See, for example, Elizabeth Ströker, ed., *Lebenswelt und Wissenschaft in der Philosophie Edmund Husserls* (Frankfurt am Main: Vittorio Klostermann, 1979).
33. For Husserl's distinction between objectivism and transcendentalism, see Husserl, *Crisis of European Sciences*, sec. 14, 68–70.
34. See Maurice Merleau-Ponty, "The Battle Over Existentialism," in *Sense and Non-Sense*, trans. Hubert L. Dreyfus and Patricia Allen Dreyfus (Evanston, IL: Northwestern University Press, 1964), 71–82.
35. See Immanuel Kant, *Critique of Pure Reason*, trans. Paul Guyer and Allen W. Wood (New York: Cambridge University Press, 1998), B274–75, 326.
36. See Martin Kusch, *Psychologism: A Case Study in the Sociology of Philosophical Knowledge* (London: Routledge, 1995). See also Mathias Rath, *Der Psychologismusstreit in der deutschen Philosophie* (Freiburg: Alber Verlag, 1994).
37. In *Philosophy as Rigorous Science*, Husserl defines "psychologism" in saying that "it "naturalizes" pure consciousness" (92).
38. See Edmund Husserl, *Logical Investigations*, 2 vols., trans. J. N. Findlay, revised by Dermot Moran, 2 vols. (London: Routledge, 2001), vol. 1, sec. 28, 316, n. 8.
39. The problem of the relation between Frege and Husserl has been studied in detail by Føllesdall and Mohanty. See D. Føllesdall, *Husserl und Frege: Ein Beitrag zur Beleuchtung der phänomenologischen Philosophie* (Oslo: Aschehoug, 1958); see also Jitendra Nath Mohanty, *Husserl and Frege* (Bloomington: Indiana University Press, 1982).

40. See David Carr, *Phenomenology and the Problem of History* (Evanston, IL: Northwestern University Press, 1974).
41. See G. W. F. Hegel, *Hegel's Philosophy of Mind*, trans. William Wallace, together with the *Zusätze*, trans. A. V. Miller (Oxford: Clarendon Press, 1971), esp. sec. 1: "Mind Subjective," 25–241.
42. See Jon Mills, *The Unconscious Abyss: Hegel's Anticipation of Psychoanalysis* (Albany: State University of New York Press, 2002).
43. See Husserl, *Crisis of European Sciences*, pt. 3: "The Clarification of the Transcendental Problem and the Related Function of Psychology," 103–265.
44. Maurice Merleau-Ponty, *The Structure of Behavior*, trans. A. L. Fisher (Boston: Beacon Press, 1963), 3.
45. Ibid., 135: "The integration of matter, life and mind is obtained by this reduction to a common denominator of physical form."
46. Ibid., 143.
47. See Merleau-Ponty, *Primacy of Perception*, 12.
48. Ibid., 12–13.
49. See Wilfrid Sellars, *Science, Perception, and Reality* (Atascadero, CA: Ridgeview, 1991), 169.
50. See Henri Bergson, *Time and Free Will: An Essay on the Immediate Data of Consciousness* (New York: Dover, 2001.
51. See Kant, *Critique of Pure Reason*, B1, 136.
52. John Locke, *An Essay Concerning Human Understanding*, 2 vols., collated and annotated by A. C. Fraser (New York: Dover, 1959), 2:19.
53. Merleau-Ponty, *Structure of Behavior*, 220.
54. According to Dan Zahavi, "Husserl never gives a clear answer to the question of whether constitution is to be understood as a creation or a restoration of reality"; see his *Husserl's Phenomenology (Cultural Memory in the Present)* (Stanford, CA: Stanford University Press, 2003), 72–73.
55. Bertrand Russell, *Mysticism and Logic* (Garden City: Doubleday Anchor, 1957).
56. See A. J. Ayer, *The Problem of Knowledge* (Baltimore, MD: Penguin, 1956), 118.
57. Ibid., 123–124.
58. Merleau-Ponty, *Primacy of Perception*, 13.
59. Ibid., 20.
60. Ibid., 27.
61. See Heidegger, *Being and Time*, sec. 44, 269.
62. See letters from Frege to Husserl, October 30 to November 1, 1906, in Edmund Husserl, *Briefwechsel*, 10 vols., ed. Karl Schuhmann (The Hague: Kluwer Academic Publishers, 1994), 6:113.
63. See Merleau-Ponty, *Primacy of Perception*, 25.
64. See G. W. F. Hegel, *Elements of the Philosophy of Right*, ed. Allen W. Wood, trans. H. B. Nisbet (New York: Cambridge University Press, 1991), 21–22.
65. See the introduction to G. W. F. Hegel, *Phenomenology of Spirit*, trans. A. V. Miller (New York: Oxford University Press, 1977), 46–57.

CONCLUSION

1. Heidegger seems in part to have been inspired by what he regarded as Aristotle's premodern form of phenomenology. For his phenomenological reading of Aristotle, see Martin Heidegger, *Phenomenological Interpretations of Aristotle: Initiations into Phenomenological Research*, trans. Richard Rojcewicz (Indianapolis: Indiana University Press, 2001).

2. Peirce apparently considered himself to be a Hegelian phenomenologist, as in the following passage: "Before we can attack any normative science, any science which proposes to separate the sheep from the goats here" [Peirce names three normative sciences: "Ethics, Esthetics, and Logic, the three doctrines that distinguish good and bad representations of truth, . . . efforts of will, . . . (and) objects considered simply in their presentation"], "it is plain that there must be a preliminary inquiry which shall justify the attempt to establish such dualism. This must be a science [sic] that does not draw any distinction of good or bad in any sense whatever, but just contemplates phenomena as they are, simply opens its eyes and describes what it sees; not what it sees in the real as distinguished from figment—not regarding any such dichotomy—but simply describing the object, as a phenomenon, and stating what it finds in all phenomena alike. This is the science that Hegel made his starting-point, under the name of the Phänomenologie des Geistes—although he considered it in a fatally narrow spirit, since he [Hegel] restricted himself to what actually forces itself on the mind. . . . I will so far follow Hegel as to call this science phenomenology although I will not restrict it to the observation and analysis of experience but extend it to describing all the features that are common to whatever is experienced or might conceivably be experienced or become an object of study in any way direct or indirect." See *Collected Papers of Charles Sanders Peirce*, 8 vols., ed. Charles Hartshorne, Paul Weiss, and Arthur Burks (Cambridge, MA: Harvard University Press, 1931–1958), 5:37.

3. See Peirce, *Collected Papers*, 1:284: "Phaneroscopy is the description of the *phaneron*; and by the *phaneron* I mean the collective total of all that is in any way or in any sense present to the mind, quite regardless of whether it corresponds to any real thing or not. If you ask present *when*, and to *whose* mind, I reply that I leave these questions unanswered, never having entertained a doubt that those features of the phaneron that I have found in my mind are present at all times and to all minds. So far as I have developed this science of phaneroscopy, it is occupied with the formal elements of the phaneron. I know that there is another series of elements imperfectly represented by Hegel's Categories. But I have been unable to give any satisfactory account of them. It will be plain from what has been said that phaneroscopy has nothing at all to do with the question of how far the phanerons it studies correspond to any realities. It religiously abstains from all speculation as to any relations between its categories and physiological facts, cerebral or other. It does not undertake, but sedulously avoids, hypothetical explanations of any sort. It simply scrutinizes the direct appearances, and endeavors to combine minute accuracy with the broadest possible generalization."

4. In that sense, Brandom's announcement of the end of representationalism only confirms the view at which Kant arrived two centuries earlier. Yet, since he does not analyze Kant's position, unlike Kant he turns to inferentialism as a replacement strategy without discussing Kantian constructivism. See Robert B. Brandom, *Making It Explicit: Reasoning, Representing and Discursive Commitment* (Cambridge, MA: Harvard University Press, 1994).

5. See Bertrand Russell, "Logical Atomism," in *The Philosophy of Logical Atomism*, ed. D. F. Pears (Chicago: Open Court, 1985), 29–34.

6. See Kant, *Critique of Pure Reason*, trans. Paul Guyer and Allen W. Wood (New York: Cambridge University Press, 1998), B862, 692.

7. Ibid., B168, 265.

8. Kant's approach suggests that there is closure with respect to the categories. This controversial claim is often contested. See, for example, Stephen Körner, *Categorial Framework* (Oxford: Blackwell, 1970).
9. Kant, *Critique of Pure Reason*, B180–81, 273.
10. Hegel, *Phenomenology of Spirit*, trans. A. V. Miller (New York: Oxford University Press, 1977), 54.
11. Ibid.
12. This theme has recently been explored in Frederick C. Beiser, *German Idealism: The Struggle against Subjectivism, 1781–1801* (Cambridge, MA: Harvard University Press, 2002).
13. Hegel, *Phenomenology of Spirit*, 53.
14. See Aristotle, *Nicomachean Ethics*, in *The Complete Works of Aristotle*, 2 vols., ed. Jonathan Barnes (Princeton, NJ: Princeton University Press, 1985), vol. 2, bk. 1, chap. 1, 1729.

INDEX

Abelard, 32
abstract art, 28
abstract versus concrete ideas, 37
aesthetic realism, 18
aisthesis, 94
aletheia, 15, 150
Allison, Henry, 51, 52, 53, 55, 225n12
Ameriks, 54
analytic philosophy, 3, 37, 68, 193
Anaxagoras, 7
anti-constructivist phenomenological approach to knowledge, 211
anti-phenomenology, 14, 24–28
anti-Platonism: causal theory of perception, 55; dualism, 45; importance of in modern formulation of knowledge, 42; return to representationalism, 31
anti-psychologism, 14–15, 108, 143
apparent retrograde motion, 61
appearance: as equivalent to phenomenon (Husserl), 126; false and true, 4, 65, 88, 89; and its cause (Kant), 45; and phenomenon, 3–4, 68, 126; as stage on way to truth (Hegel), 91
Aquinas, Thomas, 31, 32, 55, 222nn43, 44
Aristotle, 5, 6, 215; art as imitation of nature, 26–27; canonical form of problem of being, 140; distinction between activity and movement, 12; distinction between form and matter, 118; essentialism, 117, 118; form in things, 119; *Metaphysics*, 140, 168, 184–85; on method, 59; and philosophical tradition, 79; and Platonic concept of causality, 23; and Platonic theory of ideas, 21–22, 55, 140; *Poetics*, 27; theory of metaphysics, 160; third-man argument, 30; view of truth as agreement, 181
art: anti-Platonic, representative approach to, 27; mimetic approach to, 25–27; modern art, 28; religious art, 27–28
artistic representationalism, 55
atheism, 38
Augustine, Saint, 10, 31, 32, 221n42
Ayer, A. J., 205, 212, 217n3

Bacon, Francis, 28
Baden neo-Kantians, 108
Bardili, C. G., 72, 85
Beardsley, Monroe, 164
Beaufret, Jean, 146
beauty, form of, 21
Beck, J. S., 53
behaviorism, 199–200
Beiser, Frederick, 74
Beneke, Friedrich Eduard, 107, 108
Bergmann, Gustav, 110
Bergson, Henri, 201
Berkeley, George, 22, 134, 194, 223n79, 224n80; critique of Lockean empiricism, 37–38; empiricism, 28, 33, 36; on misperception, 49–50; rejection of distinction between primary and secondary ideas, 38; rejection of qualities of extramental objects, 38
blank slate, 36
Blattner, William, 240n61
Blumenberg, Hans, 58

Boethius, 32
Boghossian, Paul, 11
Bolzano, Bernhard, 30, 105, 112, 132
bracketing, 131, 167, 183, 185
Brandom, Robert, 57, 226n39, 246n4
Braque, Georges, 28
Brentano, Franz, 25, 101, 144, 172; influence on Heidegger, 142; "On the Manifold Meaning of Being since Aristotle," 118, 142; *Psychology from an Empirical Standpoint*, 199; theory of intentionality, 55, 56, 233n6; variation on Kantian representative approach, 123; view of logic, 103
British empiricism, 36, 46, 106, 202
British idealism, 68, 189
Broad, C. D., 212
Brucker, Johann Jakob: *Historia Critica*, 42, 43
Brunschvicg, Léon, 188, 195
Buridan, Jean, 32

Cairns, Dorion, 139
Cambridge Platonists, 28, 221n29
Carnap, Rudolf, 36, 101, 177, 205, 212
Cartesian occasionalists, 33
Cassirer, Ernst, 1, 2, 160, 164
categorical intuition, 15, 122, 123, 130
causality, historical span of views about, 22–24
causal theory of perception, 21, 23, 40, 52, 56, 91; anti-Platonic model of, 28–29, 55; Descartes and, 126, 155; Fichte and, 53; Hegel and, 23–24, 92; Kant and, 44–45, 54–55, 92; in modern epistemological debate, 202; and representationalism, 41, 42, 47
causal theory of reference, 55
Cézanne, Paul, 27
Christian approach to knowledge, 32
Christian art, 27
classical realism, 3
cognition: experience as source of, 93; historical relativity of, 206–7; theory of as self-consciousness, 97
cognitive objects, 3; idea as unchanging, 31; knowledge through analysis of causal relation of ideas to, 32–33; relation of phenomena to, 4; relation to human subject, 10; and representationalism, 11–12
Cohen, Hermann, 108

consciousness: Hegel and, 93–99; Husserl and, 133–34; Kant and, 97; Locke and, 202
constructivism, 41; and ancient Greek mathematics, 12–13; in German idealism, 212; Hegel and, 213–15; Kant and, 10, 11, 12, 14, 48, 49–50, 57–59, 65–67, 125, 212; and representationalism, 210; subject must "construct" what it knows, 11–13, 58
continental rationalists, 28
Copernican revolution, 58, 60, 61
Copernicus, Nikolaus: *Commentariolus*, 61; demonstration of threefold movement of earth, 62–63; *De revolutionibus*, 61–63
copy principle, 39
Cordemoy, Géraud de, 33
correspondence theory of truth, 157, 181–82, 184–85
Cotes, Roger, 58, 59, 65
Courbet, Gustave, 27
Courtine-Denamy, Sylvie, 190
Cousin, Victor, 188
Craver, Carl, 3
critical philosophers, 32, 33
critical philosophy: Fichte and, 82–84; Hegel and, 79–80, 81–84, 93; Husserl and, 101; Reinhold and, 72–73, 75. *See also* Kant, Immanuel
Cubism, 28, 55

Davidson, Donald, 37, 38, 163, 177
De Man, Paul, 241n66
denotation, 56
Derrida, Jacques, 101, 164, 188, 190, 191, 241n66
Descartes, René, 10, 28, 29, 37, 50, 145, 189; apodicticity as criterion of knowledge, 73; and causal theory of perception, 126, 155; and cogito, 148, 156, 169, 189, 196–97; *Discourse on Method*, 59; foundationalist epistemology, 34, 72; *idea* as image of thing, 35; immanence as necessarily true, 131; *Meditations*, 34, 35, 59; method as key to theory of knowledge, 59; *Passions of the Soul*, 59; and philosophical tradition, 78, 79; and psychologism, 106; rationalism, 33, 35, 222n62; reliance on God, 35–36; and scholasticism, 31–32; spectator view of subjectivity, 156; subjectivity as path to

objectivity, 98; substance ontology, 86–87; theory of ideas, 31–35
Dilthey, Wilhelm, 129
Dilthey, Wilhelm, 145, 201
direct givenness, 179, 180
dogmatic metaphysics, 93
double aspect thesis, 46, 51–54, 55, 133
Dufrenne, Mikel, 190

Ekphantus, 62
Eleatic view, 20, 164–65
Else, Gerard, 27
empathy theory, 114
empirical realism, 18
empiricism, 32, 33, 36, 91, 100, 204; Berkeley and, 28, 33, 36; British, 36, 46, 106, 202; Hegel and, 92–93; and knowledge, 111; Merleau-Ponty and, 202
Engels, Friedrich, 81
epistemological apodicticity, 73, 206
epistemological constructivism. *See* constructivism
epistemological foundationalism, 34, 72–73, 75
epistemological psychologism. *See* psychologism
epistemological relativism, 111
epistemology: as a distinct field, 140; modern, 28–40; phenomenological contribution to, 2, 17, 185–86, 208; theory of knowledge of all kinds, 1
Erdmann, Benno, 108
Erdmann, Johann Eduard, 109
essences, 119
essentialism: Aristotelian, 117, 118; Heidegger and, 167; Husserl and, 117, 118, 120, 167
Euclidean geometry, 13
exemplification, 56
existentialism, 145–47
external objects, 2
external world, 34–35, 153–55

false appearance, 4, 65, 89
Farber, Marvin, 139
Fichte, J. G., 1, 2, 14, 51, 58, 232n82, 232nn68, 69; claims to Kantianism, 76; combination of idealism and realism, 130; and critical philosophy, 82–84; *Darstellung*, 88; differences from Descartes, 86–87; and double-aspect thesis, 52–53; and form of system, 74; *Foundations of the Entire Science of Knowledge*, 87; and idealism, 53; influence on Hegel, 85, 86; and Kantian subject, 55, 89–90, 106, 214; phenomenology, 86, 88, 89; rejection of causal approach to perception, 53; rejection of thing in itself, 53, 84, 85, 86, 87, 88; reworking of Kantian distinction between false and true appearance, 88; *System of Transcendental Idealism*, 76; and three forms of experience, 53; view of positing, 90; *Wissenschaftslehre*, 85, 86, 87, 88–89

Fistioc, Mihaela, 42
force, concept of, 95
Foucault, Michel, 25
foundationalism, epistemological, 34, 72–73, 75
Frank, Manfred, 74
Franks, Paul, 74
Frege, Gottlob, 48, 57, 105, 109, 115, 206; distinction between meaning and reference, 118; distinction between sense and reference, 56; mathematical Platonism, 198
French existentialism, 145
French humanism, 147
French impressionists, 27
French phenomenology, 188–89; Heidegger's position in, 190; and translation, 189
French philosophy, 188–89
Freud, Sigmund, 97
"friends of the forms," 20
Fries, Jakob Friedrich, 107

Gadamer, Hans-Georg, 1, 15, 141, 164
Galileo, 37, 60, 204
Gassendi, Pierre, 35
German idealism, 4, 14, 55, 58, 71–72, 75, 77, 188; and constructivism, 212; Hegel and, 79–83; Leibniz and, 229n16; and philosophy as system, 228n5; and relation of system to knowledge, 74; systematicity, 73. *See also* post-Kantian German idealism
German neo-Kantians, 107–8, 159
Gestalt psychology, 200, 201
Gettier, Edmund, 56
Geulincx, Arnold, 33
Gilson, Etienne, 31

givenness, 192–93, 232n74; direct, 179, 180; experiential, 192–93; Hegel and, 232n74
Gombrich, Ernst, 27
Goodman, Nelson, 27, 56–57, 212
Grice, H. P., 56
Gris, Juan, 28
Guyer, Paul, 42, 54

Habermas, Jürgen, 174, 242n86
Hamann, Johann Georg, 42
Hanna, Robert, 240n61
Hattiangadi, Anandi, 57
Hegel, G. W. F., 1, 2, 13, 17, 50–51, 52, 57, 58; analysis of consciousness, 93–97, 99; appearance as stage on way to truth, 91; and causal theories of perception, 23–24, 92; concept of force, 95; concept of history of philosophy, 75–76; on critical philosophy as idealism in spirit but not in letter, 80; criticism of Newton, 95; critiques of metaphysics and immediate knowing, 92; on difference between Kant's intent and result, 80–81; and difference between spirit and letter of critical philosophy, 79–80, 81–84, 93; *Differenzschrift*, 74, 75, 79–83, 95; distinction between appearance and reality, 183; distinction between Fichte and Schelling, 80; distinction between subject and object within consciousness, 98; on empiricism, 92–93; *Encyclopedia of the Philosophical Sciences*, 92, 93; and Fichte, 81, 85, 86; genuine speculative philosophy, 87; and German idealism, 79–83; and givenness, 232n74; immanent consciousness of truth, 182; "invention" of post-Kantian German idealism, 71, 75, 79, 212–13; *Lectures on the History of Philosophy*, 75; phenomenological reformulation of Kant's position, 89–91; phenomenology, 14, 71, 84–86, 91–97, 97–100, 173; *Phenomenology of Spirit*, 76, 83, 89, 92, 93–100, 212; and philosophical tradition, 78, 81; philosophy of nature, 80; on Platonic ideal, 43; and problem of system, 74; *Prolegomena to Pure Logic*, 109; rejection of Kantian concept of understanding, 95; rejection of psychologism, 107; rejection of thing in itself, 89; relation to Kant, 82; separa-tion of sensation and perception, 94; shift away from transcendental analysis, 90; truth as limiting concept, 233n84; and truth of self-certainty, 96–97; view of Reinhold as leading nonphilosopher, 85
Hegelians, 81
Heidegger, Martin, 1, 3, 13, 17, 114; "The Age of the World-Picture," 148, 157, 169; anti-constructivist phenomenological approach to knowledge, 211; approach to categorical intuition, 152–53; and authentic historicity, 165–66; *Being and Time*, 15, 135, 139–45, 147, 148, 150, 152, 153–60, 162, 164–65, 167–69, 179, 211; on Cartesian concept of world as extended being, 157–59; on cognitive function of speech, 173–74; concept of intentionality, 172; concept of truth as disclosure, 174; *Contributions to Philosophy*, 148; and correspondence theory of truth, 181–82, 184; critique of Cartesian subjectivity, 156–57, 169; distinction between ready-to-hand and present-to-hand, 201–2; "The Doctrine of Judgment in Psychologism: A Critical-Positive Contribution to Knowledge," 144; essentialism, 167; etymological reconstructions, 172; on existence of external world, 153–55; French anthropological approach to, 145; grasp of philosophical tradition, 164; and history of ontology, 162–71; *History of the Concept of Time*, 152; and Husserl, 149–55, 159, 239n33; *Ideas*, 149; influence of Brentano on, 142; *Kant and the Problem of Metaphysics*, 15, 159, 160–62; *Letter on Humanism*, 146–47, 148, 189, 243n12; and metaphysical realism, 164; and National Socialism, 146, 147; ontological reading of Descartes, 155–59; on Parmenides, 180–81; phenomenological interpretation of Kant, 66; phenomenological ontology, 15, 139–43, 152, 211; phenomenology, 172–76; and philosophical anthropology, 145; philosophical relation with Husserl, 141–43; premodern view of causality, 23; priority of ontology over all other philosophical investigations, 140; and problem of meaning of being, 140, 154, 162, 165, 167–70, 174–76; "The Problem of Realism in Modern Philosophy," 153;

and psychologism, 143–49, 184; reading of Kant, 143, 155–62; and realism, 153–55; "The Reality Problem in Modern Philosophy," 144; relation between ideal entity and real thing, 182–83; representational dimension, 240n58; and the subject, 148; and textual interpretation, 164–71, 176–79; theory of *Dasein*, 144–45, 154, 156–57, 157–58, 161–62, 168–69, 171, 180, 184, 185, 196, 243n15; and theory of truth as *aletheia*, 179–85; "To the things themselves!", 172, 173, 174; translation of into French, 189; turn away from epistemology, 2

Henry, Michel, 188, 190
Heraclitus, 4, 21
Herakleides, 62
Herbart, Johann Friedrich, 112
Herder, Johann Gottfried, 85
Herz, Marcus, 50
Hicetas, 62
Hitler, Adolph, 147
Hobbes, Thomas, 34, 35, 41, 58, 97
Homer, 23, 26
humanism, and French philosophy, 147, 189
Hume, David, 28, 33, 36; attack on causality, 39, 58; contents of thoughts limited to perceptions, 39; division of contexts of mind into impressions, 37; *Enquiry*, 39; relation of simple and complex ideas, 39; skepticism, 39; *Treatise*, 39
Husserl, Edmund, 1, 2, 13, 17; anticonstructivist phenomenological approach to knowledge, 211; appearance as equivalent to phenomenon, 126; and bracketing of existence, 131, 167, 183, 185; and Brentano, 102–3; *Cartesian Meditations*, 101, 124, 135, 136–37; and categorical intuition, 151–53; central phenomenological figure for Sartre and Merleau-Ponty, 190; concept of intentionality, 172, *On the Concept of Number*, 199; concern with form in things, 119; and "constitution," 127–28, 133, 245n54; *The Crisis of European Sciences and Transcendental Phenomenology*, 135, 136, 195; and critical philosophy, 101; distinction between noema and noesis, 132, 133, 134, 202, 204; distinction between psychological and logical subject, 124; epistemology as precondition for science of being, 140; and essences, 117–18, 119, 127; essentialism, 117, 118, 120, 167; final investigation in *Logical Investigations*, 150–51; *Formal and Transcendental Logic*, 109, 114, 135; and freedom of phenomenology from presuppositions, 121, 122; *The Idea of Phenomenology*, 103, 104, 123–28, 130; *Ideas: General Introduction to Pure Phenomenology*, 109, 128, 129, 130, 219n36, 235n49; identification of phenomenology with epistemology, 143; initial concept of phenomenology as descriptive psychology, 109, 195; life-world (Lebenswelt), 119, 136, 192, 211; link between phenomenology and epistemology, 116–28; link of phenomenology to reference, 118; *Logical Investigations*, 102–5, 108, 109, 114, 117, 122–23, 131, 150–51, 152, 210; logic as a priori independent discipline, 110; *Nachlass*, 102; and parallelism, 132; phenomenological reduction, 124–27, 129, 130, 131, 132, 137, 167, 210, 236n57; phenomenologist in Kantian tradition, 3, 101–4, 233n2; phenomenology as descriptive psychology, 117–18, 210; phenomenology as foundational science of all other sciences, 121–22; phenomenology in later writings, 135–37; "Philosophy as Rigorous Science," 117, 128; *The Philosophy of Arithmetic*, 109, 143, 199; *Prolegomena to Pure Logic*, 115; and psychologism, 14–15, 101, 103–4, 108–16, 197–98, 244n37; and pure logic, 103, 105, 112, 113–14, 115, 119; and relation of phenomenology to intuition, 116–17; relation to psychology, 199; on skepticism, 111; theory of logical self-evidence, 151; and the *thing itself*, 119; transcendental idealism, 104, 109, 128–35, 137, 144, 180, 195, 197, 211; on unity of science, 112–13; view of "reism," 103

Husserlians, 139, 193
Hutcheson, Francis, 33
Hyppolite, Jean, 188

idea, 7; abstract versus concrete, 37; ancient and modern views of, 29; Descartes' position on, 31–32, 33–35; extended to

idea (*cont.*)
  mean any object of thought, 37; of God, 33; in modern philosophy, 30-31; Platonic, 29-30; simple, 36; use of in "idea" of God, 30; use of in modern epistemological contexts, 32
"idea in itself," 30
idealism: British, 68, 189; Fichte and, 53, 130; versus materialism, 68; Merleau-Ponty and, 193-94, 207; Platonism and, 67; psychological, 195; transcendental, 104, 109, 128-35, 137, 144, 180, 195, 197, 211. *See also* German idealism; post-Kantian German idealism
immediate knowing, 92
individual relativism, 111
inferentialism, 57, 226n39
infinite regress, 30
Ingarden, Roman, 143, 193
innate ideas, 33, 37
intentionality, 134, 172; modern concept of, 25; theory of, 55, 56, 103, 233n6
internalist, 3

Jacobi, F. H., 85, 87
Jaspers, Karl, 142
Jewish religious art, 27

Kant, Immanuel: advancement of phenomenology, 13; aesthetics, 27; ahistorical perspective, 77-78; analysis of preconditions of consciousness, 97; anti-anthropological reduction of subject, 72, 229n23; anti-phenomenological and phenomenological approaches, 9; anti-traditional view of philosophy, 77-78, 81; Cartesianism, 59-60; and causal theory of perception, 44-45, 54-55, 92; claim that Descartes doubted existence of external world, 34-35; and completeness of critical philosophy, 75, 77, 178; concept of subject and object and relation between them, 45, 46-47, 48, 93, 162; concept of system as unity under a single principle, 74, 113, 122; concept of thing in itself (noumenon), 6, 19, 45-46, 49, 52, 84, 225n18; constructivism, 10, 11, 12, 14, 48, 49-50, 57-59, 125, 212; Copernican turn, 1, 13, 17, 35, 225n14; critical philosophy as phenomenology, 66-67, 68; critique of Locke's physiological theory, 14; *Critique of Pure Reason*, 42, 43, 44, 46, 47-48, 51, 59-60, 80, 110; differentiation of mathematics from philosophy, 13; distinction between phenomena and noumena, 4, 5, 46, 48, 49, 58, 67, 91, 172, 202-3, 218n16, 225n13, 226n41; distinction between pure and applied logic, 112; distinction between spirit and letter of work, 76-77, 78, 142; double-aspect thesis, 46, 51-54, 55, 133; epistemological foundationalism, 73; epistemological phenomenology, 15, 17-18; experience as source of cognition, 11, 93; and false appearance, 89; and Fichte, 230n37; formulation of philosophy as system, 72; and future science of metaphysics, 14; hermeneutics, 76; Herz letter, 43, 44, 51, 57, 66; idea of philosophical tradition, 75-79; *Inaugural Dissertation*, 66; knowledge of contemporary physics, 58; and Locke, 115-16; *The Metaphysical Foundations of Natural Science*, 66; methodological revolution in metaphysics, 63-64; and modern phenomenology, 65-67; natural scientific approach to empirical knowledge, 66; and Newtonianism, 58, 94; noumenal causality, 22; and ontological reading of thing in itself, 54; and Platonism, 9-10, 27, 41, 42-43, 67-69; a posteriori existence, 118; a priori epistemology, 74, 75, 106, 213; *Prolegomena to Any Future Metaphysics*, 162, 212; and psychologism, 116; and rationalism, 33; "Refutation of Idealism," 34, 40, 197; rejection of dogmatic metaphysics, 92; rejection of Fichte's position, 82; rejection of psychologism, 106, 116; relation between objects of experience and knowledge, 10; relation to Copernicus, 63-65; representationalism, 10, 14, 44-47; role of phenomenology in view of philosophical physics, 66; subject as a transcendental unity of apperception, 10, 75, 87, 89-90, 106, 162, 170, 197; theory of knowledge of empirical reality, 130; transcendental deduction, 73, 74-75, 80, 108, 212; and transcendental logic of knowledge, 46; turn away from representationalism, 8, 47-48;

two incompatible approaches to knowledge, 4
Koffka, Kurt, 200
Kojève, Alexandre, 188, 189
Kripke, Saul, 57
Kroner, Richard, 108
Kuehn, Manfred, 42

Lachièze-Rey, Pierre, 188, 195
La Forge, Louis de, 33
Lambert, J. H., 2, 17, 65, 66, 89
La Mettrie, Julian Offray de, 38
Lange, F. A., 107, 110
Leibniz, Gottfried, 28, 33, 35, 106; "Discourse on Metaphysics," 35; and German idealism, 229n16; *Monadology*, 35; principle of sufficient reason, 54
Levinas, Emmanuel, 188
Liebmann, Otto, 110
Limnatis, Nectarios, 74
Lipps, Theodor, 114, 144
Locke, John, 14, 28, 33, 35, 50, 223n70; attack on by empiricists, 36; concept of general triangle, 37; on consciousness, 202; distinction between primary and secondary ideas, 36, 37-38, 38, 40; empiricism, 116; *Essay on Human Understanding*, 28, 36, 37; *Port Royal Logic*, 37; rejection of innate ideas, 36
logic, pure, 103, 105, 112, 113-14, 115, 119
Lotze, Hermann, 107

Maimon, Salomon, 57, 93
Malebranche, Nicolas, 33
Manet, Édouard, 27
Marburg neo-Kantians, 107-8
Marion, Jean-Luc, 188, 190
Marx, Karl, 4, 24, 58, 97, 148
Marxism, 146, 193
Marxist aesthetics, 18
materialism, 19-20, 68
mathematical psychologism, 115
McDowell, John, 156
McGrath, Sean, 239n48
Meier, Dermot, 144
Merleau-Ponty, Maurice, 1, 3, 13, 17, 101, 114, 127, 130, 143, 190; anticonstructivist phenomenological approach to knowledge, 211; argument for historical relativity of cognitive claims, 206-7; attack on transcendental idealism, 194-97; and Cartesian cogito, 196, 197; and constitution, 203-4; on continuity between Husserl and Heidegger, 190-91; critique of idealism, 193-94, 195; descriptive phenomenology, 15, 191-93; descriptive phenomenology and primacy of perception, 201-4; and empiricism, 202, 203; experiential givenness, 192-93; and Hegel, 191; and Husserl's concept of life-world, 195; influences on, 188-91; phenomenological refutation of Kant, 196-97; phenomenology and limits of knowledge, 205-7; phenomenology and psychology, 199-201; phenomenology as privileged source of knowledge, 187; *Phenomenology of Perception*, 191; and primacy of perception, 187-88, 193, 194, 202, 203-5, 207, 211; "The Primacy of Perception and Its Philosophical Consequences," 200; and psychologism, 197-98; rejection of concept of the thing in itself, 202; rejection of Kantian constructivism, 194; *The Structure of Behavior*, 199, 203; view of subjectivity, 195-97
metaphysical realism, 6-7, 18-19, 28, 41, 163, 164
metaphysics, 60, 63, 160
meta-principal interpretation, 19
Mill, John Stuart, 110; *Examination of William Hamilton's Philosophy*, 107; and psychologism, 107; *A System of Logic*, 107; view of logic, 114, 234n25
modern art, 28
modern epistemology, 28-40; anti-Platonic, 29; knowledge through analysis of causal relation of ideas to cognitive objects, 32-33; reliance on the term *idea*, 29
Mohanty, Jitendra Nath, 235n44, 236n57
Montaigne, Michel de, 10, 31, 98, 145
Moore, Henry, 37, 39, 40
Murdoch, Iris, 26
Muslim religious art, 27
myth of the given, 98

Nagel, Thomas, 11
naive realism, 153, 211
Natorp, Paul, 103, 108, 129, 143
naturalism, 3, 105-6, 129
natural science, 60

nature. *See* cognitive objects
neo-Kantians, anti-psychological attitude, 108
Neurath, Otto, 36, 177
Newton, Isaac, 37, 94–95; inverse square law, 23; *Principia*, 58, 65
Newtonian mechanics, 64
new way of ideas. *See* causal theory of perception
Nietzsche, Friedrich, 97, 241n66
noema and noesis, distinction between, 133
noetic, 111, 113, 132
noumenon. *See* Kant, Immanuel

objectivist skepticism, 111
Oetinger, F. C., 65, 228n58
old way of ideas. *See* Platonism
ontological realism, 18
ontology: and history of, 162–71; substance, 86–87; two-worlds, 19

Parmenides, 4, 19, 30, 82, 98, 180
participation, 10, 68
Paul, Saint, 76
Peirce, Charles, 18, 64, 183, 209, 246n2, 246n3
perception: Hegel's analysis of, 4; theories of, 21, 204
Pfander, Alexander, 139
phaneroscopy, 209, 246n3
phenomenological movement, 190
phenomenology: and causal explanation, 68; and distinction, 40; and external objects and sense data, 2; French, 188–89, 190; Hegel and, 14, 71, 84–86, 89–100, 173; Heidegger and, 172–76; versus phenomenalism, 2; and psychologism, 234n12; Reinhold and, 85–86; and relation of phenomena to cognitive objects, 4; relation to Platonism, 14; twentieth-century, 52. *See also* Husserl, Edmund; Kant, Immanuel; Merleau-Ponty, Maurice; post-Kantian phenomenology
phenomenon, and appearance, 3–4, 68
Philolaus, 62
philosophical anthropology, 46, 107
philosophical tradition, 77–79
philosophical writings, and textual interpretation, 163–64
philosophy of mind, 56

Picasso, Pablo, 28
Pinkard, Terry, 74
Plato: as anti-phenomenologist, 9; attack on artistic representation, 25–26; *Cratylus*, 25; distinction between object of sensory perception and object of intellection, 8–9; *Hippias Major*, 20; ideas function ontologically as causes of things, 8; *Ion*, 25; *Laws*, 5, 25; *Parmenides*, 5, 20, 21; *Phaedo*, 7, 20, 21, 22, 24, 95; *Philebus*, 20; and Platonism, 5, 18; rejection of cognitive inference from appearance to reality, 11; rejection of representational approach to knowledge, 8; *Republic*, 5–6, 7, 9, 19, 20, 25–26, 130; *Seventh Letter*, 9; *Sophist*, 5, 7, 25, 68; *Symposium*, 20; *Theaetetus*, 5, 8; theory of causality, 22–24; theory of forms (ideas), 10, 20, 21, 55, 67; *Timaeus*, 5, 20; use of term *idea*, 44; view of philosopher, 79
Platonic realism, 6–7
Platonism, 28; as causal theory, 7, 68; direct grasp of reality, 12; distinction between phenomena and appearances, 4–5, 45; as early form of idealism, 67; idea as unchanging cognitive object, 31; phenomena, 23; rejection of claims for direct knowledge, 31; rejection of representationalism, 31; relation of forms to things ontological but not epistemological, 29; theory of forms (ideas), 6, 18, 19–20, 35, 67–68; two-worlds ontology, 19
Plotinus, 31
Pöggeler, Otto, 190
Porphyry, 32
positing, 90
positivism, 18
post-Husserlian phenomenologists, 139
post-Kantian German idealism, 10, 72–75, 82–83; claim to develop critical philosophy beyond Kant, 75, 159; and epistemological anti-foundationalists, 73; a posteriori thinking, 73
post-Kantian phenomenology, 13, 41, 71
post-Kantian representationalism, 55–57
postmodernism, 187
Price, H. H., 212
Protagoras, 6, 8
psychological idealism, 195

psychologism, 46, 105–8, 148, 235n44; Heidegger and, 143–49, 184; Husserl and, 14–15, 101, 103–4, 108–16, 197–98, 244n37; Kant and, 106, 116; mathematical, 115; Merleau-Ponty and, 197–98; opposition between Lotze and Mill, 107; phenomenology and, 234n12; and skeptical relativism, 111; transcendental, 115
Ptolemy: *Almagest*, 61
Putnam, Hilary, 40, 57
Pyrrhonism, 131

quantum mechanics, 23
Quine, W. V. O., 36, 57, 79, 105, 163
Quintilian, 25

rationalism, 32, 33, 91
rational realism, 85
realism, 163; aesthetic, 18; classical, 3; empirical, 18; metaphysical, 6–7, 18–19, 28, 41, 163; naive, 153, 211; ontological, 18; Platonic, 6–7; rational, 85; representational, 8; scientific, 18; semantic, 57
reference, 56–57; and phenomenology, 118; theories of, 55
Reid, Thomas, 28, 33, 36, 37, 38, 39–40
Reinhold, Karl, 14, 58, 79, 227n48; Hegel on, 81; influence of Bardili on, 85; phenomenology as pure philosophy of nature, 85–86; restatement of critical philosophy in foundationalist form, 72–73, 75
religious art, 27–28
representationalism, 34, 38; anti-Platonic revival, 13; artistic, 55; and causal theory of perception, 41, 42, 47; and cognitive objects, 11–12; and constructivism, 210; ideas as images of mind-independent external world, 35; and modern semantic theory, 48; post-Kantian, 14, 55–57; widespread approach to knowledge, 25. *See also* Kant, Immanuel
representational realism, 8
Rescher, Nicholas, 68
Ricoeur, Paul, 188, 190
Rorty, Richard, 241n66
Russell, Bertrand, 37, 57, 204–5, 212

Sacks, Oliver, 3
Sartre, Jean-Paul, 17, 101, 130, 143, 188, 190, 193; attack in Husserlian idealism, 193; *Being and Nothingness*, 145; *Critique of Dialectical Reason*, 146; and existentialism, 189; "Existentialism Is a Humanism," 146; *The Search for a Method*, 145–46
Scheler, Max, 145
Schelling, Friedrich Wilhelm Joseph, 52, 58–59; philosophy of nature, 80; system from concept of absolute, 74; *System of Transcendental Idealism*, 80
Schlick, Moritz, 143
scholasticism, 31
scientific realism, 18
scientism, 18, 201
Scotus, Duns, 55, 239n48
Sellars, Wilfrid, 36, 98, 177, 192, 201
semantic realism, 57
semantic reference, 56
semantics, 118
sense-data theory, 204, 212
Shpet, Gustav, 139
skeptical relativism, 115
skepticism, 37, 38, 111, 112; ancient, 131; and common sense, 40; Humean, 39; Husserl on, 111
Smith, Adam, 33
Socrates, 6, 7–8, 20, 21, 30
Sokal, Alan: "Transgressing the Boundaries: Towards a Transformative Hermeneutics of Quantum Gravity," 187
Sophists, 20
speculative identity, problem of, 84
Spiegelberg, Herbert, 108–9, 190
Spinoza, Baruch, 28, 33, 35, 80, 106
Stillingfleet, Bishop Edward, 28
Strawson, Galen, 56, 57
Stumpf, Carl, 108, 199
subjectivist relativism, 111
subjectivity: and constructivism, 11–13, 58; Descartes and, 98, 156; Fichte and, 55, 89–90, 106, 214; Heidegger and, 148, 156–57, 169; Husserl and, 124, 144; Merleau-Ponty and, 195–97; modern idea of, 10, 17, 47; transcendental, 129, 144. *See also* Kant, Immanuel

textual interpretation: Heidegger and, 164–71, 176–79; and philosophical writings, 163–64; and skepticism, 241n66
Theaetetus, 6

theory of activity, 12
theory of alienation, 12
theory of forms (ideas), 6, 7–8, 9, 10, 14, 19–20; and causal explanation, 22–24; Descartes, 31–35; essential properties of a thing related to forms, 21, 28; Platonic, 21–22, 55, 140; and sensible things, 20, 22
theory of opposites, 7
theory of theory, 113
Toland, John, 28
transcendental deduction, 73, 74–75, 80, 108, 212
transcendental idealism, 104, 109, 137, 144, 180, 192, 195, 197, 211
transcendental phenomenological psychology, 199
transcendental psychologism, 115
transcendental subjectivity, 129, 144
transcendental tradition, 3

universal causal determinism, 38
universal predication, 7
universals, problem of, 32

Vico, Giambattista, 41, 58, 97
Vienna Circle, 18, 112
Vlastos, Gregory, 30
Voltaire (pseud. for François-Marie Arouet), 58
Von Helmholtz, Hermann, 107

Wahl, Jean, 188
Watson, R. A., 34, 223n62
Weinberg, Steven, 163
Wheeler, Michael, 3
William of Ockham, 32
Wilson cloud chamber, 24
Wittgenstein, Ludwig, 36, 101, 137
Wolff, Christian, 92
Wundt, Wilhelm, 110, 144, 199

www.ingramcontent.com/pod-product-compliance
Lightning Source LLC
Chambersburg PA
CBHW021940290426

44108CB00012B/908